# RUN YOUR OWN STORE

# RUN YOUR OWN STORE

## SECOND EDITION

## FROM RAISING THE MONEY TO COUNTING THE PROFITS

## IRVING BURSTINER, Ph.D.

PRENTICE HALL PRESS

New York   London   Toronto   Sydney   Tokyo

PRENTICE HALL PRESS
Gulf+Western Building
One Gulf+Western Plaza
New York, New York 10023

PRENTICE HALL PRESS and colophon are registered
trademarks of Simon & Schuster, Inc.

Library of Congress Cataloging-in-Publication Data

Burstiner, Irving
Run your own store : from raising money to counting
the profits / Irving Burstiner. — 2d ed.
p.        cm.
Includes index.
ISBN 0-13-783952-9
1. Retail trade—Management.   2. Stores, Retail—Management.
HF5429.B72   1989                                    88-38424
658.8′7—dc19                                         CIP

Designed by Irving Perkins Associates
Manufactured in the United States of America

10   9   8   7   6   5   4   3   2   1

Second Edition

*In memory of Ronald and Stuart*

# Contents

# Preface

Of the many books that guide those of you who plan to start your own businesses, no more than one or two deal with the specifics of opening a retail store. Yet store retailing is by far the most popular choice of new entrepreneurs, probably because you can launch a store with much less of an initial investment than most other types of businesses require. Another reason is that retailing is an *exciting* business. What's more exciting than your "grand opening," meeting new customers face-to-face, and listening to the *ka-ching!* of the cash register?

Just about anyone with some money and a bit of courage can start up a store of his or her own. Every week, thousands do. Unhappily, most of these promising ventures turn sour within two or three years. So your challenge is to make a success of your new store. Those who do number far fewer than those who don't.

That is precisely why this book has been written. In it, I've combined thirty years of hands-on retail experience with the theoretical know-how provided by a midlife career change to college professor of marketing and management. This is a practical "how-to" book, filled with the nuts and bolts of running a store and designed for the millions who dream of someday managing a business of their own. Its purpose? To help you translate your fantasy into reality. It's an easy-to-follow "operations manual" that provides the useful facts you need to succeed in independent store retailing.

Although this updated edition has been targeted primarily at the general public, colleges may find it an excellent text for retail entrepreneurship courses, as well as helpful supplementary reading for many of the offerings in their retailing and management curricula. It's also of value for the hundreds of small business institutes and programs provided by the continuing-education departments of such institutions and by the adult-education divisions of our evening high schools.

These days, dozens of people—like you—ask me, "Isn't this the wrong time to go into business?" They tell me the economy is faltering, that credit is hard to obtain, that the interest rates on bank loans are too high, that many stores don't seem to be faring well. I usually reply, "Why not? *Anytime* can be the right time to go into business." I say this with conviction because I believe it. A new business can be launched in good times or bad, and it can still be made to blossom into a viable, successful enterprise. Yet I do follow my response with a query of my own: "Are you certain you're the right *person* to go into business at this time?" This is, of course, a cryptic question—and a loaded one, too. What usually happens is an extended pause, followed by a confused, "Why, what do you mean?" This response leads to a fifteen-minute dialogue, after which the other party leaves—determined to burrow into the subject area, conduct a rigid self-appraisal, and get started on a master plan for the new business. At that point, the would-be retailer needs a step-by-step guide for getting started. Hence this book.

Part I introduces you to the exciting world of store retailing, indicating where today's opportunities lie and what you need to succeed in your own store.

Part II provides specifics on how to organize—and protect—your business and reviews the different ways available to you for entering the retailing sector. It shows you how to estimate how much money you need, how to understand balance sheets and operating statements, and how to prepare your comprehensive business plan.

Part III counsels you in location selection and store leases and discusses the details of store design, decor, layout, and fixture choices.

Part IV clarifies the intricacies of inventory planning and control, along with the taking of physical inventory. You discover profitable hints for buying "better," come to understand the purposes and uses of markups and markdowns, and learn the techniques of pricing for profit. Also reviewed are the wide range of services that retailers may wish to offer their customers and the more salient details of credit management.

Part V is devoted to personnel aspects: staffing your store; paying your employees; scheduling, training, and motivating them; and evaluating performance.

Part VI reviews the basics of window and in-store display and introduces you to other sales-promotion "tools" often used by retailers. It shows you how to maximize your advertising dollars and how to prepare effective ads that bring increased traffic into your store. Also offered are suggestions for improving the selling skills of your salespeople.

Part VII explains all you need to know about financial management and control. You learn what records to keep, how to prepare budgets, the value of ratio analysis, and what computers can do for you. You find out about measures you can take to reduce shoplifting and theft, and how to handle cash. Some significant aspects of business law are offered, along with up-to-date, detailed coverage of taxation. This section also includes filled-out representative tax forms.

Part VIII, finally, looks to future possibilities for your new business. It suggests directions for expansion and growth, underscores the need for reviewing your financial situation and outlining your organizational needs, shows you how to research problem situations, and offers some thoughts about management succession.

In closing this Preface, I'd like to express my warm appreciation of my wonderful wife, Razel, for her patience, support, and affection throughout the many months it took me to revise *Run Your Own Store*.

—IRVING BURSTINER

# I

# Your
# Opportunities
# in Retailing

# 1

# Exploring the Retail Sector

Retailing is an exciting way of life for the more than 17 million people who earn their livelihood in this sector of our economy. It's fun for consumers, too. Just watch the faces and behavior of the throngs visiting our shopping malls, especially on Saturdays and at preholiday times! No other type of business is as familiar to us. Retailers provide the goods that you and I need: from food, drink, and clothing to furniture, home furnishings, appliances, and other necessities—as well as an unending stream of luxury products.

Each year some 600,000 or more new business enterprises are launched.* Considerably more than one-third of these are retail operations; most of these new entrepreneurs risk their capital, invest their time, and make an extraordinary effort to open some kind of store. All are attracted by the challenge of building successful retail businesses of their own. The ventures run the gamut from clothing boutiques and health-food stores to the more prosaic groceries and superettes, hardware stores, coffee shops, bars, and so on. Among the more recent innovations on the scene are yogurt stores, "cosmetiques," suntanning parlors, computer stores and computer repair shops, and home-video rental libraries. The diversity of types is amazing!

Most retailing involves buying merchandise from wholesalers and/or manufacturers and reselling these goods directly to consumers—at a profit, of course. Each year this vital sector of our economy accounts for about 38 percent of our gross national product. As short a time ago as 1970, total retail sales reached only $368 billion; by 1981 we had passed the $1 trillion mark (see table 1–1).

Today, some 1.9 million retail establishments of all kinds are in operation in the United States. Most are store retailers, though other types are found—such as mail order houses, automatic merchandising- (vending-) machine operators, and companies engaged in direct ("door-to-door") selling.

---

\* See, for example, Jay Finegan, "The Entrepreneurial Numbers Game," *Inc.* 8 (May 1986), 31–32ff; Curtis Hartman, "Is It Easier Than Ever to Start a Business?" *Inc.* 9 (March 1987), 69.

**TABLE 1–1. ANNUAL RETAIL SALES, 1970 TO 1986**

| Year | Total Retail Sales (in billions of dollars) | Year | Total Retail Sales (in billions of dollars) |
|------|------|------|------|
| 1970 | 375.2 | 1979 | 896.8 |
| 1971 | 414.2 | 1980 | 957.3 |
| 1972 | 458.5 | 1981 | 1,038.7 |
| 1973 | 511.9 | 1982 | 1,069.3 |
| 1974 | 542.0 | 1983 | 1,171.2 |
| 1975 | 588.1 | 1984 | 1,289.4 |
| 1976 | 656.4 | 1985 | 1,379.6 |
| 1977 | 722.5 | 1986 | 1,454.4 |
| 1978 | 804.2 | | |

*Source:* U.S. Bureau of the Census, *Statistical Abstract of the United States: 1988,* 108th ed. (Washington, D.C., 1987), 737.

## WHAT RETAILING IS ALL ABOUT

Most of us are overwhelmed by the dazzling array of department stores, discount houses, and other "mass merchandisers," national and regional drugstore and variety-store chains, supermarkets, and other large-scale operations that tend to dominate the retail sector. We tend to forget we're primarily a land of small, independent merchants. In fact, most stores are small, both in size and in sales volume. Our "typical" store is a small operation, usually run by the owner alone or by a husband-and-wife team. Such small enterprises naturally lack the substantial resources, purchasing skill, and sophistication of planning and control techniques of the large-scale retailers. Where there are employees, they're few in number. One or two may be part-time workers. The store's size is, of course, related to the type of establishment: Furniture outlets, for example, require much more space than shoe stores or neighborhood groceries. A total area of less than 2,000 square feet is characteristic of most store types.

Yet, these small stores show surprising strength and resiliency in the face of competition from the more impersonal large-scale retailers. They offer the consumer convenient locations, prompt attention, more personalized service, a warmer atmosphere, and an often broader (and deeper) selection of merchandise in their particular lines. Even so, it's not easy for an independent retailer to survive these days in an economy besieged from time to time by recessionary and inflationary conditions. Nevertheless, most small store owners manage to make additional sales gains, pay their bills on time, and extract a comforting rate of return on their investment.

Yes, there's always room for the right kind of store. Geographic shifts of large numbers of consumers are characteristic of our mobile population; stores need to follow people wherever they move. The population is still growing, although at a more measured pace than in prior decades. This increase means more mouths to feed, bodies to clothe, and households to furnish. Fashions, differing lifestyles, increasing leisure, and technological advances all contribute to the need for new variations on old retailing "themes." Finally, openings in retailing continually appear as established merchants retire, sell their businesses, or close down because of poor management practices or changes in the local environment.

You never know. The small store launched today may become the largest chain operation in its field within the next decade.

## Kinds of Stores

For an overview of the major categories of retail stores, refer to table 1–2. You'll note that nearly one-third of all our stores are *eating or drinking places* and *food stores. Gasoline stations* and *automotive dealers* account for another 13.7 percent of retail establishments. These four classifications constitute more than 46 percent of all retail enterprises, and they're responsible for producing more than 60 percent of the country's retail sales. Table 1–3 is of even greater interest. In it are listed the most popular types of retail stores—and

**TABLE 1–2. RETAIL TRADE CATEGORIES, 1982: BY NUMBER OF ESTABLISHMENTS AND ANNUAL SALES**

| Major Categories of Retail Establishments | Total Number Within Category (in thousands) | Percentage of Total | Total Sales in Category (in billions) | Percentage of Total |
|---|---|---|---|---|
| Miscellaneous retail stores* | 559.0 | 29.1% | $ 111.8 | 10.5% |
| Eating and drinking places | 381.7 | 19.9 | 104.6 | 9.8 |
| Food stores | 241.7 | 12.6 | 246.1 | 23.1 |
| Apparel and accessory stores | 159.0 | 8.3 | 57.8 | 5.4 |
| Gasoline service stations | 135.5 | 7.0 | 97.4 | 9.1 |
| Furniture, home furnishings, and equipment stores | 131.7 | 6.8 | 46.8 | 4.4 |
| Automotive dealers | 129.3 | 6.7 | 193.5 | 18.2 |
| Building materials, hardware, garden supply, and mobile-home dealers | 88.5 | 4.6 | 51.0 | 4.8 |
| Drug and proprietary stores | 52.0 | 2.7 | 36.4 | 3.4 |
| General-merchandise-group stores** | 44.7 | 2.3 | 120.4 | 11.3 |
| Retail trade, total | 1,923.2 | 100.0% | $1,065.9 | 100.0% |

*Source:* U.S. Bureau of the Census, *Statistical Abstract of the United States: 1987*, 107th ed. (Washington, D.C., 1986), 762.

*A general, catchall category that includes (among others) liquor and jewelry stores, florists, stationers, used merchandise outlets, other shopping goods stores, and nonstore retailers such as mail order houses, automatic vending-machine firms, and so on.

**Includes department stores.

## TABLE 1–3. POPULAR RETAIL STORE TYPES, 1982

| Type of Establishment | Number in Category in 1982 | Approximate Sales/Unit* |
|---|---|---|
| Eating places | 301,700 | $ 315,200 |
| Grocery stores | 168,000 | 1,373,200 |
| Drinking places (alcoholic beverages) | 80,000 | 118,800 |
| Used merchandise stores | 59,000 | 79,100 |
| Women's clothing and specialty stores, and furriers | 58,800 | 378,600 |
| Drug and proprietary stores | 52,000 | 700,800 |
| Auto and home supply stores | 48,800 | 433,500 |
| Home furnishings stores | 44,300 | 213,000 |
| Liquor stores | 41,500 | 437,300 |
| Gift, novelty, and souvenir stores | 41,400 | 121,700 |
| Building materials and supply stores | 40,100 | 876,400 |
| Shoe stores | 39,400 | 289,800 |
| Jewelry stores | 38,700 | 228,100 |
| Furniture stores | 38,300 | 461,000 |
| Radio, television, and music stores | 35,200 | 392,400 |
| Sporting goods stores and bicycle shops | 34,700 | 230,900 |
| Florists | 34,700 | 107,600 |
| Hardware stores | 25,400 | 343,600 |
| Family clothing stores | 23,700 | 576,400 |
| Retail bakeries | 22,200 | 169,000 |
| Hobby, toy, and game shops | 22,000 | 157,500 |
| Sewing, needlework, and piece-goods stores | 21,900 | 122,700 |
| Men's and boys' clothing and furnishings stores | 18,600 | 419,500 |
| Bookstores | 14,900 | 219,400 |
| Household appliance stores | 13,900 | 421,200 |
| Variety stores | 13,500 | 608,200 |

*Source:* U.S. Bureau of the Census, *Statistical Abstract of the United States: 1988,* 108th ed. (Washington, D.C., 1987), 735.

*Figures derived by dividing total retail sales figures for each classification by the total number of retail establishments in the category.

how many of each were operating during 1982. Also shown are estimates of the annual sales volume reached—on the average—by the individual store in each category. Despite these statistics, which are available from the Bureau of the Census, the public doesn't readily think of bars, restaurants, gas stations, and car dealers as "retail stores."

Other than the business types already mentioned, some of the more common ones include furniture and home furnishings stores, shops that sell ladies' apparel, drugstores, auto and home supply stores, and liquor stores.

## RETAILING DIFFERS FROM OTHER TYPES OF BUSINESSES

Not everyone who wants to start a business of his or her own opens a retail store. Some are attracted to the manufacturing sector, others to the wholesale trade, still others to some sort of service business. What are these other types like? How do they differ from the retail industry?

## Manufacturing

Popular among the new entrants to small-scale manufacturing are businesses that produce metal or plastic products, ceramics or glassware, electrical and electronic equipment, various handicrafts, all kinds of apparel, and tools or machinery. Printing, too, is a common venture.

Entrepreneurs who prefer to go into manufacturing often have had prior experience in some phase of plant production. They enjoy working in such surroundings; they're at home with assembly lines and production belts, and they feel at ease with machines and factory personnel. Often, manufacturers get involved in the first place because they come across (or invent) an unusual product that appears to have a great deal of sales potential. Perhaps they realize that one machine can turn out $x$ numbers of product $z$ for each hour it operates—and that they can calculate their investment in that machine with relative ease, assuming, of course, that they can sell off its output readily enough.

A major drawback to this type of business is the initial need for a comparatively heavy capital investment—for plant, machinery, and equipment. Moreover, the new manufacturer must install the machines, gear up, schedule, and then manufacture the goods, all of which takes time. Also someone—generally a principal of the firm or perhaps a manufacturers' rep—must contact prospective buyers of these goods and secure orders. After manufacturing, the products have to be shipped to the customers in some manner, and the company may need to wait as long as thirty days (often, much longer) before receiving payment for the goods. This delay in payment occurs because manufacturers traditionally must extend "trade credit" to their accounts.

## Wholesaling

Like manufacturing enterprises, firms in wholesaling also require a substantial amount of investment capital to get started. The typical wholesaler purchases large quantities of merchandise from producers, stores this inventory in a warehouse, then sells off the goods in small quantities to hundreds—and sometimes to thousands—of retail stores. Some types, like the "drop shipper," have no need to maintain stock on hand, and hence they don't require a warehouse. Others sell primarily to industry or government, instead of to the retail stores. New wholesalers are drawn to such fields as candy and tobacco products, groceries, hardware, stationery supplies and equipment, and electrical goods.

Wholesale firms need to maintain a sizable inventory—often one that approximates the current needs of several hundred retail outlets. A large warehouse is often a must, as is a well conceived order-handling system. Orders have to be "picked" from the stacks of merchandise in the warehouse. Thus, such equipment as carts, conveyors, and forklift trucks may be needed, in addition to the more obvious skids or pallets on which to stack the cartons of goods. Transportation must be arranged for and routed. While some established wholesalers prefer company-owned-and-operated trucks, new small-scale operators would be wise to avoid this approach. They would be far better off allocating the monies required for the purchase (or rental) of such "capital goods" to inventory instead—and relying on "common carriers" for shipping merchandise.

Like manufacturing, the wholesale firm's activities center around physical things and internal systems: machines, supplies, inventories, shipments, purchasing, order-billing, and the like. There's also some contact with customers but almost none with the public-at-large. Wholesale enterprises also need to extend trade credit to their accounts—and wait up to a month or more to get paid.

## Service Businesses

The service sector of our economy has been growing at a breakneck speed in the past several decades. Such service operations as hotels and motels, movie houses, and bowling alleys are usually priced well beyond the financial capability of the new small-businessperson. More popular with newcomers to this sector are enterprises in the area of "personal services"—beauty salons, photographic studios, dry cleaners, dance schools, and the like. "Business services" are also quite popular: equipment rental, cleaning services, advertising and public relations agencies, and so on. Experienced tradespeople—electricians, locksmiths, plumbers, and the like—also tend to try their hands at small business. Similarly, many professionals open law offices, accounting services, and real estate sales offices.

A compelling feature of the service enterprise is that you need no major investment in inventory. You don't have to manufacture goods, nor purchase and store them. Of course, it's often necessary to carry a limited amount of supplies and/or materials—or perhaps spare or replacement parts—in order to conduct business. Yet the service operation primarily sells *service,* not goods. Your equity capital is therefore assigned for the most part to: (1) your business premises; and (2) promotion. Indeed, the financial requirements for the service enterprise are often far smaller than for most other business types.

Yet, even in services you have to wait to be compensated.

## STORE RETAILING: ITS ADVANTAGES AND DISADVANTAGES

Store retailing offers you a kind of business much different from all others, one in which you get to meet lots of people. The retail store is a cash-and-carry operation. The day you open your store to the public, you begin taking in money at your cash register. Capital requirements are characteristically lower than for either manufacturing or wholesaling.

The resultant "ease of entry" is a salient feature of store retailing, and it probably accounts for the large number of new stores launched every year. Another likely reason is that we consumers are more familiar with retail stores than with all other business types, by virtue of having shopped in them ever since we can remember.

Anyone can decide to go into retailing with a comparatively modest investment. Running a store isn't at all complicated. The trick is to make a success of it.

That's what this book is all about.

The evident "ease of entry" into retailing can be a disadvantage, too. As you no doubt know, a high proportion of new ventures are out of business within a few years after their start-up. Small business consultants believe the percentage of retail closings each year is higher than that in other types of business. This contention is supported in part, although somewhat indirectly, by the figures in table 1–4. Here you have the results of an analysis by Dun & Bradstreet, Inc. of more than 61,000 businesses that failed in 1987—both by business type and by the age of the enterprise. More than 41 percent of the retail failures had been operating for three years or less, as contrasted to slightly less than one-third of the manufacturing or wholesale firms.

## TABLE 1–4. AGES OF 61,209 BUSINESSES THAT FAILED IN 1987*

| Age of Business | All Types Combined** | Manu-facturing | Wholesale Trade | Retail Trade | Services |
|---|---|---|---|---|---|
| 1 year or less | 10.0% | 7.8% | 7.7% | 12.0% | 14.9% |
| 2 years | 12.4 | 13.0 | 12.5 | 15.9 | 12.7 |
| 3 years | 11.4 | 11.3 | 11.3 | 13.7 | 11.2 |
| 4 years | 9.4 | 9.9 | 9.5 | 10.1 | 8.9 |
| 5 years | 7.5 | 7.0 | 8.4 | 7.6 | 7.8 |
| Total 5 years or less | 50.7% | 49.0% | 49.4% | 59.3% | 55.5% |
| 6 to 10 years | 24.6 | 23.3 | 25.5 | 22.0 | 24.6 |
| More than 10 years | 24.7 | 27.7 | 25.1 | 18.7 | 19.9 |
| Total | 100.0% | 100.0% | 100.0% | 100.0% | 100.0% |

*Source:* The Dun & Bradstreet Corporation, *Business Failure Record: 1986 Final/1987 Preliminary* (New York: The Dun & Bradstreet Corporation, 1988), 17. Used with permission.

*These are preliminary statistics for 1987.

**Other categories included in total, although not shown, are agriculture, forestry, and fishing; mining; construction; transportation and public utilities; and finance, insurance, and real estate.

Also of interest to the aspiring retail entrepreneur are the details presented in table 1–5. Among other things, they indicate that one out of five retail failures during 1987 may be ascribed to entrepreneurial deficiencies (see *"Experience Causes"*). (The significance of the experience of small business owner to the success of the enterprise is dealt with in considerable depth in chapter 2.)

## TABLE 1–5. MAJOR CAUSES OF BUSINESS FAILURES IN RETAIL TRADE, 1987*

| Major Categories of Causes of Business Failures | Percentage of Total** |
|---|---|
| Economic Factors Causes (Insufficient profits, high interest rates, loss of market, no consumer spending, no future) | 71.7% |
| Experience Causes (Incompetence, lack of line experience, lack of managerial experience, unbalanced experience) | 20.3 |
| Sales Causes (Competitively weak, economic decline, inadequate sales, inventory difficulties, poor location) | 11.1 |
| Expenses Causes (Burdensome institutional debt, heavy operating expenses) | 8.1 |
| Other Causes (Neglect causes, capital causes, disaster causes, customer causes, fraud causes, assets causes) | 3.4 |

*Source:* The Dun & Bradstreet Corporation, *Business Failure Record: 1986 Final/1987 Preliminary* (New York: The Dun & Bradstreet Corporation, 1988), 19. Used with permission.

* These are preliminary statistics for 1987.

** As The Dun & Bradstreet Corporation points out: "Due to the fact that some failures are attributed to a combination of causes, the total of the major categories exceeds 100.0%."

## NONSTORE RETAILING

Not all retailing is store retailing. In your journeys through the countryside, you have noted the occasional roadside stand that offers ripe tomatoes, fresh corn by the bushel, freshly laid eggs, and other agricultural or dairy products—or else woven mats, towels, souvenirs and novelties, country-fresh ham, or a hundred other items. Farther down the road, you can buy grapefruits, cantaloupes, and even giant plush teddy bears and other toy animals from a produce wagon or truck. Sometimes, not even a stand or truck is in sight—simply a mound of watermelons or other sizable product, topped with a huge "For Sale" sign that can be seen easily from a distance.

Although they operate without a storefront, these sellers are retailers nevertheless, since they all sell directly to you, the consumer. While there are a number of different types of nonstore retailers (such as the flea marketer and the peddler), most such firms fall into one of three categories:

1. Mail order houses
2. Direct selling firms
3. Automatic merchandising- (vending-) machine operators

Some statistics for the three categories are presented in table 1–6.

## TABLE 1–6. MAJOR CATEGORIES OF NONSTORE RETAILERS, 1972 AND 1982

| Type of Business | Number of Establishments (in thousands) | | Total Annual Sales (in billions) | | Percentage Change ÷ Number of Establishments | Annual Sales |
|---|---|---|---|---|---|---|
| | 1972 | 1982 | 1972 | 1982 | | |
| Mail order houses | 8.0 | 12.2 | $4.6 | $11.4 | +52.5% | +147.8% |
| Direct selling firms | 8.9 | 8.7 | 2.3 | 4.2 | − 2.2 | + 82.6 |
| Vending-machine companies | 12.8 | 11.8 | 3.0 | 4.9 | − 7.8 | + 63.3 |

Source: U.S. Bureau of the Census, Census of Business, 1972 and Statistical Abstract of the United States: 1988, 108th ed. (Washington, D.C., 1987), 735.

## Mail Order Houses

Selling products or services directly to consumers via the U.S. Postal Service is an activity that dates back to the post–Civil War period, when firms such as Montgomery Ward and Sears, Roebuck & Company initiated this then-novel approach. Since then, of course, those early mail order retailers have grown into giants among today's store retailers. Most department stores now conduct mail order selling activities as a profitable sideline to their in-store selling. Many chain-store operations, big and small, count on direct mail efforts to bring in additional business. So do some small-scale independents. Printed inserts, flyers, brochures, and catalogs from all these store retailers bombard the public continually.

All such companies are omitted from the Department of Commerce's statistics on "nonstore"—or more specifically, "mail order"—retailers (table 1–6). Enterprises included in the "Mail order houses" category are just that: firms that conduct business *primarily* through the mails. These include general merchandise houses, companies that sell specialty goods of all kinds, novelty firms, various types of clubs (books, records, tapes, gifts), and so on. This segment of the economy has displayed robust growth despite sharp increases in labor and mailing costs. The number of mail order houses increased some 52.5 percent over the ten-year period from 1972 to 1982. Over the same decade, total sales for the category increased some 147.8 percent.

## Direct Selling Firms

Some of the more recognizable names in this field are Good Humor, Avon, Fuller Brush, and Tupperware. House-to-house canvassing, party plans, and route sales are among the techniques used to sell almost everything—dairy products, baked goods, soft drinks, hardware, building materials, home furnishings, books, health and beauty aids, and general merchandise. These firms enjoyed a total sales volume in 1982 of about $4.2 billion, up some 82.6 percent from 1972.

## Automatic Vending-Machine Firms

Popularly known as "vending-machine operators," these companies accounted for nearly 5 cents out of every retail sales dollar taken in during 1982. Vending received its greatest impetus during the 1960s, largely as a result of improved technology in the field. While the once-rapid growth in number of firms has slowed down substantially, the vending-machine segment reflected an enormous sales volume increase of $1.9 billion in the ten-year period ending in 1982.

Once mostly restricted to candy bars and canned sodas, today's coin-operated machines vend hot drinks, soups, milk, ice cream, snack foods, and an astonishing array of impulse goods and necessities. The machines are usually placed in high-traffic locations, such as subway stations, railroad and bus terminals, office buildings, and bars.

## THE RETAILING OF SERVICES

Selling a service (or services) to consumers usually poses more of a challenge to the retailer than does the selling of merchandise. For one thing, consumers can touch, handle, or examine goods; this is something they cannot do with services. This *tangibility* quality aids the retailer who sells merchandise. As an example, assume you're shopping for towels at a bath shop. After some searching, you locate the section on the shelves that houses the approximate color(s) you would like for your home. You then pick up several of these and proceed to unfold them, to examine them more carefully. Most likely, you want to: (1) see if you like the design; and (2) determine whether or not the material they are made of is "thirsty" enough for your use.

Shoppers cannot do this with a service. Services are *intangible;* they cannot be touched or handled. They must be *experienced*. Moreover, services reflect several other characteristics that distinguish them from goods; these qualities call for special attention by the retailer. (For more information, see the section on "Marketing Service Businesses" in chapter 12.)

For now, refer to table 1–7; it contains operating data for selected types of service retailers.

## WHERE THE OPPORTUNITIES LIE FOR THE INDEPENDENT

Almost everyone who wants to get into store retailing is determined to find "the right opportunity." This desire is natural. It also makes sense. Yet what a difficult task it can be to draw a bead on just what—or where—this opportunity might be. You may recall one

## TABLE 1–7. OPERATING INFORMATION FOR SELECTED SERVICES*

| SIC Number | Type of Business | Operating Expenses | All Other Expenses | Profit Before Taxes |
|---|---|---|---|---|
| 7933 | Bowling alleys | 93.5% | 4.3% | 2.2% |
| 7542 | Car washes | 92.5 | 3.3 | 4.3 |
| 7361 | Employment agencies | 95.7 | 0.5 | 3.8 |
| 7231, 7241 | Hair stylists | 95.2 | 1.1 | 3.7 |
| 7211, 7216 | Laundries and dry cleaners | 96.0 | 0.7 | 3.4 |
| 7011 | Motels, hotels, and tourist courts | 90.3 | 6.2 | 3.5 |
| 7221, 7333 | Photographic studios, including commercial photography | 93.2 | 1.9 | 4.9 |
| 6531 | Real estate agents and brokers | 87.4 | 4.1 | 8.5 |
| 4722 | Travel agencies | 97.9 | 0.1 | 2.0 |
| 7538 | Auto repair, general | 94.9 | 1.4 | 3.7 |
| 7299 | Health and fitness centers | 91.3 | 4.9 | 3.8 |
| 7832 | Motion picture theaters, except drive-ins | 96.2 | 2.3 | 1.5 |

*Source:* Robert Morris Associates, *'87 Annual Statement Studies* (Philadelphia: Robert Morris Associates, 1987). Copyright 1987 by Robert Morris Associates. Used with permission. (See "Interpretation of Statement Studies Figures" on page 22.)

*Based on statement studies of firms with fiscal year-ends June 30, 1986 through March 31, 1987. All statistics are expressed in terms of percentages of annual sales volume. (Note: Only data for firms with from $0 to $1 million in assets have been shown since this would be characteristic of the beginning business.)

or more occasions when you shopped in a crowded store and exclaimed to a companion or to yourself, "Wow! What a business!" You may have even thought fleetingly at the time, "What I wouldn't give to own this place!" On the other hand, there were probably times when you found yourself commiserating with store owners while they complained of poor business. Situations of the first kind tend to impel store seekers toward that particular type, while memories of the second type of encounter might turn them away.

## Some Guidelines for You

Some fashion-conscious and forward-looking retailers-to-be are attracted to high-fashion apparel stores, jewelry boutiques, and stores that sell high-quality furniture and/or home furnishings. Others may be interested in antique shops, bowling alleys, sporting goods stores, or beauty salons, mainly because they relish the atmospheres of such places. Still others, convinced there's more security in selling staple merchandise, look for retail businesses that offer simple basics or necessities, such as a grocery or a dry-goods store. How should you go about choosing among the endless variety of shops?

For one thing, you must select a field you'll enjoy. After all, you're planning to spend many years working in that environment. Thus a key question is, "In which types of stores would I like to work?"

There's another significant aspect to consider. It has to do with the amount of money you intend to invest in your business and whether it's your own or other people's money. Some retail lines require more initial capital than others. For instance, if you plan to launch a full-service restaurant, you'll need financing for remodeling and decorating the premises (and perhaps for purchasing the building itself), for kitchen equipment and utensils, for tables and chairs, and so on.

A third consideration is the extent of your preparation for the business. Your chances for success are significantly improved if you have had prior experience in the particular line or trade.

Last, and perhaps most important, the success or failure of your retail enterprise may well depend on your choice of location. (Chapter 7 is devoted to this vital subject.)

## CUSTOMARY APPROACHES TO THE PROBLEM

Retailers-to-be gravitate toward one kind of store or another by following different routes. Let's examine some of these routes, while keeping in mind that alternate avenues are proposed later in this chapter:

- Open up the type of store with which you have had experience.
- If money's no problem, buy a going business from someone else—on favorable terms, of course.
- Again, if the capital is available and you would like to cut your risk of losing your initial investment sharply, open a reputable franchised outlet.
- If your capital is limited, search for a store type that requires less of an investment.
- Try a newer type of retail business—on the assumption that the field is still wide open.

### Open the Kind of Store in Which You Have Worked

You may have worked in retailing on a part-time basis (while going through school, for instance) or even as a full-time employee. If you have, you're probably familiar with the type of store in which you worked—the fixtures, and the decor. You may also know the work inside and out: the details of merchandise selection, stock rotation, doing displays, scheduling employees and setting store hours, the proper selling techniques, and so forth. After all your "on-the-job" preparation, what would be a more natural application of your talents than to open such a store for yourself in another location?

Bear two points in mind, though:

- It may have taken your former employer five, ten, or more years to build that business up to the level you found while working there.
- Opening a facsimile of that store somewhere else is no guarantee that it will do as well as the original. No two areas are quite alike—in the extent of their trading areas,

in the local population "mix" (quantity, quality), in the character of the competition, and in many other factors. Also, *you* represent a different "quantity" from your previous employer.

Some kinds of retailing call for specific knowledge or expertise. Let's suppose, for example, you have had experience in a successful drugstore and you would like to open one of your own. As you know, the new store must be supervised (under state law) by a licensed pharmacist. You'll therefore have to either hire a pharmacist or perhaps take one on as a partner in your business. Even launching an antique shop without a working knowledge of antiques isn't easy—not if you want to succeed in business. Some store types call for technical skills or professional preparation: beauty salons, electrical supply stores, and plumbing-fixtures outlets, for example. Others require special licenses: liquor stores, restaurants, bars, and so forth.

## Buy a Going Business

Some people prefer moving into retailing via another's established business. This move is generally safer than starting a brand-new enterprise (see chapter 4). The business may be of any type, so long as it appears to have potential.

Here, several cautions are in order. Store location and prior experience in the chosen field still remain major ingredients for the continued success of the operation. Another caution is that many individuals buy businesses that aren't faring well. They're confident that they'll be able to do better than the previous owners. This assumption may or may not be true. Ego is often at play here. More than likely, the current owner knows far more about the ins and outs of his or her business than you do—and has much more hands-on experience at it too.

## Open a Franchised Outlet

As you can see in table 1–8, total franchise sales in the United States nearly quadrupled between 1970 and 1986. Over the same period, the number of franchises went up by 20.7 percent. The most notable growth among retail franchises has been in fast-food restaurants and convenience stores. As for the nonfood retailers, many types are now available: yarn stores, dry-cleaning establishments, bookstores, instant print shops, jeans shops, stores that sell automotive parts and supplies, and pharmacies (among others). These and other kinds are treated in chapter 4, where some of the more popular franchises available are listed, together with names, addresses, and telephone numbers of their home offices and other salient details.

Typically, responsible franchisors see to it that investors in their outlets have every possible chance to succeed. The success rate in the franchising field generally is reputed to be around 90 percent. Contrast this with the knowledge that the majority of brand-new ventures do not appear to last for more than four or five years!

**TABLE 1–8. THE RETAIL FRANCHISE PICTURE**

| | 1970 | 1975 | 1980 | Estimated 1987 | Percentage Change (1970–1987) |
|---|---|---|---|---|---|
| Total U.S. franchised establishments (in thousands) | 396.3 | 434.5 | 442.4 | 498.5 | + 25.8% |
| Total franchise sales (in billions) | $119.8 | $190.9 | $336.2 | $591.3 | +393.6 |

*Number of Franchise Outlets*

| Retail Franchise Types | 1970 | 1975 | 1980 | Estimated 1987 | Percentage Change (1970–1987) |
|---|---|---|---|---|---|
| Gasoline service stations | 222.0 | 189.5 | 158.5 | 117.0 | − 47.3% |
| Restaurants | 32.6 | 43.0 | 60.0 | 86.4 | +161.0 |
| Nonfood retailers | 30.7 | 37.2 | 35.2 | 50.7 | + 65.1 |
| Food retailers* | N.A.** | 11.8 | 15.5 | 23.6 | — |
| Convenience stores | 8.8 | 13.5 | 15.6 | 16.6 | + 88.6 |

*Source:* U.S. Bureau of the Census, *Statistical Abstract of the United States: 1988,* 108th ed. (Washington, D.C., 1987), 742.

*Excludes convenience stores.

**Not available.

Yet, this route to retail management has several major drawbacks:

- You usually need a fairly substantial investment for most of the reputable franchises.
- You're required to pay royalties on your sales for the life of your contract.
- You must follow the franchisor's guidelines and are, therefore, not entirely your own boss!

## Find a Type That Requires a Smaller Investment

Most retail enterprises require minimum amounts of capital—for one or two months' rent in advance and a security deposit, for utility deposits, for cash registers, and the like. Requirements for the decor, for fixturization, and for equipment may vary tremendously from one type of store to the next. The investment in *inventory,* however, is the largest part of one's total investment in the majority of cases.

Are there retail businesses that call for a comparatively small inventory? If you cull through a list of the many types of retail enterprises, you'll find quite a few. Among those that come readily to mind are plant shops, hobby and bicycle stores, instant print shops, soft ice cream and frozen yogurt stores, used book exchanges, doughnut-and-coffee places, and convenience groceries.

## Try a Newer Kind of Store

Excitement and novelty are the strengths of certain newer retail types. Both these qualities account for the extensive word-of-mouth advertising that follows their appearance in a neighborhood or shopping center. Moreover, because they're relatively few in number, you need not be concerned about "oversaturation." Examples of such businesses include costume jewelry boutiques, cookie shops, health-drink stands, suntanning parlors, computer repair stores, and fast-food salad bars. New types pop up all the time! There's always the chance that the public will come to accept this kind of store with open arms—and that the one outlet you open today may grow rapidly into a profitable chain-store operation.

## Some Alternate Suggestions

Why limit yourself to the customary approaches in choosing a store type? Other, more unusual avenues are worth exploring. Read through the "methods" outlined below. At the very least, you'll be compelled to think more about the subject. You may even come up with a valuable idea or two.

The "Follow-the-Crowd" Philosophy. To many people, it makes sense to search for a store type that's popular with consumers. *Popular,* in this sense, is equivalent to *common* or *frequently found.* For this reason, we can easily rename this approach the "Safety-in-Numbers" Philosophy. Advocates tell themselves: "If so many people own stores of this type, they *must* be profitable! So how can I go wrong?" There's a corollary to this thought: Since our population continues to grow, proportionately more of these "popular" stores will be needed than other types.

You can refer now to table 1–3 for a listing of the most frequently found retail establishments. The five most numerous types are:

| Type of Store | Number of Stores |
|---|---|
| Eating places | 301,700 |
| Groceries | 168,000 |
| Bars | 80,000 |
| Women's clothing and specialty stores, and furriers | 58,800 |
| Drug and proprietary stores | 52,000 |

A possible fallacy in this thinking is, of course, that there may already be too many of these stores in existence—that the marketplace might be "oversaturated." We have all seen neighborhoods where one of two or three supermarkets, for instance, has closed down simply because the area couldn't support so many. In such cases, location is once again the key to retail success. Opening a bar because it's a popular store type, even though another well-established bar is just down the street, might be a foolhardy route.

"The Fewer, the Better" Route. Those who subscribe to this view are positioned at the opposite end of the spectrum from the "Follow-the-Crowd" proponents. Because certain store types are relatively rare, advocates leap to the conclusion that there's ample room for more. This view also takes in the "growing population" thinking. A counter-argument, of course, is that there aren't more because additional stores cannot be supported (that is, there just isn't enough call for their merchandise).

Refer again to table 1–3, this time to those stores listed at the end of the table, such as:

| Type of Store | Number of Stores |
|---|---|
| Hobby, toy, and game shops | 22,000 |
| Men's and boys' clothing and furnishings stores | 18,600 |
| Bookstores | 14,900 |
| Household appliance stores | 13,900 |
| Variety stores | 13,500 |

You can also refer to the *Statistical Abstract* in your public library, where you'll discover some types in even shorter supply:*

| Type of Store | Number of Stores |
|---|---|
| Camera and photographic supply stores | 6,700 |
| Children's and infants' wear stores | 6,600 |
| Stationery stores | 6,600 |
| Cigar stores and stands | 3,500 |
| Luggage and leather-goods stores | 3,200 |

The "Hop-on-the-Bandwagon" Approach. Another quite novel, yet sensible method is to scout the retail sector for types whose sheer numbers show rapid growth in recent years. The assumption is that a high rate of new launches in a particular category may be considered a valid measure of current entrepreneurial interest. Every five years, the Bureau of the Census within the U.S. Department of Commerce conducts a Census of Business. If we juxtapose the numerical counts of store types from the censuses of 1972 and 1982 and compare the two series of numbers, we obtain a ten-year picture of the

---

* U.S. Bureau of the Census, *Statistical Abstract of the United States: 1986*, 107th ed. (Washington, D.C., 1985), 762.

growth (or lack of it) in the retail trades. Table 1–9 shows the results of such a comparison. I strongly recommend that you glance at the details before reading on. They're highly informative.

## TABLE 1–9. CHANGES IN NUMBERS OF STORES, 1972 TO 1982

| Type of Store | Number of Stores (in thousands) | | Percentage Change |
| --- | --- | --- | --- |
| | 1972 | 1982 | |
| Hobby, toy, and game shops | 10.5 | 22.0 | +109.5% |
| Book stores | 7.8 | 14.9 | + 91.0 |
| Gift, novelty, and souvenir stores | 24.6 | 41.4 | + 68.3 |
| Sporting goods stores and bicycle shops | 22.5 | 34.7 | + 54.2 |
| Jewelry stores | 25.3 | 38.7 | + 53.0 |
| Shoe stores | 26.9 | 39.4 | + 46.5 |
| Florists | 24.5 | 34.7 | + 41.6 |
| Family clothing stores | 18.2 | 23.7 | + 30.2 |
| Auto and home supply stores | 37.5 | 48.8 | + 30.1 |
| Eating places | 253.1 | 301.7 | + 19.2 |
| Women's clothing and specialty stores and furriers | 49.6 | 58.8 | + 18.5 |
| Radio, television, and music stores | 29.9 | 35.2 | + 17.7 |
| Retail bakeries | 19.2 | 22.2 | + 15.6 |
| Drug and proprietary stores | 51.5 | 52.0 | + 1.0 |
| Liquor stores | 42.0 | 41.5 | − 1.2 |
| Hardware stores | 26.4 | 25.4 | − 3.8 |
| Grocery stores | 194.3 | 168.0 | − 13.5 |
| Drinking places (alcoholic beverages) | 106.4 | 80.0 | − 24.8 |
| Household appliance stores | 20.3 | 13.9 | − 31.5 |
| Variety stores | 21.9 | 13.5 | − 38.4 |

*Source:* U.S. Bureau of the Census, *Census of Business, 1972* and *Statistical Abstract of the United States: 1988,* 108th ed. (Washington, D.C., 1987), 735.

Over the decade, the most rapid growth was in these five categories:

| | |
| --- | --- |
| Hobby, toy, and game shops | Up 109.5% |
| Book stores | Up 91.0 |
| Gift, novelty, and souvenir stores | Up 68.3 |
| Sporting goods stores and bicycle shops | Up 54.2 |
| Jewelry stores | Up 53.0 |

Of course, you would expect some growth in all categories because of our increasing population over those ten years. Yet some types actually *decreased* in number. Among those that experienced the sharpest declines between 1972 and 1982 are listed on the following page.

| | |
|---|---|
| Variety stores | Down 38.4% |
| Household appliance stores | Down 31.5 |
| Drinking places | |
|    (alcoholic beverages) | Down 24.8 |
| Grocery stores | Down 13.5 |
| Hardware stores | Down 3.8 |

For the present, you might be wise to shy away from these particular types. In such cases, we may make one or more assumptions:

- The field was overcrowded.
- Consumer interest or need slackened.
- Marginal operators fell by the wayside, while the remaining stores picked up much of their business.

**The "Check-the-Failure-Rate" Technique.** Each year, Dun & Bradstreet, Inc. publishes the informative *Business Failure Record*. This booklet lists the failure rates per 10,000 operating concerns for various retail lines of business (see table 1–10). Of course, you should be aware not only that these rates vary from one year to the next, but also that they are based on *failures*—not on the much larger numbers of firms that simply discontinue operations. Consulting this table may help you minimize your risk of failure by avoiding lines that show a high failure rate.

**TABLE 1–10. SOME RETAIL LINES RANKED BY FAILURE RATES, 1987\***

| Line of Business | Failure rate per 10,000 Listed Concerns |
|---|---|
| Apparel and accessory stores | 138 |
| Furniture and home furnishing stores | 100 |
| Stationery stores | 96 |
| Camera and photographic supply stores | 92 |
| Sporting goods stores | 92 |
| Eating and drinking places | 91 |
| Hobby, toy, and game shops | 77 |
| Building materials and garden supplies stores | 76 |
| Book stores | 68 |
| Gift, novelty, and souvenir shops | 66 |
| Jewelry stores | 65 |
| General merchandise stores | 60 |
| Food stores | 58 |
| Luggage and leather goods stores | 52 |
| Sewing, needlework, and piece-goods stores | 48 |
| Liquor stores | 45 |
| Used merchandise stores | 40 |
| Drug and proprietary stores | 32 |

*Source:* The Dun & Bradstreet Corporation, *Business Failure Record: 1986 Final/1987 Preliminary* (New York: The Dun & Bradstreet Corporation, 1988), 8. Used with permission.

\*These are preliminary statistics for 1987.

The retail lines with the lowest failure rates in 1986 were drug and proprietary stores (32); used-merchandise stores (40); liquor stores (45), and sewing, needlework, and piece-goods outlets (48). On the other hand, you can see from the table that the failure rate for apparel and accessory stores—at the top of the list—was more than four times greater than that for drug and proprietary stores.

**The "Biggest Payoff" Method.** These days, consumers often canvass banks for the particular long-term account that yields the highest interest and perhaps a bonus gift. This kind of approach carries appeal for many businesspeople. Indeed, the typical business owner is conditioned to seek a good return-on-investment. In this context, you should know about an excellent source of statistics on operating results for many different types of businesses—Robert Morris Associates, the national association of bank loan and credit officers. They're noted for their annual publication of statement studies' analyses.

Operating results for selected retail businesses, from their 1987 publication, are shown in table 1–11. The key column in the table for the "Biggest Payoff" method is, of course, the one headed "Operating Profit Before Taxes." As you'll note, these percentages differ from one business type to another. The five retail businesses that yielded the highest operating profit percentages that year were:

| | |
|---|---|
| Jewelry | 4.8% |
| Family clothing | 4.6 |
| Computers and software | 4.2 |
| Musical instruments and supplies | 4.2 |
| Drugstore | 4.0 |

One problem with this approach, though, is the fact that the percentages can vary considerably from one year to the next. The retail sector (like other sectors) is in a continuous state of flux!

**The "Greatest Sales Growth" Route.** Actually, you may consider this method a takeoff on the "Hop-on-the-Bandwagon" approach. Out of curiosity, I calculated the "approximate average sales per store" for the census years 1977 and 1982 for all retail store categories. With rising prices and an inflationary trend over the five-year period, I both expected and found sales gains across-the-board. Here are the retail types that showed the greatest gains:

| | |
|---|---|
| Radio, television, and music stores | Up 85.2% |
| Fruit stands, vegetable markets | Up 72.7 |
| Grocery stores | Up 66.0 |
| Hobby, toy, and game shops | Up 64.1 |
| Gift, novelty, and souvenir shops | Up 61.1 |

## TABLE 1–11. OPERATING INFORMATION FOR SELECTED RETAIL BUSINESSES*

| SIC Number | Type of Business | Cost of Sales | Gross Profit | Operating Expenses | Operating Profit Before Taxes | Cost of Sales ÷ Inventory (median values) |
|---|---|---|---|---|---|---|
| 5942, 5943 | Books and stationery | 61.5% | 38.5% | 36.7% | 1.8% | 3.4 |
| 5999 | Computers and software | 62.8 | 37.2 | 33.0 | 4.2 | 7.1 |
| 5992 | Cut flowers and growing plants | 47.6 | 52.4 | 49.8 | 2.6 | 7.7 |
| 5912 | Drugstore | 67.7 | 32.3 | 28.3 | 4.0 | 4.8 |
| 5399 | Dry goods and general merchandise | 64.2 | 35.8 | 32.0 | 3.8 | 3.3 |
| 5651 | Family clothing | 60.6 | 39.4 | 34.8 | 4.6 | 2.6 |
| 5713 | Floor coverings | 67.2 | 32.8 | 29.4 | 3.4 | 6.3 |
| 5712 | Furniture | 59.8 | 40.2 | 36.9 | 3.3 | 2.6 |
| 5541 | Gasoline service stations | 77.7 | 22.3 | 19.6 | 2.7 | 27.4 |
| 5411 | Groceries and meats | 76.3 | 23.7 | 21.7 | 2.0 | 14.7 |
| 5251 | Hardware | 65.3 | 34.7 | 31.7 | 3.0 | 2.6 |
| 5945 | Hobby, toy, and game shops | 59.7 | 40.3 | 38.2 | 2.1 | 2.9 |
| 5722 | Household appliances | 66.8 | 33.2 | 30.6 | 2.6 | 4.0 |
| 5944 | Jewelry | 54.0 | 46.0 | 41.2 | 4.8 | 1.2 |
| 5921 | Liquor | 76.7 | 23.3 | 20.8 | 2.5 | 8.3 |
| 5947, 5948 | Luggage and gifts | 55.3 | 44.7 | 40.8 | 3.9 | 2.4 |
| 5611 | Men's and boys' clothing | 58.0 | 42.0 | 39.5 | 2.5 | 2.3 |
| 5733 | Musical instruments and supplies | 58.9 | 41.1 | 36.9 | 4.2 | 2.0 |
| 5943, 5999 | Office supplies and equipment | 60.0 | 40.0 | 36.3 | 3.7 | 4.8 |
| 5231 | Paint, glass, and wallpaper | 63.5 | 36.5 | 33.3 | 3.2 | 5.2 |
| 5812 | Restaurants | 43.6 | 56.4 | 53.1 | 3.3 | 28.0 |
| 5661 | Shoes | 60.5 | 39.5 | 36.7 | 2.8 | 2.2 |
| 5941 | Sporting goods and bicycles | 66.2 | 33.8 | 30.1 | 3.7 | 2.9 |
| 5621 | Women's ready-to-wear | 59.3 | 40.7 | 37.7 | 3.0 | 3.2 |

*Source:* Robert Morris Associates, *'87 Annual Statement Studies* (Philadelphia: Robert Morris Associates, 1987). Copyright 1987 by Robert Morris Associates. Used with permission. (See "Interpretation of Statement Studies Figures" following this table.)

*Based on statement studies of firms with fiscal year-ends June 30, 1986 through March 31, 1987. All statistics are expressed in terms of percentages of annual sales volume. (Note: Only data for firms with from $0 to $1 million in assets have been shown since this would be characteristic of the beginning business.)

### Note Regarding Interpretation of Statement Studies Figures

RMA cautions that the Studies be regarded only as a general guideline and not as an absolute industry norm. This is due to limited samples within categories, the categorization of companies by their primary Standard Industrial Classification (SIC) number only, and different methods of operations by companies within the same industry. For these reasons, RMA recommends that the figures be used only as general guidelines in addition to other methods of financial analysis.

Incidentally, you may be interested in learning which stores were characterized by the slowest sales growth:

| | |
|---|---|
| Stationery stores | Up 34.6% |
| Furniture stores | Up 33.8 |
| Florists | Up 31.5 |
| Building materials and supply stores | Up 31.2 |
| Sewing, needlework, and piece-goods stores | Up 19.0 |

I'd venture to conclude that these last five types, for whatever reasons, managed to keep up with neither the economy nor the times.

## Second Thoughts About the "Biggest Payoff" Method

You'll recall that this technique involves checking through the operating results for different business types to find those with high percentages of operating profit before taxes. A major complication is the fact that inventory requirements differ substantially from one type of retailing to the next. Review the last column in table 1–11, which lists the Cost of Sales (sometimes called Cost of Goods) divided by the Inventory for each type of store in median values. *Median values* means that while some stores' operational results showed higher figures, others were lower—and that those appearing in the column are in the middle. You may assume, rather safely I think, that these are "typical" of the types in question. (Note, too, that all data in the table are from firms with $1 million or less in assets.)

*If* your initial investment must be limited and is a major consideration, this factor could present problems if inventory requirements turned out to be greater than you expected. You can, however, work this factor into the picture by following a simple procedure. Here's how you can calculate a "typical" inventory:

Let's assume you wish to open up a store of the first type on the list—a books and stationery store. You estimate that your first year's sales will be $180,000. On the strength of this estimate (let's hope it's correct!), you can determine your approximate cost of goods (or "cost of sales") by multiplying $180,000 by 61.5 percent, as listed in the third column of the table. This works out to a "COG" of $110,700. Roughly, then, *if* you reach the sales figure you have set and *if* the COG percentage holds true, you'll have to buy $110,700 worth of merchandise, at your cost, during your first year.

This calculation, however, doesn't mean that you'll have to carry this amount in stock all year long. The retailer buys goods for resale throughout the year, replenishing stock as it is sold. Take the figure in the last column that corresponds to your business (Books and stationery, 3.4), and divide it into your total cost of goods ($110,700). You'll have the approximate value of the goods you'll need to stock. In this case, it's $32,559 (at cost, of course). If your inventory is close to this figure, at least you'll know that it's in line with those of other merchants like yourself.

Just to make sure you have this procedure down pat, here are several other examples I've worked out for you from table 1–11 (all based on a projected first-year sales volume of $180,000). Check your results against them.

| Store Type | Cost of Sales | Total Cost of goods | Cost of Sales ÷ Inventory | Approximate Inventory Required |
|---|---|---|---|---|
| Groceries and meats | 76.3% | $137,340 | 14.7 | $93,429 |
| Hardware | 65.3 | 117,540 | 2.6 | 45,208 |
| Jewelry | 54.0 | 97,200 | 1.2 | 81,000 |
| Liquor | 76.7 | 138,060 | 8.3 | 16,634 |
| Family clothing | 60.6 | 109,080 | 2.6 | 41,954 |

## FOR FURTHER INFORMATION

### Books

Baumback, C. *How to Organize and Operate a Small Business,* 7th ed. Englewood Cliffs, N.J.: Prentice-Hall, 1985.

Burstiner, Irving. *Basic Retailing.* Homewood, Ill.: Irwin, 1986.

————. *The Small Business Handbook,* rev. ed. New York: Prentice Hall Press, 1989.

Fitzsimmons, James A., and Robert S. Sullivan. *Service Operations Management.* New York: McGraw-Hill, 1982.

Frantz, Forrest H. *Successful Small Business Management.* Englewood Cliffs, N.J.: Prentice-Hall, 1978.

Hughes, Robert J., and Jack R. Kapoor. *Business.* Boston: Houghton Mifflin, 1985.

Kotler, Philip, and Paul N. Bloom. *Marketing Professional Services.* Englewood Cliffs, N.J.: Prentice-Hall, 1984.

Kuriloff, Arthur H., and John M. Hemphill, Jr. *Starting and Managing the Small Business.* New York: McGraw-Hill, 1983.

Longenecker, Justin G., and Carlos W. Moore. *Small-Business Management,* 7th ed. Cincinnati: South-Western, 1987.

Lowry, James. *Retail Management.* Cincinnati: South-Western, 1983.

Musselman, V., and J. Jackson. *Introduction to Modern Business,* 9th ed. Englewood Cliffs, N.J.: Prentice-Hall, 1984.

Pintel, G., and J. Diamond. *Retailing,* 3rd ed. Englewood Cliffs, N.J.: Prentice-Hall, 1983.

### Pamphlets Available from the Small Business Administration*

#### Management Aids

MA 2.016—"Checklist for Going Into Business"
MA 2.020—"Business Plan for Retailers"

---

* Write: U.S. Small Business Administration, P.O. Box 30, Denver, CO, 80201-0030.

---

MA 2.022—"Business Plan for Small Service Firms"

MA 2.025—"Thinking About Going Into Business?"

MA 2.026—"Feasibility Checklist for Starting a Small Business of Your Own"

## Booklets Available from the Superintendent of Documents*

S/N 003-008-00194-7—*Franchise Opportunities Handbook, 1984*—$13.50.

S/N 045-000-00207-1—*Starting and Managing a Small Service Business*—$4.50.

S/N 045-000-00212-8—*Starting and Managing a Small Business of Your Own*—$4.75.

———————

* Write: Superintendent of Documents, U.S. Government Printing Office, Washington, D.C. 20402.

# 2

# What You Need to Succeed in Store Retailing

In the first chapter, you were introduced to the retailing sector of the economy. We explored this significant area in some depth and stressed how retailing differs from manufacturing and other types of business. We offered useful financial information about different kinds of retail operations. We then discussed several distinct types of "nonstore" retailers as well as the retailing of services. Finally, you were shown where opportunities may lie for small independent retailers-to-be.

This chapter has been designed, in the main, to help you come to a sensible decision about retail entrepreneurship. As you read it, bear in mind this thought: "The retailing sector is bustling, colorful, vibrant, and stimulating. No other arena of marketing activity carries more excitement or sense of immediacy. None is as close, as familiar, or more often participated in by the American consumer."*

## IS STORE RETAILING FOR YOU?

This decision isn't the kind that should be made lightly—not at all! Some intrepid spirits plunge head-on into retailing, only to discover to their chagrin (and depleted finances) that a retail merchant's way of life doesn't appeal to them.

In reality, the first decision you need to make is two-sided, as reflected in the following question: "Should I consider starting my own business, *or* am I better off staying on my job?" Of course, if you make up your mind to select the first alternative, you'll still face the challenge of choosing the *kind* of business to go into.

### A Procedure to Follow

First of all, you should try to assess the satisfactions you derive from your current job, then weigh these against the potential outcomes of managing an enterprise of your own.

---

* Irving Burstiner, *Basic Retailing* (Homewood, Ill.: Irwin, 1986), 6.

To help clarify your thinking, you might resort to preparing the kind of balance sheet format known as the *T-account*, which sales representatives sometimes use to "close" prospective buyers. Draw a line down the middle of a sheet of paper. Print the word *Job* at the top on one side of that line and the words *My Own Business* on the opposite side. Then list all the advantages and drawbacks you can think of for both alternatives. Finally, study your T-account and make your decision.

What's to be gained from going into business? For openers, you'll be independent— on your own—and you face the prospect of greater financial rewards than you would expect working for someone else.

To help you decide whether or not you're the *type* who should go into business, take a few minutes out at this point to work out the quiz in exhibit 2–1. It's by no means infallible (in fact, it's mostly for fun-and-games!), but you'll be able to gain some insights into entrepreneurship by answering the questions.

---

### EXHIBIT 2–1. A QUIZ FOR THE WOULD-BE ENTREPRENEUR

Under each question, check the answer that says what you feel or comes closest to it. Be honest with yourself.

*Are you a self-starter?*
_____ I do things on my own. Nobody has to tell me to get going.
_____ If someone gets me started, I keep going all right.
_____ Easy does it, man. I don't put myself out until I have to.

*How do you feel about other people?*
_____ I like people. I can get along with just about anybody.
_____ I have plenty of friends—I don't need anyone else.
_____ Most people bug me.

*Can you lead others?*
_____ I can get most people to go along when I start something.
_____ I can give the orders if someone tells me what we should do.
_____ I let someone else get things moving. Then I go along if I feel like it.

*Can you take responsibility?*
_____ I like to take charge of things and see them through.
_____ I'll take over if I have to, but I'd rather let someone else be responsible.
_____ There's always some eager beaver around wanting to show how smart he is. I say let him.

*How good an organizer are you?*
_____ I like to have a plan before I start. I'm usually the one to get things lined up when the gang wants to do something.
_____ I do all right unless things get too goofed up. Then I cop out.
_____ You get all set and then something comes along and blows the whole bag. So I just take things as they come.

*How good a worker are you?*
_____ I can keep going as long as I need to. I don't mind working hard for something I want.
_____ I'll work hard for a while, but when I've had enough, that's it, man!
_____ I can't see that hard work gets you anywhere.

## EXHIBIT 2–1. CONTINUED

*Can people trust what you say?*

_____ You bet they can. I don't say things I don't mean.

_____ I try to be on the level most of the time, but sometimes I just say what's easiest.

_____ Why bother if the other fellow doesn't know the difference?

*Can you stick with it?*

_____ If I make up my mind to do something, I don't let *anything* stop me.

_____ I usually finish what I start—if it goes well.

_____ If it doesn't go right away, I quit. Why beat your brains out?

*How good is your health?*

_____ I *never* run down!

_____ I have enough energy for most things I want to do.

_____ I run out of energy sooner than most of my friends seem to.

*Now count the checks you made.*

How many checks are there beside the *first* answer to each question? _____

How many checks are there beside the *second* answer to each question? _____

How many checks are there beside the *third* answer to each question? _____

If most of your checks are beside the first answers, you probably have what it takes to run a business. If not, you're likely to have more trouble than you can handle by yourself. Better find a partner who is strong on the points you're weak on. If many checks are beside the third answer, not even a good partner will be able to shore you up.

*Source:* "Checklist for Going into Business," *Small Marketers Aid No. 71* (Washington, D.C.: U.S. Small Business Administration, 1977), 4–5.

Besides taking this quiz, you should analyze yourself for other personal qualities, some of which are itemized in exhibit 2–2. If you like to meet and talk with people, if you feel that selling merchandise to consumers is a valuable service, and if you enjoy the

## EXHIBIT 2–2. PERSONAL QUALITIES NEEDED TO MANAGE A STORE

The successful manager of a small retail store:

1. Must be strongly motivated and want to get ahead
2. Prizes independence
3. Has the ability to "read" customers—to determine and supply their needs
4. Gets along well with people
5. Has a sympathetic ear and tries to understand others and their situations
6. Has a sense of fairness
7. Has the ability to adapt to change
8. Is inquisitive, imaginative, innovative, perceptive, and decisive
9. Is able to inspire and direct employees
10. Is willing to serve the people with whom he or she deals and the community as well

*Source:* Irving Schwartz, "Personal Qualities Needed to Manage a Store," *Small Marketers Aid No. 145* (Washington, D.C.: U.S. Small Business Administration, 1974), 2–7.

atmosphere of a well-kept store, then perhaps you're cut out for retailing. Think of the many stores you have shopped in over the years. Can you recall what those retail merchants were like? What did they do while in the store? What were their attitudes, interests, and concerns? What about the stores you visit today—or those owned by friends or family members? Analyze these thoughts you have collected and then ask yourself, "Will this kind of life/work/activity suit my own personality?"

## What Are the Drawbacks?

Perhaps we should get all the negatives, which you might have heard about, out on the table right now—before you commit time, energy, and money to a retail enterprise. Opening your own store means giving up your job, with its steady income, holidays with pay, vacations, and the opportunity for advancement. You'll have to exchange all this—and perhaps much more—for:

- The chance to gamble with your savings—and perhaps with borrowed capital too—with the odds really stacked against you
- Hard work and long hours, often including nights and Saturdays (the busiest day of the week for many retailers)
- Profits measured in pennies on the dollar—when they finally come in
- Months and months without even a minimum salary, in the majority of cases
- Lots of "busy work," like checking off deliveries, putting stock away into bins, housekeeping, ordering merchandise, waiting on customers, lugging cartons, and changing interior and window displays
- Concern over the possibility of shoplifters ripping you off, and worry about burglaries or, even worse, armed robbery

If none of these trade-offs frighten you, and if you would still like to try your hand at being a shopkeeper, then full steam ahead! And good luck!

## QUALIFICATIONS NEEDED FOR SUCCESS

In an earlier book on small business, I wrote that only four ingredients are essential to a new business success:

- A qualified entrepreneur
- A potential business opportunity
- A solid and detailed plan
- Sufficient capital

Upon further reflection, we should add a fifth element to that list: luck.

I see no reason for changing my thinking. Additional years of exposure to the trials and tribulations of small business owners have reinforced my belief in these ingredients. Setting aside that aspect called *luck,* as it lies largely outside our control (although some would argue this point), the nature and thrust of the second through fourth ingredients obviously depend entirely on that first item: a *qualified* entrepreneur. Without that force known as the entrepreneur welding all the other elements together and striving mightily toward his or her goals, there's no business at all.

Yet, before we start investigating what the term *qualified entrepreneur* means, a few thoughts and considerations regarding the other three ingredients are in order. Let's start from the bottom of the list and work backwards until we reach the source—or the force, if you prefer.

## Sufficient Capital

Study the statistics on small business failures, and you'll come away with an inescapable conclusion: A large proportion of these ventures must have been seriously under-capitalized. Without adequate financing, even the best laid plans can go awry. The days when you might have been able to go into business "on a shoestring," as the saying goes, have long vanished. To start a retail business these days, you need not only sufficient capital for outfitting and stocking the store but also additional funds to meet your personal needs—such as rent, clothing, food, and transportation—until you can draw some sort of salary. You also have to set aside money for "contingencies," simply because you can't predict the future. Because capitalization is so vital to your plans, all of chapter 5 has been devoted to "Planning for Your Financial Needs."

## A Solid and Detailed Plan

No one activity does more for you than the preparation of a complete "master plan" for your new business *well in advance of taking your first step.* Planning is a tremendous discipline. It forces you to think, to explore, to project, to make assumptions, to anticipate, to set objectives, and so on. Your finished plan should take into account every facet of your contemplated venture: financing; the selection of merchandise lines for resale (and the breadth and depth of your inventory); the store's location, decor, layout, and fixturization; sales promotion and advertising; managing and supervising your employees; resources to buy from; and so forth.

You'll find valuable assistance in this crucial area in chapter 6, "Developing an Effective Business Plan." Moreover, several other chapters in this book expand upon your planning needs in locating your store, in developing your insurance and store security programs, and in other important areas.

## A Potential Business Opportunity

There must be a decided need for your particular kind of store in the area you have selected. Implicit in this need is a challenge to you: how to appraise your chances for establishing and building a successful enterprise. Here are just a few of the questions for which you'll need answers:*

- Who are my potential customers?
- What are they like?
- Where do they shop now?
- What do they buy? Why?
- Can I offer the kinds of goods they want? Can I offer the services they'll expect?
- Will my prices be consistent with what my customers view as good value?
- Is the community's population expected to grow, decline, or remain static? Is there a seasonal fluctuation?
- Are incomes in the area apt to be stable?
- Can I foresee changes in the makeup of the neighborhood?
- How will my store compare with those of my competitors?
- What's the general character of the stores in my immediate vicinity? How many look prosperous? How many seem to be barely getting by?
- Can I stress a special area of appeal, such as lower prices, better quality, wider selection, convenient location, or convenient store hours?

For assistance with this particular ingredient for entrepreneurial success, you may refer to the details in chapter 7.

## The Qualified Entrepreneur

An entrepreneur is "one who undertakes a venture, organizes it, raises capital to finance it, and assumes all or a major portion of the risk."** Such individuals have been portrayed as "decision makers who identify and capitalize on opportunities through approaches that emphasize innovation, profitable venture identification, effectiveness rather than efficiency, and nonprogrammed or ambiguous situations."†

What, then, is a "qualified" entrepreneur? Some insight into the significance of that adjective can be gleaned from these five "requirements" for the successful operation of any type of business, which were outlined some years back in a business journal:

---

* For additional, insightful questions, see the following pamphlets ("Management Aids"), available from the U.S. Small Business Administration: MA 2.016—"Checklist for Going Into Business"; MA 2.020—"Business Plan for Retailers"; MA 4.012—"Marketing Checklist for Small Retailers"; MA 4.019—"Learning About Your Market."

** John G. Burch, "Profiling the Entrepreneur," *Business Horizons* 29 (September–October 1986), 13.

† Philip D. Olson, "Entrepreneurs: Opportunistic Decision Makers," *Journal of Small Business Management* 24 (July 1986), 35.

---

- The development of proper attitudes and behavior
- Technical expertise
- Managerial-entrepreneurial skills
- A viable offering
- The four critical partners every owner must have: an accountant, banker, lawyer, and insurance agent*

Note first that items 1 through 3 have to do with the entrepreneur personally. "Proper attitudes and behavior," according to the writer, include such things as the desire to learn, the ability to make decisions, the ability to delegate, being a self-starter, being energetic, having patience and self-confidence, and so on. Item 3 refers to "the sum of all the constituent parts of running a business: e.g., marketing, planning, promotion, pricing, accounting, financing, legal aspects, insurance, personnel management, etc."**

In my judgment, the odds in favor of business success are strongly enhanced when the entrepreneur is qualified along three major dimensions: *educationally, professionally,* and most important, *personally.*

**Educationally Qualified.** It's common knowledge that those fortunate enough to acquire a college education will, on the average, enjoy considerably higher lifetime earnings than will high-school graduates. This doesn't mean that less-educated individuals cannot be successful on the job or in their own businesses. Millions have, on both fronts. Indeed, many of today's millionaires never even finished high school.

Nevertheless, a higher education does broaden the "data base" in your "cranial computer," providing more reserve information to help you recognize opportunities, assess situations, and make decisions. Give yourself a sound foundation in the liberal arts and the social sciences. Take some business courses. It's not necessary to major in business administration or in retail management (though there's little wrong with doing so), but *do* take a few courses in these areas.

You can also benefit from reading widely, even voraciously. Formal schooling isn't the only way to accumulate facts or to gather insights into people, organizations, cultures, and the like. Your public library is a wonderful source of knowledge; so are the many magazines, journals, newspapers, and other periodicals. Read such publications as *Time, Business Week,* the *Wall Street Journal,* the *New York Times,* and others regularly. Doing so helps you become conversant with economic trends, changes in the sociopolitical climate, new products and ideas, technological advances, the problems of other companies, consumer attitudes, and so on. Reading the trade publications in your own field of retailing answers your more specific needs. Some examples of the hundreds of

---

* Norman R. Land, "Too Much Emphasis on Management Assistance," *Journal of Small Business Management* 13 (July 1975), 2–3.
** Ibid., p. 2.

trade periodicals are *Home Furnishings Daily, Progressive Grocer, Toy and Hobby World, Housewares,* and *Women's Wear Daily.*

**Professionally Qualified.** If you aspire to a successful retail business of your own, doesn't it make sense to come into the field properly "equipped" with some valid experience? By working in someone else's store for even six months, you will acquire firsthand experience in retail operations: keeping a clean and attractive store; filling the bins; wrapping packages; taking inventory; setting up window and interior displays; making register reconciliations and bank deposits; and the like. You will also develop skill in meeting and serving customers and in handling complaints. You will learn about store hours, night shopping, and scheduling employee hours. This sort of preparation will improve your chances for success when you finally decide to go it alone, especially if you work in a retail store of the exact same type you want to open.

It's better still if you can work up to the position of store manager. Being a manager gives you the opportunity to develop and polish managerial skills, such as planning and organizing, supervising the personnel, and learning all about buying merchandise and selecting sources of supply. These administrative capabilities will serve you well in your own business. You'll know how to motivate and inspire employees, how to train them properly, and how to coordinate their activities skillfully. Part IV of this book is devoted to those aspects; other phases of retail store operations are treated in Part III.

**Personally Qualified.** Now here's an intriguing question: Do certain personal qualities or traits correlate positively with entrepreneurial success? As we know, each of us is a complex, composite being, equipped with potential by heredity, then conditioned by our environment and fashioned by the experiences we have as we go through life. We have many facets: physical, mental, emotional, social, political, economic, and others. We reflect differing constitutions, goals, value systems, personalities, outlooks, philosophies, and so on. In a diverse world peopled by billions, individuals all, is it possible to perceive similarities among types—and to extract valid guidelines for the aspiring businessperson as to the "entrepreneurial personality?"

Some decades ago, studies of that quality called "leadership" attempted to uncover characteristics that distinguish superior leaders from the less able. This so-called trait approach—fashionable at the time—spilled over into many other areas of investigation. Among these, I recall research into "the creative person," "the successful school administrator," and "the superior salesperson." Leaders were found to be doers and self-starters. They take the initiative, are realistic in their outlook, and know how to communicate with other people.

Today, however, we have gotten away from this trait approach. We feel that there are no specific "leader types" but that, given the right circumstances, nearly everyone can be a leader. Following through on this reasoning, if we're willing to designate individuals who start small businesses of their own as "leaders" (and I certainly believe we may do so!), then by rational extension nearly everyone can be an entrepreneur!

Still, it seems to me that at least five or six personal characteristics may increase your chances for success in business. Call it intuition on my part, if you will. While a modest case might be made for many other traits, I suspect that these specific personal qualities are significant:

- A strong need to achieve
- Drive
- Abundant energy (stemming from a state of good health, both physical and mental)
- The courage to take risks
- Persistence
- Self-confidence
- Flexibility
- Innovativeness

Scan the above list of personal traits. Do you feel that you possess these qualities? If you do, then I believe you certainly have the potential to become a successful retailer!

## CHOOSING YOUR PROFESSIONAL ADVISORS

No matter how motivated you may be, launching your new venture entirely on your own, without first obtaining skilled legal and financial counsel, could be a remarkably foolish move. Doing so could even be disastrous. A business is a complicated structure, one that must operate within an infinitely more complex environment. Few people can claim even a modest competence in more than one area of specialization, such as merchandising, sales, personnel, production, and so on. Fewer still have the background necessary to handle the financial and legal aspects of the business. Recognizing their deficiencies, most prudent—and farsighted—entrepreneurs build a "general staff" of professionals who can supply the talent required not only to secure a firm foothold in the marketplace for the new enterprise but also to ensure its continued success and growth.

The nucleus of your general staff should consist of two capable experts: your attorney and your accountant. These two are your chief advisors. Others, who play lesser, though still important, roles include a responsible insurance agent or broker and an official of the bank with which you plan to do business.

### Your Attorney

You'll need to conduct your business within an intricate framework of rules, regulations, ordinances, laws, and other constraints stemming from all levels of government: federal, state, and local. Only a trained professional can make sense out of this morass for you. Search for an attorney who is familiar with retailing and, if possible, with your particular line of trade. Look for a lawyer who enjoys a good reputation among his or her peers, who can devote enough time to your business needs, and with whom you can communicate freely and easily, without discomfort. Since you want a long-term relationship with this person, consider basing the arrangement on either an hourly fee or a monthly retainer.

Among other things, your attorney can:

- Help you over the initial hurdles of starting up, by reviewing with you the laws and regulations that affect your retail operation
- Advise you as to the kinds of permits and licenses you may need
- Present the pros and cons of the different legal forms of business and suggest the one best suited to your needs
- Prepare the necessary documents to establish the legal form you select
- Interpret for you the details of the proposed store lease—and fight for better terms
- Prepare partnership (or shareholder) agreements, bearing your interests in mind
- Carefully peruse all contracts and other legal documents, pointing out all important details you need to know about (if you're planning to buy an established business or open up a franchise)
- Give counsel on all kinds of legal matters over the years, ranging from contemplated contracts, leases, and the like to changes in local ordinances or state and federal laws that may affect your business
- Aid in the collection of past-due monies from delinquent charge customers
- Assist you in resolving problems with creditors
- Defend you in litigation brought against your firm or against you

## Your Accountant

This professional advises you on all financial matters. Your accountant can set up your bookkeeping and accounting systems so that you're able to get at the facts you need to make valid business judgments. Other services provided include the periodic issuance of your basic accounting statements, the preparation of your tax returns, consultation about business outcomes and discernible trends, and recommendations as to new equipment and the improvement of internal systems where indicated. Your accountant will also call for and pore over all internal records: balance sheets, operating statements, tax returns, inventory records, and the like. Inventories, fixtures, equipment, and all other assets must be examined and evaluated, and dollar figures must be set on all.

Finally, if you're thinking of buying someone else's going business, you need to depend on your accountant's expertise in analyzing the firm's potential.

## YOUR GOVERNMENT IS READY TO HELP YOU

Our economy is imbued with the spirit of free enterprise, and small business is its mainstay. Ever since the passage of the Sherman Antitrust Act nearly a century ago, it has been evident that our government's policy has been against monopoly and in favor of competition. Back in the 1950s, Congress created the Small Business Administration (SBA); this independent agency was designed to encourage, counsel, provide assistance to, and protect the interests of American small business. It plays a leadership role in fostering the development of small firms and in strengthening their competitive position. The SBA operates in the following four areas:

- Helping small companies find adequate capital and credit
- Providing management, financial, and production counsel
- Licensing and regulating small business investment companies
- Helping small business get a fair share of government procurement contracts and surplus sales*

The first two areas—capital/credit, and counsel—are, of course, of extreme interest to the retailer. You'll find more details about capital financing and counsel in chapter 5, along with information regarding the principal lending programs of the SBA (and Small Business Investment Companies as well). Among these SBA programs are assistance loans for the handicapped, loans to minority enterprises, disaster loans, and direct loans or loan guarantees to small businesses (for construction, expansion, the purchase of equipment, and so on). The SBA also cosponsors courses in business management with educational institutions all over the country. It holds frequent conferences, workshops, and small business clinics in many cities. Through its volunteer SCORE (Service Corps of Retired Executives) and ACE (Active Corps of Executives) advisors, people who want to go into business, as well as owners of established small enterprises, can enjoy the counsel of experienced managers without charge.

Another valuable aspect of the agency's operations is its publication of many aids for small business, such as those listed at the end of each chapter in this book. Request copies of order forms #115A ("Business Development Pamphlets") and #115B ("Business Development Booklets") from the U.S. Small Business Administration, P.O. Box 30, Denver, CO 80201-0030.

Meanwhile, you might consider paying a visit to the nearest SBA field office to pick up any useful material they may have on hand that can help you in your intended venture. Be sure to set up an appointment in advance with one of the SCORE or ACE counselors to discuss your plans. The SBA maintains field offices across the country; a list of these appears in exhibit 2–3.

## DISCOVER WHAT YOUR TRADE ASSOCIATION CAN DO FOR YOU

An excellent source of help for the retail entrepreneur is the trade association. Such organizations exist to serve the needs of just about every kind of business, be it a

---

* Jack Zwick, "A Handbook of Small Business Finance," *Small Business Management Series No. 15* (Washington, D.C.: U.S. Small Business Administration, 1975), 51.

## Exhibit 2-3. Field offices, U.S. Small Business Administration

Agana, Guam
Albany, N.Y.
Albuquerque, N. Mex.
Anchorage, Alaska
Atlanta, Ga.
Augusta, Maine
Baltimore, Md.
Birmingham, Ala.
Boise, Idaho
Boston, Mass.
Buffalo, N.Y.
Casper, Wyo.
Charleston, W. Va.
Charlotte, N.C.
Chicago, Ill.
Cincinnati, Ohio
Clarksburg, W. Va.
Cleveland, Ohio
Columbia, S.C.
Columbus, Ohio
Concord, N.H.
Corpus Christi, Tex.
Dallas, Tex.
Denver, Colo.
Des Moines, Iowa
Detroit, Mich.
Eau Claire, Wis.
Elmira, N.Y.
El Paso, Tex.
Fairbanks, Alaska
Fargo, N. Dak.
Fresno, Calif.
Gulfport, Miss.
Harlingen, Tex.
Harrisburg, Pa.
Hartford, Conn.
Hato Rey, P.R.
Helena, Mont.
Holyoke, Mass.
Honolulu, Hawaii
Houston, Tex.
Indianapolis, Ind.
Jackson, Miss.
Jacksonville, Fla.
Kansas City, Mo.

Knoxville, Tenn.
Las Cruces, N. Mex.
Las Vegas, Nev.
Little Rock, Ark.
Los Angeles, Calif.
Louisville, Ky.
Lubbock, Tex.
Madison, Wis.
Marquette, Mich.
Marshall, Tex.
Memphis, Tenn.
Miami, Fla.
Milwaukee, Wis.
Minneapolis, Minn.
Montpelier, Vt.
Nashville, Tenn.
Newark, N.J.
New Orleans, La.
New York, N.Y.
Oklahoma City, Okla.
Omaha, Nebr.
Philadelphia, Pa.
Phoenix, Ariz.
Pittsburgh, Pa.
Portland, Oreg.
Providence, R.I.
Rapid City, S. Dak.
Richmond, Va.
Rochester, N.Y.
St. Louis, Mo.
Salt Lake City, Utah
San Antonio, Tex.
San Diego, Calif.
San Francisco, Calif.
Seattle, Wash.
Sioux Falls, S. Dak.
Spokane, Wash.
Springfield, Ill.
Syracuse, N.Y.
Tampa, Fla.
Washington, D.C.
Wichita, Kans.
Wilkes-Barre, Pa.
Wilmington, Del.

*Source:* C. R. Stigelman, "Franchise Index/Profile: A Franchise Evaluation Process," *Small Business Management Series No. 35* (Washington, D.C.: U.S. Small Business Administration, 1986), 55.
*Note:* For addresses and telephone numbers of the field offices, look under "United States Government" in the appropriate telephone directories.

manufacturing plant, a wholesaling firm, a retail store, or a service enterprise. To find out the name and address of the appropriate association for your particular line of business, check with other retailers in the community who operate the same kind of store, query your major suppliers, or contact your local chamber of commerce. You can also consult the *Encyclopedia of Associations* at your public library.* In this reference work, you will find listings not only of business associations but of every conceivable type of organization: cultural, civic, fraternal, and so on.

Association membership is relatively inexpensive for the store owner. Usually, the cost runs several hundred dollars annually, a tax-deductible expense. Here are some of the benefits of belonging:

- You'll be kept abreast of trends in your industry.
- The association gathers data periodically from its membership, then compiles and issues reports, such as operating results, which are extremely useful for comparison with your own figures.
- Throughout the year, you'll receive news of events and conditions that affect your phase of retailing, as well as many worthwhile hints to help your business. These hints range from merchandising, display, and other promotional information to facts about new items, sources of supply, and the like.
- Most organizations distribute their own newsletters or magazines; the ideas contained in a single issue can often return more than your annual membership fee.
- You'll meet from time to time with other retailers to share experiences, views, and ideas.

You might, at this point, wish to review the list of trade-association services in exhibit 2–4. You might also take a cursory glance at the "sample" descriptions of several trade associations that follow.

**Menswear Retailers of America (MRA), 2011 Eye St., N.W., Suite 600, Washington, DC 20006.** In existence since 1914, this organization offers its members an assortment of valuable publications including manuals on management accounting, insurance, and display; sales refresher courses and selling-skills programs; a business newsletter; monthly fashion reports; survey reports on sales and merchandising trends, and so on. It also makes available electronic data processing advice and financial services. Proposed and existing regulations that may affect the menswear industry are also monitored through Washington contacts.

**National Association of Retail Dealers of America (NARDA), 10 E. 22 St., Lombard, IL 60148.** This organization has been in existence for more than four decades. Having pioneered in the application of electronic data processing (EDP), it provides analyses of sales and gross margins on a monthly basis for many different departments in

* Published by Gale Research Company, Book Tower, Detroit, Michigan 48226.

**EXHIBIT 2–4. SOME SERVICES PROVIDED BY TRADE ASSOCIATIONS**

Promoting better accounting and record-keeping methods.

Sponsoring industry-wide meetings and developing leadership within the industry.

Operating a liaison service between federal agencies, the Congress, the industry, and its individual members.

Providing publicity and public relations programs for the industry.

Issuing special information bulletins to their members. These bulletins report on current affairs affecting the industry, on government orders and legislation, and on other similar matters.

Gathering statistics for the industry.

Publishing specialized data concerning the industry. Many of these relate to such activities as promoting sales or attracting qualified individuals into employment within the industry.

Offering training courses to employees of member companies.

Supplying other services to the industry such as credit reporting services, savings on the purchase of insurance, and varied economic studies.

Furnishing the industry with specialized technical advice that few small members, individually, would be able to afford.

*Source:* Reuel W. Elton, "How Trade Associations Help Small Business," *Management Aid No. 32* (Washington, D.C.: U.S. Small Business Administration, 1961).

the retailer's operation. Computer bookkeeping is available, as are financial-statement analyses and consultation on management problems. Regional conferences are conducted, and lobbying in Washington on behalf of its membership is active. Education sessions on advertising, merchandising, and sales training are key member benefits.

**National Grocers Association (NGA), 1825 Samuel Morse Drive, Reston, VA 22090.** This association conducts seminars and workshops for its members; supplies guides for day-to-day store operation; and publishes manuals, plans, training aids, and other helpful materials. It provides up-to-date information on government activities and financial information and issues analyses of operating results for the grocery trade.

**National Home Furnishing Association (NHFA), 305 W. High Street, High Point, NC 27260.** Representing well over 5,000 home-furnishing companies comprised of more than 13,000 individual stores in the United States and in foreign countries, this organization issues a variety of publications to its members. Included are a monthly trade magazine, annual survey of operating experiences, annual directory to equipment and services, a store planning and display guide, sales training, and other continuing-education programs. Business forms, special bank-card rates, and volume prices for various products and services are also available to members.

**International Mass Retail Association (IMRA), 570 Seventh Avenue, New York, NY 10018.** This organization has represented the discount store industry for more than two decades. It gathers, coordinates, and disseminates essential industry data and makes available a number of useful publications. Represented are more than 6,500 self-service general merchandise stores and leased departments in the United States, Canada, and other countries. The IMRA also conducts a year-round seminar program.

**National Shoe Retailers Association (NSRA), 9861 Broken Land Parkway, Columbia, MD 21046.** For over 75 years NSRA, a retail consulting organization, has aided independent shoe retailers. Benefits and services include a bimonthly newsletter, educational brochures, books and videos; seminars on management techniques and retail computer technology; an insurance program; and a discount Visa/Mastercard service. NSRA maintains a full-time professional staff and legal council in Washington to aid its members.

## FOR FURTHER INFORMATION

### Books

Baumback, C. *How to Organize and Operate a Small Business*, 7th ed. Englewood Cliffs, N.J.: Prentice-Hall, 1985.

Burstiner, Irving. *Basic Retailing*. Homewood, Ill.: Irwin, 1986.

————. *The Small Business Handbook*, rev. ed. New York: Prentice Hall Press, 1989.

Kuriloff, Arthur H., and John M. Hemphill, Jr. *Starting and Managing the Small Business*. New York: McGraw-Hill, 1983.

Longenecker, Justin G., and Carlos W. Moore. *Small-Business Management*, 7th ed. Cincinnati: South-Western, 1987.

Lowry, James. *Retail Management*. Cincinnati: South-Western, 1983.

Pintel, G., and J. Diamond. *Retailing*, 3rd ed. Englewood Cliffs, N.J.: Prentice-Hall, 1983.

### Pamphlets Available from the Small Business Administration

#### Management Aids

MA 2.016—"Checklist for Going Into Business"
MA 2.020—"Business Plan for Retailers"

### Booklets Available from the Superintendent of Documents

S/N 003-008-00194-7—*Franchise Opportunities Handbook, 1984*—$13.50.
S/N 045-000-00237-3—*Small Business Incubator Handbook: A Guide for Start-up and Management*—$8.50.

# II

# Gearing Up for Your New Business

# 3

# Organizing Your Business: Some Preliminaries

Before starting up in business, you'll need to select the legal structure that best suits your needs. There are three basic forms to choose from:

> **The sole proprietorship.** You and you alone are in charge of the business and fully responsible for all eventualities.
>
> **The partnership.** If you have selected the general partnership form, you share the management, responsibility, and profits (or losses) with one or more individuals.
>
> **The corporation.** You work within a company that has an existence of its own and that's subject to rather strict regulation.

The implications of each of these three structures are described below.

## THE SOLE PROPRIETORSHIP

The majority of small businesses in the United States reflect this form of ownership, possibly because it's the simplest and least expensive of the three legal structures to initiate. Perhaps the real reason is that it provides individual owners an opportunity to run the entire show as they please. Just about anyone with an idea, a modest amount of capital, and some courage can tackle a retail business with little more fanfare than applying for a sales tax–authorization certification in most areas and registering the business. In some places, you may need to publish your "intent to conduct business" in the local newspaper. Licenses are required for certain types of retail or service businesses, such as liquor stores, restaurants, beauty salons, and barber shops.

If you want to operate your enterprise under any name other than your own, you'll also need to file a "Certificate of Conducting Business Under an Assumed (or Fictitious) Name" with the county or town clerk. Exhibit 3–1 is a sample of a "D/B/A" ("Doing Business As") form.

**Exhibit 3–1. Certificate of Conducting Business Under an Assumed Name**

 **Blumbergs Law Products**   X 201—Certificate of Conducting Business under an Assumed Name
For Individual                    Julius Blumberg, Inc., Law Blank Publishers

# 𝕭usiness 𝕮ertificate

I HEREBY CERTIFY *that I am conducting or transacting business under the name or designation*

*of*

*at*

*City or Town of*                        *County of*                        *State of New York.*

*My full name is**
*and I reside at*

I FURTHER CERTIFY *that I am the successor in interest to*

*the person or persons heretofore using such name or names to carry on or conduct or transact business.*

IN WITNESS WHEREOF, *I have this*            *day of*                        *19*      *, made*
*and signed this certificate.*

................................................................................................................................

* Print or type name.
* If under 18 years of age, state "I am................years of age".

*STATE OF NEW YORK*          } *ss.:*
*COUNTY OF*

*On this*        *day of*                        *19*      *, before me personally appeared*

*to me known and known to me to be the individual*    *described in and who executed the foregoing*
*certificate, and    he    thereupon*            *duly acknowledged to me that    he    executed the same.*

*Source:* Forms may be purchased from Julius Blumberg, Inc., 62 White Street, New York, NY 10013, or any of its dealers. Reproduction prohibited.

**EXHIBIT 3–1. CONTINUED**

INDEX No.

# Certificate
of

..........................................

..........................................

..........................................

*CONDUCTING BUSINESS UNDER*

*THE NAME OF*

..........................................

As a sole proprietor, all decisions are up to you alone. You start up the business, run it, try to build it up—all without being subjected to criticism from anyone other than yourself. Likewise, you're able to retain all profits after taxes (or, conversely, suffer all losses) entirely by yourself. This legal form is not itself a taxable entity; whatever profit or loss you earn is taxed to you as an individual and added to any other earnings (or losses) you may have had during the year. Similarly, all debts of the business become your personal responsibility. In case of failure, your creditors can sue you personally to recover their outstanding balances.

Another disadvantage of the sole proprietorship is its extremely curtailed ability to attract additional capital. The risk for investors of a one-person business is too great. What if something should happen to you? Who will take over and run your business if you become ill? If you should die, the business goes, too. Of course, if you have adequate resources to offer as collateral, the problem is somewhat mitigated.

## THE PARTNERSHIP

This legal form carries many of the same benefits and drawbacks of the proprietorship, except that you have one or more partners to share the risks, the workload, and, of course, the profits. It's still a vulnerable type of structure in that the personal liability problem remains. Moreover, it carries an additional danger in that your risk is actually increased, since any move a partner makes, *with or without your consent,* can obligate you personally in case of business failure.

Then there's the big problem of getting along with your partner(s). The partnership concept has frequently been compared to marriage. If partners cannot get along comfortably with one another, the only escape is a "divorce"—a dissolution of the partnership or one partner buying out the other(s).

The two main attractions of this legal form seem to be (1) adding a partner brings in additional initial capital, and (2) the partner contributes skills, talents, and expertise to the enterprise that complement those of the other partner(s).

Those who participate in the active conduct of the business are referred to as "general" partners. In many states, a firm is permitted to have one or more "limited" partners; these are individuals who have invested capital in the business but are not at all involved in operations. Thus they can't be held personally liable for business debts (except to the extent of their investments).

Since the partners operate collectively under a trade name, they have to file a DBA form, as in the case of the sole proprietorship, though the form itself is different (see exhibit 3–2). Additionally, for your own protection, you should have your attorney draw up a *partnership agreement* before entering into this form of business. In it, details of the enterprise are spelled out, as well as the partners' responsibilities, important financial aspects, and the method of handling a dissolution of the partnership. Standard partner-

**EXHIBIT 3-2.** CERTIFICATE OF CONDUCTING BUSINESS AS PARTNERS

 X 74—Certificate of Conducting Business as Partners.
Individual — Corporation.

# Business Certificate for Partners

The undersigned do hereby certify that they are conducting or transacting business as members of a partnership under the name or designation of

at

in the County of                                    , State of New York, and do further certify that the full names of all the persons conducting or transacting such partnership including the full names of all the partners with the residence address of each such person, and the age of any who may be infants, are as follows:

*NAME* Specify which are infants and state ages.                    RESIDENCE

.................................................                    .................................................

.................................................                    .................................................

.................................................                    .................................................

.................................................                    .................................................

.................................................                    .................................................

.................................................                    .................................................

*WE DO FURTHER CERTIFY* that we are the successors in interest to

the person or persons heretofore using such name or names to carry on or conduct or transact business.

**In Witness Whereof,** We have this          day of          19     made and signed this certificate.

.................................................

.................................................

.................................................

.................................................

.................................................

.................................................

**State of New York, County of**                    ss.:          INDIVIDUAL ACKNOWLEDGMENT

On this          day of                    19     , before me personally appeared

to me known and known to me to be the individual     described in, and who executed the foregoing certificate, and     he     thereupon          duly acknowledged to me that     he     executed the same.

---

## EXHIBIT 3–2. CONTINUED

State of New York, County of                          ss.:                    CORPORATE ACKNOWLEDGMENT

On this                 day of                              19      , before me personally appeared

to me known, who being by me duly sworn, did depose and say, that      he resides in

that     he is the                              of

the corporation described in and which executed the foregoing certificate; that     he knows the seal of said
corporation; that the seal affixed to said certificate is such corporate seal; that it was so affixed by order
of the Board of                              of said corporation, and that     he signed h      name thereto
by like order.

*INDEX No.*

# Certificate of Partners

*CONDUCTING BUSINESS UNDER
THE NAME OF*

State of New York, County of                          ss.:                    INDIVIDUAL ACKNOWLEDGMENT

On this                 day of                              19      , before me personally appeared

to me known and known to me to be the individual     described in, and who executed the foregoing
certificate, and    he    thereupon                 duly acknowledged to me that    he    executed the same.

ship agreement forms are available at your business stationery store. A sample form is represented in exhibit 3–3.

The tax procedure for the partnership is a bit more complicated than that for the sole proprietorship. Like the sole proprietorship, the business itself is not directly taxed; income generated is added to the other earnings of the partners and reported on Form 1040, the individual income tax form. However, each year it is still necessary to file Form 1065, the "U.S. Partnership Return of Income," which is essentially a reporting form. (Refer to chapter 20 for an expanded discussion of business taxes.)

## THE CORPORATION

This legal form represents the most complex of the three basic structures and the most closely regulated of all. To form a corporation, the necessary number of "legally qualified incorporators" (usually three) must file a "Certificate of Incorporation" with the Secretary of State in the particular state where the business will be located (see exhibit 3–4). Although it's possible to handle all the necessary paperwork by yourself or with the aid of your accountant, it's certainly more advisable to engage the services of an attorney in seeking a corporate charter. Although a lawyer may charge you a few hundred dollars for the service, this initial investment is money well spent.

The corporate form of organization is attractive to many entrepreneurs for a variety of reasons, the most important of which are that:

- The personal liability aspect is avoided.
- As a separate entity, the corporation has its own legal existence and consequently continues in business even after the death of a principal.
- The corporation is of more interest to investors and lenders than the other two basic legal forms.
- Ownership in the corporation is transferred easily simply by selling stock.

At this juncture, you may wish to review the pros and cons of all three legal forms, which are graphically described in exhibit 3–5.

## PLANNING YOUR INSURANCE (RISK-MANAGEMENT) PROGRAM

In addition to the near-total commitment of your time and personal energies, the new enterprise you're about to start represents a major investment of funds. You need to arrange for adequate insurance to protect that investment. The wisest approach is to discuss your business needs with an insurance representative who is familiar with your particular line of retailing. Moreover, the program you settle on should be reviewed annually.

You can never insure your business fully (100 percent) against all the hazards that

---

## EXHIBIT 3–3. PARTNERSHIP AGREEMENT FORM

107—Article of Co-Partnership.                                        W                        JULIUS BLUMBERG, INC., LAW BLANK PUBLISHERS

# Articles of Agreement,

Made the                          day of                          one thousand nine hundred and
BETWEEN

WITNESSETH: *The said parties above named have agreed to become co-partners and by these presents form a partnership under the trade name and style of*

*for the purpose of buying, selling, vending and manufacturing*

*and all other goods, wares and merchandise belonging to the said business and to occupy the following premises:*

*their co-partnership to commence on the                          day of                          19
and to continue*

*and to that end and purpose the said*

*to be used and employed in common between them for the support and management of the said business, to their mutual benefit and advantage. AND it is agreed by and between the parties to these presents, that at all times during the continuance of their co-partnership, they and each of them will give their attendance, and do their and each of their best endeavors, and to the utmost of their skill and power, exert themselves for their joint interest, profit, benefit and advantage, and truly employ, buy, sell and merchandise with their joint stock, and the increase thereof, in the business aforesaid. AND ALSO, that they shall and will at all times during the said co-partnership, bear, pay and discharge equally between them, all rents and other expenses that may be required for the support and management of the said business; and that all gains, profit and increase, that shall come,*

*Source:* Forms may be purchased from Julius Blumberg, Inc., 62 White Street, New York, NY 10013, or any of its dealers. Reproduction prohibited.

**EXHIBIT 3–3. CONTINUED**

*grow or arise from or by means of their said business shall be divided between them, as follows:*

*and all loss that shall happen to their said joint business by ill-commodities, bad debts or otherwise shall be borne and paid between them, as follows:*

*AND it is agreed by and between the said parties, that there shall be had and kept at all times during the continuance of their co-partnership, perfect, just, and true books of account, wherein each of the said co-partners shall enter and set down, as well all money by them or either of them received, paid, laid out and expended in and about the said business, as also all goods, wares, commodities and merchandise, by them or either of them, bought or sold, by reason or on account of the said business, and all other matters and things whatsoever, to the said business and the management thereof in anywise belonging; which said book shall be used in common between the said co-partners, so that either of them may have access thereto, without any interruption or hindrance of the other. AND ALSO, the said co-partners, once in*

*or oftener if necessary, shall make, yield and render, each to the other, a true, just and perfect inventory and account of all profits and increase by them or either of them, made, and of all losses by them or either of them, sustained; and also all payments, receipts, disbursements and all other things by them made, received, disbursed, acted, done, or suffered in this said co-partnership and business; and the same account so made, shall and will clear, adjust, pay and deliver, each to the other, at the time, their just share of the profits so made as aforesaid.*

*AND the said parties hereby mutually covenant and agree, to and with each other, that during the continuance of the said co-partnership,          of them shall nor will endorse any note, or otherwise become surety for any person or persons whomsoever, nor will sell, assign, transfer, mortgage or otherwise dispose of the business of the co-partnership, nor each of          share, title and interest therein without the written consent of the parties hereto. And at the end or other sooner termination of their co-partnership the said co-partners each to the other, shall and will make a true, just and final account of all things relating to their said business, and in all things truly adjust the same; and all and every the stock and stocks, as well as the gains and increase thereof, which shall appear to be remaining, either in money, goods, wares, fixtures, debts or otherwise, shall be divided between them as follows:*

*after the payment of the co-partnership liabilities; and should said co-partners be unable to ascertain the value of any of the assets belonging to the co-partnership at the termination of their co-partnership, the said assets shall then be sold either at private or public sale to be agreed upon by the parties hereto and a division of the proceeds of said sale shall be made as herein provided.*

**Exhibit 3–3. Continued**

IT IS FURTHER AGREED *that during the continuance of the co-partnership herein, all notes, drafts or money received for and in behalf of the said co-partnership by the parties hereto shall be deposited in a bank to be agreed upon by the parties hereto and the moneys credited to said co-partnership shall only be withdrawn by check signed by*

*who shall also receive said notes, drafts or moneys or other orders for payment of moneys of the said co-partnership for the purpose of making said deposits.*

IT IS FURTHER AGREED *that during the continuance of said co-partnership the parties hereto shall mutually agree in writing, upon a weekly allowance, to be paid to each of the parties hereto for services to be rendered, and said allowance shall be charged as an item of expense of the co-partnership business, or if otherwise agreed upon in writing may be charged against their personal interest in said business.*

IN THE EVENT *of the death of a party hereto, the surviving co-partner   shall within a period of          weeks, make and give, to the legal representative of the deceased co-partner, a true, just and final account of all things relating to the co-partnership business, and within a period of          months, in all things truly adjust the same with the legal representative of the deceased co-partner. The surviving co-partner   shall have the privilege of purchasing the interest of the deceased co-partner from his legal representative, upon a true and proper valuation of the interest of the deceased co-partner; and until the purchase of said interest by the surviving co-partner   , or a division as herein agreed upon, the legal representative of the deceased co-partner during reasonable business hours shall have access to the books of the co-partnership and examine same personally or with the aid of other persons and make copies thereof or any portion thereof without any interruption or hindrance, and the said legal representative of said deceased co-partner shall have equal and joint control of the said co-partnership with the surviving partner or partners.*

*This instrument may not be changed orally.*

IN WITNESS WHEREOF, *the parties hereto have hereunto set their hands and seals the day and year first above mentioned.*

*In presence of:*

## EXHIBIT 3–3. CONTINUED

STATE OF

      *of*                        } *ss.:*

County of

              *On the*              *day of*                      *in the year*
*one thousand nine hundred and*              *before me personally came*

*to me known, and known to me to be the individual*   *described in, and who executed the foregoing in-*
*strument, and*                         *acknowledged to me that*   *he*   *executed the same.*

*and*

## Article of Co=Partnership

*Dated,*           *, 19*

# EXHIBIT 3–4. CERTIFICATE OF INCORPORATION

**Blumbergs Law Products**  A 234—Certificate of Incorporation
Business Corporation Law §402: 9-87

© 1975 BY JULIUS BLUMBERG, INC.
PUBLISHER, NYC 10013

## Certificate of Incorporation of

### under Section 402 of the Business Corporation Law

### IT IS HEREBY CERTIFIED THAT:

(1) The name of the proposed corporaton is

(2) The purpose or purposes for which this corporation is formed, are as follows, to wit:
To engage in any lawful act or activity for which corporations may be organized under the Business Corporation Law. The corporation is not formed to engage in any act or activity requiring the consent or approval of any state official, department, board, agency or other body.*

The corporation, in furtherance of its corporate purposes above set forth, shall have all of the powers enumerated in Section 202 of the Business Corporation Law, subject to any limitations provided in the Business Corporation Law or any other statute of the State of New York.

*If specific consent or approval is required delete this paragraph, insert specific purposes and obtain consent or approval prior to filing.

*Source:* Forms may be purchased from Julius Blumberg, Inc., 62 White Street, New York, NY 10013, or any of its dealers. Reproduction prohibited.

EXHIBIT 3–4. CONTINUED

(3) The office of the corporation is to be located in the County of
State of New York.

(4) The aggregate number of shares which the corporation shall have the authority to issue is

EXHIBIT 3–4. CONTINUED

(5) The Secretary of State is designated as agent of the corporation upon whom process against it may be served. The post office address to which the Secretary of State shall mail a copy of any process against the corporation served upon him is

(6) A director of the corporation shall not be liable to the corporation or its shareholders for damages for any breach of duty in such capacity except for

(i) liability if a judgment or other final adjudication adverse to a director establishes that his or her acts or omissions were in bad faith or involved intentional misconduct or a knowing violation of law or that the director personally gained in fact a financial profit or other advantage to which he or she was not legally entitled or that the director's acts violated BCL § 719, or

(ii) liability for any act or omission prior to the adoption of this provision.

The undersigned incorporator, or each of them if there are more than one, is of the age of eighteen years or over.

IN WITNESS WHEREOF, this certificate has been subscribed on _____ 19___ by the undersigned who affirm(s) that the statements made herein are true under the penalties of perjury.

| Type name of incorporator | Signature |
|---|---|
| Address | |
| Type name of incorporator | Signature |
| Address | |
| Type name of incorporator | Signature |
| Address | |

**EXHIBIT 3–4. CONTINUED**

# Certificate of Incorporation

of

under Section 402 of the Business Corporation Law

Filed By:

*Office and Post Office Address*

EXHIBIT 3–5. THE THREE LEGAL FORMS OF BUSINESS

# WHAT FORM OF BUSINESS ORGANIZATION?

## SINGLE PROPRIETORSHIP

**ADVANTAGES**
1. Low start up costs
2. Greatest freedom from regulation
3. Owner in direct control
4. Minimal working capital requirements
5. Tax advantage to small owner
6. All profits to owner

**DISADVANTAGES**
1. Unlimited liability
2. Lack of continuity
3. Difficult to raise capital

## PARTNERSHIP

**ADVANTAGES**
1. Ease of formation
2. Low start up costs
3. Additional sources of venture capital
4. Broader management base
5. Possible tax advantage
6. Limited outside regulation

**DISADVANTAGES**
1. Unlimited liability
2. Lack of continuity
3. Divided authority
4. Difficulty in raising additional capital
5. Hard to find suitable partners

## CORPORATION

**ADVANTAGES**
1. Limited liability
2. Specialized management
3. Ownership is transferrable
4. Continuous existence
5. Legal entity
6. Possible tax advantages
7. Easier to raise capital

**DISADVANTAGES**
1. Closely regulated
2. Most expensive form to organize
3. Charter restrictions
4. Extensive record keeping necessary
5. Double taxation

*Source:* Wendell O. Metcalf, "Starting and Managing a Small Business of Your Own," *The Starting and Managing Series, Vol. 1,* 3d ed. (Washington, D.C.: Small Business Administration, 1973), 24.

might occur. You could never afford the cost. It's better to think in terms of separating the risks you face into two categories:

- Those over which you have little or no control and which, if they occur, can seriously jeopardize your business
- Those misfortunes that your business can absorb without much inconvenience and pain

The cracked window pane, for example, might cost you some money to replace, but it may not pay you to insure against such an eventuality. Of course, you can do much yourself to reduce the chance of perils befalling your operation: For example, you can install an automatic sprinkler system. (See chapter 19, "Safety Measures for Your Store," for other steps you can take.)

Three types of insurance coverage are just about mandatory for most retail businesses. These are fire, liability, and workers' compensation insurance; each type is discussed in the next several pages.

## Fire Insurance

One of the major concerns in your risk-management program must be the insuring of your store against the peril of fire. While the chances of your business suffering a major fire may be small, the consequences of such an occurrence can be so great as to wipe out your operation in a matter of minutes.

A standard fire-insurance policy is available; its terms are nearly identical in every state. It protects your store against property loss due to fire and lightning. It also covers losses to merchandise that must be removed temporarily from your premises because of a fire. It doesn't cover the loss of certain kinds of property, such as deeds, securities, and currency. The rate you pay depends on a number of factors: the area in which you're located (and the "loss experience" in that area); the type of building that houses your store; the condition of your premises; and so on.

Your best bet is to purchase a "multiperil" policy that insures you not only against loss from fire and lightning but also from such additional perils as smoke, windstorm, explosion, hail, and the like. A commercial-property insurance policy, attached to the standard fire policy as an endorsement, gives you all-risk protection of inventories, fixtures, and any improvements you may have made on the building as a tenant.

Also, *inland marine floater policies* are designed for specific types of retailers not covered by the commercial-property form, such as furriers, jewelry stores, dry-cleaning establishments, and others.

Coinsurance. The coinsurance clause in a fire policy requires you to carry a specified percentage of insurance, based on the property's cash value, or to bear part of a partial loss yourself. This clause discourages the "underinsurer." The percentage required is commonly 80 percent of the value.

The following example will serve to illustrate the coinsurance concept:

> Suppose you own a building valued at $140,000. Because you doubt that you'll be hit with a *total* loss, you carry only $64,000 worth of fire insurance to keep down your premium.
>
> According to the "80-percent rule," you should be carrying insurance to the tune of $112,000—so you're *underinsured*. You're insured to only about four-sevenths of the required amount ($64,000 ÷ $112,000). Should your premises suffer a $20,000 loss, the insurance company will pay only 4/7 of the loss; you'll have to bear the other 3/7.

## Liability Insurance

The retail store depends on traffic for its existence. As the owner of a retail enterprise, you're consequently quite vulnerable to being sued for negligence by anyone injured on or near your premises. A single liability judgment against you could bankrupt your firm.

A comprehensive general liability policy, then, is just as essential as fire insurance (if not more so). This policy covers the costs of defending legal actions, pays liability judgments, medical and surgical expenses, and so on. Premiums are computed on the basis of the area, type of occupancy, parameters of the coverage, and other details.

## Workers' Compensation Insurance

Under state law, employees are afforded protection against loss of income due to injury on the job or occupational disease. They may file for compensation regardless of whether negligence is involved. As an employer, you're supposed to provide your help with a safe working environment. Yet there's always the possibility that one of your employees may bring suit against you, in case of accidental injury. Moreover, legal liability limits of $1 million or more are no longer considered unreasonable in the courts.

Workers' compensation insurance, then, should be a must for you the moment you hire your first employee. Premiums in retailing are generally rather low; by employing safety and loss-prevention measures, you may be able to reduce them even more. Premiums are based in part on the size of your payroll and the hazards in your business.

## OTHER TYPES OF INSURANCE TO CHECK INTO

No one, of course, ought to operate any kind of business whatsoever without carrying fire, liability, and workers' compensation coverages. These perils bear the potential for the total destruction of your business. In setting up your store's insurance program, consider also the merits of other, additional protection. Available types include health and business life insurance (discussed later in this chapter) and a variety of policies designed to insure against specific, less serious, hazards. These latter types are treated in the next section.

## Automobile Insurance

If you require the use of an automobile in your business or, for that matter, a truck (for delivering packages or other business purposes), you need to think about protection against two kinds of hazards. One type is the possibility of physical damage to, or the actual loss of, the vehicle itself through collision, fire, or theft. The other consideration is the threat of legal action against your firm in the case of damage caused by the vehicle to property or to persons, as might occur in accidents. Your insurance representative can help prepare a comprehensive policy for your needs. The premium you pay depends on a number of factors: the territory in which you're located, the type(s) of vehicles used, the distance generally traveled, who's doing the driving, and the amount of coverage you need. Premiums may be kept down somewhat by using higher deductibles.

## Business Interruption Insurance

Should your retail store need to be closed down for an extended period, as would be likely in the case of a serious fire, you still need to continue paying your bills: utilities, taxes, interest on outstanding loans, and the like. Moreover, you may wish to continue paying salaries to some of your key people so as not to lose them. This type of insurance coverage is designed for just such a purpose. It pays you approximately the amount of fixed expenses and profits your business would normally have earned during the period of shutdown.

## Crime Insurance

Small stores are particularly susceptible to both *robbery* (loss of property by force or under threat of violence) and *burglary* (property loss from the premises accompanied by visible signs of forced entry). You'll find that a basic storekeeper's burglary and robbery policy is available in most locations to the small retailer. Crime-insurance rates are relatively high; they depend, of course, on such factors as the area in which you're located, your type of business, loss-prevention measures you have taken (such as the installation of an alarm system), and so on. Insurance companies are understandably reluctant to issue crime-insurance policies in high-risk areas. If you find it difficult to obtain such coverage in your particular neighborhood, talk to your insurance agent about the Federal Crime Insurance Program that's available in many states.

## Fidelity Bonds

These may be secured from insurance or bonding companies. They're used to bond employees, on either an individual or a group basis, in situations where they have access to large sums of money. Claims for fidelity losses must, of course, be supported with facts and figures. This means that your record-keeping practices ought to be exemplary.

### Glass Insurance

Glass is an important structural and design element in store retailing. This kind of policy provides you with all-risk coverage on show windows, glass doors, countertops and showcases, mirrors, and the like. In addition to replacing glass, the policy also covers the cost of replacing frames or the boarding up of windows, if necessary. Excluded, of course, is glass damage that's due to fire, war, or nuclear destruction.

### Power Plant Insurance

Also referred to as *boiler and machinery insurance*, this type of policy is generally of more significance to the manufacturing firm than to the store retailer. However, if you own your own building, you may want to investigate its merits. Such insurance covers losses due to the explosion of furnaces, steam boilers, engines, and electrical equipment. These items are normally excluded from the standard fire policy. Part of the premium you pay goes to defray the insuring corporation's regular inspections of your equipment to detect possible problems or deficiencies early.

### Water Damage Insurance

It's possible for a retail firm to sustain damage to merchandise, fixtures, or other assets through the accidental release of water in any form. Some of the possibilities are steam that escapes from deteriorated fittings or broken pipes, the overflow of water from refrigeration or air-conditioning equipment, and snow on the building's roof that melts and leaks through. Insurance is, of course, available for just such contingencies.

## CONSIDER HEALTH AND BUSINESS LIFE INSURANCE, TOO

Two additional types of insurance should appeal to you as the owner of a new business: health and business life insurance.

### Health Insurance

While not aimed at reducing your risk of a particular hazard, health insurance can be part and parcel of your general employee compensation package. It also contributes to good organizational morale. Employee group health (and life) insurance is usually available without medical examination. Such plans can be *noncontributory* (the employer pays the entire premium) or *contributory* (costs are shared between employer and employees). Three general types of group health insurance are available: (1) the basic medical and hospitalization plan; (2) the major medical plan; and (3) the disability income plan.

Talk over your needs with your insurance representative. You should know that employees who leave your business for any reason can usually retain their coverage by converting within thirty days to an individual plan.

## Business Life Insurance

Typically, new entrepreneurs consider the purchase of business life insurance as an unnecessary frill, a luxury that can't be afforded until their businesses have been firmly established. This just isn't so. Such insurance definitely has its uses, some of which are indicated in exhibit 3–6.

The major types of life insurance available are:

- Whole life
- Term life
- Limited payment life
- Endowment life

**Whole Life Insurance.** The name of this type is derived from the fact that premiums must be paid throughout the course of your lifetime, generally to age eighty-five. For the same reason, it's often referred to as *straight-life* or *ordinary life* insurance. Upon the

---

**EXHIBIT 3–6. PURPOSES OF BUSINESS LIFE INSURANCE**

Business life insurance can be written for numerous specific purposes. Chief among these are:

1. A sole-proprietorship plan to provide for maintenance of a business upon the death of the sole proprietor.
2. A partnership insurance plan to retire your partner's interest at death and vice versa.
3. A corporation insurance plan to retire your shareholder's interest at death and vice versa.
4. Key-man protection to reimburse for loss and to provide a replacement in the event of your key employee's death. Such insurance helps to prevent a setback that develops because of losing a vital employee.
5. Group plan for employees. A group annuity or pension plan may be desirable where the number of employees is sufficiently large. Where only a few are involved, some form of individual retirement policy could be used, with the cost shared by employer and employees in any proportion desired.
6. Reserve for emergencies. Most business life insurance plans utilize life insurance which has cash value. This cash value, growing over the years, provides the firm with a valuable reserve for emergencies in the event of any sharp dislocation in business conditions. When necessary, the policy cash value can be used as the basis for loans.
7. Where your estate consists entirely of your interest in the business, insurance on your life, payable to your family on your death, provides them with ready cash and aids in liquidating your interest in the business.

---

*Source:* Institute of Life Insurance, "Business Life Insurance," *Management Aid No. 222* (Washington, D.C.: U.S. Small Business Administration, March 1975), 3.

---

demise of the insured, the *face amount*—the specific amount for which the policy is written—is paid out to the stipulated beneficiaries. Over time, a limited amount of cash accumulates in the policy; this is the *cash value*. Hence, the policy may be cashed in if it's surrendered at any time, and you may take out loans against the cash value, should you need to, at a comparatively low interest rate. Should you die, in the interim, before paying back the loan, your indebtedness is, of course, deducted from the face amount. Premiums are quite low, in consideration of the many years of payments to be made.

**Term Life Insurance.** Term life policies carry the lowest premiums of all, since there's no cash accumulation and, consequently, no loan privileges. When you purchase a term policy, you're buying "pure insurance." Such policies are written for a specified number of years (the *term*). Among the more popular varieties are the *renewable term* and the *decreasing term*. The first type is renewable at the end of the term, at a higher premium because of advancing age. The second pays out the face amount of the policy in the event of the insured's demise during the first year it's in effect, reducing the payout each subsequent year until the entire term contracted for has ended. Decreasing term life insurance is often sought in connection with home mortgages to cover the remaining balance due the mortgage holder.

**Limited Payment Life Insurance.** In this type of policy, premiums are scheduled for payment over a limited number of years, such as fifteen or twenty, instead of throughout your lifetime. After the last payment has been made, the policy has been fully paid up and remains in force until the death of the insured. Because premiums under this arrangement are substantially higher than under the "whole life" type, the cash accumulation and, of course, loan privileges are considerable.

**Endowment Life Insurance.** Somewhat similar in intent to limited payment life, endowment life insurance requires the payment of premiums for a set number of years. The face amount of the policy is, naturally, paid out to the beneficiary should the insured die. However, should the insured still be alive at the end of the contracted time span, the full amount is paid to the insured, usually in a lump sum (or *endowment*). Since such policies are designed to incorporate future "savings" as well as life insurance, both the rates and the accumulated cash value are high.

## FOR FURTHER INFORMATION

### Books

Greene, M., and O. Serbein. *Risk Management: Text and Cases,* 2d ed. Englewood Cliffs, N.J.: Prentice-Hall, 1983.

Hemphill, C. *Basic Business Law.* Englewood Cliffs, N.J.: Prentice-Hall, 1984.

White, E., and H. Chasman. *Business Insurance,* 5th ed. Englewood Cliffs, N.J.: Prentice-Hall, 1980.

## Pamphlets Available from the Small Business Administration

**Management Aids**

MA 6.004—"Selecting the Legal Structure for Your Business"

## Booklets Available from the Superintendent of Documents

S/N 045-000-00184-9—*Risk Management and Insurance*—$4.50.
S/N 045-000-00209-8—*Insurance and Risk Management for Small Business*—
$5.00.

# 4

# How to Enter the Retailing Field

Ordinarily, aspiring retail entrepreneurs get to own their own stores in only three ways:

- By launching a brand-new business
- By buying an existing operation
- By contracting for a franchised outlet

You might argue on behalf of a fourth possibility, that of leasing a department of some type in a discount or department store. In reality, however, this fourth route represents one or another of the three choices listed above.

My personal experience across many retail lines indicates that the chances of your ultimate success with a retail enterprise run in the reverse of the order in which the three avenues are shown—or (3), (2), and (1). All three approaches are discussed in this chapter. The launching of a new retail enterprise is, of course, the theme of the entire book and so merits only abbreviated treatment here.

## LAUNCH YOUR OWN RETAIL STORE

You may suspect—and rightly so—that this approach to entrepreneurship consistently draws more would-be retailers than the other two avenues. Why? Because it provides these individuals with a blank slate on which to write their futures. There's the challenge of doing your own thing, unimpeded. All the choices are yours alone to make: where to locate, what inventory to carry, how to merchandise and promote your goods, how much to charge for them, and so on. Despite drawbacks—such as the lack of both customer and supplier bases, the many mistakes you make as you learn from hands-on experience, and the fact that you may not be able to draw even a minimum salary for quite some time—this avenue is often the most psychologically satisfying of all.

### Rent, Buy, or Build?

As an incidental note, another major factor (which is bound to affect your financial needs) is your decision as to renting, buying, or building your retail premises.

Most small independent retailers begin by renting, probably because this option places the lowest demands on capital requirements. Renting involves the signing of a lease, payment of one or two months' rent in advance, and payment of another, perhaps equal, amount as security so that you don't disappear into the night leaving your landlord holding a worthless lease. When you rent a store, problem areas such as property taxes, building upkeep, insurance coverage, and the like remain in the building owner's hands. Yet leases eventually expire, leaving you vulnerable despite having built up the trade at the location. (The trick, of course, is to protect yourself via a favorable lease.)

Buying the property eliminates some of the undesirable aspects of renting, although the landlord's problems then become yours. The same goes for having your own retail premises constructed to order. Naturally, a much larger investment is required in either case, but you also benefit from the depreciation allowances in your tax liabilities. Moreover, when you own your own property free and clear, you can always take out a mortgage on it, should you find yourself in a tight cash position. There's also the bright prospect of earning a capital gain at some future date, when you decide to sell the property.

## BUY AN EXISTING RETAIL OPERATION

This approach seems to be less perilous—and is certainly simpler—than trying to launch your own new enterprise (see exhibit 4–1). When you buy an established store,

---

**EXHIBIT 4–1. BUYING A GOING BUSINESS: PROS AND CONS**

Certain advantages may be gained in buying a going business:

1. You may be able to buy the business at a bargain price. For personal reasons, an owner may be sufficiently anxious to sell to give you a favorable buy.
2. Buying a business will save you time and effort in setting up your establishment with equipment and stock.
3. You may acquire customers who are accustomed to trading with the establishment. Thus you eliminate an initial waiting period for business while you are getting started.
4. The owner should be able to give you the benefit of his experience in the business and in the community.

Such benefits may be offset by disadvantages, however:

1. You may pay too much for the business because of your inaccurate appraisal or the former owner's misrepresentation.
2. The owner may have had a bad reputation. You would then be battling prejudices of former customers and, perhaps, of merchandise and equipment suppliers.
3. The location may be poor.
4. The former owner's choice of fixtures and equipment may have been poor. Or they may be outmoded or in bad condition.
5. Too much of the merchandise or materials on hand may have been poorly selected.

---

*Source:* Wendell O. Metcalf, "Starting and Managing a Small Business of Your Own," *The Starting and Managing Series, Vol. 1*, 3d ed. (Washington, D.C.: U.S. Small Business Administration, 1973), 33–34.

---

you get many of the benefits you would expect from a franchise: ready-made customers, known sources of supply, a basic store inventory, fixtures, decor, experienced employees, and so forth. Moreover, the location is a known quantity and can be checked carefully.

The key question, of course, is whether the business you purchase is really in a healthy state. The assumption is that you'll be exceedingly careful in evaluating the merits of any store you consider. Naturally, the owner can be expected to praise the operation to the skies—and to try to get the highest possible price for it. Be leery of high-pressure tactics. Try to find out, if you can, the owner's real reason for selling the business; any talk of "two sets of books" ought to turn you off completely. Never, never attempt to reach a decision without the advice of both an excellent accountant and an attorney.

There's much more to it, of course. Read over the suggestions outlined in exhibit 4–2 for background advice. While this material is aimed at people seeking to enter the retail shoe business, most of it is just as applicable to any other kind of retail operation.

---

**EXHIBIT 4–2. SUGGESTIONS ON BUYING A GOING BUSINESS (SHOE STORE)**

Let's talk first about buying a going business from someone else. What are the advantages—and disadvantages? What should you be cautious about? First, here are some of the advantages:

1. You have an established income (sales dollars) from the start.
2. You have a ready-made clientele.
3. You have records of sales, purchases, and so on.
4. You have a customer mailing list.
5. You have established resources and lines.
6. You have established goodwill.
7. The need for the store in the locality has been proved.
8. The store is already stocked for the existing clientele.

Before you buy, however, there are a lot of questions you must ask of the seller, of yourself, and of others. And keep in mind that when you buy you'll be paying out a good piece of your starting capital in one lump. This will leave a limited amount for operating reserve. But let's get to those questions to ask:

1. Why is the business for sale? Is it because the seller wants to retire and has no relatives to pass the business on to? Or is he trying to unload a business that is going downhill?

2. What do the records show? The sales volume, the growth pattern, the efficiency of the management, and so on? This helps give you a good insight into how the business has been conducted.

3. What is the condition of the inventory? Is it fresh and current? Or is much of it outmoded? You'll be paying for the quality of this stock—but its quality will also indicate whether the business itself, like the stock, has grown tired and senile.

4. What is the store's local image, the status of its goodwill and reputation? If it's good, fine. If it's questionable, then remember that you'll be required to repair and rejuvenate it, which is often hard to do.

5. What has been the trend of the business over the past five years—up or down or at a standstill? Has the momentum gone out of it? If so, why?

EXHIBIT 4–2. CONTINUED

6. What about the neighborhood or locality or trading area? Is it a growth or declining area? Is the clientele or makeup of the local population changing? Check this out carefully with the local banker, because you may be buying a business that was good for yesterday but will not be good for tomorrow.

7. How much of the business will you lose? The business might be closely dependent on the personality of the seller. The new management does not automatically inherit all the former business.

8. Is it exactly or nearly the kind of store and business you really have in mind—the kind you consider your experience best equips you to operate?

9. Is the business worth the asking price? How long will it take for you to get back your investment?

10. What is the breakdown in sales by departments or categories? If it's a family store, for example, what portion of the sales is in men's footwear, in women's, children's, accessories, and so on? This is very important for you to know because it indicates the kind of clientele you'll be working with.

11. What is the quality of the store's brands or lines? Are they of good reputation? And can you, representing new management, retain them? Check this out with the store's resources (suppliers).

12. Is it chiefly a fashion business or a basic shoe business? Either way, is this the kind of business you have in mind?

13. What about the local competition? Have you investigated the area for a competitive store count—the quantity and quality of it? Who in the area will be your chief competition? How has the store itself held up against local competition?

14. What is the store's credit standing—with its resources, with banks, and so on? Even though you yourself may have or can establish an excellent credit rating, you'll be inheriting some of the effects of the previous credit rating.

15. What about the store's leasing arrangements with the landlord? How long is the lease for? What are its terms? What can and can't you do under its agreement?

16. Has the store reached its maximum earning capacity? Is there room to grow under your new management?

Some of these questions you can decide or answer for yourself. But make sure to call in other qualified people as investigators and advisers: your banker; one or more friends who operate their own stores (but who won't be direct competitors of yours). They'll see things, good or bad, that will slip past you. If everything checks out favorably, then buying a going business can be a good step. But if there are any serious questions unanswered or answered unfavorably—steer clear.

*Source:* William A. Rossi, "Starting and Managing a Small Shoestore," *The Starting and Managing Series, Vol. 24* (Washington, D.C.: U.S. Small Business Administration, 1974), 16–18.

## Estimating How Much to Pay

Once you have decided you're interested in buying a business, you face a most difficult problem: how to estimate the price you're willing to pay for it.

Basically, two methods are used in evaluating the worth of any enterprise: (1) the net-worth method; and (2) the return-on-investment method.

**Net-Worth Method.** The more common technique (although the less sensible of the two, at least for *your* purposes) is by appraising the net worth of the business (assets less liabilities). This is the easier approach by far; hence its popularity. One of its major shortcomings is that it doesn't take into account the future of the business in any way. To put it more simply, you're merely buying property: fixtures, equipment, inventory, accounts receivable, and the like. The other something you purchase, called *goodwill,* is nearly impossible to evaluate.

Asset valuation should be done by an impartial expert appraiser in the particular field of retailing. Further, when using this method, make certain to deduct the liabilities of the firm from its assets, since those debts become *your* responsibility when you take over. You will then arrive at the actual "net worth" of the enterprise. (See the major accounting statements in chapter 5.)

**Return-on-Investment Method.** The second technique for determining the value of a business involves forward thinking. What kinds of profits may you expect? And how much of a rate of return will you get on your investment? This "return-on-investment" (or "ROI") approach stresses the logic of an equitable return for the money you're risking on the business. Were you to put $20,000 into a federally insured long-term certificate of deposit at your local bank, you would be assured of a perfectly safe haven for your investment, along with a growth rate of your capital of some 7 to 10 percent or more, depending on the current economic climate. Consequently, if you decide to invest instead in a business, you should want your capital to earn a *much higher* rate for you—high enough to compensate for the appreciable risk you face of losing your investment. A logical target ROI should be 20 percent as a bare minimum; if possible, a 25-percent return would be ideal.

In determining how much to pay for someone else's operation, you need to pore over past financial records, paying special attention to the firm's earnings history. If, for example, the business has been showing an average annual bottom line of $9,000, then that business should be worth five times that figure to you (or $45,000)—if you're willing to settle for a 20 percent ROI. Similarly, if you prefer to recoup your investment in four years, rather than five (a 25 percent ROI), your offering price would be $36,000.

Just one suggestion: Check the retailer's operating statements to learn how much of a salary the owner has been drawing. This amount may have to be modified up or down if you buy the firm to match the salary you're now earning by working for someone else. Remember that when investing in a certificate of deposit, your salary remains intact, and so it doesn't enter into your expected ROI at all. Of course, the store's past operating statements may have to be adjusted somewhat to account for this need.

## SELECT A RETAIL FRANCHISE

Although the franchising of retail outlets has been around since the turn of the century (with the advent of the automobile dealership and the gas station), we have witnessed a tremendous growth in this form of distribution since the 1960s. Moreover, retailing dominates the entire franchising area, accounting for "87 percent of all franchising receipts in 1986. The retail sales of all firms associated with franchising reached about $487 billion in 1986, or 33 percent of all U.S. retail sales, which are estimated at $1.5 trillion."*

According to available estimates, approximately nine out of every ten franchised stores are profitable; this figure, of course, is based only on *reputable* parent companies, not on the more shady operations that have plagued the franchising field. Contrast this figure with the certain knowledge that well over one-half of all new enterprises go out of business within five to ten years.

## What Franchising Is

The U.S. Department of Commerce defines franchising as "A form of licensing by which the owner (the franchisor) of a product, service, or method obtains distribution through affiliated dealers (the franchisees). The holder of the right is often given exclusive access to a defined geographical area."**

Those of you who are eager to explore opportunities in the franchising sector should understand that two distinct forms of this approach to distribution exist. These are (1) product and trade-name franchising and (2) business-format franchising.

Here's how the Commerce Department differentiates between the two:

> *Product and trade-name franchising* began in the United States as an independent sales relationship between supplier and dealer in which the dealer acquired some of the identity of the supplier. Franchised dealers concentrate on one company's product line and to some extent identify their business with that company. Typical of this segment are automobile and truck dealers, gasoline service stations, and soft drink bottlers.
>
> *Business-format franchising* is characterized by an ongoing business relationship between franchisor and franchisee that includes not only the product, service, and trademark, but the entire business format itself—a marketing strategy and plan, operating manuals and standards, quality control, and continuing two-way communications. Restaurants, non-food retailing, personal and business services, rental services, real estate services, and a long list of other service businesses fall into the category of business-format franchising.†

**Business-format franchising** is the type of franchising that American consumers know quite well. Some of the more popular and successful business-format franchises around the country that come readily to mind are Athlete's Foot, A to Z Rental Centers, Baskin-Robbins, Century 21, Domino's Pizza, Dunkin' Donuts, Holiday Inns, Insty-Prints,

---

* U.S. Department of Commerce, *Franchising in the Economy: 1985–1987* (Washington, D.C.: Department of Commerce, 1987), 14.
  ** U.S. Department of Commerce, *Franchise Opportunities Handbook* (Washington, D.C.: Department of Commerce, November 1986), xxix.
  † *Franchising in the Economy,* 1, 3.

International House of Pancakes, Little Professor Book Centers, MAACO, McDonald's, Putt-Putt Golf Courses, Snelling and Snelling, Supercuts, T-Shirts Plus, and Taco Bell.

## Opening a Franchised Store: Pros and Cons

By investing in a franchise of this type, you're opening an individual business under the beneficial umbrella of an established, usually well-publicized, company image. Outside of providing the necessary capital and receiving training in operations, just about everything else has already been managed for you by the time you open your door. Your layout and decor, inventory, equipment, and systems all have been evolved and proven over time, and merchandising and promotion programs are well established and in place. As the owner of a franchised outlet, you operate your store as though it were another unit of a large retail chain. Consumers are already familiar with the chain and its reputation; this head start gives you immediate business on opening day.

Moreover, you can capitalize on the franchisor's tried-and-proven management methods and financial expertise to assist you over the hurdles.

Naturally, as part of a chain-store organization, you have to observe the rules laid down by the parent company. In this respect, then, you cannot entirely be "your own boss." You need to decide in advance whether or not you can live with this "subjugation of your personal identity" and enjoy your role as franchisee.

For a quick review of the advantages and disadvantages of going the franchise route, refer to exhibit 4–3.

---

**EXHIBIT 4–3. FRANCHISING: ADVANTAGES AND DISADVANTAGES**

Some advantages of franchising to you, as a franchisee, are that you can start a business with:

1. Limited experience
2. A relatively small amount of capital and a strengthened financial and credit standing
3. A well-developed consumer image and goodwill with proven products and services
4. Competently designed facilities, layout, displays, and fixtures
5. Chain buying power
6. The opportunity for business training and continued assistance from experienced management in proven methods of doing business
7. National or regional promotion and publicity

All of these factors can help increase your income and lower your risk of failure.
Now, what are the disadvantages of franchising? Some of them are the:

1. Submission to imposed standardized operations
2. Sharing of profits with the franchisor
3. Lack of freedom to meet local competition
4. Danger of contracts slanted to the advantage of the franchisor
5. Time consumed in preparing reports required by the franchisor
6. Sharing the burden of the franchisor's faults

---

*Source:* Wendell O. Metcalf, "Starting and Managing a Small Business of Your Own," *The Starting and Managing Series, Vol. 1,* 3d ed. (Washington, D.C.: U.S. Small Business Administration, 1973), 43–46.

---

## Choosing a Franchise

In your search for the right franchise operation, deal only with reputable companies. Stay away from the occasional franchise "deal" promoted by unknown, often shady operators. In analyzing all offers, be sure to refer to the checklist in exhibit 4–4.

---

**EXHIBIT 4–4. CHECKLIST FOR EVALUATING A FRANCHISE**

*The Franchise*

1. Did your lawyer approve the franchise contract you are considering after he studied it paragraph by paragraph?
2. Does the franchise call upon you to take any steps which are, according to your lawyer, unwise or illegal in your state, county, or city?
3. Does the franchise give you an exclusive territory for the length of the franchise or can the franchisor sell a second or third franchise in your territory?
4. Is the franchisor connected in any way with any other franchise company handling similar merchandise or services?
5. If the answer to the last question is "yes," what is your protection against this second franchisor organization?
6. Under what circumstances can you terminate the franchise contract and at what cost to you, if you decide for any reason at all that you wish to cancel it?
7. If you sell your franchise, will you be compensated for your goodwill or will the goodwill you have built into the business be lost by you?

*The Franchisor*

8. How many years has the firm offering you a franchise been in operation?
9. Has it a reputation for honesty and fair dealing among the local firms holding its franchise?
10. Has the franchisor shown you any certified figures indicating exact net profits of one or more going firms which you personally checked yourself with the franchisee?
11. Will the firm assist you with:
    (a) A management training program?
    (b) An employee training program?
    (c) A public relations program?
    (d) Capital?
    (e) Credit?
    (f) Merchandising ideas?
12. Will the firm help you find a good location for your new business?
13. Is the franchising firm adequately financed so that it can carry out its stated plan of financial assistance and expansion?
14. Is the franchisor a one-man company or a corporation with an experienced management trained in depth (so that there would always be an experienced man at its head)?
15. Exactly what can the franchisor do for you which you cannot do for yourself?
16. Has the franchisor investigated you carefully enough to assure itself that you can successfully operate one of their franchises at a profit both to them and to you?
17. Does your state have a law regulating the sale of franchises and has the franchisor complied with that law?

*You—the Franchisee*

18. How much equity capital will you have to have to purchase the franchise and operate it until your income equals your expenses? Where are you going to get it?

---

19. Are you prepared to give up some independence of action to secure the advantages offered by the franchise?
20. Do *you* really believe you have the innate ability, training, and experience to work smoothly and profitably with the franchisor, your employees, and your customers?
21. Are you ready to spend much or all of the remainder of your business life with this franchisor, offering his product or service to your public?

*Your Market*

22. Have you made any study to determine whether the product or service which you propose to sell under franchise has a market in your territory at the prices you will have to charge?
23. Will the population in the territory given you increase, remain static, or decrease over the next five years?
24. Will the product or service you are considering be in greater demand, about the same, or less demand five years from now than today?
25. What competition exists in your territory already for the product or service you contemplate selling?
    (a) Nonfranchise firms?
    (b) Franchise firms?

---

*Source:* U.S. Department of Commerce, *Franchise Opportunities Handbook* (Washington, D.C.: U.S. Department of Commerce, November 1986), xxxiii–xxxiv.

When you have made your decision and chosen a specific franchise, engage an attorney for counsel regarding the franchise contract you'll have to sign. *Never* enter into any agreement without legal advice!

## Some Popular Offerings

Table 4–1 offers brief descriptions of some representative retail franchise opportunities. These listings are intended to furnish you with a sampling of available offerings, and they do not constitute either an endorsement or a recommendation of any of these firms. Note that a more complete listing of more than 1,300 franchising organizations appears in the U.S. Department of Commerce's *Franchise Opportunities Handbook,* issued in November 1986.*

---

\* Compiled by Andrew Kostecka. Available from the Superintendent of Documents, U.S. Government Printing Office, Washington, D.C. 20402 (Stock #003-009-00241-9).

---

## TABLE 4–1. A SAMPLING OF RETAIL FRANCHISING ORGANIZATIONS*

| Name and Address of Franchisor | Type of Operation | Number of Franchisees |
|---|---|---|
| AEROBIC FITNESS CENTERS<br>c/o Fitness Systems, Inc.<br>P.O. Box 266<br>Independence, MO 64050 | Exercise program for men and women | 150 in 15 states |
| ATHLETE'S FOOT MARKETING ASSOCIATES, INC.<br>3735 Atlanta Industrial Parkway<br>Atlanta, GA 30331 | Specialty stores that sell athletic shoes | 473 in the U.S., Japan, France, and Australia |
| BASKIN-ROBBINS, INC.<br>31 Baskin-Robbins Place<br>Glendale, CA 91201 | High-quality ice cream stores | More than 3,000 stores in the U.S. and Canada |
| BATHTIQUE INTERNATIONAL, LTD.<br>Carnegie Place<br>247 Goodman Street<br>Rochester, NY 14607 | Specialty shops that offer bath and bath-related items and gifts | 91 units in 35 states |
| BRESLER'S 33 FLAVORS, INC.<br>999 East Touhy Avenue<br>Suite 333<br>Des Plaines, IL 60018 | Multiflavor specialty ice cream shops | Approximately 375 in 34 states and Canada |
| BURGER KING CORPORATION<br>P.O. Box 520783<br>(M.S. #1643)<br>Miami, FL 33152 | Limited-menu restaurants specializing in hamburgers | More than 4,635 units worldwide |
| CHEESE SHOP INTERNATIONAL, INC.<br>255 Greenwich Avenue<br>Greenwich, CT 06830 | Retail shops that sell fine cheese, gourmet foods, and related gift items | 50 in 16 states |
| CHILD ENRICHMENT CENTERS<br>6 Passaic Street<br>Hackensack, NJ 07601 | A prestige preschool, kindergarten, and summer camp | 15 in 3 states |
| CONFECTIONERY SQUARE CORPORATION<br>968 James Street<br>P.O. Box 6969<br>Syracuse, NY 13078 | Retail candy and nut shops (Jo-Ann's Nut House, Chez Chocolat) | 175 stores in 25 states (including company-owned) |

*Source: Franchise Opportunities Handbook* (Washington, D.C.: U.S. Department of Commerce, November 1986).

TABLE 4–1. CONTINUED

| Name and Address of Franchisor | Type of Operation | Number of Franchisees |
|---|---|---|
| COUNTRY KITCHEN INTERNATIONAL, INC. 7800 Metro Parkway Minneapolis, MN 55420 | Sit-down service restaurant, family type | 250 in 24 states and 2 provinces in Canada |
| DIET CENTER, INC. P.O. Box 160 Rexburg, ID 83440 | Weight-control program through private counseling and weekly classes, plus sales of vitamins and other nutritional products | 2,100 in the U.S. and Canada |
| H & R BLOCK INC. 4410 Main Street Kansas City, MO 64111 | Preparation of individual income-tax returns | More than 9,000 offices in the U.S., Canada, and overseas (more than 4,000 franchisees; balance operated by parent company) |
| INSTY-PRINTS, INC. 1215 Marshall Street, N.E. Minneapolis, MN 55403 | Full-service printing center | 330 locations in 40 states, Washington, D.C., Puerto Rico, and Israel |
| JUST PANTS 201 North Wells Street Suite 1530 Chicago, IL 60606 | Stores that sell quality branded jeans, slacks, tops, and accessories for young people | 18 franchisees (118 units) in 22 states |
| KAMPGROUNDS OF AMERICA, INC. P.O. Box 30558 Billings, MT 59114 | America's largest system for recreational vehicles | More than 650 in the U.S. and Canada |
| KARMELKORN SHOPPE, INC. 101 31st Avenue P.O. Box 1058 Rock Island, IL 61204 | Make and sell original Karmelkorn popcorn candy and other confections and related snack-food items | 250 in 44 states |
| LAWN DOCTOR INCORPORATED P.O. Box 512142 Highway #34 Matawan, NJ 07747 | Professional, automated lawn services | More than 300 in 27 states |
| LEE MYLES ASSOCIATES CORPORATION 25 East Valley Avenue Maywood, NJ 07607 | Complete, one-stop transmission service | 140 in 9 states and Puerto Rico |

TABLE 4–1. CONTINUED

| Name and Address of Franchisor | Type of Operation | Number of Franchisees |
|---|---|---|
| LITTLE PROFESSOR BOOK CENTERS, INC. 110 North Fourth Street Suite 400 Ann Arbor, MI 48104 | Full-line, full-service retail bookstores | 100 units in 31 states |
| MANPOWER, INC. 5301 North Ironwood Road P.O. Box 2053 Milwaukee, WI 53201 | Offers a complete line of contemporary help services | More than 300 offices in the U.S. |
| MARTIN FRANCHISES, INC. 2005 Ross Avenue Cincinnati, OH 45212 | One-hour Martinizing dry-cleaning establishments | 1,100 units throughout the U.S. |
| MEDICINE SHOPPE INTERNATIONAL, INC. 10121 Paget Drive St. Louis, MO 63132 | Retail prescription and health-care centers | 708 in 48 states |
| MINI-GOLF, INC. 202 Bridge Street Jessup, PA 18434 | Prefabricated miniature golf courses | 394 in 47 states, Canada, and Aruba |
| MISTER DONUT OF AMERICA Multifoods Tower Box 2942 Minneapolis, MN 55402 | Doughnut and coffee shops (drive-in and walk-in units) | 637 in 35 states, Puerto Rico, Canada, and overseas |
| SERVICE PERSONNEL, INC. 826 Memorial Boulevard Suite 208 Murfreesboro, TN 37130 | Full-service employment agency offering discount fees; full-line temporary service | 40 in 12 states |
| SPRING CREST COMPANY 505 West Lambert Road Brea, CA 92621 | Drapery centers that offer draperies, drapery hardware, and accessories | 300 stores in 39 states, Canada, and overseas |
| SUBWAY 25 High Street Milford, CT 06460 | Shops that sell foot-long specialty sandwiches (submarines) and salads | 710 stores in 39 states, Washington, D.C., Canada, and England |
| SWISS COLONY STORES, INC. 1 Alpine Lane Monroe, WI 53566 | Specialty food shops offering cheeses, sausage, pastries, candies, and gifts | 105 stores in 35 states |
| THE SCREENMOBILE, INC. 538 East Dalton Avenue Glendora, CA 91740 | Mobile window and door screening and rescreening service | 11 in 4 states |

**TABLE 4–1. CONTINUED**

| Name and Address of Franchisor | Type of Operation | Number of Franchisees |
|---|---|---|
| THE SOUTHLAND CORPORATION<br>2828 North Haskell Avenue<br>Box 719<br>Dallas, TX 75204 | Convenience grocery stores (7-Eleven) | 2,849 in 20 states plus Washington, D.C. |
| TASTEE DONUTS, INC.<br>2121 Ridgelake Drive<br>Suite 105<br>Metairie, LA 70001 | Doughnut and coffee shops | 42 in 3 states |
| TRAVEL AGENTS INTERNATIONAL, INC.<br>8640 Seminole Boulevard<br>Seminole, FL 33542 | Retail travel-agency franchise | 208 in 31 states and Washington, D.C. |
| T-SHIRTS PLUS, INC.<br>P.O. Box 20608<br>3630 I-35 South<br>Waco, TX 76702 | Family-oriented specialty stores selling T-shirts and associated garments (personalized) | 250 in 42 states |
| WESTERN AUTO<br>2107 Grand Avenue<br>Kansas City, MO 64108 | Stores selling automotive items, hardware, appliances, and other hard goods | More than 1,800 in the U.S. |

## FOR FURTHER INFORMATION

### Books

Goldstein, Arnold S. *The Complete Guide to Buying and Selling a Business.* New York: Wiley, 1983.

Hagendorf, Stanley. *Tax Guide for Buying and Selling a Business,* 6th ed. Englewood Cliffs, N.J.: Prentice-Hall, 1986.

Longenecker, Justin G., and Carlos W. Moore. *Small-Business Management,* 7th ed. Cincinnati: South-Western, 1987.

Mangold, M. J. *How to Buy a Small Business,* rev. ed. New York: Pilot Books, 1986.

Siegel, William L. *Franchising.* New York: Wiley, 1983.

Small, Samuel, and Pilot Books Staff. *Directory of Franchising Organizations,* rev. ed. New York: Pilot Books, 1986.

### Pamphlets Available from the Small Business Administration

#### Management Aids

MA 2.016—"Checklist for Going into Business"

MA 2.020—"Business Plan for Retailers"

MA 7.007—"Evaluating Franchise Opportunities"

## Booklets Available from the Superintendent of Documents

S/N 003-008-00194-7—*Franchise Opportunities Handbook, 1984*—$13.50.

S/N 045-000-00125-3—*Franchise Index/Profile*—$4.50.

S/N 045-000-00218-8—*Starting and Managing a Small Business of Your Own*—$4.75.

S/N 045-000-00164-4—*Buying and Selling a Small Business*—$5.00.

## 5

# Planning for Your Financial Needs

Sooner or later, every person who plans a retail store of his or her own faces the inevitable question: "How much money will I need to make a success of my business?" This is a most thoughtful question. It deserves a much better answer than, "As little as I must have to cover the basics," or, "I'll make do with whatever I can scrape together."

The amount of money you'll need to finance your business adequately has a great deal to do with the individual *way* you choose to join the entrepreneurial ranks in the first place. Besides your personal plans and decisions, there are still other factors: whether you rent, build, or buy the store premises; the type of merchandise you'll be carrying; the storefront and interior decor you envision; and so on. So many variables are involved that no expert can tell you precisely how much capital you're going to need. Calculating your total investment requirements is *your* responsibility; you must do it yourself. Fortunately, "rule-of-thumb" guidelines based on trade averages are available. You need some knowledge, of course, and a method to work out approximate figures. Reading through the balance of this chapter will help you on both counts.

## CAPITAL AND ITS USES

When mounting a full-scale attack on the how-much-money problem, it's helpful to think in terms of the *uses* to which you'll put your finances:

**Initial capital.** You'll need this either to start up your new business, to buy someone else's business, or to sign up with a franchisor, depending on which of these routes you choose. You'll also need it to arrange for the legal form of your business, for necessary licenses and permits, as well as to open accounts with both the telephone and electric companies, to secure fixtures and equipment, and so on.

**Working capital.** This money is needed to take care of things once you have launched the retail operation and until you start to recover profits that can be reinvested. It's also used to purchase the goods to stock your store, to pay salaries to your employees, and the like.

**Reserve capital.** A reserve fund is necessary for those unexpected contingencies that crop up from time to time in virtually all enterprises.

**Promotional capital.** This is money you'll need to get the business off the ground in the first place and to ensure its viability in the second place. You start spending it in advance of your grand opening, and you continue to spend it to build your store image and popularity.

**Growth capital.** Of little importance to the new small business owner, this form of capital will be of concern to you at some future date, when you're contemplating the expansion of your retail enterprise.

## MONEY SOURCES: A QUICK REVIEW

Many people who consider going into business are wary of risking their own financial reserves. They're quick to solicit funds from lending institutions, friends, and family. Indeed, some even boast of their "shrewdness" in using other people's money instead of their own. This sort of thinking is fallacious, if not dangerous; all it means is that they lack sufficient confidence in their own plans.

Your own funds are always the best to resort to when starting a business. For one thing, when you borrow money, you're charged interest on it, which needs to be paid back from the business operation. And bank interest charges are high, high, high! Your first "source," then, ought to be *your own savings*. People who have managed to accumulate several thousand dollars by working for a few years before tackling their own business have at least the kernel of the financial backing needed for entrepreneurship. It's safe to assume that others will be reluctant to lend you money unless you have demonstrated your own faith in your new business by putting up funds of your own.

Indeed, according to a 1986 survey by *Venture* magazine: "Personal funds are by far the most common primary source of start-up capital."*

Here are some other useful sources of financing for your business:

**Property you own.** If you own a building or a vacation home, land, an automobile, or any other tangible asset, you may wish to either sell that property or take out a mortgage on it to raise capital for your business. This possibility also applies, by the way, to any life insurance you may have been carrying which has built up a substantial cash or loan value. Usually, the rate of interest charged by the insurance company is much lower than what you would be charged by a commercial bank. Moreover, you need never repay the loan principal. On your demise, the insurance company simply deducts the outstanding loan balance from the benefits to be paid out.

**Your family.** A rather common way for the entrepreneur to raise capital for a business venture is to discuss the possibilities with family members—all the way through to great-uncles and third cousins (especially those who may be blessed with extensive holdings!). You can borrow money as an outright loan or invite the family member(s) to hold part ownership of the business. In the first instance (and in today's climate), it

---

* "The Venture Survey: Financing Your Business," *Venture* 8 (October 1986), 24.

would be wise for you to insist on a sensible repayment schedule and on returning some rate of interest along with the repayments. After all, your relatives are losing their normal bank interest while you're using their money. If the funds are going to be used as "equity capital" instead of "loan capital," I'd recommend that you set up a corporation and sell shares of stock to your family. Another possibility, of course, is to form a partnership, although I ordinarily advise against doing this.

**Your friends.** In much the same vein, friends and even business associates may be willing either to lend you money for your venture or to put equity funds into it. Handle these individuals much as you would your family; friends are hard to come by.

**Banks.** Nearly everyone who has established an acceptable credit history, owns a savings account, and holds a steady job will have little trouble in getting a personal bank loan for several thousand dollars. Your savings account may also be used to borrow from rather easily. The bank will lend you up to your balance, and your account will continue to earn its regular interest as you're paying back the loan in installments. Barring the personal or savings account, though, you'll find that banks are rarely interested in lending money to someone first starting out in business. They're more interested in lending funds to established firms, on a short-term basis, to buy merchandise or equipment or to expand. Be assured that they won't even consider your start-up needs unless you already have sufficient capital to invest on your own. *Sufficient*, in this case, usually means at least 50 percent of the funds required. Of course, to gain their attention, you need to furnish all sorts of documentation about your business plans, including a "pro forma" balance sheet and operating statement (see exhibit 5–1).

The entrepreneur who seeks a bank loan must understand that the financial institution is interested not only "in the repayment ability and credit worthiness of the loan applicant" but also in "how the loan will help improve the productivity and profitability of the recipient."\* Thus, the good loan application ought to contain the following eight basic sections:

- Executive summary
- Business description
- Owner/manager profiles
- Business projections
- Financial statements
- Purpose of loan
- Amount of loan
- Repayment schedules\*\*

**Finance companies.** These firms, whether they offer personal or commercial services, are potential lending sources too. The commercial type requires collateral on your loan, such as the pledge of your accounts receivable or your inventory. Because of their extremely high interest rates, though, you're better off trying to secure the funds from a bank or other sources.

---

\* Robert T. Justis, "Starting a Small Business: An Investigation of the Borrowing Procedure," *Journal of Small Business Management* 20 (October 1982), 23.

\*\* Ibid.

## EXHIBIT 5–1. IS YOUR FIRM CREDIT-WORTHY?

The ability to obtain money when you need it is as necessary to the operation of your business as is a good location or the right equipment, reliable sources of supplies and materials, or an adequate labor force. Before a bank or any other lending agency will lend you money, the loaning officer must feel satisfied with the answers to the following questions:

1. What sort of person are you, the prospective borrower? By all odds, the character of the borrower comes first. Next is his ability to manage his business.

2. What are you going to do with the money? The answer to this question will determine the type of loan—short- or long-term. Money to be used for the purchase of seasonal inventory will require quicker repayment than money used to buy fixed assets.

3. When and how do you plan to pay it back? Your banker's judgment as to your business ability and the type of loan will be a deciding factor in the answer to this question.

4. Is the cushion in the loan large enough? In other words, does the amount requested make suitable allowance for unexpected developments? The banker decides this question on the basis of your financial statement which sets forth the condition of your business and/or on the collateral pledge.

5. What is the outlook for business in general and for your business particularly?

*Source:* "The ABC's of Borrowing," *Management Aid No. 170* (Washington, D.C.: U.S. Small Business Administration, 1977), 2.

**Credit from suppliers.** When your suppliers ship merchandise to you and bill you for it, giving you thirty days (or sometimes more) to pay, they are in fact lending you capital. This *trade credit* is always an excellent source of short-term financing. To keep this avenue open throughout your business's career, always pay your bills on time (or earlier) and gradually build your credit standing.

**Leasing.** Closely related to trade credit is leasing. You'll find that equipment such as cash registers, showcases, and the like can often be leased, rather than purchased, from your suppliers. Leasing such goods will help you keep your investment costs down.

**Venture capitalists and small business investment companies.** Much has been written in small business management books and journals about these sources of capital for the new enterprise. Venture capital firms, investment groups, or individuals are usually not at all interested in providing financial assistance to the small retail store. Their major concern is with companies that display exceptional growth possibilities; with such firms, they may be interested in furnishing equity capital for expansion *if* they feel they can recover their investment in a few short years. In short, they seek capital gains.*

Small business investment companies (SBICs) and their counterparts for minority-group members, the MESBICs (minority enterprise small business investment companies) may supply long-term financing for modernization and expansion as well as

---

* For helpful suggestions about the raising of venture capital, see: "Venture Capital: Part I—Tapping the Money Pool," *Small Business Reporter* 10 (July 1985), 52–57; "Venture Capital: Part II—A Successful Strategy to Secure Capital," *Small Business Reporter* 10 (August 1985), 85–88; W. Keith Schilit, "How to Obtain Venture Capital," *Business Horizons* 30 (May–June 1986), 76–81; David J. Gladstone, *Venture Capital Handbook,* rev. ed. (Englewood Cliffs, N.J.: Prentice-Hall, 1987).

equity capital. These privately owned firms are licensed by the Small Business Administration. Once again, if you're looking for *initial* capital for your retail business, chances are that you won't be able to find it here.

**The Small Business Administration.** This agency was designed by the federal government to aid and assist the interests of small business in an effort to preserve competitive enterprise. Among its many activities and programs since its creation in 1953 are its lending programs. The SBA provides financial assistance to small firms for business construction, conversion, or expansion; for the purchase of equipment, facilities, machinery, supplies, or materials; and for working capital. They will consider either participating with a bank in a loan or guaranteeing up to 90 percent of the loan. If funds are available, a direct SBA loan is sometimes a possibility. Your first step, if considering this type of financing, is to interest a bank in lending you money for your business. If you're turned down, your next move is to visit with an agency loan officer at an SBA field office to discuss your situation. He or she will review the problem and suggest a course of action. If the situation looks promising, you'll receive instructions for proceeding from that point.

## THE BALANCE SHEET

This accounting device is a statement of the financial condition of a firm at a given point in time. Most often, it's prepared annually, after the close of each year's business activity. The facts it contains are most useful as a springboard for management decision making. Consequently, many business consultants strongly recommend that the new enterprise have its balance sheets prepared quarterly throughout the year.

The basis for this statement is a simple formula that you ought to commit to memory:

$$\text{ASSETS} - \text{LIABILITIES} = \text{NET WORTH}$$

In exhibit 5–2, you'll find a simplified balance sheet for a small retail operation such as the one you may now be considering. Study it. You'll find most of the terms in it explained below:

**Assets.** Whatever the firm owns that is worth money: cash, stocks and bonds, property, land, inventory, equipment, fixtures, and the like.

**Liabilities.** Debts your business has to repay: the claims of creditors from whom you purchased goods or services, bank loans, promissory notes, taxes you already owe but have not yet paid, and so on.

**Net worth.** Often referred to as the *Owner(s)' Equity,* this element represents the owner(s)' investment in the business plus any retained profits. It's what's left over when all liabilities are subtracted from the firm's assets.

**Current assets.** Cash (either on hand, in the bank, or in the "petty cash" box), securities that you can convert quickly into cash, monies owed to your store by

## EXHIBIT 5–2. SAMPLE BALANCE SHEET FOR A SMALL STORE

B & L DRY GOODS
BALANCE SHEET
DECEMBER 31, 1989

ASSETS

Current Assets:

| | | |
|---|---|---|
| Cash on hand | $    525 | |
| Cash in bank | 18,440 | |
| Marketable securities | 4,850 | |
| Accounts receivable (less allowance for bad debts) | 3,125 | |
| Merchandise inventory | 38,910 | |
| Supplies | 760 | |
| Total Current Assets | | $66,610 |

Fixed Assets:

| | | |
|---|---|---|
| Equipment, less depreciation | 6,070 | |
| Fixtures, less depreciation | 8,235 | |
| Delivery truck, less depreciation | 6,940 | |
| Total Fixed Assets | | 21,245 |
| Total Assets | | $87,855 |

LIABILITIES

Current Liabilities:

| | | |
|---|---|---|
| Account payable | $ 8,725 | |
| Note payable, 1990 | 3,000 | |
| Accrued payroll taxes | 860 | |
| Total Current Liabilities | | $12,585 |

Long-term Liabilities:

| | | |
|---|---|---|
| Note payable, 1992 | 9,000 | |
| Note payable, 1995 | 12,500 | |
| Total Long-term Liabilities | | 21,500 |
| Total Liabilities | | $34,085 |

NET WORTH

| | |
|---|---|
| Owner's Equity, December 31, 1989 | $53,770 |
| Total Liabilities and Net Worth | $87,855 |

*Source:* Compiled by the author.

customers to whom you have extended credit (called *accounts receivable* or simply *receivables*), and inventory. The term *current assets* applies, in general, to whatever you own that can be cashed in or marketed within a year.

**Allowance for bad debts.** When you extend credit, you can be certain that a small number of customers will default. To give a more accurate valuation to your accounts receivable, then, you need to subtract some percentage of the total outstanding. A year or two of actual experience will help you decide on how much to subtract. If you have had no prior history, a telephone call to your trade association or to a few merchants in the same business (noncompetitors, of course!) should help you resolve the problem.

**Fixed assets.** These assets represent the tangible property you have acquired for use in your operation over the long term. Included in this category are fixtures, equipment, furniture, machinery, plant, and land, if you have purchased it. All of these fixed assets, except land, depreciate in value over time. They're recorded on your balance sheet at their original cost, less depreciation.

**Current liabilities.** Debts that must be paid within the year following the date of the balance sheet: the accounts payable (what you owe your suppliers), any loans outstanding, accrued taxes, and other expenses.

**Long-term liabilities.** Debts owed by your firm that need to be repaid in the future, more than one year after the balance-sheet date.

## THE OPERATING STATEMENT

Also referred to as an *income statement* or a *profit and loss statement* (more familiarly, a *P&L*), the operating statement records the *results* of running a business over a period of time. In it, all income and expenses are summarized, and the net profit or loss is indicated for the period covered. Every business is required by the IRS to furnish an annual operating statement, so that taxes may be levied against the profits earned. Yet the information contained in a P&L is so valuable to the firm's management that many consultants recommend that new business owners arrange for income statements to be developed on a quarterly, or even monthly, basis. To wait an entire year before learning whether your store has earned a profit is not smart. On the other hand, discovering shortly after the end of, say, March that you had a loss for the first quarter prompts you to improve activity in April so that you recoup the earlier loss. When you know what's going on in your business, you can make adjustments in your marketing tactics and strategies from one month to the next. By year's end, you have come in on target with that "bottom line" figure—profit, the last item on your operating statement.

Exhibit 5–3 shows a sample operating statement. Note its major parts: net sales, cost of goods sold, gross margin, operating expenses, other income, and net profit. In reality, three important formulae are illustrated in the statement:

SALES − COST OF GOODS SOLD = GROSS MARGIN (or GROSS PROFIT)

GROSS MARGIN − OPERATING EXPENSES = OPERATING PROFIT

OPERATING PROFIT + OTHER INCOME − INCOME TAXES = NET PROFIT

## ESTIMATING HOW MUCH MONEY YOU NEED

Congratulations! You have arrived at the point where you're ready to tackle the job of calculating the total investment you'll need to launch your new retail venture. By way of an overview, here's the method you ought to follow:

1. Set a realistic figure for your first year's sales volume.
2. Using the targeted annual sales as a base, begin constructing your first year's operating statement.
3. Estimate all the expenses you expect to incur in operating your store, then total them up.

## EXHIBIT 5–3. A SAMPLE OPERATING STATEMENT (P&L) FOR A SMALL STORE

MARIE'S GIFTS AND NOVELTIES
INCOME STATEMENT FOR AUGUST 1989

| | | |
|---|---:|---:|
| Gross Sales for August | | $12,335 |
| Less returns and allowances | | 240 |
| Net Sales | | $12,095 |
| Less Cost of Goods Sold: | | |
| Opening inventory, August 1 | 20,870 | |
| Purchases during August | 3,075 | |
| Freight charges | 85 | |
| Total merchandise handled | 24,030 | |
| Less closing inventory, August 31 | 17,165 | |
| Total Cost of Goods Sold | | 6,865 |
| Gross Margin | | 5,230 |
| Operating Expenses: | | |
| Payroll | 1,910 | |
| Rent | 850 | |
| Utilities | 210 | |
| Telephone | 120 | |
| Insurance | 160 | |
| Advertising | 45 | |
| Displays | 130 | |
| Depreciation | 355 | |
| Interest expense | 50 | |
| Delivery expense | 180 | |
| Stationery | 40 | |
| Travel and entertainment | 45 | |
| Dues and subscriptions | 35 | |
| Bad Debts | 70 | |
| Miscellaneous | 65 | |
| Total Operating Expenses | | 4,265 |
| Operating Profit | | 965 |
| Other Income: | | |
| Dividends | 20 | |
| Interest on bank account | 65 | |
| Total other income | | 85 |
| Total Income before Taxes | | 1,050 |
| Less provision for income taxes | | 320 |
| Net Profit | | 730 |

*Source:* Compiled by the author.

4. Complete your "pro forma" operating statement.
5. Fill out the worksheet in exhibit 5–4 to determine the cost of furniture, fixtures, and equipment.
6. Post all figures from both your P&L and the fixtures worksheet to the estimated monthly expenses worksheet in exhibit 5–5.
7. Complete Column 2 in the latter worksheet.

**EXHIBIT 5–4. WORKSHEET: FURNITURE, FIXTURES, AND EQUIPMENT**

### LIST OF FURNITURE, FIXTURES, AND EQUIPMENT

| Leave out or add items to suit your business. Use separate sheets to list exactly what you need for each of the items below. | If you plan to pay cash in full, enter the full amount below and in the last column. | If you are going to pay by installments, fill out the columns below. Enter in the last column your downpayment plus at least one installment. | | | Estimate of the cash you need for furniture, fixtures, and equipment |
|---|---|---|---|---|---|
| | | Price | Downpayment | Amount of each installment | |
| Counters | $ | $ | $ | $ | $ |
| Storage shelves, cabinets | | | | | |
| Display stands, shelves, tables | | | | | |
| Cash register | | | | | |
| Safe | | | | | |
| Window display fixtures | | | | | |
| Special lighting | | | | | |
| Outside sign | | | | | |
| Delivery equipment if needed | | | | | |
| TOTAL FURNITURE, FIXTURES, AND EQUIPMENT (Enter this figure also in worksheet 2 under "Starting Costs You Only Have To Pay Once ".) | | | | | $ |

*Source:* "Checklist for Going into Business," *Small Marketers Aid No. 71* (Washington, D.C.: U.S. Small Business Administration, 1977), 12.

## Some Helpful Pointers

Your expected sales volume for the first year of operation should be planned with care. This is the most important figure of all in your calculations, because all else stems from that amount. Often your trade association can provide average figures for small stores in locations similar to yours. Sometimes, sales-per-square-foot information is available; in this case, you can multiply this figure by the square footage of your selling area to approximate your annual sales. Your own appraisal of the location and community, along with estimates you may be able to secure from other, noncompeting merchants in your line of retailing, will also be of value to you.

Refer to the sample operating statement in exhibit 5–3 as you begin making up your own pro forma P&L for Year 1 of operations. Bear in mind, of course, that you're preparing an *annual* statement, not a *monthly* one such as that of Marie's Gifts and Novelties. As you study the format in exhibit 5–3, you'll notice that you have only one of the figures at this time: the expected gross sales for Year 1. Other dollar figures—such as those for returns and allowances and, more importantly, the cost of goods sold and gross

# EXHIBIT 5–5. WORKSHEET: ESTIMATED CASH NEEDED

| | ESTIMATED MONTHLY EXPENSES | | |
|---|---|---|---|
| Item | Your estimate of monthly expenses based on sales of $_____ per year | Your estimate of how much cash you need to start your business (See column 3.) | What to put in column 2 (These figures are typical for one kind of business. You will have to decide how many months to allow for in your business.) |
| | Column 1 | Column 2 | Column 3 |
| Salary of owner-manager | $ | $ | 2 times column 1 |
| All other salaries and wages | | | 3 times column 1 |
| Rent | | | 3 times column 1 |
| Advertising | | | 3 times column 1 |
| Delivery expense | | | 3 times column 1 |
| Supplies | | | 3 times column 1 |
| Telephone and telegraph | | | 3 times column 1 |
| Other utilities | | | 3 times column 1 |
| Insurance | | | Payment required by insurance company |
| Taxes, including Social Security | | | 4 times column 1 |
| Interest | | | 3 times column 1 |
| Maintenance | | | 3 times column 1 |
| Legal and other professional fees | | | 3 times column 1 |
| Miscellaneous | | | 3 times column 1 |
| STARTING COSTS YOU ONLY HAVE TO PAY ONCE | | | Leave column 2 blank |
| Fixtures and equipment | | | Fill in worksheet 3 and put the total here |
| Decorating and remodeling | | | Talk it over with a contractor |
| Installation of fixtures and equipment | | | Talk to suppliers from whom you buy these |
| Starting inventory | | | Suppliers will probably help you estimate this |
| Deposits with public utilities | | | Find out from utilities companies |
| Legal and other professional fees | | | Lawyer, accountant, and so on |
| Licenses and permits | | | Find out from city offices what you have to have |
| Advertising and promotion for opening | | | Estimate what you'll use |
| Accounts receiveble | | | What you need to buy more stock until credit customers pay |
| Cash | | | For unexpected expenses or losses, special purchases, etc. |
| Other | | | Make a separate list and enter total |
| TOTAL ESTIMATED CASH YOU NEED TO START WITH | $ | | Add up all the numbers in column 2 |

*Source:* "Checklist for Going into Business," *Small Marketers Aid No. 71* (Washington, D.C.: U.S. Small Business Administration, 1977), 6–7.

margin—call for some real detective work on your part. Luckily, accountants have developed a helpful technique for analyzing profit and loss statements which you can put to use: You can consider the net-sales entry as 100 percent of the total on the P&L, since everything else on the sheet represents a subtraction from that amount. All other major sections can therefore be easily expressed as percentages of sales.

On this premise, you'll need to ascertain the overall markup enjoyed by the "average" store of the kind you own. In this case, you can interpret the markup as net sales minus the cost of goods sold. (You'll find more on markup in chapter 11.) For example, if the typical markup in your line is 45 percent of sales, then your cost-of-goods percentage is necessarily 55 percent. The applicable percentage is easily discovered by talking to your trade association or to other retailers.

As a simple example, let's assume that you're planning to open a neighborhood variety store next year, and you have estimated first-year sales at $230,000. You don't expect much of a problem with returns and allowances, and so you have allocated only $3,000 to that entry. You have also learned from your trade group that stores such as yours typically end up with a maintained markup overall of about 45 percent. Exhibit 5–6 shows how your operating statement for next year might look as you begin to fill in the details.

You can, for the time being, ignore those first five question marks that appear under the "Less Cost of Goods Sold" heading. These entries are useful for calculating the cost of goods sold in the first place, a figure you already have, as we shall shortly see. You can, however, pencil in amounts at this point for the last two question marks, by following this logic:

1. Your targeted gross sales are $260,000, from which you have subtracted $3,000 for returns and allowances.
2. Your net sales, therefore, are $257,000.

---

## EXHIBIT 5–6. PARTIAL PRO FORMA INCOME STATEMENT

### STORE NAME
#### INCOME STATEMENT FOR 1989

| | | | |
|---|---|---|---|
| Gross Sales for Year | | $260,000 | |
| Less returns and allowances | | 3,000 | |
| Net Sales | | $257,000 | (100%) |
| Less Cost of Goods Sold: | | | |
| Opening inventory, January 1 | ? | | |
| Purchases during 1989 | ? | | |
| Freight charges | ? | | |
| Total merchandise handled | ? | | |
| Less closing inventory, | | | |
| December 31 | ? | | |
| Total Cost of Goods Sold | | ? | (55%) |
| Gross Margin | | ? | (45%) |

*Source:* Compiled by the author.

---

GEARING UP FOR YOUR NEW BUSINESS

3. Net sales represent 100 percent of all monies shown subsequently on the operating statement.
4. Your expected markup is 45 percent of that 100 percent. Your markup, then, equals 45 percent of $257,000. When you work out this amount, you discover that it comes to $115,650. (Use a calculator; it's easier that way!)
5. Do you recall the point made earlier that markup can be interpreted as "net sales minus the cost of goods sold"? By glancing at the income statement again, you will see that gross margin and markup mean the same thing. So pencil in $115,650 in place of the final question mark.
6. Now ask yourself: What sum, subtracted from $257,000, yields a figure of $115,650? Fine! You have come up with $141,350. (Note that you can also arrive at this figure by multiplying the net sales of $257,000 by the decimal equivalent of 55 percent—or .55.) Now, pencil in this figure where indicated on your evolving P&L.

## Calculating Your Operating Profit

In the next section of your pro forma operating statement, the one entitled "Operating Expenses," list the expense categories you're likely to incur as you operate your new store. (Refer again to exhibit 5–3.) While you may be quite certain at this point as to the amount of rent you'll be paying and can easily approximate your total payroll costs (salaries for you as well as for your employees), you'll probably need to research many of the other entries in order to come up with realistic estimates. With some luck, you may find that operating percentages are available from your trade association; one such example can be seen in table 5–1. (Note that the most useful figures in that table are those for the "median firm.") After entering all your operating costs, total them and enter that total in its proper place on your P&L. Then subtract that amount from your gross-margin figure to derive your expected operating profit.

At this point, it shouldn't be too difficult for you to finish your pro forma P&L on your own. Have fun!

## WORKING UP YOUR CAPITAL REQUIREMENTS

Once you have completed your operating statement, tailored to your own particular store and needs, you can then resort to the two worksheets provided by the SBA in their "Checklist for Going into Business" (exhibits 5–4 and 5–5). Read the column headings in the worksheet in exhibit 5–5; note that the expenses shown in column 1 are *monthly* expenses. So you need to divide those figures on your P&L by twelve before you insert them into column 1. Then read the directions in column 3 for all entries. Following those suggestions, enter the proper amounts in column 2.

At this juncture, fill out the worksheet in exhibit 5–4. Again, you'll need to do some research. Transfer your total estimate to the line in the estimated monthly expenses (exhibit 5–5) worksheet that reads "Fixtures and equipment." Thereafter, complete all remaining entries in column 2, following the notes indicated in column 3. Finally, total column 2. This total is the *total estimated cash you need to start with*.

Your completed estimated monthly expenses worksheet will look something like the one in exhibit 5–7, although the numbers will, of course, be different.

# TABLE 5-1. COMPOSITE OPERATING STATEMENT FOR 1978—MENSWEAR STORES

| PLEASE NOTE THAT NET WORKROOM COST IS NOW TREATED AS A SEPARATE EXPENSE CENTER. TAKE THIS INTO CONSIDERATION WHEN COMPARING GROSS MARGIN AND TOTAL EXPENSES TO LAST YEARS DATA PRIOR TO 1980. (*EXPENSE DIVISION NUMBERS AND DEFINITIONS ARE IN ACCORDANCE WITH MRA's FINANCIAL & OPERATIONS GROUP "MENSWEAR BASIC MANAGEMENT ACCOUNTING MANUAL".) | GROUP I FIRMS ANNUAL SALES under $300,000 (15 Firms) | | GROUP II FIRMS ANNUAL SALES $300,000 to $499,999 (31 Firms) | | |
|---|---|---|---|---|---|
| | Range of Common Experience | Median Firm | Range of Common Experience | Median Firm | YOUR FIRM |
| COST OF GOODS SOLD (Percent of net sales, excluding leased departments, except as noted.) | | | | | |
| 1. Ending inventory at cost | 21.6-44.0 | 36.4 | 20.6 -32.4 | 26.4 | _____% |
| 2. Total cost of merchandise sold | 55.8-70.1 | 59.6 | 50.8 -61.1 | 56.4 | _____ |
| 3. Gross margin, excluding leased department income and sales | 29.9-44.2 | 40.5 | 38.9 -49.2 | 43.6 | _____ |
| 4. Income from leased departments | NA | NA | NA | NA | _____ |
| 5. Gross margin, including income from leased departments, as a percent of total net sales | 29.9-44.2 | 42.6 | 38.9 -49.2 | 43.6 | _____ |
| Expense Div. No.* | | | | | |
| 6. 00 Net Alteration Cost | | | | | |
| a. Alterations payroll | 1.0- 4.1 | 1.2 | 1.1 - 3.8 | 2.2 | _____ |
| b. All other workroom expenses | .6- 2.3 | 1.1 | .1 - 1.3 | .5 | _____ |
| c. Less: Alteration Income | NA | NA | .3 - 1.1 | .8 | _____ |
| d. Net Alterations Costs (line a plus line b, minus line c) | 1.1- 2.5 | 1.4 | .8 - 2.0 | 1.3 | _____ |
| 7. 01 Payroll (total) | 8.6-24.0 | 18.5 | 14.3 -23.4 | 19.3 | _____ |
| a. Payroll of owners and officers | 2.0-11.1 | 8.0 | 5.7 - 9.8 | 7.2 | _____ |
| b. Selling payroll (includes commissions & "spiffs") | 6.7-12.9 | 9.4 | 7.4 -10.0 | 9.3 | _____ |
| c. Non-selling payroll (excludes workroom & advertising payroll) | NA | NA | 1.2 - 3.7 | 2.8 | _____ |
| 8. 03 Advertising | 2.6- 3.9 | 3.1 | 2.0 - 3.7 | 3.0 | _____ |
| 9. 04 Taxes (total) | 1.1- 1.8 | 1.3 | 1.5 - 2.3 | 1.9 | _____ |
| a. All state and local taxes (including licenses) with the exception of payroll taxes and Federal income taxes | .1- .7 | .3 | .1 - .7 | .5 | _____ |
| b. Social security and unemployment taxes | .6- 1.6 | 1.2 | 1.2 - 1.8 | 1.6 | _____ |
| 10. 06 Supplies | 1.4- 4.3 | 2.5 | 1.6 - 3.9 | 2.7 | _____ |
| a. Wrapping and packing supplies | .8 - 1.7 | 1.2 | .6 - 1.5 | 1.1 | _____ |
| b. Other supplies (cleaning, stationery) | .4- 1.5 | 1.0 | .1 - .7 | .5 | _____ |
| c. Utilities (heat, light, water, sewer, etc.) | 1.3- 2.6 | 2.1 | .9 - 1.7 | 1.2 | _____ |
| 11. 07 Services Purchased (Total) | NA | 2.1 | .8 - 3.8 | 2.2 | _____ |
| a. Accounts receivable factoring charges | NA | NA | NA | NA | _____ |
| b. Data processing/service bureau charges | NA | NA | .5 - 2.0 | 1.1 | _____ |
| c. Credit card service fees | .2- .8 | .5 | .3 - 1.1 | .5 | _____ |
| d. Cleaning service, delivery, alarm service, attorney fees for account collection, buying office, etc. | .2- 1.1 | .6 | .1 - .7 | .3 | _____ |
| 12. 08 Unclassified (cash shortages, want ads, dues, subscriptions, employee prizes, etc.) | .2- 1.4 | .4 | .5 - 1.3 | .8 | _____ |
| 13. 09 Traveling | .3- 1.0 | .7 | .4 - 1.2 | .7 | _____ |
| 14. 10 Communications | .4- 1.0 | .5 | .4 - .9 | .5 | _____ |
| 15. 11 Pensions | NA | NA | .7 - 3.0 | 2.1 | _____ |
| 16. 12 Insurance (total) | 1.3 - 3.8 | 2.3 | 1.3 - 3.0 | 2.2 | _____ |
| a. Workmen's compensation insurance; sickness, accident, group medical, group hospital and life insurance premiums | .8- 2.4 | 1.4 | .7 - 1.8 | 1.4 | _____ |
| b. All other insurance premiums | .5- 1.3 | .8 | .6 - 1.2 | .9 | _____ |
| 17. 13 Depreciation (total) | .7- 1.4 | .9 | .5 - 1.9 | 1.1 | _____ |
| 18. 14 Professional services | .3- 1.0 | .5 | .3 - .9 | .6 | _____ |
| 19. 15 Donations | .1- .7 | .2 | .1 - .3 | .2 | _____ |
| 20. 16 Bad Debts | .1- .4 | .2 | .1 - .4 | .1 | _____ |
| 21. 17 Equipment costs | .2- 1.1 | .3 | .1 - .6 | .3 | _____ |
| 22. 20 Real property rentals | 1.7- 5.5 | 4.3 | 2.0 - 4.6 | 3.3 | _____ |
| 23. Total expenses | 25.1-44.2 | 37.1 | 33.9 -44.7 | 40.0 | _____ |
| NET GAIN (Percent of total net sales, except as noted.) | | | | | |
| 24. Operating profit, including income from leased departments | 2.1- 7.8 | 6.4 | (1.1)- 8.7 | 3.5 | _____ |
| 25. a. Interest income | .3- 2.7 | .6 | .2 - 1.3 | .6 | _____ |
| b. Net other income | .1- 2.1 | .6 | .2 - 1.2 | .6 | _____ |
| c. Interest expenses | .5- 3.0 | 1.2 | .4 - 2.3 | 1.2 | _____ |
| d. Net other expenses | NA | NA | .2 - .5 | .5 | _____ |
| 26. Net profit, before Federal income taxes | .7- 6.7 | 5.9 | .5 - 9.0 | 2.5 | _____ |

*Source: MRA Annual Business Survey: 1987 Men's Store Operating Experiences* (Washington, D.C.: Menswear Retailers of America, 1988), 40.

## EXHIBIT 5–7. COMPLETED MONTHLY EXPENSES WORKSHEET

### ESTIMATED MONTHLY EXPENSES

| Item | Your estimate of monthly expenses based on sales of $ 100,000 per year | Your estimate of how much cash you need to start your business (See column 3.) | What to put in column 2 (These figures are typical for one kind of business. You will have to decide how many months to allow for in your business.) |
|---|---|---|---|
| | Column 1 | Column 2 | Column 3 |
| Salary of owner-manager | $ 833 | $ 1,666 | 2 times column 1 |
| All other salaries and wages | 667 | 2,001 | 3 times column 1 |
| Rent | 475 | 1,425 | 3 times column 1 |
| Advertising | 150 | 450 | 3 times column 1 |
| Delivery expense | 45 | 135 | 3 times column 1 |
| Supplies | 108 | 324 | 3 times column 1 |
| Telephone and telegraph | 90 | 270 | 3 times column 1 |
| Other utilities | 150 | 450 | 3 times column 1 |
| Insurance | 125 | 500 | Payment required by insurance company |
| Taxes, including Social Security | 200 | 800 | 4 times column 1 |
| Interest | 83 | 249 | 3 times column 1 |
| Maintenance | 100 | 300 | 3 times column 1 |
| Legal and other professional fees | 80 | 240 | 3 times column 1 |
| Miscellaneous | 50 | 150 | 3 times column 1 |
| STARTING COSTS YOU ONLY HAVE TO PAY ONCE | | | Leave column 2 blank |
| Fixtures and equipment | | 5,600 | Fill in worksheet 3 and put the total here |
| Decorating and remodeling | | 1,500 | Talk it over with a contractor |
| Installation of fixtures and equipment | | 1,200 | Talk to suppliers from whom you buy these |
| Starting inventory | | 8,500 | Suppliers will probably help you estimate this |
| Deposits with public utilities | | 300 | Find out from utilities companies |
| Legal and other professional fees | | 450 | Lawyer, accountant, and so on |
| Licenses and permits | | 110 | Find out from city offices what you have to have |
| Advertising and promotion for opening | | 500 | Estimate what you'll use |
| Accounts receiveble | | — | What you need to buy more stock until credit customers pay |
| Cash | | 1,000 | For unexpected expenses or losses, special purchases, etc. |
| Other | | 750 | Make a separate list and enter total |
| TOTAL ESTIMATED CASH YOU NEED TO START WITH | | $ 28,870 | Add up all the numbers in column 2 |

Source: "Checklist for Going into Business," Small Marketers Aid No. 71 (Washington, D.C.: U.S. Small Business Administration, 1977).

## One Last, Vital Thought

These computations do not take into account two factors: (1) reserve funds to live on until you begin to earn profits on your store operation; and (2) "contingency funds" that should be available just in case you have erred in your calculations or something unexpected affects your business. How much you allocate to handle these factors is, of course, your decision to make.

## FOR FURTHER INFORMATION

### Books

Batterson, L. *Raising Venture Capital and the Entrepreneur*. Englewood Cliffs, N.J.: Prentice-Hall, 1986.

Carey, Omer L., and Dean F. Olson. *Financial Tools for Small Business*. Reston, Va.: Reston, 1983.

Dible, D. *How to Plan and Finance a Growing Business*. Reston, Va.: Reston, 1981.

Gladstone, David J. *Venture Capital Handbook,* rev. ed. Englewood Cliffs, N.J.: Prentice-Hall, 1987.

Mancuso, Joseph R. *How to Prepare and Present a Business Plan*. Englewood Cliffs, N.J.: Prentice-Hall, 1983.

Pratt, Stanley E. *How to Raise Venture Capital*. New York: Scribner's, 1982.

————, ed. *Guide to Venture Capital Sources,* 6th ed. Englewood Cliffs, N.J.: Prentice-Hall, 1982.

Silver, A. David. *Venture Capital: The Complete Guide for Investors*. New York: Wiley, 1982.

### Pamphlets Available from the Small Business Administration

#### Management Aids

MA 1.001—"The ABC's of Borrowing"
MA 1.004—"Basic Budgets for Profit Planning"
MA 1.009—"A Venture Capital Primer for Small Business"
MA 1.015—"Budgeting in a Small Business Firm"
MA 1.016—"Sound Cash Management and Borrowing"
MA 1.019—"Simple Breakeven Analysis for Small Stores"
MA 2.016—"Checklist for Going into Business"
MA 2.020—"Business Plan for Retailers"
MA 2.022—"Business Plan for Small Service Firms"

### Booklets Available from the Superintendent of Documents

S/N 045-000-00142-3—*Financial Recordkeeping for Small Stores*—$5.50.
S/N 045-000-00174-1—*Evaluating Money Sources*—$5.00.
S/N 045-000-00193-8—*Capital Planning*—$4.50.
S/N 045-000-00194-6—*Understanding Money Sources*—$4.75.
S/N 045-000-00208-0—*Handbook of Small Business Finance*—$4.50.
S/N 045-000-00233-1—*Financial Management: How to Make a Go of Your Business*—$2.50.

# 6

# Developing an Effective Business Plan

As you have already noted, the odds for succeeding in your new enterprise are decidedly *not* in your favor. Doesn't it make sense, then, to exercise consummate care in developing a thorough, well-detailed *master plan* for your new business? Even if it takes you an entire month or longer to work it out?

## PLANNING: YOUR KEY TO A SUCCESSFUL LAUNCH

Here are some of the activities you engage in when you tackle the preparation of a master plan for your new retail store:

- Setting goals (both long- and short-range)
- Working out ways of attaining those goals
- Arranging priorities
- Trying to anticipate obstacles
- Preparing strategies
- Conceiving contingency plans
- Scheduling events
- Developing budgets
- Setting timetables
  . . . and much, much more.

### Planning Is Hard Work

Like inventive genius, serious planning is about 1 percent inspiration and 99 percent perspiration. Planning requires thinking—and thinking requires intense concentration. Planning also demands an extraordinary amount of self-discipline. Yet, so many would-be entrepreneurs neglect this essential activity.* For many entrepreneurs, the creation of

---

* See, for example, Carson R. Kennedy, "Thinking of Opening Your Own Business? Be Prepared!" *Business Horizons* 28 (September–October 1985), 38–42; Richard L. Osborne, "Planning: The Entrepreneurial Ego at Work," *Business Horizons* 30 (January–February 1987), 20–24; Fred L. Fry and Charles R. Stoner, "Business Plans: Two Major Types," *Journal of Small Business Management* 23 (January 1985), 1–6.

a business is so intoxicating that they feel an almost irrepressible compulsion to plunge headlong into the venture without doing much sensible planning at all. The entrepreneurial personality is more action-oriented than analytical and deliberative. Further, since most entrepreneurs instinctively realize that the future is largely unpredictable, they tend to shy away from "wasting" their time and energy on what they perceive to be sheer speculation. Moreover, the average person has had little practice at planning.

Even people with years of experience in lower- or middle-management positions show an appalling lack of interest in this area. Such individuals are, for the most part, caught up in day-to-day operations and find little time for developing well-conceived plans. Generally, they follow the mandates handed down by top management, initiating few plans of substance except for the small-scale, short-term, operations-oriented variety. Consequently, they acquire little practice at the type of conceptual planning you need to launch a new retail enterprise.

If you think of any plan as a blueprint for action—a scheme to get you where you want to go—you won't have such problems. As a government pamphlet points out:

> A business plan:
>
> Gives you a path to follow. A plan with goals and action steps allows you to guide your business through turbulent, often unforeseen, economic conditions.
>
> A plan shows your banker the condition and direction of your business so that your business can be more favorably considered for a loan because of the banker's insight into your situation.
>
> A plan can tell your sales personnel, suppliers, and others about your operations and goals.
>
> A plan can help you develop as a manager. It can give you practice in thinking and figuring out problems about competitive conditions, promotional opportunities, and situations that are good or bad for your business. Such practice over a period of time can help increase an owner-manager's ability to make judgments.
>
> A sound plan tells you what to do and how to do it to achieve the goals you have set for your business.*

For an overview of the areas in which you need to plan, refer to the chart in exhibit 6–1.

## The Basic Management Tasks

Like managers in all fields, administrators and other executives expend most of their time and energy conducting four distinct types of activities. These four areas—planning, organizing, directing, and controlling—are collectively known as the *four basic management functions,* or *tasks.* As an aspiring retail entrepreneur, then, you should understand that the conceptualization of a plan must precede the other three activities. Once you have developed the plan, you then need to organize all the necessary resources (time,

---

* "Business Plan for Retailers," *Management Aid No. 2.020* (Washington, D.C.: U.S. Small Business Administration, April 1981 reprint), 2.

## EXHIBIT 6–1. THE RETAIL STORE OPERATION

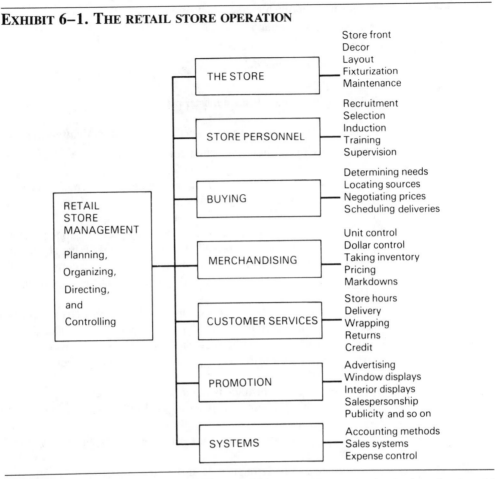

*Source:* Irving Burstiner, *The Small Business Handbook: A Comprehensive Guide to Starting and Running Your Own Business*, rev. ed. (New York: Prentice Hall Press, 1989), 313.

energy, finances, personnel, materials, methods, and so forth) to carry out the plan. This step is called *organizing*. Having successfully organized your resources, your next moves are to put the plan into operation and to manage or *direct* it. You also need to monitor both actions and results as the plan unfolds, so you can make adjustments where necessary to keep your plan on target. We call this last phase *controlling*.

Bear these four steps in mind when planning your new business—and when running it in the years ahead.

## THE PLANNING PROCESS

Some years ago, an article in the *Journal of Small Business Management* suggested that, to some extent, you can measure the small firm's strength by "how well it succeeds in performing each of six crucial tasks." The author suggested the six tasks listed on the next page.

- Making a thorough market analysis
- Developing an attractive product line
- Developing an effective sales effort
- Achieving financial stability
- Developing managerial expertise
- Developing and following a master plan*

Since each of these tasks merits serious thought and attention to proper planning procedures, here's one such procedure for you to follow, step by step:

1. *Analyze your present situation.* Study your current state of preparedness. Examine your capabilities, your finances, and your other resources. Investigate your opportunities; estimate your chances of success.

2. *Forecast the future situation.* This is the heart of your planning. Assess the economic climate that will prevail at that future time. What about your customers? Your competitors? Your resources? Gather information from your trade association, government agencies, business journals and trade magazines, your suppliers, and your customers.

3. *Set your major objectives.* Only clear-cut goals enable you to plan all the activities, events, schedules, and so on that help you achieve success. Vague objectives don't help you; they must be specific. More general objectives—such as sheer survival, profit, and growth—can't provide enough illumination to light your way in serious planning.

Here are a few illustrations of more specific objectives:
- To reach my break-even point of $135,000 in sales within eight months after opening day
- To attain a growth rate of 10 percent annually during my first three years in business
- To add a second store in my fourth year of operation and another two stores in the following year
- To develop competent managers for those new stores
- To earn a return-on-investment of 15 percent per year

4. *Divide your major objectives into subgoals.* It's far easier to make plans for portions of your business, one by one, than to come up with one overall plan for the entire enterprise. Similarly, by analyzing each of your main goals with care, you will discover that they can be further subdivided into three, four, or more narrowly circumscribed objectives, which are much easier for you to plan for.

5. *Link the present situation to the future situation.* Now's the time to think about how to attain your objectives, about your strategies and tactics, about the timing and sequence of planned activities, about the wise deployment of your resources, and so on. Now is when you can use your imagination and creativity. Now, too, you need to budget and conserve your resources carefully—and to build in controlling mechanisms that will enable you to "fine-tune" the details, once you have put the plan into operation and are directing it.

---

\* Panos Apostolidis, "Criteria for Success in Small Business," *Journal of Small Business Management* 15 (January 1977), 48–51.

## PREPARING YOUR RETAIL BUSINESS PLAN

Lacking sufficient financial resources to launch a new business, would-be entrepreneurs sometimes seek to interest a venture capital group or company in their operation. With the assistance of a consultant and/or a CPA, they prepare a type of business plan called a *venture proposal* (see exhibit 6–2 for a description of the usual contents of such documents). These proposals are detailed and lengthy. Few such documents receive a positive reaction because venture capital companies prefer to invest in enterprises that are already established and that show a good track record. For the most part, these investors are interested in placing equity capital in firms with growth potential because their major objective is to make capital gains.

The business plan you prepare shouldn't be destined for the eyes of a venture company but for your own eyes and use. Your finished plan will serve as your guide in the months and years ahead. Of course, it must be flexible; modifications are not only desirable but also necessary, as you "fine-tune" the details along the way.

---

### EXHIBIT 6–2. ELEMENTS OF A VENTURE PROPOSAL

1. *Purpose and Objectives*—a summary of the what and why of the project;

2. *Proposed Financing*—the amount of money you'll need from the beginning to the maturity of the project proposed, how the proceeds will be used, how you plan to structure the financing, and why the amount designated is required;

3. *Marketing*—a description of the market segment you've got now or plan to get, the competition, the characteristics of the market, and your plans (with costs) for getting or holding the market segment you're aiming at;

4. *History of the Firm*—a summary of significant financial and organizational milestones, description of employees and employee relations, explanations of banking relationships, recounting of major services or products your firm has offered during its existence, and the like;

5. *Description of the Product or Service*—a full description of the product (process) or service offered by the firm and the costs associated with it, in detail;

6. *Financial Statements*—both for the past few years and pro forma projections (balance sheets, income statements, and cash flows) for the next 3–5 years, showing the effect anticipated if the project is undertaken and if the financing is secured (This should include an analysis of key variables affecting financial performance, showing what could happen if the projected level of revenue is not attained.);

7. *Capitalization*—a list of shareholders, how much is invested to date, and in what form (equity/debt);

8. *Biographical Sketches*—the work histories and qualifications of key owners/employees;

9. *Principal Suppliers and Customers*

10. *Problems Anticipated and Other Pertinent Information*—a candid discussion of any contingent liabilities, pending litigation, tax or patent difficulties, and any other contingencies that might affect the project you're proposing.

11. *Advantages*—a discussion of what's special about your product, service, marketing plans, or channels that gives your project unique leverage.

---

*Source:* LaRue Tone Hosmer, "A Venture Capital Primer for Small Business," *Management Aid No. 235* (Washington, D.C.: U.S. Small Business Administration, 1978), 3.

---

## Working Up Your Business Plan

The time to begin preparing your new business plan is now—today. Get yourself a looseleaf notebook. Set up the following five sections in the notebook:

- My Store Plan
- My Stock Plan
- My Promotion Plan
- My Personnel Plan
- My Financial Plan

Then begin to work on each of the sections in turn, following the outline suggested in exhibit 6–3.

---

### EXHIBIT 6–3. MY BUSINESS PLAN

A. MY STORE PLAN
- Thorough description of my location.
- Analysis of my competition.
- What my customers are like.
- Terms of lease.
- Licenses, permits, local ordinances, and other legal requirements.
- The storefront.
- Interior decor.
- Store layout.
- Store lighting.
- Show windows.
- Fixturization.
- Equipment.
- Supplies.

B. MY STOCK PLAN
- Merchandise line(s) to be carried.
- Depth of merchandise offerings.
- Merchandise resources: list of suppliers' names and addresses, terms, credit and delivery policies, and the like.
- Price ranges; quality levels.
- Opening stock.
- Expected turnover rate (overall; by classification).
- Markdown and discount policies.
- Inventory and stock control method.
- Customer services.
- Customer credit extension program.

C. MY PROMOTION PLAN
- One-year promotional calendar.
- Display and advertising budgets.
- Window display program.
- Interior display program.

---

- Selection of advertising media.
- Cooperative advertising efforts.
- Public relations program.
- Sales training program.

D. MY PERSONNEL PLAN
- Employee needs assessment.
- Job specifications for all positions.
- Sources of prospective employees.
- Compensation plans and pay guidelines.
- Employee benefits to offer.
- Promotional ladder.
- Training program.

E. MY FINANCIAL PLAN
- Pro forma accounting statements (P&Ls, balance sheets).
- Bookkeeping method to be followed.
- Cash flow projections.
- Payroll and other record-keeping approaches.
- Insurance program.
- Internal risk-reduction measures.
- Tax liability and responsibilities.
- Bank relations.

---

*Source:* Compiled by the author.

Of course, you should have an intensive grounding in the fundamentals before you tackle this planning task. Work in one of the five areas at a time. As a beginning, read through the chapters in this book that deal with the respective areas, and take copious notes for reference.

Here are the pertinent chapters in each case:

| | |
|---|---|
| My Store Plan | Chapters 7, 8 |
| My Stock Plan | Chapters 9, 10, 11 |
| My Promotion Plan | Chapters 15, 16, 17 |
| My Personnel Plan | Chapters 13, 14 |
| My Financial Plan | Chapters 5, 18, 19 |

For each area, you'll be able to gather additional useful information and further insights by referring to one or more of the books listed at the end of each chapter in the "For Further Information" section. Finally, make sure to obtain a copy of the "Marketing Checklist for Small Retailers" (MA 4.012), which contains a superb list of questions you'll want answers to as you prepare your plan.

Two more forms will be of help to you in preparing your financial plan. The first (exhibit 6–4) is useful as a guide in working up your operating statements, especially since it provides a breakdown of the percentages for hardware stores as an illustration. The second (exhibit 6–5) is of value in making your cash-flow projections.

# EXHIBIT 6–4. EXPENSES WORKSHEET FOR MONTHLY P&L STATEMENTS

**Worksheet**

| | Sample figures for Hardware Stores (% of Sales) Percent of Sales | % of Your Sales | Your Dollars JAN | Your Dollars FEB | Your Dollars MAR | Your Dollars APR | Your Dollars MAY | Your Dollars JUN | Your Dollars JUL | Your Dollars AUG | Your Dollars SEPT | Your Dollars OCT | Your Dollars NOV | Your Dollars DEC | Your Annual Sales Dollar |
|---|---|---|---|---|---|---|---|---|---|---|---|---|---|---|---|
| Net Sales | 100.00 | | | | | | | | | | | | | | |
| Cost of goods Sold | 66.05 | | | | | | | | | | | | | | |
| Margin | 33.95 | | | | | | | | | | | | | | |
| Salary Expense: | | | | | | | | | | | | | | | |
| Owners and managers | 7.15 | | | | | | | | | | | | | | |
| Salespeople, office, and other | 9.60 | | | | | | | | | | | | | | |
| Total Salaries | 16.75 | | | | | | | | | | | | | | |
| Other Expense: | | | | | | | | | | | | | | | |
| Office supplies and postage | 0.40 | | | | | | | | | | | | | | |
| Advertising | 1.55 | | | | | | | | | | | | | | |
| Donations | 0.05 | | | | | | | | | | | | | | |
| Telephone and Telegraph | 0.30 | | | | | | | | | | | | | | |
| Losses on notes and accounts receivable | 0.15 | | | | | | | | | | | | | | |
| Delivery expense (exclusive of wages) | 0.50 | | | | | | | | | | | | | | |
| Depreciation of delivery equipment | 0.25 | | | | | | | | | | | | | | |
| Depreciation of furniture, fixtures, and tools | 0.35 | | | | | | | | | | | | | | |
| Rent | 2.70 | | | | | | | | | | | | | | |
| Repairs to building | 0.10 | | | | | | | | | | | | | | |
| Heat, light, water, and power | 0.80 | | | | | | | | | | | | | | |
| Insurance | 0.80 | | | | | | | | | | | | | | |
| Taxes (not including Federal income tax) | 1.10 | | | | | | | | | | | | | | |
| Interest on borrowed money | 0.05* | | | | | | | | | | | | | | |
| Unclassified (including store supplies) | 1.20 | | | | | | | | | | | | | | |
| Total Expense (Not including interest on investment) | 27.05 | | | | | | | | | | | | | | |
| Net Profit | 6.90 | | | | | | | | | | | | | | |

* The interest on funds used for start-up costs if yours is a new store.

Source: "Business Plan for Retailers," *Management Aid 2.020* (Washington, D.C.: U.S. Small Business Administration, reprinted April 1981), 11.

EXHIBIT 6–5. FORM FOR ESTIMATING YOUR CASH FLOW

| ESTIMATED CASH FORECAST | | | | | | | | | | | | |
|---|---|---|---|---|---|---|---|---|---|---|---|---|
| | Jan. | Feb. | Mar. | April | May | June | July | Aug. | Sept. | Oct. | Nov. | Dec. |
| (1) Cash in Bank (Start of Month) | | | | | | | | | | | | |
| (2) Petty Cash (Start of Month) | | | | | | | | | | | | |
| (3) Total Cash (add 1) and (2) | | | | | | | | | | | | |
| (4) Expected Cash Sales | | | | | | | | | | | | |
| (5) Expected Collections | | | | | | | | | | | | |
| (6) Other Money Expected | | | | | | | | | | | | |
| (7) Total Receipts (add 4, 5 and 6) | | | | | | | | | | | | |
| (8) Total Cash and Receipts (add 3 and 7) | | | | | | | | | | | | |
| (9) All Disbursements (for month) | | | | | | | | | | | | |
| (10) Cash Balance at End of Month. in Bank Account and Petty Cash (subtract (9) from (8)* | | | | | | | | | | | | |

*This balance is your starting cash balance for the next month.

*Source:* Office of Management Assistance, "Business Plan for Retailers," *Small Marketers Aid No. 150* (Washington, D.C.: U.S. Small Business Administration, 1972), 17.

# FOR FURTHER INFORMATION

## Books

Brooks, Julie K., and Barry A. Stevens. *How to Write a Successful Business Plan.* New York: AMACOM, 1987.

Mancuso, J. *How to Write a Winning Business Plan.* Englewood Cliffs, N.J.: Prentice-Hall, 1985.

Stoner, Charles R., and Fred L. Fry. *Strategic Planning in Small Business.* Cincinnati: South-Western, 1987.

## Pamphlets Available from the Small Business Administration

### Management Aids

MA 1.019—"Simple Breakeven Analysis for Small Stores"
MA 2.010—"Planning and Goal Setting for Small Business"
MA 2.020—"Business Plan for Retailers"
MA 2.022—"Business Plan for Small Service Firms"

# III

# Getting It All Together

# —— 7 ——

# Selecting Your Store Location

With regard to finding a store location, the SBA is quick to point out the unfortunate fact that "Amazingly, many location decisions are based on the personal preferences of the owner-manager. . . . Such preferences can mean anything from locating the business within walking distance of your home to buying a building from a friend because that friend wants to sell."*

To rely solely on intuition in choosing your store location is to cast your fate before the wind. Never, never allow your impulses or emotions to influence this vital decision. Serious, painstaking analysis is required. Of course, tried-and-true guidelines are available, but these are only guides and are not infallible. Even with seasoned location experts, multivariable rating schemes, and the benefit of advanced computers, major retail chains and department stores still make costly errors of judgment in selecting their new store locations. You may still err even with a sensible plan, but your chances of securing an above-average spot are considerably enhanced.

## THE CITY'S RETAIL STRUCTURE

Basically, you may consider two categories of "retail shopping areas" in selecting your store location: (1) the older, largely unplanned shopping areas; and (2) the planned shopping centers (neighborhood, community, regional).

### Older Retail Shopping Areas

Within a typical American city, you can generally discern several distinct types of long-established shopping areas. These include:

- The central business district, or *CBD* (also known as *downtown* or *center city*)
- Secondary business districts

---

* Fred I. Weber, Jr., "Locating or Relocating Your Business," *Management Aid No. 2.002* (Washington, D.C.: U.S. Small Business Administration, n.d.), 2.

- Neighborhood shopping streets
- Occasional small groups of stores spotted throughout residential areas

**The Central Business District.** Bustling with activity during the day (especially between the hours of noon and 2 P.M., the central business district is the heart of the city's business and commerce. Traffic, both vehicular and pedestrian, is extremely heavy. City dwellers, suburbanites, and even out-of-towners come here to work, shop, and play. This section houses office buildings, banks, theaters, department and chain stores, restaurants, and hotels as well as an extensive "mix" of retail types. The stores here reflect considerable street frontage and ample windows; their interiors are spacious and well-merchandised; the breadth, depth, and assortment of goods carried is greater here than anywhere else. Store rents are the highest in the city.

Yet, despite the heavy concentration of traffic, I believe that the new small retailer generally ought to shy away from the central business district. Not only are rents there nearly prohibitive nowadays, but many downtown areas across the country have been deteriorating for years. Of course, many cities have successfully revitalized their downtown areas in recent years.

**Secondary Business Districts.** These are scaled-down versions of the CBD. Most have developed over the decades (as the city grew) along the major roads leading out of the downtown section toward the city's perimeter. The store mix here is similar to that of downtown, except that a larger percentage of the shops are devoted to convenience goods, and the stores themselves are typically smaller in size. Although some people travel to these areas from distant neighborhoods, the majority of shoppers are from apartment buildings or houses not more than ten or fifteen minutes away by car.

Since these secondary business districts enjoy considerable street traffic, rents are still high, but they're more in line with your new enterprise's sales potential. You may be able to find an available location; it also may be possible for you to purchase someone else's established retail business here.

**Neighborhood Shopping Streets.** These areas generally extend for a few city blocks in several directions. Traffic is usually brisk. The store mix encompasses just about every type needed to service a well-populated neighborhood: pharmacies, hardware stores, meat markets and fruit stands, bakeries, clothing stores (men's, women's, children's), supermarkets and/or superettes, fast-food and service restaurants, beauty salons and barber shops, shoe stores, gift shops, and so on. Interspersed among these types of stores can be found occasional establishments conducting both wholesale and retail activities in such areas as electrical or plumbing supplies, party goods, and soft drinks (by the case).

**Other Retail Areas.** Seen sporadically throughout the city are small groupings of four, five, or perhaps more stores. In these *retail clusters,* you will usually find a grocery, drugstore, dry cleaner or laundromat, small luncheonette or perhaps a pizza parlor, and other independent retailers of convenience goods.

Here and there, too, may also be found an occasional large discount or variety store that stands apart from other retail outlets and that has its own facilities for parking. These *freestanding* stores depend, in the main, on frequent newspaper and possibly radio advertising to attract their clientele from miles around.

## Planned Shopping Centers

A relatively new development on the American scene that had its beginnings in the early 1950s, planned shopping centers proliferated on the American scene over the next several decades. Thousands of such centers—of all sizes—now exist across the country.

The typical center's site is selected for easy access and convenience, so that shoppers can drive in, park, and walk to the complex. Preplanned as a merchandising unit, the center contains a deliberate "mix" of retail stores designed to attract consumers, sometimes from considerable distances. When classified by size, three distinct types of planned centers are readily apparent:

- Neighborhood shopping centers
- Community shopping centers
- Regional shopping centers

**The Neighborhood Shopping Center.** The smallest of the three types, the typical neighborhood center consists of about 50,000 square feet of leasable space on a four-acre site. Many are built as a straight line, or *strip,* of retail stores; these are often referred to as *strip centers.* Others are constructed in the shape of an L or a U.

Neighborhood shopping centers cater to the needs of a few thousand to as many as 30,000 or 40,000 people who live within a six- to ten-minute drive from the site. The parking area may accommodate from as few as twenty or thirty to as many as one hundred or more cars. The major tenant may be a supermarket or a sizable unit of a national or regional drug chain; this large outlet is often located at one end of the center. Other stores are mostly of the convenience-goods type. Here, too, you may find an occasional beauty salon, dry cleaner, shoe store, women's ready-to-wear shop, convenience grocery, or laundromat.

**The Community Shopping Center.** Usually, this type is more than twice the size of the neighborhood shopping center. It's typically erected on some ten acres of land and may offer as much as 140,000 or more square feet of retail space. Its trading area, of course, is a good deal larger than that of the neighborhood shopping center; people come to shop from as far away as five to eight miles around. The center is designed to serve a population that may range from as few as 25,000 to as many as 150,000. Frequently, the dominant store (or *anchor store*) is a mass-merchandising retailer (like a K Mart or Zayre's outlet), a junior department store, or a large supermarket. In addition to shops selling convenience goods and services, there are considerably more outlets that carry shopping goods, as well as a liberal sprinkling of specialty shops.

**The Regional Shopping Center.** Typically covering a tract of thirty or more acres and leasing upwards of 300,000 to 400,000 square feet, this is the largest of the three types. Regional centers can adequately serve between 100,000 and 200,000 people living within a circumference of up to forty minutes or more away by automobile (ten to fifteen miles around). Some modern-day centers run to as large as one-half to one million square feet of retail space. Sometimes built on several levels, most are fully enclosed and climate controlled, so that consumers are able to shop without care year-round. There are parking accommodations for a thousand cars or more.

Often, a department store is located at each end. Spread out between these two anchors are independent retail shops of every description and units of nationally known chains. Kiosks may be found in the main passageways, displaying a wide range of merchandise, from greeting cards or jewelry to house plants, candy, and the like. The tenant mix has been so designed as to satisfy just about all the needs of the public; here you can find clothing, home furnishings, food, giftware, sewing machines and craft supplies, drugs and sundries, appliances and television sets, and so on.

In addition to banks, restaurants, and variety stores, today's regional centers frequently house offices, motels, bowling alleys, movie theaters, banks, and even large meeting rooms for community activities.

## WHICH IS FOR YOU: IN-CITY LOCALE OR SHOPPING CENTER?

You would do well to avoid opening your new store in the downtown area. For the most part, the central business districts in our cities are unattractive to small retailers not only because of the inordinately high rents and intense competition from surrounding stores, but also because these areas are no longer growing. Indeed, many of them continue to deteriorate.

For most retail lines, your chances of building a successful trade are much better in the secondary business districts and in the neighborhood shopping streets. Your chances are especially promising in well-populated sections that draw shoppers from nearby apartment houses and that have substantial numbers of young marrieds and young families moving in. In such locales, though, you need to select the "right" side of the street; pedestrian traffic is often up to five or six times greater on one side than on the other. (In these areas, the *traffic count* comes in handy, an element that's discussed later in this chapter.) You should also weigh the advantages of a corner location against those of an in-street spot, even though the rent for the former is typically much higher. You'll also find that the type of location you need for your business is dictated by the kind of merchandise you sell. If you carry, in the main, convenience goods, then the proper place for you might be on a busy thoroughfare or in a shopping center. If you sell specialty merchandise, your store can easily be housed in an out-of-the-way, off-street location simply because shoppers will travel farther to ferret you out. (Similarly, the space you need varies according to your type of business: space for your selling activities, for display and work areas, for storage, and so forth.)

As a final thought, check whether the stores that flank your location are, in your judgment, detrimental to or supportive of your particular type of business—and whether the vicinity can support another store such as yours.

## Consider the Planned Shopping Center

For the long pull, though, you might be better off opening in a planned community or regional shopping center that has proved successful. Today's consumer is better educated, more mobile, more a seeker after the good life, and apparently inclined to feel more comfortable in the shopping-center milieu than the consumer of the 1950s and 1960s. Shopping in this type of environment is certainly relaxed and casual. Moreover, many centers are open for business five or six nights a week, and some on Sundays. This schedule isn't characteristic of the older in-city retail shopping areas.

Traffic—that lifeblood of retailing—is generated not only by the mere massed presence of a conglomeration of stores, big and small, but also by the many promotional activities coordinated by the center's tenants' association: center-wide sales, special exhibitions and shows, fairs, concerts, visits by leading sports figures (or Santa and his reindeer), and other public-relations events.

**Disadvantages of Shopping Centers.** Of course, these centers do have some drawbacks. You're required to join the tenants' association, pay your dues, and contribute your share of the shopping center's maintenance costs. You're subject to all rules and regulations set forth by "the management": what your store hours will be, which holidays you must remain open or closed, what you can or cannot place in or on your windows or above your store entrance, and so on.

Should you decide to seek space in a brand-new center, you may be surprised to learn that its developers intend to provide only the bare walls, the roof, and the square footage of space inside. In many instances, you're expected to provide the rest: ceilings, wall coverings, flooring, plumbing and air conditioning equipment, and the like. Many shopping-center managements, however, provide an allowance toward the completion of your store interior. Frequently, this allowance is spelled out in your lease (as a dollar amount representing some percentage of the cost).

## HOW TO NARROW DOWN YOUR CHOICES

We have already established that you ought to have a sensible *plan* before tackling the store-location problem. In actuality, selecting the best location for your new retail enterprise is not a single decision but a *process* that involves a series of successive decisions—from broadening your horizons so as not to neglect opportunities elsewhere to deciding on the exact site and location within the state of your choice. Exhibit 7–1 summarizes this process.

---

### EXHIBIT 7–1. CHOOSING A LOCATION

Three factors confront an owner-manager in choosing a location: selection of a city; choice of an area or type of location within a city; and identification of a specific site.

If you are going to select a new *city,* naturally you consider the following factors:

- Size of the city's trading area.
- Population and population trends in the trading area.
- Total purchasing power and the distribution of the purchasing power.
- Total retail trade potential for different lines of trade.
- Number, size, and quality of competition.
- Progressiveness of competition.

In choosing an *area* or *type of location* within a city you evaluate factors such as:

- Customer attraction power of the particular store and the shopping district.
- Quantitative and qualitative nature of competing stores.
- Availability of access routes to the stores.
- Nature of zoning regulations.
- Direction of the area expansion.
- General appearance of the area.

Pinpointing the *specific site* is, as you know, particularly important. In central and secondary business districts, small stores depend upon the traffic created by large stores. Large stores in turn depend upon attracting customers from the existing flow of traffic. (However, where sales depend upon nearby residents, selecting the trading area is more important than picking the specific site.) Obviously, you want to know about the following factors when choosing a specific site:

- Adequacy and potential of traffic passing the site.
- Ability of the site to intercept traffic en route from one place to another.
- Complementary nature of the adjacent stores.
- Type of goods sold.
- Adequacy of parking.
- Vulnerability of the site to unfriendly competition.
- Cost of the site.

---

*Source:* James R. Lowry, "Using a Traffic Study to Select a Retail Site," *Small Marketers Aid No. 152* (Washington, D.C.: U.S. Small Business Administration, 1973), 3.

---

Here's the procedure I'd recommend:

1. *Don't limit your choices; consider the entire country.* Read widely in books and periodicals about the different sections of the country and about the various states in each region. Talk to people about where the opportunities may lie for your new retail business.

2. *Select two or three states where you feel your store can be successful and where, just as important, you would enjoy living for the next five or ten years.* Bone up on these states; write away for information about the climate, local economy, types of industry, and population demographics. A valuable reference work in this connection is the latest *Statistical Abstract of the United States,* published annually by the U.S. Department of Commerce and available at most public libraries. This publication is filled with valuable consumer market statistics such as incomes, employment figures, and other population characteristics. Also, the annual *Survey of Buying Power,* put out by *Sales Management,* not only furnishes valuable data by states, counties, and metropolitan areas but also indicates retail sales for a number of major lines.

3. *Choose the state that best meets your criteria and personal preferences.* Survey that state for up to a half-dozen cities. Then, get help through correspondence with the state development agency, the various cities' planning commissions, chambers of commerce, utility companies, and banks. (You can make good use of the Commerce Department's *County and City Data Book,* which presents all sorts of information from the latest available censuses on population, housing, retail and wholesale trades, and other topics. Even unincorporated places of 25,000 inhabitants or more are covered in this book.)

4. *Rate the selected cities according to criteria, such as those suggested in exhibit 7–1 or any others you may think of.* You might, for instance, consider the "quality of life for me" as an additional criterion! Then compare the ratings and choose the one with the highest.

5. *Repeat the process indicated in entry 4, first with the general areas within the city you have selected and then with specific sites within the most favored area or areas.* By this time in your planning, actual visits to the selected city, to the areas, and to the sites are a *must!* Again consult exhibit 7–1 for guidelines to follow in your investigations during this process. Now correspondence becomes supplanted by oral communication on a one-to-one basis, not only with local banks and real estate firms but also with many of the store owners and with people residing or shopping in the area.

## Gain Valuable Information by Analyzing Census Data

The material in this section describes useful statistical data made available to the public through the U.S. Bureau of the Census. Thorough reading of both exhibits 7–2 and 7–3 should help you to clarify the location problem even more and enable you to make a better choice. Exhibit 7–2 informs you of the kinds of facts covered in the census reports; further details as to the meaning of census tracts and block statistics are provided in exhibit 7–3.*

---

\* Bureau of the Census publications are available for reference purposes at many libraries. They may also be purchased at district offices of the U.S. Department of Commerce. For an order form listing tract and block reports, write to the Publications Distribution Section, Bureau of the Census, Social and Economic Statistics Administration, Washington, D.C. 20233.

## Exhibit 7–2. Store locations and census data

No decision is more important to a retail-store owner than selecting the location for his business. Even if you have ample financial resources and above-average managerial skills, they can't offset the handicap of a poor location. Moving is costly. Legal complications of a lease can be difficult to untangle—not to mention other location-related problems that could arise. Clearly, your careful examination of alternative sites is a worthwhile endeavor. By studying the relevant Bureau of the Census reports, you can develop valuable insights about the characteristics of prospective customers as well as knowledge about the economic strengths and weaknesses of your trading area.

Every store has a trading area—in other words, the geographic region from which it draws its potential customers. Data for trading areas, regardless of size, generally can be assembled by combining a number of census tract tables. These may be your best single source of information. However, if you are going to make a complete store location analysis, they should be supplemented with other material.

Unlike a manufacturing operation which usually can ship its products elsewhere, the potential business of a retail store is limited to its trading area. The primary area can range from a number of blocks for a small neighborhood store to a thirty-five-mile radius for a store located in a large shopping center.

If you are the prospective owner of a single store, your main concern will be the factors that have direct relevance to your store's trading area. Far too many small retailers select a store site by chance. (In fact, the most common reason given is "noticed vacancy.") Their high turnover rate would be considerably lower had they analyzed in advance the trading area's population characteristics, housing characteristics, nature and quality of competition, traffic count, and accessibility. It is also of fundamental importance to determine total consumer purchasing power and the store's expected share of this total. Each location analysis must be done on a custom study basis, focusing on your particular line of retailing. Answers to questions like the following can be found in the census reports.

1. How many persons or families are there in the trading area and how has this changed over time?
2. Where do they work?
3. How many young or old persons are there, how many children or teenagers?
4. How many families with small children or with teenagers?
5. How many one-person households, how many small or large families?
6. What is the income of the families or individuals?
7. What do they do for a living?
8. Is the area an older established one or one where most residents are newcomers?
9. How many families own their homes? How many rent?
10. What is the value of the homes? What is the monthly rent?
11. What is the age and quality of the homes?
12. Do the homes have air conditioning; other appliances?
13. How many of the families own an automobile? How many own two or more?

---

*Source:* Louis H. Vorzimer, "Using Census Data to Select a Store Site," *Small Marketers Aid No. 154* (Washington, D.C.: U.S. Small Business Administration, 1974), 2–3.

---

**EXHIBIT 7–3. GEOGRAPHICAL BREAKDOWNS OF CENSUS DATA**

The *Standard Metropolitan Statistical Area (SMSA)* is a geographical designation that includes a county (or counties) containing a central city of at least 50,000 inhabitants, plus contiguous counties which are socially and economically integrated with the central county. In some cases, there may be twin cities with a total population of 50,000 or more (the smaller of the two cities with at least 15,000 people). There are 267 tracted standard SMSAs in the United States and Puerto Rico.*

*Census tracts* are subdivisions of SMSAs. Large cities and adjacent areas have been divided for the purpose of showing comparable small-area statistics. The average tract has about 4,000 to 5,000 residents. One report is published for each SMSA. It includes statistical information about each tract and also includes a map for reference. The information is based on the 1970 Census of Population and Housing. Altogether, this amounts to some 34,000 tracts.

While the census tract usually constitutes a geographical unit small enough for a retail store location analysis, you may want to examine even smaller units. *Block statistics* within a census tract are available for urbanized areas. (An urbanized area for the 1970 Census consists of a central city or cities, as well as surrounding closely settled territory.) These reports by city blocks present data on general characteristics of housing and population for some 1.8 million blocks. Because these are such small geographic units, they provide less census information than the reports from census tracts. You may not be interested in any specific block as such, but you can combine blocks into special trading areas. Again, appropriate maps are included with block statistics.

*Source:* Louis H. Vorzimer, "Using Census Data to Select a Store Site," *Small Marketers Aid No. 153* (Washington, D.C.: U.S. Small Business Administration, 1974), 3.
* As of 1973.

## TRAFFIC COUNTS CAN HELP

In making your final decision, you can make good use of a rather simple retailer's technique: the traffic count. For most store types, the numbers of people or vehicles passing by the particular location is a measure, however rough, of the amount of business that can be expected in that location. Traffic counts are especially valuable for comparing the relative expected value of several locations. Obviously, a store situated where some 400 or more people pass each hour, on the average, should enjoy far greater sales than one with only 50 or 60 passersby per hour.

Of course, quantity isn't the only factor to be considered; the type and quality of traffic is often equally as important. For example, if you sell primarily young women's sportswear, street traffic principally composed of older people or of men wouldn't be of much value to you. Similarly, if your business is selling jeans or if you have a frozen-custard stand, you would be primarily interested in younger people.

### How to Make Traffic Counts

To get the right kind of information to help you make a decision, you need a little notebook and a counter. You also need to decide in advance *who* should be counted—and *when* they're to be counted. Rather than remaining in one spot for days on end, work up a sampling plan. Try to "cover" the location on all the days of the week (Saturday and Sunday, too, if the other stores are open) and at different times of the day and evening. To do so, divide the day into one-hour segments, such as 9–10 A.M., 10–11 A.M., 11 A.M.– noon, and so on. Cover different hours on different days. You'll find that the traffic fluctuates tremendously; for example, it may increase sharply in most locations between 12 and 2 P.M. Bear in mind also that traffic during holiday periods isn't at all representative of year-round traffic and that you ought to do your "clocking" during normal times.

**Utilizing the Information.** Experienced retailers can estimate the percentage of passersby who will, on the average, come into the store. From past experience, they can also judge the proportion of store entrants who will make a purchase, as well as the "average sale" rung up at the register. This information is enough for the storekeeper to calculate the approximate annual sales volume for the location.

By way of illustrating this point, consider the following example:

Some 1,500 people (of the type needed for your business) pass by each day, on the average. You know that about 4 out of every 100 passersby will come in. Further, you're confident that you'll be able to sell at least 8 out of every 10 of these "prospects." Past sales records (either yours or those of your trade association) indicate an average sale of $9.75.

Here's how you estimate your annual sales:

| | |
|---|---:|
| Daily traffic | 1,500 |
| 4 percent will come in | 60 prospects |
| 80 percent of these will buy | 48 sales |
| Estimated daily sales   (48 × $9.75) | $468 |
| Estimated yearly sales   (300 days × $468) | $140,400 |

## YOUR STORE LEASE

After you have decided on your location, your next challenge is to negotiate a lease. The store lease is a legal contract between the landlord and the tenant. In effect, the landlord grants the tenant the use of the premises for the latter's business for a specified period of time and at a specified charge (or *rental*). All sorts of things are spelled out in the lease: your responsibilities, rights, and privileges, along with those of your landlord. A cursory glance at the side headings of the sample lease in exhibit 7–4 will show you the thoroughness of this document.

*Never, never* sign any lease without first having your lawyer examine it and discuss all its terms and conditions with you. This step should always be taken despite the fact that many building owners use a standard form of lease, such as that shown in exhibit 7–4. Bear in mind that you're committing yourself to a binding, long-term agreement to remain at that location (often for five or ten years), regardless of your business' progress—or lack of it.

# Exhibit 7–4. A Sample Lease

A 880—Lease of Business Premises.                                JULIUS BLUMBERG, INC., LAW BLANK PUBLISHERS

**This Lease,** dated the      day of      19

Between

hereinafter referred to as the Landlord, and

**Parties**

hereinafter referred to as the Tenant,
WITNESSETH: That the Landlord hereby demises and leases unto the Tenant, and the Tenant hereby hires and takes from the Landlord for the term and upon the rentals hereinafter specified, the premises described as follows, situated in the      of
County of      and State of

**Premises**

**Term**

The term of this demise shall be for
beginning      19      and ending      19    .

**Rent**

The rent for the demised term shall be
($      ), which shall accrue at the yearly rate of

The said rent is to be payable monthly in advance on the first day of each calendar month for the term hereof, in instalments as follows:

**Payment of Rent**

at the office of
or as may be otherwise directed by the Landlord in writing.

### THE ABOVE LETTING IS UPON THE FOLLOWING CONDITIONS:

**Peaceful Possession**

*First.*—The Landlord covenants that the Tenant, on paying the said rental and performing the covenants and conditions in this Lease contained, shall and may peaceably and quietly have, hold and enjoy the demised premises for the term aforesaid.

*Second.*—The Tenant covenants and agrees to use the demised premises as a

**Purpose**

and agrees not to use or permit the premises to be used for any other purpose without the prior written consent of the Landlord endorsed hereon.

**Default in Payment of Rent**

**Abandonment of Premises**

**Re-entry and Reletting by Landlord**

**Tenant Liable for Deficiency**

**Lien of Landlord to Secure**

**Performance Attorney's Fees**

*Third.*—The Tenant shall, without any previous demand therefor, pay to the Landlord, or its agent, the said rent at the times and in the manner above provided. In the event of the non-payment of said rent, or any instalment thereof, at the times and in the manner above provided, and if the same shall remain in default for ten days after becoming due, or if the Tenant shall be dispossessed for non-payment of rent, or if the leased premises shall be deserted or vacated, the Landlord or its agents shall have the right to and may enter the said premises as the agent of the Tenant, either by force or otherwise, without being liable for any prosecution or damages therefor, and may relet the premises as the agent of the Tenant, and receive the rent therefor, upon such terms as shall be satisfactory to the Landlord, and all rights of the Tenant to repossess the premises under this lease shall be forfeited. Such re-entry by the Landlord shall not operate to release the Tenant from any rent to be paid or covenants to be performed hereunder during the full term of this lease. For the purpose of reletting, the Landlord shall be authorized to make such repairs or alterations in or to the leased premises as may be necessary to place the same in good order and condition. The Tenant shall be liable to the Landlord for the cost of such repairs or alterations, and all expenses of such reletting. If the sum realized or to be realized from the reletting is insufficient to satisfy the monthly or term rent provided in this lease, the Landlord, at its option, may require the Tenant to pay such deficiency month by month, or may hold the Tenant in advance for the entire deficiency to be realized during the term of the reletting. The Tenant shall not be entitled to any surplus accruing as a result of the reletting. The Landlord is hereby granted a lien, in addition to any statutory lien or right to distrain that may exist, on all personal property of the Tenant in or upon the demised premises, to secure payment of the rent and performance of the covenants and conditions of this lease. The Landlord shall have the right, as agent of the Tenant, to take possession of any furniture, fixtures or other personal property of the Tenant found in or about the premises, and sell the same at public or private sale and to apply the proceeds thereof to the payment of any monies becoming due under this lease, the Tenant hereby waiving the benefit of all laws exempting property from execution, levy and sale on distress or judgment. The Tenant agrees to pay, as additional rent, all attorney's fees and other expenses incurred by the Landlord in enforcing any of the obligations under this lease.

**Sub-letting and Assignment**

*Fourth.*—The Tenant shall not sub-let the demised premises nor any portion thereof, nor shall this lease be assigned by the Tenant without the prior written consent of the Landlord endorsed hereon.

**Condition of Premises, Repairs**

*Fifth.*—The Tenant has examined the demised premises, and accepts them in their present condition (except as otherwise expressly provided herein) and without any representations on the part of the Landlord or its agents as to the present or future condition of the said premises. The Tenant shall keep the demised premises in good condition, and shall redecorate, paint and renovate the said premises as may be necessary to keep them in repair and good appearance. The Tenant shall quit and surrender the premises at the end of the demised term in as good condition as the reasonable use thereof will permit. The Tenant shall not make any alterations, additions, or improvements to said premises without the

*Source:* Forms may be purchased from Julius Blumberg, Inc., 62 White Street, New York, NY 10013, or any of its dealers. Reproduction prohibited.

# EXHIBIT 7–4. CONTINUED

**Alterations and Improvements**

**Sanitation, Inflammable Materials**

**Sidewalks**

prior written consent of the Landlord. All erections, alterations, additions and improvements, whether temporary or permanent in character, which may be made upon the premises either by the Landlord or the Tenant, except furniture or movable trade fixtures installed at the expense of the Tenant, shall be the property of the Landlord and shall remain upon and be surrendered with the premises as a part thereof at the termination of this Lease, without compensation to the Tenant. The Tenant further agrees to keep said premises and all parts thereof in a clean and sanitary condition and free from trash, inflammable material and other objectionable matter. If this lease covers premises, all or a part of which are on the ground floor, the Tenant further agrees to keep the sidewalks in front of such ground floor portion of the demised premises clean and free of obstructions, snow and ice.

**Mechanics' Liens**

*Sixth.*—In the event that any mechanics' lien is filed against the premises as a result of alterations, additions or improvements made by the Tenant, the Landlord, at its option, after thirty days' notice to the Tenant, may terminate this lease and may pay the said lien, without inquiring into the validity thereof, and the Tenant shall forthwith reimburse the Landlord the total expense incurred by the Landlord in discharging the said lien, as additional rent hereunder.

**Glass**

*Seventh.*—The Tenant agrees to replace at the Tenant's expense any and all glass which may become broken in and on the demised premises. Plate glass and mirrors, if any, shall be insured by the Tenant at their full insurable value in a company satisfactory to the Landlord. Said policy shall be of the full premium type, and shall be deposited with the Landlord or its agent.

**Liability of Landlord**

*Eighth.*—The Landlord shall not be responsible for the loss of or damage to property, or injury to persons, occurring in or about the demised premises, by reason of any existing or future condition, defect, matter or thing in said demised premises or the property of which the premises are a part, or for the acts, omissions or negligence of other persons or tenants in and about the said property. The Tenant agrees to indemnify and save the Landlord harmless from all claims and liability for losses of or damage to property, or injuries to persons occurring in or about the demised premises.

**Services and Utilities**

*Ninth.*—Utilities and services furnished to the demised premises for the benefit of the Tenant shall be provided and paid for as follows: water by the _____ ; gas by the _____ ; electricity by the _____ ; heat by the _____ ; refrigeration by the _____ ; hot water by the _____ .

The Landlord shall not be liable for any interruption or delay in any of the above services for any reason.

**Right to Inspect and Exhibit**

*Tenth.*—The Landlord, or its agents, shall have the right to enter the demised premises at reasonable hours in the day or night to examine the same, or to run telephone or other wires, or to make such repairs, additions or alterations as it shall deem necessary for the safety, preservation or restoration of the improvements, or for the safety or convenience of the occupants or users thereof (there being no obligation, however, on the part of the Landlord to make any such repairs, additions or alterations), or to exhibit the same to prospective purchasers and put upon the premises a suitable "For Sale" sign. For three months prior to the expiration of the demised term, the Landlord, or its agents, may similarly exhibit the premises to prospective tenants, and may place the usual "To Let" signs thereon.

**Damage by Fire, Explosion, The Elements or Otherwise**

*Eleventh.*—In the event of the destruction of the demised premises or the building containing the said premises by fire, explosion, the elements or otherwise during the term hereby created, or previous thereto, or such partial destruction thereof as to render the premises wholly untenantable or unfit for occupancy, or should the demised premises be so badly injured that the same cannot be repaired within ninety days from the happening of such injury, then and in such case the term hereby created shall, at the option of the Landlord, cease and become null and void from the date of such damage or destruction, and the Tenant shall immediately surrender said premises and all the Tenant's interest therein to the Landlord, and shall pay rent only to the time of such surrender, in which event the Landlord may re-enter and re-possess the premises thus discharged from this lease and may remove all parties therefrom. Should the demised premises be rendered untenantable and unfit for occupancy, but yet be repairable within ninety days from the happening of said injury, the Landlord may enter and repair the same with reasonable speed, and the rent shall not accrue after said injury or while repairs are being made, but shall recommence immediately after said repairs shall be completed. But if the premises shall be so slightly injured as not to be rendered untenantable and unfit for occupancy, then the Landlord agrees to repair the same with reasonable promptness and in that case the rent accrued and accruing shall not cease or determine. The Tenant shall immediately notify the Landlord in case of fire or other damage to the premises.

**Observation of Laws, Ordinances, Rules and Regulations**

*Twelfth.*—The Tenant agrees to observe and comply with all laws, ordinances, rules and regulations of the Federal, State, County and Municipal authorities applicable to the business to be conducted by the Tenant in the demised premises. The Tenant agrees not to do or permit anything to be done in said premises, or keep anything therein, which will increase the rate of fire insurance premiums on the improvements or any part thereof, or on property kept therein, or which will obstruct or interfere with the rights of other tenants, or conflict with the regulations of the Fire Department or with any insurance policy upon said improvements or any part thereof. In the event of any increase in insurance premiums resulting from the Tenant's occupancy of the premises, or from any act or omission on the part of the Tenant, the Tenant agrees to pay said increase in insurance premiums on the improvements or contents thereof as additional rent.

**Signs**

*Thirteenth.*—No sign, advertisement or notice shall be affixed to or placed upon any part of the demised premises by the Tenant, except in such manner, and of such size, design and color as shall be approved in advance in writing by the Landlord.

**Subordination to Mortgages and Deeds of Trust**

*Fourteenth.*—This lease is subject and is hereby subordinated to all present and future mortgages, deeds of trust and other encumbrances affecting the demised premises or the property of which said premises are a part. The Tenant agrees to execute, at no expense to the Landlord, any instrument which may be deemed necessary or desirable by the Landlord to further effect the subordination of this lease to any such mortgage, deed of trust or encumbrance.

**Sale of Premises**

*Fifteenth.*—In the event of the sale by the Landlord of the demised premises, or the property of which said premises are a part, the Landlord or the purchaser may terminate this lease on the thirtieth day of April in any year upon giving the Tenant notice of such termination prior to the first day of January in the same year.

**Rules and Regulations of Landlord**

*Sixteenth.*—The rules and regulations regarding the demised premises, affixed to this lease, if any, as well as any other and further reasonable rules and regulations which shall be made by the Landlord, shall be observed by the Tenant and by the Tenant's employees, agents and customers. The Landlord reserves the right to rescind any presently existing rules applicable to the demised premises, and to make such other and further reasonable rules and regulations as, in its judgment, may from time to time be desirable for the safety, care and cleanliness of the premises, and for the preservation of good order therein, which rules, when so made and notice thereof given to the Tenant, shall have the same force and effect as if originally made a part of this lease. Such other and further rules shall not, however, be inconsistent with the proper and rightful enjoyment by the Tenant of the demised premises.

**Violation of Covenants, Forfeiture of Lease, Re-entry by Landlord**

**Non-waiver of Breach**

*Seventeenth.*—In case of violation by the Tenant of any of the covenants, agreements and conditions of this lease, or of the rules and regulations now or hereafter to be reasonably established by the Landlord, and upon failure to discontinue such violation within ten days after notice thereof given to the Tenant, this lease shall thenceforth, at the option of the Landlord, become null and void, and the Landlord may re-enter without further notice or demand. The rent in such case shall become due, be apportioned and paid on and up to the day of such re-entry, and the Tenant shall be liable for all loss or damage resulting from such violation as aforesaid. No waiver by the Landlord of any violation or breach of condition by the Tenant shall constitute or be construed as a waiver of any other violation or breach of condition, nor shall lapse of time after breach of condition by the Tenant before the Landlord shall exercise its option under this paragraph operate to defeat the right of the Landlord to declare this lease null and void and to re-enter upon the demised premises after the said breach or violation.

EXHIBIT 7–4. CONTINUED

**Notices**

*Eighteenth.*—All notices and demands, legal or otherwise, incidental to this lease, or the occupation of the demised premises, shall be in writing. If the Landlord or its agent desires to give or serve upon the Tenant any notice or demand, it shall be sufficient to send a copy thereof by registered mail, addressed to the Tenant at the demised premises, or to leave a copy thereof with a person of suitable age found on the premises, or to post a copy thereof upon the door to said premises. Notices from the Tenant to the Landlord shall be sent by registered mail or delivered to the Landlord at the place hereinbefore designated for the payment of rent, or to such party or place as the Landlord may from time to time designate in writing.

**Bankruptcy, Insolvency, Assignment for Benefit of Creditors**

*Nineteenth.*—It is further agreed that if at any time during the term of this lease the Tenant shall make any assignment for the benefit of creditors, or be decreed insolvent or bankrupt according to law, or if a receiver shall be appointed for the Tenant, then the Landlord may, at its option, terminate this lease, exercise of such option to be evidenced by notice to that effect served upon the assignee, receiver, trustee or other person in charge of the liquidation of the property of the Tenant or the Tenant's estate, but such termination shall not release or discharge any payment of rent payable hereunder and then accrued, or any liability then accrued by reason of any agreement or covenant herein contained on the part of the Tenant, or the Tenant's legal representatives.

**Holding Over by Tenant**

*Twentieth.*—In the event that the Tenant shall remain in the demised premises after the expiration of the term of this lease without having executed a new written lease with the Landlord, such holding over shall not constitute a renewal or extension of this lease. The Landlord may, at its option, elect to treat the Tenant as one who has not removed at the end of his term, and thereupon be entitled to all the remedies against the Tenant provided by law in that situation, or the Landlord may elect, at its option, to construe such holding over as a tenancy from month to month, subject to all the terms and conditions of this lease, except as to duration thereof, and in that event the Tenant shall pay monthly rent in advance at the rate provided herein as effective during the last month of the demised term.

**Eminent Domain, Condemnation**

*Twenty-first.*—If the property or any part thereof wherein the demised premises are located shall be taken by public or quasi-public authority under any power of eminent domain or condemnation, this lease, at the option of the Landlord, shall forthwith terminate and the Tenant shall have no claim or interest in or to any award of damages for such taking.

**Security**

*Twenty-second.*—The Tenant has this day deposited with the Landlord the sum of $ as security for the full and faithful performance by the Tenant of all the terms, covenants and conditions of this lease upon the Tenant's part to be performed, which said sum shall be returned to the Tenant after the time fixed as the expiration of the term herein, provided the Tenant has fully and faithfully carried out all of said terms, covenants and conditions on Tenant's part to be performed. In the event of a bona fide sale, subject to this lease, the Landlord shall have the right to transfer the security to the vendee for the benefit of the Tenant and the Landlord shall be considered released by the Tenant from all liability for the return of such security; and the Tenant agrees to look to the new Landlord solely for the return of the said security, and it is agreed that this shall apply to every transfer or assignment made of the security to a new Landlord. The security deposited under this lease shall not be mortgaged, assigned or encumbered by the Tenant without the written consent of the Landlord.

**Arbitration**

*Twenty-third.*—Any dispute arising under this lease shall be settled by arbitration. Then Landlord and Tenant shall each choose an arbitrator, and the two arbitrators thus chosen shall select a third arbitrator. The findings and award of the three arbitrators thus chosen shall be final and binding on the parties hereto.

**Delivery of Lease**

*Twenty-fourth.*—No rights are to be conferred upon the Tenant until this lease has been signed by the Landlord, and an executed copy of the lease has been delivered to the Tenant.

**Lease Provisions Not Exclusive**

*Twenty-fifth.*—The foregoing rights and remedies are not intended to be exclusive but as additional to all rights and remedies the Landlord would otherwise have by law.

**Lease Binding on Heirs, Successors, Etc.**

*Twenty-sixth.*—All of the terms, covenants and conditions of this lease shall inure to the benefit of and be binding upon the respective heirs, executors, administrators, successors and assigns of the parties hereto. However, in the event of the death of the Tenant, if an individual, the Landlord may, at its option, terminate this lease by notifying the executor or administrator of the Tenant at the demised premises.

*Twenty-seventh.*—This lease and the obligation of Tenant to pay rent hereunder and perform all of the other covenants and agreements hereunder on part of Tenant to be performed shall in nowise be affected, impaired or excused because Landlord is unable to supply or is delayed in supplying any service expressly or impliedly to be supplied or is unable to make, or is delayed in making any repairs, additions, alterations or decorations or is unable to supply or is delayed in supplying any equipment or fixtures if Landlord is prevented or delayed from so doing by reason of governmental preemption in connection with the National Emergency declared by the President of the United States or in connection with any rule, order or regulation of any department or subdivision thereof of any governmental agency or by reason of the conditions of supply and demand which have been or are affected by the war.

*Twenty-eighth.*—This instrument may not be changed orally.

IN WITNESS WHEREOF, the said Parties have hereunto set their hands and seals the day and year first above written.

Witness: ...........................................................(SEAL)
                                                       Landlord

..................................................   By...........................................................

..................................................   ...........................................................(SEAL)
                                                       Tenant

**EXHIBIT 7–4. CONTINUED**

## GUARANTY

In consideration of the execution of the within lease by the Landlord, at the request of the undersigned and in reliance of this guaranty, the undersigned hereby guarantees unto the Landlord, its successors and assigns, the prompt payment of all rent and the performance of all of the terms, covenants and conditions provided in said lease, hereby waiving all notice of default, and consenting to any extensions of time or changes in the manner of payment or performance of any of the terms and conditions of the said lease the Landlord may grant the Tenant, and further consenting to the assignment and the successive assignments of the said lease, and any modifications thereof, including the sub-letting and changing of the use of the demised premises, all without notice to the undersigned. The undersigned agrees to pay the Landlord all expenses incurred in enforcing the obligations of the Tenant under the within lease and in enforcing this guaranty.

Witness :...........................................................................          .......................................................................................( SEAL )

            ...........................................................................          .......................................................................................( SEAL )

Date :......................................................................

**Lease**

Landlord

to

Tenant

Premises leased :

From :

To :

## ASSIGNMENT AND ACCEPTANCE OF ASSIGNMENT

For value received the undersigned Tenant hereby assigns all of said Tenant's right, title and interest in and to

the within lease from and after                                                        unto

heirs, successors, and assigns, the demised premises to be used and occupied for

                                                                    and for no other purpose, it being expressly agreed that this assignment shall not in any manner relieve the undersigned assignor from liability upon any of the covenants of this lease.

Witness :...........................................................................          .......................................................................................( SEAL )

            ...........................................................................          .......................................................................................( SEAL )

Date :......................................................................

In consideration of the above assignment and the written consent of the Landlord thereto, the undersigned assignee,

hereby assumes and agrees from and after                                              to make all payments and to perform all covenants and conditions provided in the within lease by the Tenant therein to be made and performed.

Witness :...........................................................................          .......................................................................................( SEAL )

            ...........................................................................          .......................................................................................( SEAL )

Date :......................................................................

## CONSENT TO ASSIGNMENT

The undersigned Landlord hereby consents to the assignment of the within lease to

on the express conditions that the original Tenant

                                          , the assignor, herein, shall remain liable for the prompt payment of the rent and the performance of the covenants provided in the said lease by the Tenant to be made and performed, and that no further assignment of said lease or sub-letting of any part of the premises thereby demised shall be made without the prior written consent of the undersigned Landlord.

                                                         ..........................................................................................
                                                                            Landlord

Date :......................................................................          By ........................................................................................

## Types of Leases

Leases come in a number of forms. One frequently seen type is the *fixed-rent lease*. Here, the tenant is required to pay the same amount of rent each month over the term of the lease. Another popular type is the *percentage-of-sales lease*. In this form, your rental expense is determined by the sales volume you enjoy. One variation is the *straight percentage,* such as 4 or 5 percent of your sales (usually with a guaranteed minimum for the building owner just in case your sales fail to measure up to expectations).

In some instances, the landlord may offer you a *turnkey lease*. Under such a lease, the store is essentially ready to be turned over to you—all the construction requirements having been satisfied. All you need do is put in your fixtures and your merchandise stock, turn the key in the door, and open for business. In other cases, landlords may severely limit their contributions and expect you to complete many aspects: ceilings, walls, and floor coverings; the air conditioning and ductwork; electrical work; show windows; and so on. Many of the new shopping centers give *shell-and-allowance leases,* whereby the builders provide no more than the walls and the back of the store, leaving the bulk of construction to the tenant. In this case, of course, all such details are spelled out in the lease, including (perhaps) the size of the contribution *(allowance)* to be made by the developers.

## FOR FURTHER INFORMATION

### Books

Davis, R. L., and David S. Rogers, eds. *Store Location and Assessment Research.* New York: Wiley, 1984.

Ghosh, Avijit, and Sara L. McLafferty. *Location Strategies for Retail and Service Firms.* Lexington, Mass.: Lexington Books, 1987.

Schmenner, R. *Making Business Location Decisions.* Englewood Cliffs, N.J.: Prentice-Hall, 1982.

Thompkins, James A., and John A. White. *Facilities Planning.* New York: Wiley, 1984.

White, John A., and Richard L. Francis. *Facility Layout and Location: An Analytical Approach.* Englewood Cliffs, N.J.: Prentice-Hall, 1974.

## Pamphlets Available from the Small Business Administration

### Management Aids

MA 2.002—"Locating or Relocating Your Business"
MA 2.017—"Factors in Considering a Shopping Center Location"
MA 2.021—"Using a Traffic Study to Select a Retail Site"

# 8

# Planning Your Store

A store's primary function is to sell merchandise. You'll need to bear this fundamental truth in mind all throughout your store planning. All other activities performed within the store are ancillary to that function.

From a coldly structural point of view, a store represents boxed-in space—space contained by storefront, walls, ceiling, and floor. It's as simple as that. Yet what you do with that structure—and, more significantly, with the contained space—can make or break your business.

Planning your premises is no simple matter. It demands your prolonged concentration on myriad details: the construction aspects of both exterior and interior; the decor; the showcases, fixtures, and equipment you need; the very arrangement of all of these components; and the deliberate, considered creation of a pleasant, sales-stimulating atmosphere. The store environment is a dynamic one. Within it, activities of various sorts continually take place, not the least of which are the consummations of sales. Because of this dynamism, store planning, design, and layout all become challenges that require consultation with knowledgeable professionals, such as architects, interior designers, and lighting engineers.

## THE IMPORTANCE OF STORE ATMOSPHERE

The value of the store environment cannot be overestimated. As a case in point, two researchers sought to investigate the effects of store atmosphere on shoppers' *emotions* in a variety of retail outlets: department stores, hardware stores, apparel and shoe boutiques, liquor stores, supermarkets, drugstores, sporting goods outlets, and several other types. A major finding of their study was that "the correct emotional combination of pleasantness and arousal created by store atmosphere can stimulate shopping behavior within the store."*

---

* Robert J. Donovan and John R. Rossiter, "Store Atmosphere: An Environmental Psychology Approach," *Journal of Retailing* **58** (Spring 1982), 34–57.

As the researchers pointed out:

> Some practical implications follow . . . . If consumers rate your store as pleasant, then their enjoyment, shopping time, spending, etc. can be increased by raising the arousal level of the store's atmosphere with bright lighting, upbeat music, and so forth. However, if your store cannot easily be made pleasant—if it is, perhaps, an industrial outlet or a bargain-basement operation—then the arousal level should be kept low through the use of subdued lighting, spaced displays, and relaxing music or no music at all.*

In this context, it may be well worth your time to read Philip Kotler's substantive article on "Atmospherics As a Marketing Tool."** This professor of marketing at Northwestern University described *atmospherics* as "the effort to design buying environments to produce specific emotional effects in the buyer that enhance his purchase probability."† In his article, he also pointed out that at times the atmosphere of a place has more to do with a purchasing decision than the product itself. Of course, Professor Kotler referred not only to the use of color in appealing to the shopper's sense of sight (see the section on the use of color in store decor, page 127) but also to brightness, size, and shapes. Moreover, he stressed attention to aspects that stimulate other senses as well.

Because they sell intangibles, not merchandise, service retailers especially need to concentrate on offering the kind of stimulating environment that will differentiate their premises from those of competitors. Banks, motels and hotels, restaurants and bars, exercise salons, photography studios, health clubs and spas, and others are among the many kinds of service operations that should seek to produce a special ambience. The decor of the premises is, of course, the main component to consider in establishing the desired image; factors such as lighting, signage, background music, and even pleasant odors (in some cases) can all be brought into play.‡

## THE STORE EXTERIOR

The aim of the storefront, or *façade,* as it's sometimes called, is to serve as the major focus of contact between the general public and the retail firm. In brief, the store exterior must help the selling job. Moreover, it ought to communicate to passersby the kind of image you want to project: the type of store it is, the kinds of merchandise and services the shopper may expect to find inside, and so forth.

---

* Ibid., 56.

** Philip Kotler, "Atmospherics As a Marketing Tool," *Journal of Retailing* **49** (Winter 1973–74), 48–64.

† Ibid., 8.

‡ See Tansu Barker and Martin L. Gimpl, "Differentiating a Service Business," *Journal of Small Business Management* 20 (April 1982), 1–7.

## Try This Beneficial Exercise

Here's a fruitful morning's exercise for those of you who live in or near a sizable city. Pay a visit to a shopping street of your choice. Position yourself at the curb, and study the store you're facing. Look at it from top to bottom and from one side to the other. Check the exterior surfaces, the sign over the window and the surface over which it has been erected, the show window or windows, the entrance, the awning (if any), and any other elements you notice. By doing this, you'll be able to register, indelibly, the components that collectively make up the storefront.

Next, take a slow stroll down and across the street. Consider the variety of shapes, sizes, surface materials, signage, and the like that you're able to discern on other stores. As ideas occur to you, jot them down in a small notebook for later reflection. Note the wide range of "images" that are projected: the shabby or chintzy façade, the high-toned "quality" storefront, shops that present a homey and comfortable feeling, others that appear lively and bustling, still others that seem to turn you off completely. Then on another morning—or still better, an evening—visit a regional shopping center and go through the same process. In doing so, you will gain more first-hand, valuable knowledge than you ever anticipated. To help you in this "study," these major parts of the store exterior are described briefly in the next section:

- The overhead sign
- The awning
- The show window(s)
- The store entrance

## The Overhead Sign

Like all other components of the storefront, the overhead sign's tone, character, and design should be perfectly congruent with the total image you're trying to project. For the sake of that "oneness" principle, no element should conflict with the total. The sign itself, of course, has two basic purposes: (1) to identify the store and give the public some hint as to the kind(s) of merchandise that's sold inside; and (2) to attract attention.

Signs come in many varieties: lettering (in block or script) made of wood, plastic, or metal and set against a background of metal, stone, wood, stucco, or other material; light boxes covered with translucent facings that carry imprinted lettering and/or designs; glass tubing with neon for nighttime illumination; and so forth. The varieties of hues and shades are legion.

One caution to bear in mind about that outside sign, whatever it may be made of and however it may be constructed: It should be well maintained and kept clean at all times. Chipped or damaged letters, sections of glass tubing that fail to light up, electric bulbs that go out or are broken, and other defects should be remedied at once.

## The Awning

Awnings are rather simple contraptions. Their major purposes are to shade merchandise and the display materials in the window(s) from both the direct rays of the sun and from reflected glare; and to protect passersby from rain or snow. The typical awning is made of heavy canvas mounted on a metal frame. Some awnings are of metal or plastic only. Raise or lower the awning as needed; generally, it rolls up into a receptacle *(awning box)* above the window. Incidentally, the pole used to put it up or down should never be left outside; it should always be kept in the store. Keep it near the front. Retailers are always "watching the window" to avoid discoloration or fading of their merchandise. It might also be necessary to purchase window strips of canvas, similar in color and design to the awning, to shut off the sun's rays, which have a habit of "sneaking past" the awning at times.

## The Show Window(s)

While window displays are treated rather intensively in chapter 15, a brief discussion of window structure is appropriate here. The principal promotion medium for the majority of small retail firms, the show window is often referred to as "the eyes of the store." A window is an enclosed area that faces the street (or walkway, in the case of the larger shopping center). Often it starts several feet above the sidewalk, has a flat or elevated wooden base, and is protected on several sides by panes of glass.

Lighting fixtures are set into the ceiling; sometimes, they're also set along one wall that is solid, not glass.

Window Backs. The window back is commonly left open in many stores, on the assumption that consumers looking at the window display will be able to see directly into the store. Thus, the interior displays and decor serve as additional attractions that may induce the shoppers outside to come in. You'll find this *open-back* arrangement in groceries, beauty parlors, confectionery shops, liquor stores, and so forth. There's one handicap, though, to this kind of back: When the store is obviously empty, or perhaps overcrowded, the shopper may be reluctant to enter.

A completely closed window back, such as is found in shoe stores, women's apparel shops, luggage stores, menswear shops, and so on, enables the window trimmer to exercise much more creativity in the display, because there's no "interference" from the store interior. The closed back is also preferable in stores where consumers like to do their shopping without eyes peering at them, as is the case in a lingerie shop or an exclusive women's sportswear store. Some retail merchants try to gain the best of both worlds by using a partially closed back in their window. The typical drugstore is one example.

**The Store Entrance**

Logic alone informs you that both door and doorway ought to facilitate entering and leaving the premises. The doorway should be wide enough to permit people to pass either way easily. It should also, of course, be kept immaculately clean and inviting. The door itself, whether constructed of glass enclosed by a wooden or metal frame or of all glass, should be sturdy. Clearly marked "PUSH" and "PULL" handles are preferable by far to the old-fashioned door knob. The door(s) should be easy to open and close. Of course, in the enclosed, all-weather shopping malls, doors are often done away with completely. This encourages browsers and shoppers alike to saunter in and exit at their leisure.

As a final note, be sure to sweep the sidewalk in front of your store each morning and several times throughout the day. Similarly, in northern climes, the sidewalk should be kept free of snow or ice. It's a good idea to keep a bag of rock salt in the back room or basement during the wintertime.

## INSIDE YOUR STORE

Aspects of the store interior that are of concern include:

- The flooring
- The ceiling
- The walls
- The decor
- The lighting
- Fixturization
- Equipment
- Store layout

**The Flooring**

In considering the many available materials for flooring in your new store, look for surfaces that wear well, especially those that can bear lots of traffic. Durability is a particularly important consideration in entrances and near cash registers or checkout stands. You have a choice of asphalt, vinyl, and other tiles in an infinite variety of shades and patterns, along with carpeting of many kinds. Your floors can be of wood, stone, or terrazzo, or you can cover them with linoleum. In addition to durability, look for floor coverings that are pleasant to look at and safe to walk on. Think also of your long-term costs of maintaining the floor.

If you're handy, you can save some of your initial capital by installing the floor covering yourself. Incidentally, the same applies to wallpapering or painting the interior walls, as well as to covering them with paneling or other types of surfaces.

---

## The Ceiling

Ceilings may simply be painted, or they may be covered with such materials as plaster-board, acoustic tiles, and cork. They may be high or dropped quite low, depending on the effect you would like to project. The low ceiling affords a feeling of informality and warmth in some types of stores; in others, it gives rise to a sense of closeness and confinement in shoppers. On the other hand, the high ceiling conveys a spacious atmosphere that's often equated in the consumer's mind with quality of merchandise and with leisurely shopping. Yet to some, there's an aura of impersonality, even coldness, in the large, high-ceilinged store. Of course, the lighting in your store also has a great deal to do with how your customers feel about your ceiling. Naturally, you have to be concerned with the acoustics in your shop as well.

## The Walls

The interior walls and perhaps one or more necessary partitions can be treated in an almost infinite number of ways. These range from paints of every conceivable shade to cloth materials, tiles, paneling, wood and plastic strips, printed and photographic murals, and wallpaper, to mention just a few. Again, the primary considerations here are the initial cost, the attractiveness of the wall coverings, their resistance to "normal wear and tear," and the expense involved in keeping them looking good. Often, display shelves of glass, wood, chrome, or other materials are affixed to one or more walls. Mirrors can make the store look wider or longer than it is, and shadow boxes, illuminated from within, are often used to feature special merchandise.

## Decor—and the Use of Color

Skillfully applied by an experienced interior decorator, color can breathe life into your premises. It can set tone and mood, as well as create the kind of atmosphere that enhances your entire presentation.

As an example, a store that sells homemade candies and fudge may do well to use gleaming white showcases to offset the chocolate look of their contents, flooring of brown and tan tiles, light yellow walls, and so on.

As another example, a shop that sells high-quality men's footwear might be furbished with thick, luxurious, dark red or maroon carpeting; wood paneling on the walls; gleaming chrome-and-glass stands for displaying the shoes; impressive chandeliers to illuminate the selling area; and the like—all to convey a sedate, clublike atmosphere.

In one of the many pamphlets formerly distributed by the SBA, the author makes this comment:

> Inside the store, the layout and the decor reinforce customers' impressions about your products and salespeople. For example, fixtures which are classic in design usually

appeal to older and more conservative groups. Very plain, inexpensive-appearing fixtures help to build an image with young families whose incomes are limited. Low ceilings may make the store more personal, and indirect lighting usually makes the customer think of higher quality. Some color schemes are more masculine than others.*

## Lighting

You'll need the services of a lighting engineer, as well as those of a decorator, to provide the proper illumination for your store. Lighting is essential to your operation, simply because people like to see what they buy. Its function, though, isn't just to illuminate; you should use lighting as a sales tool to increase the effectiveness of your displays. In this latter sense, the kind of lighting you use should enable the shopper to see details of the merchandise as well as bring out its best features.

Lighting levels for various merchandising areas are recommended by the Illuminating Engineering Society in terms of *footcandles* (see table 8–1). Specific suggestions for using lighting to increase the attractiveness of goods on display are provided in exhibits 8–1 and 8–2.

### TABLE 8–1. RECOMMENDED ILLUMINATION LEVELS FOR STORES

| | *Footcandles** | | *Footcandles** |
|---|---|---|---|
| Circulation areas | 30 | Alteration rooms | |
| | | General | 50 |
| Merchandising areas | | Pressing | 150 |
| Service | 100 | Sewing | 200 |
| Self-service | 200 | | |
| Showcases and wall cases | | Show windows (daytime or nighttime) | |
| Service | 200 | Main business districts | |
| Self-service | 500 | General displays | 200 |
| | | Feature displays | 1,000 |
| Feature displays | | | |
| Service | 500 | | |
| Self-service | 1,000 | Secondary business districts or small towns | |
| | | General displays | 100 |
| Fitting rooms | | Feature displays | 500 |
| Dressing area | 50 | | |
| Fitting area | 200 | | |

*Source:* Charles B. Elliott, "Pointers on Display Lighting," *Small Marketers Aid No. 125* (Washington, D.C.: U.S. Small Business Administration, 1967), 4.

*A footcandle equals the illumination falling on a surface 12 in. × 12 in. in size from a candle 1 ft. away.

---

* Roger D. Blackwell, "Knowing Your Image," *Small Marketers Aid No. 124* (Washington: Small Business Administration, 1977), 5.

## Exhibit 8–1. Using lighting to make merchandise more attractive

Proper lighting can make common merchandise appear more attractive. For example, the vertical surfaces can be shown to the best advantage by using incident light on a display of opaque merchandise. Incident light is a beam of light falling on a surface. Aim the beam at an oblique angle. If the lower shelves stick out further than upper shelves, they will intercept the light beam more readily.

Glassware, small appliances, and similar items look better when free of distracting shadows. Shadows can be cut out by lighting each open shelf individually. Use thin fluorescent lamps with shields and locate them just under the front edge of each shelf. A more elaborate method would be to use double translucent glass shelves. Between the two panes of glass there is a thin strip-type lighting fixture which is shielded by a narrow, semiopaque front pane.

Emphasizing the decoration and glazing on china increases its appeal. Do it with vertical fluorescent strips in front of the display case. As part of the room lights in a china department, decorative incandescent fixtures can, for example, simulate lighting in the shopper's home.

The attractiveness of merchandise can also be increased by lighting which brings out its true color. Lamps with complete light-energy spectrum and tinted light help do it.

In addition, color-tinted sources can be used to create various atmospheres. For example, pale-pink lamps glamorize lingerie, and moonlight blue lamps enhance summer evening wear.

Dramatic displays can be made with color-tinted lamps casting black, gray, or colored shadows. For example, a display of trench coats can be dramatized by the use of shadows to suggest intrigue and identification with the character of spy thriller movies or "private-eye" television shows.

However, a word of caution on the use of colored lights. Make sure that the customer can examine the merchandise under a light which brings out the true color of the item.

*Mirror* lighting is important because a shopper rejects or accepts a frock depending on how it looks on her. Mirror lights should illuminate the figure from head to toe. The angle of the light beams is critical. The wrong angle throws long shadows which emphasize both wrinkled apparel and complexions. If you want to make older people look younger, supplement directional light with a generous amount of diffused lighting.

*Source:* Charles B. Elliott, "Pointers on Display Lighting," *Small Marketers Aid No. 125* (Washington, D.C.: U.S. Small Business Administration, 1967), 4–5.

## Exhibit 8–2. Lighting tips for specific merchandise

1. Use large area lighting fixtures plus incandescent downlighting to avoid heavy shadows when displaying major appliances and furniture.

2. Use general diffuse lighting, accented with point-type spotlights to emphasize the beauty of china, glass, home accessories, and giftware.

3. Bring out the sparkle and luster of hardware, toys, auto accessories, highly polished silver, and other metalware by using a blend of general light and concentrated light sources—spotlights.

4. Use concentrated beams of high-brightness incandescent sources to add brilliant highlights to jewelry, gold and silver, or cut glass.

5. Highlight the colors, patterns, and textures of rugs, carpets, upholstery, heavy drapes, and bedspreads by using oblique directional lighting plus general low-intensity overhead lighting.

6. Heighten the appeal of men's wear by using a cool blend of fluorescent and incandescent—with fluorescent predominating.

EXHIBIT 8–2. CONTINUED

7. Highlight women's wear—especially the bright, cheerful colors and patterns—by using natural white fluorescents blended with tungsten-halogen.

8. Bring out the tempting colors of meats, fruits, and vegetables by using fluorescent lamps rich in red energy, including the deluxe cool white type. Cool reflector incandescent lamps may also be used for direct-type lighting.

*Source:* Charles B. Elliott, "Pointers on Display Lighting," *Small Marketers Aid No. 125* (Washington, D.C.: U.S. Small Business Administration, 1967), 5.

## Fixtures

Having paid due consideration to the major structural elements of the store and its decor, you need to think next about the types of fixtures required by your particular operation. If your retail business is typical, you'll need fixtures for several purposes: display, selling (or self-service), stock, and certain work activities.

Here are some of the kinds you may need:

| | |
|---|---|
| back counters | pegboards |
| baskets | racks |
| build-ups | register stands |
| carts | sales counters |
| counters | self-service stands |
| display cases | shelving |
| display shelves | showcases |
| display tables | stock bins |
| dumbbells | storage cabinets |
| easels | tiered tables |
| floor stands | work tables |
| island displayers | wrapping desks |

If you have had enough foresight to have spent some time working in a store of the same type prior to starting your business, you'll be familiar with the kinds and the amounts of fixtures needed. Visits to similar stores, along with a chat or two with your trade association, will also help you to firm up your requirements.

Be prudent. Look for fixtures that will stand up under heavy usage, that will be easy to maneuver about (should this be necessary), and that are flexible enough to use in several ways. Don't invest too much of your initial capital in fixtures or equipment; you'll need every excess dollar for unexpected contingencies! Many shrewd new store owners seek out used fixtures that can be purchased for perhaps one-fifth or even one-tenth of the cost of new ones—and then paint or otherwise refurbish them to blend with the store decor.

## Equipment

A cautious approach should also be followed in purchasing equipment. Depending on the kind of operation you have, you most likely will need to buy some of the following:

| | |
|---|---|
| air conditioners | pricing machines |
| bells | refrigerated cases |
| brooms | scales |
| cash registers | sewing machines |
| conveyors | skids |
| dollies | soap dispensers |
| duplicating machines | tape machines |
| floor trucks | ticketing machines |
| labeling machines | towel machines |
| mannequins | wrapping machines |
| mops | |

For the more costly items you need, try to obtain several quotes before making your decision, or see if you can't buy used ones in good condition.

## EFFECTIVE STORE LAYOUT

Designing the layout of a store consists of allocating internal space to specific activity areas, such as storage, selling, display, work rooms, receiving sections, and the like. It also includes the strategic deployment of all fixtures and equipment. Moreover, it involves the facilitating of several kinds of in-store traffic: shopper traffic, employee traffic, and even the movement of merchandise and supplies. Naturally, this design for operation must also follow the dictates of the overall decor, so as to contribute to that principle of "oneness." It must be commensurate with your desired store image. You may need to take into consideration a number of other requirements, such as the boxing off or disguising of building columns, an occasional interior wall or partition, staircases, escalators, elevators (if you operate on more than one level), and the like. For the convenience of your customers, you need aisles wide enough to permit shoppers to pass to and fro without knocking into each other. Similarly, you want to allow passageways behind counters and showcases of at least twenty-eight to thirty inches for salespeople to travel back and forth. Because so many factors are involved, I strongly advise consultation with an architect experienced with your type of store.

### Managing Your Space Efficiently

Always keep in the back of your mind the fact that every foot of your store costs you a certain number of dollars per year; this *cost per square foot* can be calculated by dividing one year's rental by the number of square feet of store space. Such an attitude will lead you to to be extremely careful about how you apportion that space. Usually, the largest area in your store is the selling area. Indeed, many retailers actually "departmentalize" in accordance with the sales-per-square foot concept. A menswear shop, for example, may devote 15 percent of its selling space to sport jackets because past sales figures have indicated that this is the percentage of total sales accounted for annually by those jackets. Your trade association probably has this kind of information for your type of store. Similar information may be available from the National Retail Merchants Association.

## Types of Layouts

Two major approaches are common in retail store layout: the grid and the free-form. By far the more popular of the two is the *grid* (or *gridiron*) layout. Based on rectangles, squares, and other geometric patterns, it's found in most small stores. Most often, shoppers enter and begin walking to the right. They pass showcases or sales counters, make a sharp left turn and walk by displays, and then come up along the other side of the store toward the register stand. The classic example of the grid layout is the modern-day supermarket, where customers are compelled to go up and down aisles and make right- or left-angle turns at the ends. Many retailers prefer the grid format because it ensures maximum exposure of store merchandise to the shopper.

Stores laid out on the *free-form* principle are characterized by curves, arcs, and ovals; this type of design permits traffic to ebb and flow at will, *without* compelling the shoppers inside to follow predetermined paths. Of course, such designs are far more graceful and pleasing to the eye than grid layouts.

In some cases designers attempt to combine the two basic forms, especially in those stores where the planners intend to set up a number of uniquely different departments or perhaps boutiques within the store.

Whether you're more attracted to the grid, free-form, or combination layout, be sure to seek out a competent store architect to help you make your decision. You need the kind of layout that will produce the best possible results for your new retail business.

## FOR FURTHER INFORMATION

### Books

Barr, V., and C. Broudy. *Designing to Sell: A Complete Guide to Retail Store Planning and Design.* New York: McGraw-Hill, 1985.

Green, William R. *The Retail Store: Design and Construction.* New York: Van Nostrand Reinhold, 1986.

Novak, Adolph. *Store Planning and Design.* New York: Lebhar Friedman, 1977.

Thompkins, James A., and John A. White. *Facilities Planning.* New York: Wiley, 1984.

White, John A., and Richard L. Francis. *Facility Layout and Location: An Analytical Approach.* Englewood Cliffs, N.J.: Prentice-Hall, 1974.

# IV

# Managing Your Goods and Services Mix

# 9

# Merchandise Management and Control

With a bit of imagination, you might think of your retail store as a money-making machine. (Isn't that exactly what you would like it to be?) Further, the merchandise you stock for resale is the fuel that powers your business. Providing the kinds of products (and services) that satisfy the needs and wants of your customers—at the right prices and in the correct quantities—produces sales. Of course, better fuel generates higher sales. To vary the analogy slightly, if you keep your "tank" full, you will get more mileage out of your vehicle. Thus, there's a case for maintaining a sizable inventory. Carrying a wide assortment of merchandise, in considerable depth as well, helps you meet the needs of more shoppers and reduces the number of lost sales due to *stockouts.*

On the other hand, your store's stock represents capital that's tied up. Indeed, the store inventory is usually the retailer's single largest investment. Simply maintaining an inventory of any size costs you additional money. You pay *carrying costs,* that is, some allocated share of your rent, insurance, utilities, and other overhead expenses. You pay the cost of *frozen money* as well—that is, the interest you would be drawing from the bank had you invested some of that tied-up capital in a savings account. Finally, you incur another type of cost, the *opportunity cost* of not having funds available for the purchase of other, perhaps more readily salable, goods—because you have every cent invested in merchandise. These hidden costs can run as high as 20 or even 25 percent of your inventory valuation, an excellent rationale for keeping your stock tight, or *lean,* as they say in retailing.

Evidently, then, you need an inventory that's ample enough for your needs and at the same time has little or no fat in it. Of such stuff is merchandise management made!

## INVENTORY PLANNING AND CONTROL

In actuality, merchandise planning runs the entire gamut of stocking activities from the initial planning (for a month or a season) through all the purchasing steps, to the judicious monitoring of inventory movement. For the sake of simplicity, however, the merchandising area has been broken down into two separate chapters. The buying area is treated in considerable detail in chapter 10 and so need not concern us further at this point.

Controlling your merchandise—or, if you prefer, managing your inventory—requires not only that you purchase goods for resale but also that you buy *according to plan.* Your primary challenge is to stock only as much merchandise as you need and to "turn it over" as rapidly as possible so that you recover some of that tied-up capital. The faster the capital is returned to you, the sooner you'll be able to reinvest that money into more goods—again and again. Implicit in this principle is the concept of *stock turnover,* often simply called *stockturn.* You need to identify items that sell quickly (a fast turnover), so you can replenish your stock more often. You must be equally sensitive to the slow movers; are they the right items for your customers? If they aren't, plan on dropping them from your regular inventory, and perhaps sell off the few you have left by marking them down to a lower selling price. To keep your finger right on the pulse of store sales, take inventory of your stock on a regular basis instead of relying on only "eyeball control" (a quick visual check) to decide on what's moving and what you should order. The importance of stock control to the independent retailer is underscored in exhibit 9–1.

## Stockturn

One of the surest indicators of how well or how poorly your business is doing (provided you maintain enough inventory on hand to satisfy your customers) is the rate at which

---

**EXHIBIT 9–1. IMPORTANCE OF STOCK CONTROL IN THE SMALL STORE**

Maintaining effective control over stock is important in all kinds and sizes of retail operations, but it can be critical in a small one. At best, the owner-manager of a small retail store flirts with loss when stock becomes unbalanced.

The type of merchandise you handle will largely determine the kind and amount of paperwork needed for effective stock control. For example, control of perishables—such as in a delicatessen—requires no paperwork. Stocks are controlled visually. Many deliveries—such as milk and bread—are daily, and others are frequent. In addition, the suppliers' routepeople have a self-interest in helping keep stocks fresh.

But even so, the owner-manager may need some sort of reminder—perhaps a note on the calendar—to make periodic checks. The important thing is to watch for changing customer demands requiring changes in your purchases.

The situation is different, though, with parts inventory in a service operation and with sizes and styles in an apparel store. For example, the owner-manager of a shop that specializes in motor tuneup may keep track of the parts used every day with little effort. But what about those used only once a month? Some sort of record is necessary if the right parts are to be on hand when needed.

In shoes, ladies ready-to-wear, and other soft-goods stores, style, color, and size complicate the problem of stock control. A great deal of paperwork may be necessary in order to serve customers properly and to prevent over- or underbuying.

---

*Source:* Edward L. Harling, "Stock Control for Small Stores," *Management Aid No. 3.005* (Washington, D.C.: U.S. Small Business Administration, n.d.), 2.

---

your stock moves, or "turns over." Of course, you need to compare your stockturn rate with those of similar stores, because rates differ from one type of store to the next. For example, a florist's entire inventory may turn over twenty-five times a year, while the stockturn rate of a shoe store or a boys' clothing store may be less than two over the year. Further, the stockturn rate differs within a single store among classifications of merchandise—and even from one item to the next within a single classification (see exhibit 9–2).

A more rapid-than-average stockturn can mean fresher merchandise in your store and consequently fewer outmoded or shopworn products and fewer markdowns. It also reflects the more efficient use of your assets and a higher return on your investment in inventory. In addition, of course, it reduces your inventory carrying costs, which can mount up appreciably over a year's time.

## How to Calculate Stockturn

Most retailers calculate stock turnover on their stores' inventories as a whole, instead of on classifications or subclassifications of merchandise, as they may be computed in department stores or large chain operations. While stockturn can be calculated for any period of time, its most common applications are annually and possibly semiannually. Although it may be calculated in three ways, all three approaches employ basically the same formula.

Here are the three approaches:

1. Stockturn based on *costs:*

$$ST_{cost} = \frac{\text{Cost of Goods Sold}}{\text{Average Inventory at Cost}}$$

2. Stockturn based on *retail prices:*

$$ST_{retail} = \frac{\text{Retail Sales}}{\text{Average Inventory at Retail}}$$

3. Stockturn based on *units of merchandise:*

$$ST_{units} = \frac{\text{Sales in Units}}{\text{Average Inventory in Units}}$$

In all three formulas, the term *average inventory* refers to the average stock available for sale during the period in question. It's calculated by totaling the number of inventory counts made during the period and averaging them. For example, should you want to determine your stockturn for the month of May, total your beginning-of-the-month inventory count (usually taken after the close of business April 30) and your end-of-the-month inventory (May 31), then divide the result by two to arrive at the average inventory for May.

## EXHIBIT 9–2. STOCKTURN RATES FOR MENSWEAR: BY MERCHANDISE CLASSIFICATION
### ALL FIRMS OPERATING EXPERIENCES

#### 1987 INVENTORY TURNOVER BY MERCHANDISE CLASSIFICATION*

| (Classification Numbers, 010-890, are taken from MRA's Financial & Operations Group "Menswear Basic Management Accounting Manual.") | ALL FIRMS (50 Firms) | | YOUR FIRM | FIRMS HANDLING MEN'S WEAR ONLY (20 Firms) | | FIRMS HANDLING WOMEN'S WEAR (30 Firms) | |
|---|---|---|---|---|---|---|---|
| | Range of Common Experience | Median Firm | | Range of Common Experience | Median Firm | Range of Common Experience | Median Firm |
| **MEN'S CLOTHING** | | | | | | | |
| 010 Men's Suits | 1.2-2.0 | 1.6 | ____ % | .9-2.3 | 1.5 | 1.2-2.0 | 1.6 |
| 040 Men's Coats | 1.1-1.9 | 1.4 | ____ | .7-2.7 | 1.1 | 1.3-1.9 | 1.4 |
| 060 Sport Coats | 1.1-1.9 | 1.3 | ____ | .8-2.1 | 1.2 | 1.1-1.9 | 1.4 |
| 080 Dress Slacks | 1.4-2.3 | 1.8 | ____ | 1.2-2.5 | 1.9 | 1.5-2.2 | 1.8 |
| Total Men's Clothing | 1.3-2.0 | 1.6 | ____ | 1.0-2.4 | 1.6 | 1.3-1.9 | 1.6 |
| **MEN'S SPORTSWEAR** | | | | | | | |
| 100 Sport Shirts | 1.9-3.0 | 2.3 | ____ | 1.8-2.8 | 2.1 | 1.9-3.1 | 2.5 |
| 130 Sweaters | 1.6-2.9 | 2.5 | ____ | 1.5-3.4 | 2.4 | 1.6-2.8 | 2.5 |
| 150 Actionwear | 1.9-3.5 | 2.5 | ____ | 1.1-3.9 | 1.9 | 2.0-3.4 | 2.5 |
| 180 Casual Slacks | 1.6-2.7 | 2.1 | ____ | 1.1-2.4 | 2.1 | 1.6-3.0 | 2.1 |
| 200 Jeans | 1.1-2.5 | 1.7 | ____ | 1.1-3.2 | 1.4 | 1.0-2.4 | 2.1 |
| 220 Jackets & Heavy Outerwear | 1.2-3.4 | 1.9 | ____ | .9-2.7 | 2.0 | 1.4-3.5 | 1.9 |
| 240 Coordinated Leisurewear | 1.3-3.8 | 1.8 | ____ | 1.4-4.4 | 3.2 | 1.3-2.7 | 1.7 |
| Total Men's Sportswear | 1.7-2.7 | 2.3 | ____ | 1.5-2.5 | 2.2 | 1.7-2.9 | 2.3 |
| **MEN'S FURNISHINGS** | | | | | | | |
| 260 Dress Shirts | 1.1-2.5 | 1.6 | ____ | 1.0-2.6 | 1.6 | 1.2-2.3 | 1.6 |
| 290 Neckwear | 2.0-3.1 | 2.3 | ____ | 2.0-3.8 | 2.6 | 1.9-2.7 | 2.3 |
| 300 Hosiery | 1.5-2.5 | 1.9 | ____ | 1.1-2.7 | 1.6 | 1.6-2.4 | 2.0 |
| 310 Men's Belts | 1.0-2.1 | 1.4 | ____ | .8-2.4 | 1.0 | 1.1-2.0 | 1.5 |
| 320 Men's Accessories | 1.2-1.9 | 1.5 | ____ | 1.3-2.3 | 1.5 | 1.1-1.8 | 1.4 |
| 340 Underwear | .7-1.8 | 1.2 | ____ | .6-1.9 | 1.0 | .8-1.9 | 1.3 |
| 360 Sleepwear | .9-2.1 | 1.5 | ____ | .9-2.1 | 1.9 | .8-2.1 | 1.4 |
| 380 Men's Headwear | .8-1.8 | 1.1 | ____ | .7-2.0 | .8 | .9-1.8 | 1.2 |
| Total Men's Furnishings | 1.3-2.2 | 1.7 | ____ | 1.2-2.4 | 1.6 | 1.4-2.1 | 1.7 |
| **BOYS' AND TEENS'** | | | | | | | |
| 400–440 Clothing | .8-1.8 | 1.5 | ____ | NA | NA | 1.5-1.8 | 1.7 |
| 450–510 Sportswear | .9-2.2 | 1.3 | ____ | NA | NA | 1.0-2.2 | 1.3 |
| 520–560 Furnishings | .9-1.8 | 1.7 | ____ | NA | NA | 1.5-1.8 | 1.7 |
| Total Boys' and Teens' | 1.4-2.3 | 1.6 | ____ | 1.1-2.5 | 1.5 | 1.4-2.1 | 1.6 |
| **MEN'S AND BOYS' SHOES** | | | | | | | |
| 570–595 | .9-1.7 | 1.2 | ____ | .9-1.6 | 1.2 | .9-1.8 | 1.2 |
| **WOMEN'S WEAR** | | | | | | | |
| 600–699 Misses | 2.0-3.0 | 2.3 | ____ | NA | NA | 2.0-3.0 | 2.3 |
| 700–773 Junior | 1.9-3.7 | 2.3 | ____ | NA | NA | 1.9-3.7 | 2.3 |
| Total Women's Wear | 2.0-2.7 | 2.3 | ____ | NA | NA | 2.0-2.7 | 2.3 |
| **WESTERN WEAR** | | | | | | | |
| 810–890 | NA | NA | ____ | NA | NA | NA | NA |
| OVERALL TOTAL | 1.5-2.2 | 1.9 | ____ | 1.3-2.2 | 1.7 | 1.5-2.2 | 1.9 |

*For each merchandise classification, only those stores reporting that classification are included in the tabulation.
Inventory turnover is the number of times during a given period, in this case one year, that the average inventory on hand at retail has been sold and replaced. The rate of turnover is computed by dividing net sales by average retail inventory.

Source: *MRA Annual Business Survey: 1987 Men's Store Operating Experiences* (Washington, D.C.: Menswear Retailers of America, 1988), 33.

Now for a bit of practice, just to get things down pat.

*Example 1.* You've just finished up your inaugural year in your sporting-goods emporium. Your operating statement for the year tells you that your cost of goods sold came to $72,400. Checking through your inventory records, you calculate that you maintained an average stock of some $28,500, at cost. What rate of stockturn did you enjoy? Here's how to work it out:

1. Use the first formula:

$$ST_{cost} = \frac{\text{Cost of Goods Sold}}{\text{Average Inventory at Cost}}$$

2. Now plug in the figures:

$$ST_{cost} = \frac{\$72,400}{\$28,500} = 2.5X$$

Your stock turned over—at cost—two and a half times (2.5X).

*Example 2.* This one you'll have to do by yourself. The sales for three months in your new grocery store amount to $37,000. You total up the retail values of the *four* monthly inventories you have taken: one at the beginning of the period, say January 1, and then the three successive inventories on January 31, February 28, and March 31. You then divide the sum by four to derive the *average inventory at retail* of $7,200. Now, work out the rate of stockturn for the quarter.

You should come up with a stockturn—at retail—of 5.1 (to be more exact, though you needn't be in working on stockturn rates, 5.138889).

You should understand that your rate of stock turnover may be influenced in either direction by decisions you make. For instance, should you overstock your store, thereby inflating the denominator in the stockturn ratio, your rate will necessarily slow down. This occurs when an independent retailer stocks up well in advance of a coming season.

The stockturn rate is also a useful management tool for determining how much inventory to carry. Projecting your stock needs for an entire year or season is relatively simple on the basis of your expected sales and your overall turnover rate.

*Example 3.* You own a music store. For your second year in business, you have targeted $140,000 in sales, a figure you believe to be thoroughly realistic. From your inaugural year's experience and from checking with your trade association's industry survey, you have decided that your rate of stockturn (at retail) should be 3.5X. Resorting to the by-now familiar formula, you insert these numbers into the proper slots:

1. $$ST_{retail} = \frac{\text{Retail Sales}}{\text{Average Inventory at Retail}}$$

2. $$3.5 = \frac{\$140,000}{x}$$

3. $$3.5x = \$140,000$$

4. $$x = \$40,000$$

The calculations in this example followed the principles you learned long ago in elementary algebra. First the letter $x$ was substituted for the one unknown quantity in the equation; it stands for *average inventory at retail*. Then we worked out the equation; the solution indicates that you can expect to turn over your average inventory of $40,000—at retail—3.5 times over the year.

To determine how much you need to invest in inventory, it's necessary to convert that $40,000 retail figure into a *cost* figure. Again, this is a simple process when you know your *overall markup* or *gross-margin percentage*. This figure should be available from your last annual operating statement. If your gross margin came to 41 percent, for instance, then your *cost-of-goods-sold* percentage was 59 percent. (The two figures must total 100 percent.) The $40,000 worth of inventory that you need to carry must be multiplied by .59 in order to calculate how much you have to spend for the goods. Working this calculation through, you find that it comes to $23,600.

## MORE ABOUT YOUR STOCK

Knowing your annual average-stock figure is helpful, of course, but it becomes just a departure point in your inventory planning. As you may realize, your store will enjoy brisk sales during some months of the year and experience rather lifeless movement in other months. As an illustration, the monthly percentages of annual sales registered last year in one type of retailing are as follows:

| | | | |
|---|---|---|---|
| January | 5.8% | July | 4.1% |
| February | 9.6 | August | 4.5 |
| March | 8.5 | September | 6.1 |
| April | 9.1 | October | 8.2 |
| May | 6.3 | November | 11.7 |
| June | 5.7 | December | 22.4 |

If you study this store's distribution of sales, you will easily conclude that it needs relatively little stock on hand during July and August and that it can use an especially heavy inventory in November and December. Check with your own line of retail merchandising for its particular "average" sales distribution pattern for direction in planning your monthly stocks. Remember: If you plan on a month's sales figure of, say, $10,000 at retail, you'll need *far more* in stock than $10,000 worth of merchandise. For one thing, you want to be left with a representative inventory in your store the day after that month ends—to start taking in the next month's sales. For another, it's impossible to sell out evenly across all types and classifications of merchandise and within all categories, no matter how well you may have planned your stock assortment. An example of purchasing plans for a small retail shoe store can be seen in exhibit 9–3. Note that it employs monthly sales percentages as planning guides.

# EXHIBIT 9–3. STOCK PURCHASING PLANS BASED ON SALES PROJECTIONS

Store _____

Location _____

Date _____

| Period | Actual sales last year | | | Planned sales this year | | | Actual sales this year | | |
|---|---|---|---|---|---|---|---|---|---|
| | Sales | Cost | Percent of year's total | Sales | Cost | Percent of year's total | Sales | Cost | Percent of year's total |
| January | $ 11,340 | $ 6,804 | 6.3% | $ 12,600 | $ 7,560 | 6.3% | | | |
| February | 11,160 | 6,696 | 6.2 | 12,400 | 7,440 | 6.2 | | | |
| March | 17,820 | 10,692 | 9.9 | 19,800 | 11,880 | 9.9 | | | |
| Total for Quarter | $ 40,320 | $ 24,192 | 22.4% | $ 44,800 | $ 26,880 | 22.4 | | | |
| April | $ 18,180 | $ 10,908 | 10.1% | $ 20,200 | $ 12,120 | 10.1% | | | |
| May | 16,020 | 9,612 | 8.9 | 17,800 | 10,680 | 8.9 | | | |
| June | 12,420 | 7,452 | 6.9 | 13,800 | 8,280 | 6.9 | | | |
| Total for Quarter | $ 46,620 | $ 27,972 | 25.9% | $ 51,800 | $ 31,080 | 25.9% | | | |
| July | $ 11,880 | $ 7,128 | 6.6% | $ 13,200 | $ 7,920 | 6.6% | | | |
| August | 14,400 | 8,640 | 8.0 | 16,000 | 9,600 | 8.0 | | | |
| September | 18,000 | 10,800 | 10.0 | 20,000 | 12,000 | 10.0 | | | |
| Total for Quarter | $ 44,280 | $ 26,568 | 24.6% | $ 49,200 | $ 29,520 | 24.6% | | | |
| October | $ 17,820 | $ 10,692 | 9.9% | $ 19,800 | $ 11,880 | 9.9% | | | |
| November | 13,680 | 8,208 | 7.6 | 15,200 | 9,120 | 7.6 | | | |
| December | 17,280 | 10,368 | 9.6 | 19,200 | 11,520 | 9.6 | | | |
| Total for Quarter | $ 48,780 | $ 29,268 | 27.1% | $ 54,200 | $ 32,520 | 27.1 | | | |
| Year's total | $180,000 | $108,000 | 100.0% | $200,000 | $120,000 | 100.0% | | | |

*Source*: Adapted from William A. Rossi, "Starting and Managing a Small Shoestore," *The Starting and Managing Series, Vol. 24* (Washington, D.C.: U.S. Small Business Administration, 1974), 52–53.

Small retailers need annual and even monthly sales goals to provide overall direction, but they must then translate these objectives into specific, day-to-day operational details. They must decide on how wide an assortment to carry (that is, how many different categories or classifications of goods to stock, the *breadth* of the assortment), as well as how many varieties to carry within each category (the *depth* of the assortment). The breadth decision takes into account the kind of store you have and the store image you seek to project. This consideration translates to "what your customers expect you to carry in stock." To make decisions as to depth, you need to think in terms of *product variants*—such details as the more popular styles, brands, colors, sizes, price lines, and the like. You cannot stock every conceivable variant. You must therefore learn to be selective, thinking in terms of *substitutability,* which is the factor in a shopper's outlook that induces him or her to accept a "substitute" brand, color, quality, and so on when you don't have in stock what he or she is originally searching for. Then, too, you want to stock up fully on what are called the *heart items* in your inventory—articles that sell very well. At the same time, you can carry a relatively light stock of the *fringe items* in inventory to please the occasional customer.

It's best to work up your store's basic stock plan with paper and pencil. If yours is a seasonal business or if you sell fashion merchandise, you may need to prepare several *model stocks* for your store.

Exhibit 9–4 offers a sound procedure for the preparation of your stock plan.

---

### EXHIBIT 9–4. HOW TO PREPARE A STOCK PLAN

1. Begin with the overall sales expected for the period. Put that figure at the top of your page.

2. Draw a number of columns, depending on how many classifications or major categories of goods you maintain in inventory. Write the category names at the heads of the columns.

3. From your records, ascertain the percentage of total sales for that period last year that can be attributed to each classification. Translate that percentage into dollars; these are the rough figures you hope to attain (all other things being equal) in the coming period.

4. Adjust these figures for (a) classes whose sales are growing in your judgment and for (b) those that appear to be slowing down. Write the new figures underneath the respective column heads. These become your new guidelines.

5. Now consider each classification individually. List the more popular and the less popular items that you carry. Assign to each item some plausible percentage of the total sales in that category. Be specific; put down dollar amounts.

6. Finally, work out the quantities needed in product variants for each item. Again, plan to stock more of the popular items and less of the "fringes."

7. As a last thought, remember that you have worked with *retail* prices all along. You now have to convert all figures to *cost* prices, so you can prepare your buying plan.

---

*Source:* Compiled by the author.

---

# THE PRODUCT LIFE CYCLE

To do a better job of merchandising, every new retailer should become familiar with the concept of the product life cycle, or PLC. It's a key to understanding the market behavior of new products; it also provides useful direction for you when buying merchandise for resale in your store.

Every new product that is successfully introduced into the marketplace appears to reflect a "life cycle" of its own. For most merchandise, we can identify four distinct phases in that cycle: the introductory, growth, maturity, and decline stages. No one, of course, can predict the overall "longevity" of any particular product. Some innovations may prove popular for decades; others may last for several years; still others (like some "fads") may fall completely out of use within a few months after their appearance.

Here is a brief description of each of these stages, along with their effects on the manufacturing firm that originated the product:

**Introductory stage.** This commences at the time the new product is first made available for sale. Characteristically, there's little consumer awareness of the product at this point. Nor can interested shoppers locate the item easily, since few retailers have elected to carry it. For a successful "launch," the manufacturer will need to spend considerable sums to promote the product and devote much time and expense to gaining wider distribution. Thus, the producer can usually expect to show a loss rather than profit during this initial phase of the PLC.

**Growth stage.** As increasing sales volume keeps pace with growing consumer demand, more wholesalers and retailers can be expected to agree to stock the new item. Even as more gross-margin dollars are taken in, the originating company will work at refining its production methods. As the firm succeeds in bringing down its cost of goods, it starts to earn profit. And *more* profit . . .

Unfortunately, though, competitors start to enter the marketplace at some point during this stage. To meet the increasing competitive challenge, the original producer will need to increase substantially its expenditures for both advertising and distribution.

**Maturity stage.** By the time this phase of the PLC arrives, competition has become keen. Each competitor offers its own version of the basic product; each claims its own is superior to the rest.

For the innovator, sales growth slows and begins to level out. Competitors strive to increase their own particular market shares through product improvement, significant pricing maneuvers, and accelerated promotional efforts. To maintain its own share of market, the originating firm steps up activity in all these areas. Because of increasing expenses, its profits start to weaken.

**Decline stage.** Eventually, consumer demand for the item begins to wane. As sales volume slackens, the company that developed the item in the first place will begin thinking about phasing out its manufacture. Before it does, however, it may attempt to rekindle consumer enthusiasm through a variety of approaches: by promoting new uses for the product; by redefining the firm's target markets; by repositioning the item; and so on. At some point, though, arrangements will have to be made to discontinue production and dispose of whatever inventory is still on hand.

## What the PLC Signifies for the Retailer

When considering merchandise offerings for resale in their stores, retailers should first try to determine at which stage of the product life cycle each item submitted to them most likely is. This knowledge will enable them to buy more sensibly. Here are some helpful hints on each of the four PLC stages:

> **Introductory stage.** Be careful with brand-new goods. Since consumers as yet know little about them, demand can be expected to be slight. If you feel the merchandise has appeal for your regular customers, test it out by ordering only a small quantity. Also, see if you can get supportive (cooperative) advertising from your supplier, as well as a few promotional aids (for example, free signs or banners). If the goods sell well, you can then reorder according to the continued demand you may come to expect.
>
> **Growth stage.** As your sales of the new product continue to grow, the manufacturer may make additional variants available to you: other colors, sizes, shapes, or materials. Consider adding some of these, again taking pains to observe the results carefully.
>
> Since competitors start to enter the picture during this stage, you may be able to substitute another source's better-quality merchandise—or buy the product at a lower price, secure better terms, gain more frequent delivery of goods, and so on. Or, you may be able to convince your original supplier to meet competitive offers.
>
> **Maturity stage.** Most merchandise now in the marketplace is in this stage of product life cycle. Since this indicates that there are a number of competitors sharing the total pie, this is the time for the retail firm to discard marginal suppliers and choose to buy only from the strongest, and most cooperative, source. In essence, the retailer can be quite independent when it comes to dealing with producers of mature products.
>
> **Decline stage.** With merchandise that is clearly in its last stage of the PLC, you'll need to think about gradually cutting back on reorders. Start narrowing the range of the assortment you carry, insofar as sizes, colors, and other variants are concerned. Finally, clear out your inventory completely by marking down all remaining goods.

## INVENTORY PROCEDURES

Typically, independent retailers look over their stock from time to time with an eye to ordering more of items that are low. This is known as *eyeball control* of the store's inventory. It enables retailers to avoid the time-consuming task of taking physical inventory, which requires the counting of every package, all bulk goods, and every carton or case they stock—in the bins, on display, or in storage areas. Nevertheless, every retail business owner must take an accurate physical count of inventory at least once each year in anticipation of closing the books and issuing annual statements for income tax reasons.

In my judgment, there are more important considerations in this area of inventory than income taxes. There's the valuable knowledge of stock-movement rates, which enables store management to make decisions throughout the year. Most small store owners ought to take inventory more often, at least quarterly, to coincide with seasonal changes. Indeed, in many retail lines, inventory should be taken every month. A grocery store, for example, carries literally hundreds of items; there is no way that eyeball control can do an adequate job. Monthly physical inventory is also important in the preparation of monthly profit and loss statements, which measure your progress all along and provide direction for changes in your marketing strategies.

When you take monthly inventory, you're able to order more effectively and more often. Greater frequency of ordering results in fresher merchandise on hand and in goods that are more in vogue. Consequently, you most likely will have to contend with fewer markdowns and at the same time will lower your storage costs.

## Taking Physical Inventory

The procedure for taking inventory of your merchandise is quite simple. The small store usually prepares its own inventory form, which consists of one or more sheets of paper (dictated by the number of items you carry) divided into columns. The merchandise is often arranged first by logical groupings or categories and again by size or retail price within those groupings. Usually, the first three columns are headed with terms such as "Size," "Description of Item," and "Retail Price." Under those headings in a grocery store, for instance, you might find listed under the category "Canned Fruits" such entries as:

| 8 oz. | Apricots | .99 |
| 12 oz. | Apricots | 1.29 |
| 16 oz. | Apricots | 1.59 |
| 8 oz. | Fruit Cocktail | .65 |
| 16 oz. | Fruit Cocktail | 1.19 |

You would probably find the various brands listed as well.

Additional columns on the inventory sheet are provided for writing in the quantities counted, for totals, and for the dollar extension of each item total (quantity × price at retail). The sheets are often printed up (or mimeographed, at the very least) in quantity and stored away for future use. The physical inventory is best taken by two people: One searches through every nook and cranny of the premises, counts the merchandise, and calls out the figures to the second person, who enters the totals on the inventory sheets. While counting, the counter can also check the merchandise for its condition, freshness, salability, and the like.

## RECEIVING AND MARKING MERCHANDISE

When shipments of goods arrive at your store, your first order of business is to *check the delivery*. If you're lucky enough to have a back door that leads directly into your stockroom, the delivery should be made through that door, with the trucker most likely using a dolly to bring in the cartons. Many small stores, however, have to accept their deliveries through the front. In this situation, the storekeeper must make sure that the cartons are stacked up neatly to one side so customer traffic is not impeded.

Each shipment is accompanied by an invoice or packing slip. Before signing the sheet (for the receipt of the merchandise), be certain to count the number of cartons in the delivery and match that number against the invoice. Discuss any discrepancy with the trucker. Your next step is to check the invoice against your own purchase order to see whether or not you have received everything you ordered. Each carton is usually marked as to its contents. As you open the cartons to put the merchandise into stock, check to see if the items inside are exactly what they're supposed to be, that they're in good condition, and that the carton count is correct. Occasionally, for example, a carton that should contain one dozen of an item is found to be short one or two pieces. Boxes of bulk merchandise that is sold by weight should be checked on your scale to make certain you have been shipped the right amount. With such goods, check also for quality. All merchandise should be marked with the necessary information—retail price, cost code, weight, contents, or whatever else the item requires—before consigning it to the stockroom or to ready stocks (shelves, bins, and the like).

## FOR FURTHER INFORMATION

### Books

Burstiner, Irving. *Basic Retailing.* Homewood, Ill.: Irwin, 1986.

Depaola, H., and C. Mueller. *Marketing Today's Fashion,* 2d ed. Englewood Cliffs, N.J.: Prentice-Hall, 1986.

Grace, E. *Introduction to Fashion Merchandising.* Englewood Cliffs, N.J.: Prentice-Hall, 1978.

Janson, R. *Handbook of Inventory Management.* Englewood Cliffs, N.J.: Prentice-Hall, 1986.

Kneider, Albert P. *Mathematics of Merchandising,* 3rd ed. Englewood Cliffs, N.J.: Prentice-Hall, 1986.

Kotler, P. *Marketing Essentials.* Englewood Cliffs, N.J.: Prentice-Hall, 1984.

Mason, J. Barry, and Morris L. Mayer. *Modern Retailing: Theory and Practice,* 3rd ed. Plano, Tex.: Business Publications, 1984.

Shuch, Milton L. *Retail Buying and Merchandising: A Decision-Making Approach.* Boston: Little, Brown, 1982.

Troxell, Mary D. *Retail Merchandising Mathematics: Principles and Procedures.* Englewood Cliffs, N.J.: Prentice-Hall, 1980.

### Pamphlets Available from the Small Business Administration

#### Management Aids

MA 3.005—"Stock Control for Small Stores"

## Booklets Available from the Superintendent of Documents

S/N 045-000-00152-1—*Small Store Planning for Growth*—$5.50.

S/N 045-000-00167-9—*Purchasing Management and Inventory Control for Small Business*—$4.50.

S/N 045-000-00178-4—*Retail Merchandise Management*—$4.75.

S/N 045-000-00190-3—*Inventory Management—Wholesale/Retail*—$4.50.

# 10

# Buying Merchandise

The continuous task of purchasing goods for resale in your retail store is a complex process. Among other things, it involves these activities:

1. Determining the needs and wants of your customers (from past sales, a want-list system, comparison shopping, trade papers, suppliers, and other sources of information
2. Forecasting sales for an upcoming period
3. Planning the merchandise assortment needed to attain the forecasted sales
4. Seeking and selecting the right resources (sources of supply)
5. Negotiating prices, terms, and conditions with suppliers
6. Writing orders
7. Receiving and checking the merchandise
8. Keeping records of stock movement for future decisions

## BUYING FOR THE NEW, SMALL STORE

Invariably, at the beginning, owners of new retail businesses do all the buying personally, for they consider (and rightfully so) this aspect of store operations as one of the most crucial phases. Since owners must remain in the store most of the time, their contacts with sales representatives constitute the major approach to buying merchandise.

Another characteristic of the small retailer's purchasing is *hand-to-mouth buying*, or buying only as needed to replace items that have moved off the shelves. This method necessitates buying frequently and, of course, in small quantities. The effect isn't bad at all; this approach provides flexibility in merchandise planning, and it avoids the building up of an unnecessarily heavy inventory.

Occasionally, retail merchants may have someone else "cover the store" so they can travel to "the market" to explore other sources of supply. However, if your store's located in New England, the Midwest, or the South, trips to the major market areas such as New York City or Chicago can cost you a great deal of both money and time away. In such cases, using an independent buying office (discussed later in this chapter) or purchasing from catalogs through the mails can help to round out your inventory. Occasional visits to manufacturers' and wholesalers' showrooms and to trade shows are other possibilities.

## MERCHANDISE SOURCES

Most store merchants buy their goods from local wholesalers and at times directly from manufacturers. A few, such as the retailer of fruits and vegetables, may purchase directly from producers in the vicinity. Shopkeepers who carry imported goods obtain their merchandise either from import houses or from catalogs provided by the importers. Naturally, buying from the manufacturer usually results in the merchant's paying lower prices for the goods; this practice is fairly common in such retail enterprises as music stores, confectionery or cheese shops, most types of apparel stores, furniture stores, and so on. There's also the possibility that, if you order in sufficient quantity from the manufacturer, you will be able to request changes in the merchandise or, at the very least, in the packaging. This is called *specification buying;* the store seeks to differentiate what it carries from the inventories of its competitors.

For most retail lines, you'll be able to locate sources of supply (*resources* or *suppliers*) simply by checking the Yellow Pages of the telephone directory under the category of interest to you. Here are just a few examples taken from one directory:

Apparel—Children's, Infants' & Teens' Wear—Whol. & Mfrs.
Apparel—Men's & Boys' Shirts—Whol. & Mfrs.
Automobile Parts & Supls.—Whol. & Mfrs.
Carpet & Rug Distrs. & Mfrs.
Giftwares—Whol. & Mfrs.
Health Food Products—Whol. & Mfrs.
Shoes—Whol. & Mfrs.
Sporting Goods—Whol. & Mfrs.
Toys—Whol. & Mfrs.

Other sources of information regarding potential suppliers include your trade association, trade publications (especially those companies advertising in them), the wholesalers' salespeople and the manufacturers' sales representatives who visit your store, and other retailers in the same line who have stores in other areas and are therefore not your competitors.

## WHAT WHOLESALERS DO

Typically, the wholesale enterprise buys in large quantities from various manufacturing companies, stores the goods till needed in a warehouse, then distributes the products in small quantities to retailers—and perhaps to other types of businesses, institutions, government agencies, and other organizations. (Incidentally, the terms *wholesaler, jobber,* and *distributor* all have essentially the same meaning.) The *full-service* (or *full-function*) wholesaling firm provides a wide variety of services, in addition to the sale of merchandise—such as storage, transportation, the extension of credit, providing market information, and so forth. Most wholesalers in this country are of this type.

Three different types of full-service companies exist, distinguished by the products they offer: the general-merchandise distributor, the single-line wholesaler, and the specialty wholesaler. The first type offers its customers a wide-ranging variety of merchandise lines; the second concentrates on one specific line (hardware, flowers, carbonated beverages, housewares, and so on); the third specializes within a single line by offering only a limited number of items.

You should be aware of some special types of distributors: the rack jobber, the cash-and-carry wholesaler, the mail order distributor, and the truck jobber. Only the first type is a full-service firm; the others are referred to as *limited-service* wholesalers because they do not offer all of the usual services. Each type is described below:

> **The rack jobber.** These wholesalers are found in a variety of merchandise lines, such as inexpensive plastic toys and novelties, cookies, pantyhose, paperback books, beauty aids, and hardware items. The rack jobber introduces one or more, usually freestanding, racks into your store at no cost to you, stocks these self-service fixtures with merchandise, then visits the store from time to time to replenish the stock and to keep the entire presentation looking fresh and neat. You, the merchant, usually pay only for the items sold. Many retailers welcome the addition of racked merchandise that's not normally carried in the store if they have the space for it; the sales of these items help defray part of the monthly rent and other operating expenses.
>
> **The cash-and-carry wholesaler.** An example of this type is the beverage and grocery distributor who caters to local grocery stores, restaurants, and bars. Retailers can purchase at wholesale bottled soft drinks by the case, institution-size cans of soup, large canisters of pretzels or potato chips, and so on. They pay for the goods with cash. As a point of information, cash-and-carry wholesalers prefer storefronts where they can also offer merchandise to consumers in the neighborhood. Prices to consumers are generally somewhat lower than those found in the supermarkets.
>
> **The mail order distributor.** This kind of firm displays its wares in catalogs it mails to retail establishments, thus avoiding the need for maintaining a sales force. Orders are both placed and shipped by mail. This service is especially helpful to retail merchants situated in the more isolated communities around the country. There are many mail order distributors found in a variety of retail lines including jewelry, dry goods, and musical instruments and supplies.
>
> **The truck jobber.** Still called *wagon jobbers* by some (a throwback to the days when these distributors used a horse and wagon to conduct business), truck jobbers service food stores for the most part. Working from a well-stocked truck, they provide produce, bread, candy, dairy products, or other perishables to the stores. Daily deliveries are generally made along an established route.

## A BUYING OFFICE CAN HELP

Department stores and large chain-store organizations maintain internal buying staffs or set up their own buying offices in close proximity to the major metropolitan markets.

Their professional buyers continually scout the market for information on (in many cases) the thousands of different items they need to carry. For the most part, the small retailer can't afford to maintain even one part-time buyer on the payroll to do a more professional job of buying goods for resale. Yet in many retail lines, assistance is available in the form of *independent buying offices.*

These firms serve as market representatives for smaller stores around the country. They're found in such lines as apparel (men's, women's, and children's), fashion accessories, furniture, home furnishings, housewares, appliances, millinery, and furs. Most of these companies are located in New York City, Chicago, Los Angeles, and several other metropolitan areas. Some of the services they perform are described in exhibit 10–1.

The most common type of independent buying office is the *salaried* (or *fee*) type. The firm usually requires the retailer to sign an annual contract. The cost to the retailer typically runs to about 0.5 percent of annual sales. When sales are quite low, the buying office may substitute a minimum fee of several hundred dollars for the customary percentage arrangement. The fee is payable over the year in equal monthly installments.

A second type of buying office can be helpful to the small-scale retail merchant: the *merchandise broker.* No contract is signed, and you need not affiliate your store with such firms. They furnish smaller stores, at no charge, with information regarding merchandise, prices, sources of supply, and the like. They're compensated by the manufacturers they represent on a commission basis.

---

### EXHIBIT 10–1. THE SERVICES OF A BUYING OFFICE

You can expect a well-staffed buying office to furnish certain basic services, such as:

1. Advising on the best sources of merchandise.
2. Keeping constant contact with the market—particularly with the new styles, new products, price changes, and good buys.
3. Buying merchandise for you with your approval when you are unable to come to market.
4. Following up on orders so that you receive merchandise on time. (This in itself can be a major competitive advantage, justifying the fee in many cases.)
5. Handling adjustments—returns and cancellations.
6. Providing office space and clerical-secretarial services for you and your buyers when you are in the market city.
7. Notifying manufacturers that you plan to come to market.
8. Assigning buyers to accompany you on visits to manufacturers' showrooms.

Some resident buying offices also sponsor formal and informal meetings where you can discuss your operations with stores similar to your own. They organize fashion clinics to examine the market's offerings. They sometimes offer fashion coordination services.

They assist you in analyzing your various operational costs, help you plan a branch store opening, prepare Christmas and other holiday catalogs on a group-saving basis, and suggest ways to improve your advertising.

---

*Source:* Ernest A. Miller, "How to Select a Resident Buying Office," *Small Marketers Aid No. 116* (Washington, D.C.: U.S. Small Business Administration, 1976), 2.

---

## POINTERS ON HOW TO BUY BETTER

"Better buying" means more than simply trying to purchase merchandise at good prices. Of course, reducing the cost-of-goods entry on your profit and loss statement increases the gross margin earned during the accounting period. Provided that you hold your operating costs constant, your bottom line will show more profit. In the typical retail enterprise, the total amount in the cost-of-goods figure is larger by far than all other operating expenses combined. For many retail lines, it hovers around 60 percent; in other words, 60 cents out of every dollar taken in as sales goes to pay for the merchandise sold. This average is mentioned only to accent the seriousness with which you should approach your buying endeavors.

In addition to the prices you pay for your goods, you need to think about other aspects in conducting negotiations with your suppliers:

- Terms of sale: dating and discounts and passing of title
- Quality guarantees
- Storage until need by the buyer
- Delivery: when and how
- Assumption of transportation charges
- Packing and packaging for shipment and for resale
- Ticketing by the seller
- Reorder availability and price guarantees on reorders
- Return privileges
- Promotional aids and allowances
- Possible changes in the product itself or in the standard size and color assortments provided
- Long-term business relationship between the parties, including at times financial assistance to the seller*

To help yourself "buy better," consider first those buying principles outlined in exhibit 10–2. Then, you may wish to commit to memory the random suggestions offered in exhibit 10–3.

## CHECK INTO YOUR SUPPLIERS' SERVICES

A review of the prime reasons for selecting certain sources of supply, as against others, will no doubt reveal some or all of the following:

- They carry the type and quality of merchandise your customers purchase readily.
- Their prices are fair; terms and conditions are favorable to your needs.

---

\* John W. Wingate and Joseph S. Friedlander, *The Management of Retail Buying*, 2d ed., © 1978, 279. Reprinted by permission of Prentice-Hall, Inc., Englewood Cliffs, N.J.

**EXHIBIT 10–2. SOME BUYING PRINCIPLES**

The following rules or principles for buying have stood the test of experience:

1. Purchases should be made frequently to avoid "out of stock" conditions, to provide fresh stock, and to achieve maximum stock turnover.

2. Buy in smaller quantities in a falling market. This avoids losses due to lower prices, stock shrinkage, markdowns, and idle capital tied up in inventory.

3. In a rising market, avoid the temptation to overbuy or speculate. But do not neglect buying to protect your competitive position.

4. Buy the right merchandise. Clever sales talks, brilliant advertising, and smart displays cannot sell old stock which is not salable. Only when the goods are "right" can other sales aids help you succeed.

5. Know your merchandise and your market. It pays to study the trading community carefully, whether you sell staple or specialty goods. Find out what the people need and want. Guessing is gambling and accounts for many losses in the retail business. When the merchant knows what he can sell, how much and at what price, he can make sound purchasing plans—but not otherwise.

6. Keep adequate sales and stock records. Too many merchants rely on their memories and actually guess about the most important facts affecting their businesses. The best merchandise buyers keep and use detailed records so they may buy enough but no more than they need of the right brands, styles, materials, sizes, colors, and price lines.

*Source:* New York State Department of Commerce, *Your Business: A Small Business Management Handbook* (Albany, N.Y.: NYS Department of Commerce, 1976), 27.

---

**EXHIBIT 10–3. FIFTEEN SUGGESTIONS TO HELP YOU BUY BETTER**

1. Investigate the possibility of buying together with other merchants who carry the same merchandise in order to earn quantity discounts. Many independent retailers form small "associations" for the purpose of buying goods and exchanging information and ideas.

2. Keep a listing of your resources in a notebook. In addition to the name, address, and telephone number of each supplier, show the name of the person to be called; information about delivery, terms, and conditions; special services offered; and the like.

3. If selling fashion goods, remember to stock your store with a broad assortment and little depth at the beginning of each season. As the season progresses, you'll be able to spot the weaker numbers, which you can try to phase out—and the fast-moving merchandise, whose depth you need to increase.

4. Keep your customers prominently in mind whenever you examine merchandise offered to you.

5. Be in control of your buying. Avoid overstocking your store; it's easy to get carried away during a visit to a supplier's showroom. Go there with a definite plan in mind, as well as a dollar limit for your purchasing requirements.

6. Check into the vendor's policies on deliveries (when and how often they're made), returned merchandise, transportation charges, promotional assistance, and other facets of interest to you.

7. Think about the kinds of "extras" you would like to get from the vendor *before* you start negotiating prices and terms.

8. Before negotiating price, first try to estimate the selling price *your* customer would most likely be willing to pay for the item. Then subtract your customary markup from this price; the resulting figure should be the *top* price you should be willing to pay for the item.

EXHIBIT 10–3. CONTINUED

9. A useful technique to practice, when discussing price, is to show dissatisfaction with the initial price quoted by the vendor. State simply that you cannot readily sell the merchandise in your store with your usual markup. Negotiating a price involves bargaining; the first price quoted, more often than not, is not the price finally agreed to.

10. When you and the supplier are rather close to agreement on the price of goods but at an apparent impasse, you might offer to *split the difference* with him or her. This tactic often works.

11. Once the price has been set, you need to work on some of the other aspects. Discuss cash, quantity, and seasonal discounts (see chapter 13). Strive for favorable terms, such as future dating and deliveries FOB your store.

12. Have your goods "preticketed" or "prelabeled" if this service is available from the supplier.

13. Ask about any special promotions that may be coming up in the near future.

14. Always pay your bills ahead of time to be able to deduct your cash discounts.

15. Investigate the usefulness to your business of offers of job lots or closeout merchandise. Often, these can be valuable additions to your store's inventory. To estimate the value of these goods, sort them into two groups: those your customers will readily purchase and those you'll have to sell at markdown. Remember, however, that such merchandise frequently doesn't represent a balanced assortment of sizes, colors, and styles and that it is usually offered toward the close of a season.

---

*Source:* Compiled by the author.

- They're honorable in their business dealings and are evidently in sound financial shape.
- Stocks are ample to fill repeat orders.
- Deliveries are made promptly.
- You and they get along well together.

Over and above these conditions, as well as the others normally discussed during negotiations, suppliers are often prepared to extend a variety of other useful services to their customers. It would be well worth your while to familiarize yourself with them. Simple awareness on your part can become the prelude to a close and helpful relationship that may increase your profit picture, in addition to making things easier for you in your store. These services can be grouped under three headings:

- Providing market information
- Giving promotional assistance
- Offering financial aid*

## Providing Market Information

Because of its position as an intermediary in the marketing channel, the wholesaling company enjoys innumerable contacts with both retailers and producers. Thus, the

---

* Richard M. Hill, "Profit by Your Wholesalers' Services," *Small Marketers Aid No. 140* (Washington, D.C.: U.S. Small Business Administration, 1970).

wholesale house continually gathers information about new products, new methods, supply conditions, competitive prices, merchandise that is selling well or poorly, and so on. Information can then be relayed to the retailers through the firm's sales representatives or through newsletters or bulletins.

## Giving Promotional Assistance

Suppliers often provide display materials and point-of-purchase posters or signs; these may be free of charge or supplied at a nominal cost to the retail store. Sometimes the wholesale firm provides information about how to build effective window and counter displays. During a special promotion, the firm may even be willing to send in an employee to help out. Moreover, since the wholesaler often benefits by receiving cooperative advertising dollars from the manufacturers from whom they buy, the firm generally pushes the retailers' items through newspaper and air-media advertising. Finally, price concessions obtained by the wholesale distributor are often passed along to their retail merchants.

## Offering Financial Aid

Among the activities provided by some distributors are:

- The extension of direct financial assistance through the practice of delayed billing
- Long-range financing for modernization or the erection of a new building
- Help in finding new locations or other businesses that are for sale
- Facilitating or actually rendering accounting services

Management assistance is also common. Suggestions on setting policy and improving methods may be made in all areas of retail operations: administration, housekeeping, personnel, insurance, public relations, expansion, and so forth. As an example, should you some day need to hire a competent specialist, such as a buyer or a store manager, your supplier may be able to locate one for you.*

## FOR FURTHER INFORMATION

### Books

Depaola, H., and C. Mueller. *Marketing Today's Fashion,* 2d ed. Englewood Cliffs, N.J.: Prentice-Hall, 1986.
Diamond, J., and G. Pintel. *Retail Buying,* 2d ed. Englewood Cliffs, N.J.: Prentice-Hall, 1985.

---

* For a useful set of guidelines to follow in maintaining good vendor relations, see Marc J. Dollinger and Michael G. Kolchin, "Purchasing and the Small Firm," *American Journal of Small Business* 10 (Winter 1986), 33–45.

Janson, R. *Handbook of Inventory Management.* Englewood Cliffs, N.J.: Prentice-Hall, 1986.

Kneider, Albert P. *Mathematics of Merchandising,* 3d ed. Englewood Cliffs, N.J.: Prentice-Hall, 1986.

Shuch, Milton L. *Retail Buying and Merchandising: A Decision-Making Approach.* Boston: Little, Brown, 1982.

Stern, L., and A. El-Ansary. *Marketing Channels,* 2d ed. Englewood Cliffs, N.J.: Prentice-Hall, 1982.

Troxell, Mary D. *Retail Merchandising Mathematics: Principles and Procedures.* Englewood Cliffs, N.J.: Prentice-Hall, 1980.

Wingate, J., and J. Friedlander. *The Management of Retail Buying,* 2d ed. Englewood Cliffs, N.J.: Prentice-Hall, 1978.

## Pamphlets Available from the Small Business Administration

### Management Aids

MA 3.005—"Stock Control for Small Stores"

## Booklets Available from the Superintendent of Documents

S/N 045-000-00167-9—*Purchasing Management and Inventory Control for Small Business*—$4.50.

S/N 045-000-00178-4—*Retail Merchandise Management*—$4.75.

S/N 045-000-00190-3—*Inventory Management—Wholesale/Retail*—$4.50.

# ——— 11 ———

# Pricing for Profit

After consultation with several dictionaries, followed by the perusal of half a dozen textbooks on economics, you may possibly conclude (as I have) that the *price* of something is what someone will *pay* for it. (Of course, money isn't necessarily the only mode of settlement; payment can be in trade or in effort.)

## WHAT'S A PRICE?

In retailing, the price of an article appears to be the amount of money that store management will *ask* for the item. This definition, I'm confident, doesn't furnish you with much in the way of useful guidelines for pricing your merchandise.

As a practical-minded person, you're not much concerned with the theory or philosophy of pricing, nor do you care to get into the nitty-gritty of the laws of supply and demand—and rightly so. Recognizing that price is one of the few variables within your control, you want to know how to *administer* your prices. How do you arrive at the "right" prices for your goods (whatever this means)? And, conversely, what makes a "poor" price?

It's wise to consider the subject from several distinct vantage points: from your customers' point of view, from your own viewpoint, and in view of your competitors. Each angle lends a different perspective to your thinking. Moreover, you need to decide on your basic pricing philosophy: Will your prices be somewhat above the market, competitive, or somewhat below the market? This question has to do, of course, with your intended "store image."

Then you need to realize that your prices have to be high enough to cover all your costs and to yield some profit. Oddly enough, it would seem that many firms fail to charge enough for the goods they sell.* Yet, your prices must still attract shoppers into

———

*Charles W. Kyd, "Pricing for Profit," *INC*. 9 (April 1987), 119.

your store. What the consumer is willing to pay for an item is one consideration. However, additional considerations, such as the regularly advertised prices on popular brand-name items and the fact that your competitors also stock many of the same items, place constraints on your own pricing practices. Many other factors also tend to influence selling price: cost factors, economic factors, seasonality, product characteristics such as perishability and style, how fast or slow the merchandise sells, and others.

You'll find the thorough treatment of markups and their applications later in this chapter quite helpful in your pricing endeavors. Toward the chapter's end, you'll discover a listing of many of the *promotional pricing* techniques that retailers use. Read these over for additional ideas for your new store.

## RETAIL PRICING APPROACHES

How do retailers ordinarily approach the pricing problem? How do they set the retail selling prices of the merchandise they offer for sale to consumers? Usually, each firm's management first decides on its own, preferred orientation toward the pricing of goods. Then, as it does in all other phases of its business operation, management will choose a specific, major objective to pursue in the pricing area.

In making their pricing decisions, retailers try to take into consideration such aspects as:

- The extent of consumer demand for their merchandise (as indicated by the prices that shoppers seem willing to pay for it)
- Their competitive stance: Should they price their goods at, above, or below the prices of their leading competitors?
- The "suggested retail prices" as proposed by their suppliers
- Such qualities or characteristics of the merchandise as style, perishability, and seasonality

Here are the pricing objectives most commonly pursued by retail organizations; careful consideration of each in turn may help you decide on your own firm's attitude:

- *The target ROI.* Establishing retail selling prices that will yield a specific return-of-profit percentage on your investment.
- *Profit maximizing.* Setting prices designed to produce the highest possible profit percentage you might expect to earn on the goods you sell.
- *The target sales increase.* Working up prices that should produce a specified percentage increase in overall store sales (usually by reducing prices sufficiently to sell much more merchandise).
- *Cash-flow improvement.* Establishing prices designed to bring more sales dollars into the firm's treasury (usually a short-term strategy).

Once they have decided on their pricing philosophy, the majority of retail organizations make use of *markup* techniques to establish their selling prices. Some, especially service retailers, work on *average-cost pricing*. In this approach to price setting, the retailer takes into consideration the costs of direct labor, materials (if used), a portion of overhead expenses, and a reasonable profit margin.

The subject of markups is discussed fully in the next section. Before you proceed, though, be sure to look over the useful "pricing checklist" that appears in exhibit 11–1.

---

### EXHIBIT 11–1. A PRICING CHECKLIST

| **Have you established a set of pricing policies and goals?** | Yes | No |
|---|:---:|:---:|
| Have you determined whether to price below, at, or above the market? | ☐ | ☐ |
| Do you set specific markups for each product? | ☐ | ☐ |
| Do you set markups for product categories? | ☐ | ☐ |
| Do you use a one-price policy rather than bargain with customers? | ☐ | ☐ |
| Do you offer discounts for quality purchases, or to special groups? | ☐ | ☐ |
| Do you set prices to cover full costs on every sale? | ☐ | ☐ |
| Do the prices you have established earn the gross margin you planned? | ☐ | ☐ |
| Do you clearly understand the market forces affecting your pricing methods? | ☐ | ☐ |
| Do you know which products are slow movers and which are fast? | ☐ | ☐ |
| Do you take this into consideration when pricing? | ☐ | ☐ |
| Do you experiment with odd or even price endings to increase your sales? | ☐ | ☐ |
| Do you know which products are price sensitive to your customers; that is, when a slight increase in price will lead to a big dropoff in demand? | ☐ | ☐ |
| Do you know which of your products draw people when put on sale? | ☐ | ☐ |
| Do you know the maximum price customers will pay for certain products? | ☐ | ☐ |
| If the prices on some products are dropped too low, do buyers hesitate? | ☐ | ☐ |
| Is there a specific time of year when your competitors have sales? | ☐ | ☐ |
| Do your customers expect sales at certain times? | ☐ | ☐ |
| Have you determined whether or not a series of sales is better than one annual clearance sale? | ☐ | ☐ |
| Have you developed a markdown policy? | ☐ | ☐ |
| Do you take markdowns on a regular basis, or as needed? | ☐ | ☐ |
| Do you know what role you want price to play in your overall retailing strategy? | ☐ | ☐ |
| Are you influenced by competitors' price changes? | ☐ | ☐ |
| **Are there restrictions regarding prices you can charge?** | Yes | No |
| Do any of your suppliers set a minimum price below which you cannot go? | ☐ | ☐ |
| Does your state have fair-trade-practice laws which require you to mark up your merchandise by a minimum percentage? | ☐ | ☐ |
| Are you sure you know all the regulations affecting your business, such as two-for-one sales and the like? | ☐ | ☐ |
| Do you issue "rainchecks" to customers when sale items are sold out so they can purchase later at sale price? | ☐ | ☐ |

*Source:* Michael W. Little, "Marketing Checklist for Small Retailers," *Management Aid No. 4.012* (Washington, D.C.: U.S. Small Business Administration, revised 1985), 3–4.

---

## MASTERING MARKUPS

You have recently opened a women's shoe store on a busy neighborhood street. Other merchants on the block have spoken to you about the benefits of *scrambled merchandising*—adding one or more new lines to one's regular business to help defray overhead costs. You have room for another line, without detracting in any way from your shoe sales. Women's accessories seem as though they would readily fit in; sales on such merchandise would amount to some very nice extra business for you. Moreover, you might be able to attract "nonshoe" shoppers into your store for these items—and wind up selling them shoes at that time or in the future. A definite plus!

You decide to take on a line of low- and moderate-priced handbags, which you display on wire floor racks supplied by the jobber. The two styles, both attractive canvas bags covered with initials reminiscent of several expensive brands, come in four basic colors: brown, blue, red, and gray. You're convinced that your clientele will love them—and that many of your customers can be sold one of the bags along with the purchase of a pair of shoes.

Your costs are $70 per dozen for one style, $130 per dozen for the other. The distributor has told you that one group sells for $10 to $15; the other, for between $20 and $25.

What selling price do you set for them?

If you're like the majority of retailers, you apply a *keystone markup:* you double your cost to arrive at the retail selling price.

### How to Calculate Markups

Let's take the less expensive pocketbook as an example. The wholesale price of $70.00 per dozen figures out to a cost per unit of $5.85 for "Bag A." Were you to sell Bag A at $11.70 (or perhaps at $11.99 or $12.00, depending on your pricing philosophy), you would be earning approximately $6.00 over your cost with each sale. Of course, you realize that the word *cost* in this case excludes all your other costs of doing business, such as your rent, cost of utilities, labor, and so forth. This *cost* refers exclusively to the cost of the handbag—to what is more accurately termed your *cost of goods.*

This figure, the difference between the cost of merchandise and the price you get for it, is your *gross margin* (or *gross profit*) on the single item. It's also your *markup* or *markon* (these terms are interchangeable in practice). You marked $5.85 (or $6.14 or $6.15, as the case may be) on to your original cost. When retailers mark up an article of merchandise, they actually add a desired amount to the cost price to determine the retail selling price. Thus, a markup can be defined as *the difference between the cost of goods and the selling price.* To put this thinking into a simple and useful formula, which you can easily remember:

$$\text{Markup} = \text{Selling Price} - \text{Cost Price}$$

Or, even more simply:

$$MU = SP - C$$

In the case of Bag A, then, the worked-out formula looks like this:

$$MU = \$11.70 - \$5.85 = \$5.85$$

In this instance, the markup is expressed in monetary terms, as a dollars-and-cents figure. Markups can also be calculated in *percentages,* either of cost or of selling price. Here's how to do so:

*Markup Percentage, Based on Cost:*

$$MU\%_{cost} = \frac{\text{Markup (in dollars)}}{\text{Cost (in dollars)}} \times 100$$

*Markup Percentage, Based on Retail Price:*

$$MU\%_{retail} = \frac{\text{Markup (in dollars)}}{\text{Retail Price}} \times 100$$

Referring again to Bag A, here are the calculations for both approaches:

$$MU\%_{cost} = \frac{\$5.85}{\$5.85} \times 100 = 100\%$$

$$MU\%_{retail} = \frac{\$\ 5.85}{\$11.70} \times 100 = 50\%$$

Train yourself to work only with the *retail* markup percentage: retail markup in dollars, divided by the retail selling price, multiplied by one hundred. Although manufacturers and wholesalers generally compute their markups on their costs, most astute retailers rely on the second (retail) type because it provides quick and useful insights into the financial aspects of their businesses. (This advantage will become more evident later in this chapter.) Of course, some store types—such as bakeries, appliance repair shops, stores that sell custom-made draperies, and other retail enterprises where direct labor must enter the cost picture—are perhaps better off calculating their markups on the cost basis.

Back to the original question: What should be the selling price for Bag A? Bag B? In brief, is a 50-percent markup at retail right or wrong? Such conjecturing leads us to the next section.

## PLANNING YOUR OVERALL MARKUP

How much of a markup—*on the average*—do you need to operate your business profitably? Further, how much of a profit should you make? If you attack these problems with unemotional logic, you will realize that whatever markup you decide on, it must contain room enough to (1) cover the cost of merchandise, (2) pay all your operating expenses, and (3) present you with some leftover profit at the year's end.

When we examine markup from this long-term point of view, we're looking at it from a completely different angle—not the amount that you would tack on to the cost of a single unit of merchandise, but the *gross margin* you earn overall on the total sales you take in. If you can work up this figure in advance (and you can!), then you shouldn't have much trouble pricing *any* item for your inventory. I'm not suggesting you mark up all goods by the same percentage. Not at all! What I do suggest, however, is that you think in terms of *averaging* all markups. Your goals are to make your end-of-year operating statement reflect the cost-of-goods percentage that you have targeted and to make your "bottom-line" figure approximate the one you have planned. As far as pricing your merchandise is concerned, aiming at an *overall* (or *maintained*) markup leaves you ample room to consider placing higher markups on some goods and lower markups on others.

Reference to an actual P&L at this point would be valuable. If you have been in business for some time, you can bring out your own for purposes of comparison. If you're just starting up, you have probably prepared a pro forma statement to which you can refer (see chapter 5). Either way, let's take someone else's situation for the sake of illustration. Here's a P&L for last year (highly abbreviated; only the major headings are shown):

| | |
|---|---|
| Net sales | $134,600 |
| Cost of goods | 78,350 |
| Gross margin | 56,250 |
| Expenses | 54,630 |
| Net profit (before taxes) | $ 1,620 |

Taking that top "Net sales" figure as 100 percent of sales, let's work up the percentages of sales represented by all the other entries. Simply divide each figure by $134,600.

Here are the results:

| | |
|---|---|
| Net sales | 100.0% |
| Cost of goods | 58.2 |
| Gross margin | 41.8% |
| Expenses | 40.6 |
| Net profit (before taxes) | 1.2% |

By way of interpretation, these figures indicate that, of every dollar made in sales, the merchandise purchased for resale cost the store owner (on the average) 58.2 cents. On each dollar of sales, the retailer earned an overall gross margin of 41.8 cents. From this figure, 40.6 cents had to be deducted to defray the store's operating expenses, thereby earning the proprietor a *pretax* profit of little more than one penny.

Hardly seems worthwhile? Surprisingly enough, the owner of this particular store thought she'd covered everything properly. Like so many other retail merchants, she automatically marked up just about every item carried during the year by doubling her cost (a 50 percent markup at retail). Yet her P&L showed only a 41.8 percent gross margin. She had neglected to consider a number of things: Over the year, many articles were marked down to sell at lower-than-retail prices; other merchandise deteriorated and became unsalable; employees were granted discounts on things they bought for their own use; pilferage and shoplifting further reduced her margin. Evidently, then, a keystone markup was insufficient in this case.

## Work from the P&L

Let's assume that the percentages in our example P&L represent your own operating statement for the year just ended and that you're dissatisfied—and rightly so—with the poor profit showing. On studying the figures, you should conclude that you could do three things to rectify the situation for this year:

> **Increase Your Sales.** Naturally, your cost of goods will also rise, but, if you can manage to hold your operating expenses to last year's level, your net profit before taxes will, of course, be higher. Assuming the same overall markup, you'll enjoy another 41.8 cents of gross margin for each additional dollar of sales.
> **Cut Your Expenses Where Possible.** Lowering your operating expenses by as little as 1 percent of sales—all other things being equal—will nearly double your profit figure.
> **Reduce Your Cost of Goods.** Trimming this cost by the same percentage will accomplish the identical increase in profit as in the previous entry.

It goes without saying that if you can accomplish all three objectives, things will *really* perk up!

Since the first two items are treated in other chapters, we're mainly interested in that third item: Just *how* can you decrease your cost of goods? The answer: by deliberately seeking to raise your markups—through *better buying* and *better pricing*. This answer requires thoughtful analysis and some key decisions.

Here's an actual case in point:

> The owner of a confectionery and ice cream store located in a regional shopping center in the Northeast was piqued by the tiny profit shown on his first-year's operating statement. When translated into a percentage of annual sales, the bottom-line figure came to only 0.7 percent. This, he knew, was way below the average for his type of outlet. Since the shopping center's management had expressed their satisfaction with his sales figures (indicating that they were just about what had been expected) and since he believed he had done an outstanding job of controlling store expenses, he concluded that somehow his cost of goods must have been out of line.

Luckily, he had had the foresight to follow his accountant's recommendations in setting up his books at the beginning. He had been advised to arrange his records so as to be able to determine the total sales volume earned by each of the four major merchandise lines carried. (Analyzing your stock movement by merchandise categories is essential to proper inventory management; see chapter 9.) On a sheet of paper, he listed the total sales in each of the categories during the prior year. These figures, shown below, have been rounded off for the sake of simplification:

| Classification | Last Year's Sales |
|---|---|
| Boxed chocolates (known brands only) | $ 97,700 |
| Bulk ice cream | 24,250 |
| Bulk candies | 22,100 |
| Novelties | 8,600 |
| Total Sales | $152,650 |

Next, the store owner checked through his purchase orders to the various suppliers and was able to arrive at an approximation of the markup percentage for each category. With the aid of a pocket calculator, he then computed the total contribution of each merchandise classification to the operation's gross margin.

The resulting table looked like this:

| Classification | Sales | Markup Percentage | Gross Margin Earned |
|---|---|---|---|
| Boxed chocolates | $ 97,700 | 42% | $41,034 |
| Bulk ice cream | 24,250 | 56 | 13,580 |
| Bulk candies | 22,100 | 52 | 11,492 |
| Novelties | 8,600 | 50 | 4,300 |
| Totals | $152,650 | | $70,406 |

To obtain the average markup across all classes of goods, the proprietor then divided the total gross margin earned by the total sales, following a formula that you'll recognize as an adaptation of the basic markup formula:

$$1. \ \text{MU\% (retail)} = \frac{\text{Gross Margin}}{\text{Sales}} \times 100$$

$$2. \ \text{MU\% (retail)} = \frac{\$70,406}{\$152,650} \times 100$$

$$3. \ \text{MU\% (retail)} = 46.1\%$$

After scrutinizing these figures and again reviewing the various expense categories with an eye to possible cutting back, the owner concluded that (1) the overall markup had been insufficient for his needs and would have to be increased; and (2) the boxed-chocolates classification had been the most significant contributor of all to the firm's gross profit, while the novelties didn't amount to very much at all.

With this analysis firmly in mind, the retailer proceeded to take the following steps:

- He decided against instituting any price increase, however small, on the boxed chocolates so as not to endanger the one major line that brought in nearly two-thirds of his sales and close to 60 percent of his gross-margin dollars. For one thing, these were known brands with prices that had been well advertised. For another, there were two competitive stores in the same shopping complex. Moreover, the retailer felt that a price increase might knock out the marginal customer simply because boxed chocolates were luxury goods, not necessities.
- He successfully renegotiated prices with his three major suppliers of boxed chocolates, getting them to concede to a slight reduction in his wholesale costs, not to mention a more favorable set of terms.
- He replaced the six ice cream scoops in the store with ones that were slightly smaller. Essentially, these would reduce the amount of ice cream in an individual cone by about a half-ounce, while the selling prices of the ice cream cones wouldn't be altered.
- He fought the temptation to drop all novelties from his store on the strength of his conviction that overall sales would fall by somewhere between 5 and 6 percent.
- He applied a 3 percent price increase across-the-board to all bulk candies and novelties. He doubted that this minor increase would be noted by most of his customers.
- He took on another basic merchandise category: shelled nutmeats (peanuts, cashews, almonds, pistachios, and so forth). The new line was priced to yield a markup at retail of about 56 percent. In his judgment, a reasonable estimate of nut sales for the first year—in view of the sizable display case he planned to use for them—was $6,000.

To ascertain just how he would have fared the year before had these changes been in effect, he reworked his original figures:

| Classification | Last Year's Sales | Revised Markups | Hypothethical Gross Margin |
|---|---|---|---|
| Boxed chocolates | $ 97,700 | 43.5% | $42,499 |
| Bulk ice cream | 24,250 | 61.0 | 14,792 |
| Bulk candies | 22,100* | 55.0 | 12,520 |
| Novelties | 8,600* | 53.0 | 4,695 |
| Nutmeats | 6,000** | 56.0 | 3,360 |
| Totals | $159,571 | | $77,866 |

*Based on a 3 percent price increase and assuming no falloff in sales.

**Estimated sales for new line.

By dividing the gross margin ($77,866) by the total sales ($159,571), he discovered that he would have obtained an overall hypothetical markup amounting to some 48.8 percent—as compared with an actual markup of 46.1 percent. At first blush that doesn't seem to be much of an improvement. Based on these moves, he would have earned an additional $7,460 in sales ($77,866 − $70,406). Bear in mind, however, that the firm's actual net profit before taxes the year before had totaled 0.7 percent of sales. These new calculations had unearthed a potential of an additional 2.7 percent, which would bring the total profit figure to 3.4 percent. This last percentage represents almost a *quintupling* of the original bottom line!

Every retailer faces challenging price problems like these from time to time. Could the confectionery store owner have done more in this case? Was he correct in his assessment of the boxed-chocolates situation, or should he have raised prices? What's your opinion of his decision to reduce the size of individual servings of ice cream? Ought he to have discontinued all novelties, or should he instead have sought to expand that line, perhaps by adding more items that afforded a 55- or even a 60-percent markup?

Of such stuff are pricing decisions made.

## MAINTAINED MARKUP: PLANNING'S THE KEY!

Our confectionery merchant's resolution of the situation suffered from one glaring imperfection: All markups used in his calculations were based on his *original costs* of the merchandise—as tallied from purchase orders. These costs were, of course, subtracted from the selling prices he had established. The markups, then, were *initial* markups. As noted earlier in this chapter, the first markup placed on goods when they arrive at the store isn't necessarily the markup actually realized at the time of sale. Such eventualities as subsequent markdowns in price (some articles may even be marked down twice!), employee and customer discounts, and inventory shortages all reduce the overall markup percentage obtained.

A healthy approach is to plan your *maintained markup* in advance. This sort of planning can be done; indeed, it's done all the time by department and chain stores and by other knowledgeable retailers. Of course, you need to make some educated guesses along the way, but the procedure, once understood, is fairly easy to follow. If you recall, the formula for calculating markup was:

$$MU = \text{Selling Price} - \text{Cost}$$

In this formula, markup is expressed in dollars; it's what's left after subtracting the item's cost from the selling price you have placed on it. If, however, the selling price is reduced for some reason (such as a markdown or discount), you can readily see that the MU in the formula must be lowered. In this case, the formula really should be rewritten to look like this:

$$MU = \text{Selling Price} - \text{Cost} - \text{Reductions}$$

In practice, such a reduction is what happens to your gross-margin picture during the year. That's what happened to our friend who owned the confectionery store. His "cost of retail reductions" ran to several thousands of dollars, thus reducing his planned 50-percent markup to the point where he ended up with a gross profit of only 41.8 percent for the year.

The way out of this dilemma is to take the reins with a firm hand by deciding to *direct* what happens, not just *allow it to happen*. You plan for the next year or for the next season by making projections for *all* the elements that make up your maintained markup. This figure has to be high enough to cover your cost of goods, any retail reductions, the kind of profit you're looking for, and all your store expenses. When you have worked it out to your satisfaction, this figure then becomes the *initial markup* to place on merchandise when it first arrives at your store. (It's still an average figure, not necessarily applicable to each and every item.) If your projections are approximately on target, your initial markup and final maintained markup ought to be very close, if not identical!

Here's the formula we suggest you use in your planning:

$$\text{Initial MU\%} = \frac{\text{Expenses} + \text{Reductions} + \text{Desired Profit}}{\text{Sales} + \text{Reductions}} \times 100$$

where:

**Initial MU%** is your average markup target to seek in pricing your goods.

**Expenses** include all of the costs of operating the store (rent, labor, utilities, insurance, and the like).

**Reductions** include markdowns, customer discounts, employee discounts, and stock shortages (*shrinkage*).

**Desired Profit** means just that! How much profit do you want?

To apply the formula, refer to your P&L (either last year's, if you have been in business, or your proposed pro forma statement for your new enterprise). The P&L's figures are of assistance to you in working up your best "guestimates" for next year. Then replace the terms in the formula with the appropriate numbers. As an example, let's assume you have come up with the following set of statistics:

| Category | Estimated Amounts | Percentage of Sales |
|---|---|---|
| Anticipated: | | |
| Sales | $135,000 | 100.0% |
| Expenses | 52,350 | 38.8 |
| Markdowns | 10,700 | 7.9 |
| Employee discounts | 1,850 | 1.4 |
| Customer discounts | 1,550 | 1.1 |
| Stock shortages | 2,800 | 2.1 |
| Desired profit for year | $ 8,500 | 6.3% |

You proceed to work out the formula:

$$\text{Initial MU\%} = \frac{\$52,350 + \$16,900 + \$8,500}{\$135,000 + \$16,000} \times 100$$

$$= \frac{\$77,750}{\$151,900} \times 100$$

$$= 51.2\%$$

According to these figures, when initially pricing your merchandise, you should aim at an average markup of 51.2 percent. Alternatively, if you know the percentage of sales that each figure represents, you can use those percentages directly in the same formula (omitting the "× 100" at the end):

$$\text{Initial MU\%} = \frac{38.8\% + 12.5\% + 6.3\%}{100\% + 12.5\%}$$

$$= \frac{57.6\%}{112.5\%}$$

$$= 51.2\%$$

This approach is, of course, much simpler to compute.

Having determined that you need to aim at a 51.2 percent initial markup, you're ready to price the three items you have just put into your line: Item A costs $2.82; Item B costs $3.67; and Item C costs $7.88. Simply divide your cost price by the *complement of the markup*, which is equal to 100 percent minus the markup percentage. In this case, the complement is 100 percent minus 51.2 percent—or 48.8 percent. Dividing the three costs, in turn, by 48.8 percent, you obtain the following "rough" selling prices: Item A, $5.78; Item B, $7.52; and Item C, $16.15. In practice, experienced retail merchants improve on these rough figures to make them sound more like customary retail prices; they would probably end up being priced more like $5.95, $7.50, and $15.95 (or $16.50). Then, of course, other factors would most likely be taken into consideration, such as those mentioned in the first pages of this chapter.

## MARKDOWNS NEED TO BE TAKEN

Some retailers strongly resist marking down the prices of merchandise; instead, they permit goods to accumulate in their back rooms or basements. Their "logic" seems to be that selling merchandise at lesser markups cuts down on their gross margin. So they carry ever-heavier inventories, continuing to list their out-of-style and shopworn items at their original values. This practice makes their P&Ls look good, though not quite accurate.

Capital tied up in such articles does more harm than good, in the long run. Markdowns need to be taken, if only to make room for other merchandise that can be turned over more quickly. Of course, the extra cash comes in handy, too. Markdowns will always be with us. If you're looking for reasons, try the following list:

- Adverse weather conditions
- Buying at the wrong time
- Changes in fashion

- Customer handling of merchandise
- Errors in selecting product variants (sizes, colors, brands, materials, and the like)
- Fading of goods
- Inefficient merchandise management and control
- Overbuying
- Poor stock rotation
- Pricing mistakes

## PRICING SERVICES

We have already seen how most store owners arrive at the retail selling prices for the merchandise they buy for resale. By and large, they utilize markups that are high enough to cover both their cost of goods sold and all operating expenses—while still leaving room for an adequate profit margin.

Like most manufacturers, service retailers tend to approach the pricing problem from a somewhat different perspective. They prefer a cost-oriented method. To illustrate, let's observe the pricing process at work in the following situation:

A small toy-manufacturing plant distributes its products to retail stores in five contiguous states through the services of three large wholesalers. At this point in time, the producer is attempting to arrive at the "suggested retail price" to place on Item Q, a new product that has just been added to the company's extensive line.

After some analysis, all applicable *per-unit costs* were determined; these are shown below, along with the amount of profit *per unit* the firm would like to earn.

| | |
|---|---|
| Cost of materials used | $2.38 |
| Direct labor | .76 |
| Percentage of indirect labor | .43 |
| Percentage of fixed overhead | 1.26 |
| Total Costs | $4.83 |
| + Profit | 3.90 |
| Grand Total | $8.73 |

The company may then decide to set the wholesale price of Item Q at $8.75 per unit. It can then offer its distributors cartons of one dozen each, at $105.00 per dozen ($8.75 × 12). In turn, the wholesaling firms may be expected to price the goods accordingly, adding perhaps another one-third or more of their cost from the manufacturer to cover their own expenses and desired profit. Assuming that they do so, they will sell the merchandise to retailers at perhaps $150.00 per dozen ($12.50 per unit). Depending on their individual pricing approaches, the retailers may price the individual Item Q at anywhere from $20.95 to $25.00, or even higher.

After working through this procedure, the manufacturer may choose to place a "suggested retail price" of $25.00, $27.50, or even $30.00 on Item Q.

## Pricing by the Service Retailer

The *cost-plus* approach is common among service retailers. Although the cost of materials used is often a small, sometimes even insignificant, factor, labor costs generally represent a substantial proportion of overall costs. As is the case in manufacturing, some percentage of the firm's overhead expenses is also assigned to the particular service being priced. Another amount is then added, to serve as a profit margin.

Consider, for example, a beauty salon where the following figures have been worked out for a particular service:

| | |
|---|---:|
| Cost of beauty supplies used | $1.60 |
| Direct labor (for operators) | 3.50 |
| Assigned percentage of variable overhead (uniforms, laundry, water, and so on) | 1.25 |
| Assigned percentage of fixed overhead (owners' salaries, rent, insurance, depreciation of equipment, office expenses, and so on) | 2.85 |
| Total Costs | $9.20 |
| + Profit Margin | 5.70 |
| Grand Total | $14.90 |

Most likely, the retailer will charge the customer $15.00 for this service.

## AN INTRODUCTION TO DISCOUNTS

Discounts have a nearly universal appeal. Just about everyone loves to buy things at below their customary prices.

*To discount* means *to deduct from an account, a charge, or a debt.* A discount is a reduction from a set amount or price. Discounts are offered in the business world for a variety of purposes; here are the types most frequently seen in store retailing:

**Cash discount.** A reduction in the face amount of an invoice, offered to encourage prompt payment. Usually the amount of the discount appears as a percentage under the "terms of sale" on the bill. For example, terms that read "2/10, N/30" (actually, "2 percent/10 days, Net 30 days") indicate that (a) you have thirty days from the invoice date to pay the full amount (a normal business procedure); or (b) you may elect to pay the bill within ten days and deduct 2 percent of the total. As a small retailer, paying your bills early over the year can save you a lot of money!

**Early-bird discount.** A deduction from the regular selling price offered in advance of an upcoming season to encourage the early purchase of merchandise. Such discounts typically run from 5 to 15 percent off the list price, with a fairly safe median of about 10 percent.

**Employee discount.** An employee benefit that can be offered by any retail merchant and that enables employees to purchase store merchandise for their own use at a reduction from the regular selling price. It's usually expressed as an overall percentage, such as 20 percent. In practice, the employee discount is often not granted for sale items or certain merchandise classifications.

**Introductory discount.** A technique that manufacturers and distributors frequently resort to in order to encourage retail firms to take on a new product or a new line of merchandise. It can also be used quite profitably by store retailers in introducing new items to their customers.

**Quantity discount.** Extended to customers who make large purchases or who buy in quantity. A supplier, for example, from whom you ordinarily buy Item X at the regular wholesale price of $60 per dozen, may offer you a 10 percent discount from this figure if you order a gross at a time. Some retailers offer this type of discount to consumers who purchase a dozen of one type of article (neckties, shirts, and so on); others may offer it to any customer making an extraordinarily large purchase. Indeed, many buyers expect it and ask for it.

**Seasonal discount.** A tactical maneuver often employed by producers and sometimes by wholesalers, usually to clear out their warehouses or to generate cash flow. The regular price of merchandise is reduced to induce before-season purchasing, thus relieving the pressures on the supplier. (Imagine the heavy inventory piled up by a toy manufacturer long before the Christmas holidays!)

**Trade discount.** A deduction from the regular selling price of goods offered to the wholesaler or retailer for performing their usual functions in the marketing channel. These discounts result in the customary wholesale and retail distributor costs.

## PROMOTIONAL PRICING TECHNIQUES

To increase store sales, retailers may draw upon a variety of well-known promotional pricing approaches. A few of these techniques, like bait pricing and comparative pricing, are clearly deceptive. Honest merchants will refuse to engage in such practices. On the other hand, such strategies as leader pricing, price lining, and multiple pricing are thoroughly acceptable and often used.

As the owner of a new store, you owe it to yourself to become familiar with these and other promotional pricing techniques found in the retailing sector:

**Bait pricing.** A deliberate and illegal ploy by a retail concern whereby an article of merchandise—usually a popular item with a well-known price—is advertised at an extraordinarily low selling price in order to attract shoppers to the store. This tactic is generally used in connection with the *bait-and-switch* technique. The retailer has no intention in the first place of selling the advertised merchandise at the stated price; once inside the store, the shopper is "switched"—that is, persuaded to buy a more expensive variety.

**Comparative pricing.** Another deceptive strategy, whereby an article is pretagged or preticketed with two (or possibly more) selling prices. The higher price is crossed out, perhaps with a red slash through it (though it's still legible). The consumer is thus led to believe that the merchandise has been marked down by the retailer. Another variation is to use a phrase on the price ticket, such as *Usually $35.00, Formerly $19.95,* or *At Our Competitor's Shop, $49.50.* In any of these instances, however, store management really intended to sell the item at the low price in the first place, and shoppers mistakenly believe that they're getting a true bargain.

**Flexible pricing.** Actually, a pricing philosophy that's directly opposed to the "one-price-to-all" attitude of most retailers. The item's usual selling price becomes the initial kick-off point for further negotiations between seller and buyer. Among those who employ this approach—often called *variable pricing*—are antique dealers, stores that sell used office furniture or store fixtures, and used car dealers.

**Leader pricing.** A frequently used promotional technique that involves taking a shorter-than-usual markup on merchandise in order to generate additional store traffic. It's most often used with popular or brand merchandise, the prices of which are well known to consumers.

**Multiple pricing.** A method that's especially effective with low-priced items. The retailer offers the product in multiples, such as in a three-, four-, or six-pack. This often induces the shopper to purchase more at one time, at a considerable savings from the regular selling price.

**Odd- or even-pricing.** Some retail firms, notably those seeking a higher-than-average price/quality image, prefer to set their selling prices in round numbers or in figures that end in even numerals, such as $6.00, $14.50, or $35.00. However, many prefer odd-figure price endings, such as $2.79, $9.95, or $19.99. These are often used on the assumption that such prices appear to present more of a bargain to the consumer.

**Prestige pricing.** Stores that sell high-quality furniture or home furnishings, fine restaurants, shops that sell expensive women's dresses or coats, and the like may deliberately set their prices at a higher level than their competitors'. The retail merchants' conviction is that consumers perceive a direct relationship between higher selling prices and the quality of the merchandise. They're seeking to build a "prestige image" for their stores.

**Price lining.** A merchandise strategy found in many types of retail establishments, this involves grouping similar merchandise into several *price lines,* fixed at different *price points.* For example, the women's accessories department may carry three "grades" of scarves, one at $6.00, another at $10.00, and a third at $17.95. The retailer may have paid widely varying prices for the scarves within any *one* of the three lines, let alone across the three. By grouping the items in this manner, however, making a choice is simplified for the customer. Then, too, it becomes easier for the experienced salesperson to "trade up" the shopper from a lower to the next higher price line.

**Push money (PM).** Money allocated to the salespeople in the store, generally by suppliers, in order to encourage them to push specific articles of merchandise. For each unit sold, the salesperson is paid a small sum.

Incidentally, there's no reason why retail-store owners can't employ this technique on their own to move certain stock off the shelves! In addition to small amounts of cash, many retailers offer prizes to those employees who sell the most of "Product X" for the day, week, or longer period.

**Trade-ins.** Some retail merchants offer cash rebates to buyers of their products who bring in their old models as "trade-ins." This technique is a favorite with auto-tire dealers (especially for snow tires), retail outlets selling household appliances, new car dealers, and others.

**Unit pricing.** This is more of a customer service (often mandated by local ordinances) than a promotional pricing technique. Of special importance to the grocery or food store, unit pricing enables shoppers to compare the prices for different-size packages of the same item in terms of a basic unit of measurement.

## FOR FURTHER INFORMATION

### Books

Gabor, Andre. *Pricing: Concepts and Practices for Effective Marketing.* Brookfield, VT: Gower, 1987.

Hirshleifer, J. *Price Theory and Applications,* 3d ed. Englewood Cliffs, N.J.: Prentice-Hall, 1984.

Marshall, A. *More Profitable Pricing.* New York: McGraw-Hill, 1980.

Monroe, Kent B. *Pricing: Making Profitable Decisions.* New York: McGraw-Hill, 1979.

Nagle, Thomas T. *The Strategy and Tactics of Pricing: A Guide to Profitable Decision Making.* Englewood Cliffs, N.J.: Prentice-Hall, 1987.

Oxenfeldt, Alfred R. *Pricing Strategies.* New York: AMACOM, 1982.

Symonds, Curtis W. *Pricing for Profit.* New York: AMACOM, 1982.

### Pamphlets Available from the Small Business Administration

#### Management Aids

MA 1.019—"Simple Breakeven Analysis for Small Stores"

### Booklets Available from the Superintendent of Documents

S/N 045-000-00137-7—*Guides for Profit Planning*—$4.50.
S/N 045-000-00192-0—*The Profit Plan*—$4.50.
S/N 045-000-00195-4—*Understanding Costs*—$3.25.

# Customer Services in Retailing

On a blustery winter's day, try offering the incoming shopper a cup of coffee or steaming hot chocolate. This kind of unexpected yet most welcome service can help to build up, over time, a loyal clientele. You'll note instantly a warm smile of appreciation cross the shopper's face.

A frill? An unnecessary gesture that's bound to increase your operating costs? Not at all! Your initial expense is a minor one; you need to buy an automatic coffeemaker or a hot-chocolate machine. After that, your only outlay is for a supply of paper cups, some plastic spoons (or stirrers), and the necessary ingredients. This expense is hardly a massive investment on your part—definitely less than the cost of a single good newspaper advertisement—and you can charge the expense off to your promotion budget just as easily! Moreover, it's right in line with that major strength of the small retail merchant: personal attention.

In creative hands, services can be more than just gimmicks that differentiate your store from those of your competitors. They can add a dimension that complements and rounds out your merchandise offerings and that leads to consumers regarding your shop as a gratifying and attractive place to visit.

## SERVICES TODAY'S CUSTOMER EXPECTS

The public, of course, normally expects the retailer to provide certain general services entirely free of charge. These you too are expected to provide; nowadays, they're part and parcel of normal store operations:

- Convenient store hours
- Courteous treatment by salespeople
- A pleasant store environment
- Prompt and efficient service
- The bagging (or wrapping) of items purchased
- The satisfactory resolution of complaints

Shoppers also associate other, more particular, services with certain kinds of stores or with the types of products they sell. Examples of these include *alterations* in apparel stores; *instructions,* as necessary, in stores selling sewing machines, cameras, arts and crafts supplies, and the like; *home delivery* of floor coverings, refrigerators, and other heavy or bulky merchandise; and *installation* of carpeting or linoleum, air conditioners, and so on. In the majority of instances, customers understand that these services may all involve time, effort, expertise, and expense, and they're perfectly willing to defray the charges, if reasonable.

## OTHER SHOPPER SERVICES TO CONSIDER

Catering to your customers' needs—for recognition, for ego-gratification, for convenience, or for comfort—can only help your business grow. Some services, of course, are quite inexpensive to provide, yet they can foster a great deal of goodwill. Others may be completely out of reach for your limited budget. Nevertheless, you ought to evaluate the following list of additional services, which are commonly encountered in retailing, in terms of your own store's needs. They appear in alphabetical order, not in order of their importance:

| | |
|---|---|
| bulletin board | restrooms |
| check acceptance | returns and adjustments |
| equipment rental | shopping baskets |
| gift certificates | special services |
| gift wrapping | telephone |
| quantity discounts | water fountain |
| refreshments | |

### Bulletin Board

If you own a food market, bakery, or other type of outlet that can generate lots of traffic, a bulletin board is an inexpensive yet welcome device to consider. Usually, the bulletin board is erected near the store entrance, as long as there's enough room for shoppers to pass to and fro without clogging the doorway. It's used by the public to post notices of local happenings; of articles for sale, trade, or purchase; and the like.

### Check Acceptance

Although it's entirely possible for you to be "stuck" occasionally with a bad check, most retail merchants need to and should accept checks. Note that I'm recommending the *acceptance* of checks, not necessarily the *cashing* of checks. You may, of course, wish to cash the check of a regular customer in an emergency. Under the right circumstances, your risk can be reduced considerably; at the same time, your customer welcomes the convenience you have provided and becomes more "store loyal." Which conditions reduce your risk? You lessen your chances of being stuck if the check is written for the exact amount of the purchase, if you examine two major forms of identification, and so on. (Other suggestions are given in chapter 19.)

## Equipment Rental

Hardware, garden supply, and appliance stores are among the many types of retail establishments that may find it useful to rent out tools and other equipment (floor waxers, lawn mowers, rug-shampooing machines, and the like) to their customers on a daily or weekly basis. This type of service can be priced so as to break even or, more commonly, to generate additional revenue for the store. Some service firms that do repair work lend out, free of charge, a substitute for the item under repair, such as a television set, sewing machine, steam iron, or electric toaster-oven.

## Gift Certificates

These represent not only a service, especially around holidays, but also an effective method of promoting sales. Printing up a few hundred each of several denominations ($5, $10, and $25, for instance) should prove relatively inexpensive if you use a stock form at your local printer's. Of course, you should number certificates individually and exert tight control over them in your store. You can advertise them through a simple point-of-purchase display card in your window and/or by the store register.

## Gift Wrapping

This is always appreciated. Many purchases are destined to be used as gifts, and the store's regular wrapping or bagging procedure isn't suitable. You can stock a variety of gift-wrap papers in various colors and designs for birthdays, weddings, and other purposes. You can purchase ready-made stick-on bows for decoration or buy a bow-making machine. Of course, if you want to, you can buy some rolls of ribbon in different widths, colors, and designs and tie your own bows. Either way, a nominal fee can be charged that defrays your costs and/or produces a tiny amount for extra profit. A related service for some retail businesses (gift shops, confectionery stores, and the like) is the packaging of merchandise for parcel-post shipment, either by the customer or by the store. Needed for this service are a supply of mailing cartons in a few different sizes, a roll of corrugated cardboard, sealing tape, and parcel-post labels.

## Quantity Discounts

Like gift certificates or equipment rental, this service can be useful as a promotional tool to boost sales. A higher sales volume can be encouraged by offering a discount of, say, 5 or 10 percent on a sale where the shopper buys perhaps six or more of an item—or on a purchase of $50 or $100. You might also give a free gift, worth perhaps $2 to $4, with a large purchase. A variation on this theme might be a "collect-the-register-tapes" promotion. In such a program, the customer who accumulates $100 or $200 in register tapes may choose from among a variety of gifts or perhaps be entitled to $10 or $20 in store merchandise. Another possibility is the extension of a discount on purchases made by religious or other organizations for purposes of fund-raising. Students who show their I.D. or G.O. cards may be granted discounts.

## Refreshments

As noted earlier, offering hot beverages or a cup of hot soup in cold weather is the kind of unexpected service that delights the shopper. In the same vein, why not consider giving out cool drinks of lemonade, soda, or even an ice cream pop in the dog days of summer. A women's apparel shop located in a metropolitan area created a flurry of excitement in the vicinity during an exceptionally hot and humid week, when the owners distributed free cups of ice cream to all who came in. The promotion was limited to the hours between 9:30 A.M. and noon, ordinarily a slow time of day. A banner on the store window announced the event. With a bit of thought, you may be able to come up with even more sales-stimulating variations on this theme.

## Restrooms

In most localities, you're legally obligated to provide restrooms for your employees. Yet many store retailers discourage the use of these facilities by the public, claiming that they can't keep out either strangers who enter without any intention of making a purchase or possible shoplifters. They also seem to have the attitude that restrooms are both difficult and costly to keep clean and stocked with the necessary supplies.

When you think about this attitude, it doesn't seem quite fair to the people from whom you derive your livelihood, does it? As an additional point to ponder, research conducted in supermarkets informs us that the longer the shopper remains in the store, the greater the size of the order rung up at the checkout point. While this may or may not be true at other kinds of stores, I suspect that if you make your place of business a more comfortable one in which to shop, you'll increase sales in the long run.

## Returns and Adjustments

As mentioned earlier, you're expected to resolve shopper complaints readily to your customers' satisfaction. In line with this attitude, you need to set store policy for handling returned merchandise. Good retail practice dictates that you immediately exchange any defective or store-damaged goods, along with an apology. Many articles are, however, brought back by customers for other reasons: wrong sizes, colors, brands, materials, and so on. Sometimes the customer complains about the quality, the price, or perhaps of having just received an identical item from someone else as a gift. When the returned merchandise is in apparently excellent, resalable condition, it would be far better to honor the request for a refund than to deny it. The cost of losing one customer is so much more expensive than the loss of the profit margin you earned on the sale of the one item.

Posting your policy on returns near the register is also wise. You may wish to put a time limit on returns, such as within two weeks or one month from the date of purchase, and request that they be accompanied by the sales check or register receipt. If shoppers bring back articles of merchandise after your "deadline" or without the receipt, you may wish to issue a credit slip for the amount of the purchase, exchangeable for other store merchandise (usually within thirty or sixty days). Sometimes a downward adjustment in the selling price may help solve the customer's problem; for example, you might deduct $5 or so from the price of a returned blouse because of slight damage or an imperfection.

## Shopping Baskets

A familiar sight for decades in our supermarkets and discount outlets, the shopping cart can, by extension or modification, be useful in other types of stores. Drugstores, arts and crafts supply shops, variety stores, and gift shops are a few examples. Putting in miniature carts that are half the size of their big supermarket brothers or just "carryalls" may be a welcome shopper convenience. These latter are inexpensive portable baskets, often of canvas stretched over a wire frame, with handles of either wire or canvas. They're usually stacked near the store checkout point, where customers can pick them up as they enter.

## Special Services

Whether provided free or for a nominal charge, certain services cater to customer wants and can actually help increase the sale of some articles of merchandise. Such services include engraving, monogramming, or affixing preformed initials to jewelry, women's pocketbooks, men's shirts, and many other ready-to-wear items. This type of service also includes the transfer of designs to T-shirts and other products.

## Telephone

Some retailers like to have a public pay telephone installed both as a service and as an attractor of additional traffic to the store. Other merchants permit the use of their own business telephone for necessary local calls. Either way, this is a service you can offer to your clientele at little or no cost.

## Water Fountain

This is often a welcome sight to the weary shopper, especially during the hot summer months. It can also be a blessing to the many older people who take medication one or more times each day, to control high blood pressure, for example. Of course, you can make things even more pleasant by supplying cups or by having a step in front of the fountain for small children.

## MARKETING SERVICE BUSINESSES

Operating profits for retailers of services compare favorably with those earned by merchandise retailers. (See tables 1–7 and 1–11 in chapter 1.) By way of illustration, here are the profit-before-taxes percentages of sales for a few of the services mentioned in table 1–7:

| | |
|---|---|
| Auto repairs | 3.7% |
| Car wash | 4.3 |
| Employment agency | 3.8 |
| Hair stylist | 3.7 |
| Health and fitness center | 3.8 |
| Photographic studio | 4.9 |

For purposes of comparison, consider the profit-before-taxes earned by these merchandise retailers (from table 1–11):

| | |
|---|---|
| Hardware store | 3.0% |
| Household appliances store | 2.6 |
| Restaurant | 3.3 |
| Shoe store | 2.8 |
| Jewelry store | 4.8 |
| Furniture store | 3.3 |
| Women's ready-to-wear store | 3.0 |

## How Services Differ from Products

As we have pointed out earlier, services differ markedly from products in several ways. The most obvious distinction is that while products are tangible, services are not. Moreover, most services also reflect the qualities of *perishability* and *inseparability*. Evidently, then, services need to be marketed in quite a different manner from the customary marketing of goods.*

---

* See: Dan R. E. Thomas, "Strategy Is Different in Service Businesses," *Harvard Business Review* 56 (July–August 1978), 158–65; Duane L. Davis, Joseph P. Guiltinan, and Wesley H. Jones, "Service Characteristics, Consumer Search, and the Classification of Retail Services," *Journal of Retailing* 55 (Fall 1979), 3–23.

Each of these distinguishing characteristics of services is discussed briefly below:

**Intangibility.** The consumer who pays for a Caribbean cruise or a ski weekend, optometric or dental services, a facial or a permanent at a beauty salon, an overnight stay at a motel, or an evening at the theater is unable to feel or touch the service. He or she can only *experience* the service. On the other hand, when consumers shop for bedspreads, sheets, or pillowcases; a new or used car; a child's bicycle or a set of golf clubs; or a suit or dress, they're able to touch, handle, and examine the goods closely before making the decision to buy.

This quality of products, as distinct from the intangibility of services, makes it easier for buyers to arrive at purchase decisions.

**Perishability.** Goods of all kinds can be warehoused, stocked in bins or on shelves, or put on display. They can be stored and held over for future sale. Services, on the other hand, cannot be stored, nor can they be manufactured in advance of their use by customers. Moreover, most services that aren't used go to waste; in short, they can be considered perishable. This quality of perishability creates difficulty for service retailers, who cannot store their services for use during peak periods.*

**Inseparability.** Again, unlike goods, services cannot be readily separated from the people who perform or provide them.** Manufacturers enlist the aid of intermediaries such as wholesalers and retailers to help distribute their products. Service retailers deliver their services directly to their customers.

Now, let's address the following problem: Given these three unusual characteristics of service offerings, what can retailers do to improve their marketing efforts?†

One helpful approach is to try to add some degree of tangibility, or "reality," to a service through the technique of *personalization*. As an example, you might consider enlisting the aid of several well-known figures, such as politicians or sports personalities, who have used (or will endorse) your service. Or, you might take pictures of your employees in the act of delivering the service, and then send the photos along with news releases to the media. If, for instance, your firm performs bookkeeping services for small companies, you might publicize several owners of those companies. If you service musical instruments by mail, your catalogs or brochures can carry endorsements by popular musicians or by professional music associations. If you offer laboratory services to the world of medicine, you can turn to noted physicians, medical schools, or hospitals.

Of course, you should seek as much publicity as you can by sending news releases to local newspapers and other publications, and to radio and television stations.

You can also benefit by preparing a concise code of ethics for your service firm.

---

* J. Patrick Kelly and William R. George, "Strategic Management Issues for the Retailing of Services," *Journal of Retailing* **58** (Summer 1982), 34.

** A. J. Magrath, "When Marketing Services, 4 Ps Are Not Enough," *Business Horizons* 29 (May–June 1986), 50.

† For some insights into how the service enterprise can increase productivity in marketing and other aspects, see James L. Heskett, "Lessons in the Service Sector," *Harvard Business Review* 65 (March–April 1987), 118–26.

Have it printed up, and post a copy of it in the store. Another worthwhile approach is to offer a firm guarantee of satisfaction, in writing, to your customers.

Finally, nothing will add more believability to your service operation than to demonstrate to the public that your employees are not only knowledgeable about, and skilled in, the work they perform but they are also courteous and completely honest.

## CREDIT—AND WHAT IT CAN DO FOR YOU

Can you visualize a situation where a new salesclerk calls out to the store manager, "Do we take cash?" You chuckle at this picture, for it's still a gross exaggeration. Yet it does point up the fact that credit in retailing is a way of life today. To consumers, credit is a convenience they have come to expect. Indeed, at times, when confronted with a big-ticket purchase, it can be a necessity.

As an SBA pamphlet explains:

> Retail credit is a part of everyday living in America. Retailers sell on credit and buy on credit from their suppliers who, in turn, order on credit from the companies who manufacture the merchandise. Many of their customers rely on credit because it allows them to buy what they want, when they want it, and to pay for it from future earnings. This wide use of credit in the Nation's economic system helps to maintain a balance between production, distribution, and consumption of goods.*

Yet many retailers don't like to extend credit, not only because of the attendant paperwork but also because they fear getting "stuck." Because they *do* get stuck on occasion, they have all the more reason to be ultra-careful with respect to who gets credit and how much credit to extend! Nevertheless, for retailers, credit can be a boon to sales as well as a way of differentiating their stores in a positive way from those of competitors. It's important for you to recognize the fact that people ordinarily do *not* carry large sums of money on their person, nor do they maintain sizable balances in their checking accounts. The majority of shoppers run quite low on funds each week until the next paycheck arrives to loosen things up for them.

Credit encourages these individuals to buy today, not tomorrow.

### Should You Offer Credit to Shoppers?

Should you extend credit to your customers? Consider this proven point: Shoppers who have charge accounts or open credit tend to spend more and to buy merchandise of better quality than "noncredit" (cash) customers. Customers with credit privileges are also more inclined toward store loyalty; they tend to shop at the store where they enjoy credit

---

* Wm. Henry Blake, "Retail Credit and Collections," *Small Business Bibliography No. 31* (Washington, D.C.: U.S. Small Business Administration, 1974), 2.

rather than visit other outlets of the same type. Moreover, when a retail firm extends credit, it's easy enough to build up, over time, a useful list of its charge customers. This list can then be worked occasionally, by mail or by telephone, to produce additional sales volume.

If you're still reluctant about extending credit, you should, at the very least, consider accepting the major credit cards (Visa, MasterCard, and the like). Despite the fact that you have to pay the issuing bank or organization a small percentage of such sales, you can be assured that the additional business brought in by the credit cards will more than compensate for your efforts.

## Types of Charge Accounts

In addition to honoring bank and other credit cards, several major types of purchase credit are offered by retailers. These include:

- The regular charge account (also called *open* or *regular* credit)
- The installment account
- The revolving charge account
- The layaway plan

**The Regular Charge Account.** This is the most frequently encountered type of credit in small-scale retailing. It's also the simplest of all to set up and maintain. Customers are permitted to buy goods without any down payment; they're simply billed for the amount owed. No service charges are added; customers are expected to pay within a specified time, usually thirty days from the date of invoice. A credit limit is usually set for each individual, and each may purchase merchandise up to that limit.

**The Installment Account.** This type of credit is used most often in connection with the purchase of expensive articles of merchandise, such as jewelry, fur coats, major appliances, and the like. The purchaser is asked to place a down payment on the item and to sign a conditional sales contract or perhaps a chattel mortgage. The balance due on the purchase is then paid out in installments over a specified period of time. The retailer adds a finance charge to cover the costs of extending this privilege. However, in some variations of this installment account (such as the ninety-day account or the budget plan), there may be no carrying charges added. It should be noted that some retail organizations sell their installment contracts to a bank or finance company to raise immediate cash; in such cases, the original customers continue to pay their installment payments to the new owners of the contracts.

**The Revolving Charge Account.** This type gets its name from the fact that the shopper is entitled to charge merchandise at the store up to a specific level, called the *credit* *ceiling.* Then, as payments on the account are received, the customer is entitled to make additional purchases on credit, again up to the ceiling. A finance charge is assessed against the account for the unpaid balance.

A popular variation is the *option credit* account, whereby the customer may elect to pay the bill in full within the usual time limit (frequently, thirty days) or make a partial payment on the account. If the first option is exercised, no finance charge is added.

**The Layaway Plan.** This method is used often by small retail firms because of the reduced risk involved. The store puts away merchandise for the shopper and holds it until the customer is ready to pay for it in full. A down payment is, of course, required; typically, it runs from 10 to 20 percent of the total amount. Since the retailer holds the merchandise, the only risk involved would seem to be the danger that the articles may become dated or "out-of-style," should the shopper decide not to buy. If this happens, the store may have to sell the merchandise off by marking down the selling price. The answer to this problem, of course, is to place a sensible time limit on such purchases.

## What to Do About Unpaid Bills

You must assume that, despite all precautions, some small percentage of your credit customers will be delinquent in paying their bills. For the most part, it's better that you think about trying to retain these accounts as customers than chafing over their outstanding balances. The loss of a regular customer can be more costly in the long run.

Keep careful records of your credit transactions and issue monthly statements to your accounts. A good procedure is to schedule your statements for mailing five or six days before the beginning of each month. This measure usually ensures that they are delivered before bills from other creditors arrive to vie for the same consumer dollars.

When an account is overdue, the subsequent statement should carry a notation to this effect, as a reminder to the customer. If this reminder fails to generate any action within a reasonable period of time, you may then have to think about initiating correspondence with the tardy payer.

Exhibit 12–1 offers a few useful suggestions regarding collection letters.

---

### EXHIBIT 12–1. ADVICE ABOUT COLLECTION LETTERS

One of the best methods to collect past-due accounts is through the use of personalized collection letters. Here, above all, tact must be used and the appeal varied because not everyone responds to the same appeal.

The first letter of the series should be a friendly reminder. There must be no hint of suspicion that the debtor does not fully intend to pay. In fact, willingness must be assumed, and the merchant must make the assumption evident. The debtor who is treated with suspicion responds in kind.

Pride is one of the strongest appeals to the debtor who has few or no tangible assets. The publicity accompanying suit . . . exposure of the fact that he is without assets . . . the humiliation

---

**EXHIBIT 12–1. CONTINUED**

of letting friends and neighbors know that he does not pay his debts . . . these may be used to good effect but only after frank and friendly appeals have proved to no avail.

Future need is another strong appeal. The customer should be shown what it means to have his right to credit destroyed by not paying promptly. He should be told that he might require credit in the future and be unable to obtain it if the right is abused.

Merchants usually use a series of four or five collection letters. Each becomes slightly more firm and more urgent than the last. The final letter usually sets a time limit and warns that legal action will be taken without further notice unless payment is made. Threats should never be made unless all other means have failed. Then, the merchant should do exactly what he says he will do.

These letters should be personal and written on the store's letterhead. They should be typed, not mimeographed, lithographed, or printed. Mailings which are ten days to two weeks apart are preferred. They should be mailed so that the debtor receives them on a Wednesday or Thursday rather than the first or the last day of the week.

*Source:* NCR Corporation, *Credits & Collections* (Dayton, Ohio: NCR Corporation, 1972), 19.

## TRUTH-IN-LENDING

In 1969 the Consumer Credit Protection Act became law. Familiarly known as *Truth-in-Lending,* this is essentially a disclosure law that you, the merchant, must comply with whenever you extend credit that carries a finance or other charge. It requires you to inform the customer of the terms and conditions of your credit arrangements, including the finance charge and the annual percentage rate.

With *closed-end* credit transactions (where you grant credit for a fixed amount over a fixed period of time, such as with a purchase made on the installment plan), you need to advise the buyer of certain information before credit is extended. Such disclosures are commonly made directly on the face of the contract to be signed. Among other facts, they include the cash price for the merchandise, the down payment required, the amount financed, the annual percentage rate charged, and the amounts and due dates of payments (see exhibit 12–2).

Finally, you should also know that, under the law, customers have the right to change their minds about the purchase of "big-ticket" items on the installment plan within three days of signing the contract. This is called the *right of rescission.*

## FOR FURTHER INFORMATION

### Books

Collier, David A. *Service Management: The Automation of Services.* Reston, Va.: Reston, 1985.

Connor, Richard A., Jr., and Jeffrey P. Davidson. *Marketing Your Consulting and Professional Services.* New York: Wiley, 1985.

## EXHIBIT 12–2. A RETAIL INSTALLMENT CONTRACT

Seller's Name: _____    Contract #_____

#### RETAIL INSTALLMENT CONTRACT AND SECURITY AGREEMENT

The undersigned (herein called Purchaser, whether one or more) purchases from _____ _____ (seller) and grants to _____ a security interest, in, subject to the terms and conditions hereof, the following described property.

| QUANTITY | DESCRIPTION | AMOUNT | |
|---|---|---|---|
| | | | |
| | | | |
| | | | |
| | | | |
| | | | |
| | | | |
| | | | |

Description of Trade-In:

| | Sales Tax | |
|---|---|---|
| | Total | |

#### Insurance Agreement

The purchase of insurance coverage is voluntary and not required for credit.    (Type of Ins.)
Insurance coverage is available at a cost of $_____ for the term of credit.

I desire insurance coverage

Signed _____ Date _____

I do not desire insurance coverage

Signed _____ Date _____

PURCHASER'S NAME _____
PURCHASER'S ADDRESS _____
CITY _____ STATE _____ ZIP _____

1. CASH PRICE                                    $_____
2. LESS: CASH DOWN
           PAYMENT        $_____
3.          TRADE-IN       _____
4.          TOTAL DOWN
            PAYMENT        _____ $_____

5. UNPAID BALANCE OF CASH
   PRICE                                          $_____
6. OTHER CHARGES:
   _____                               $_____
   _____                               $_____
7. AMOUNT FINANCED                                $_____
8. FINANCE CHARGE                                 $_____
9. TOTAL OF PAYMENTS                              $_____
10. DEFERRED PAYMENT PRICE
    (1+6+8)                                       $_____
11. ANNUAL PERCENTAGE RATE        _____%

Purchaser hereby agrees to pay to _____
_____ at their offices shown above the "TOTAL OF PAYMENTS" shown above in _____ monthly installments of $_____(final payment to be $_____) the first installment being payable _____ 19._____, and all subsequent installments on the same day of each consecutive month until paid in full. The finance charge applies from __(Date)__

Signed _____

Notice to Buyer: You are entitled to a copy of the contract you sign. You have the right to pay in advance the unpaid balance of this contract and obtain a partial refund of the finance charge based on the "Actuarial Method." [Any other method of computation may be so identified, for example, "Rule of 78's," "Sum of the Digits," etc.]

*Source:* Benny L. Kass, "Understanding Truth in Lending," *Small Marketers Aid No. 139* (Washington, D.C.: U.S. Small Business Administration, 1974), 7.

Kotler, P., and P. Bloom. *Marketing Professional Services.* Englewood Cliffs, N.J.: Prentice-Hall, 1984.

Lovelock, Christopher H. *Services Marketing: Text, Cases, and Readings.* Englewood Cliffs, N.J.: Prentice-Hall, 1983.

Wheatley, Edward W. *Marketing Professional Services.* Englewood Cliffs, N.J.: Prentice-Hall, 1983.

## Pamphlets Available from the Small Business Administration

### Management Aids

MA 1.007—"Credit and Collections"

## Booklets Available from the Superintendent of Documents

S/N 045-000-00165-2—*Managing the Small Service Firm for Growth and Profit*—$4.25.

S/N 045-000-00180-6—*Credit and Collections: Policy and Procedures*—$4.75.

S/N 045-000-00203-9—*Management Audit for Small Service Firms*—$4.50.

# V

# Managing Your Employees

# — 13 —

# Management Basics for the Small Store Owner

On the typical retail entrepreneur's ladder of priorities, any thoughts about store employees, the characteristics of good personnel administration, and how to manage people can most likely be located on the next-to-last rung. Small store retailers are usually more concerned about the "impersonal" phases of the business, such as the layout and decor of the store, the fixtures, the merchandise to be carried in stock, proper pricing procedures, and managing the ebb and flow of finances. Yet people are just as important as, if not more important than, any of these other facets of retail business administration—even in a self-service operation.

Why, then, do retail merchants take on this uninspired attitude toward their employees? Perhaps they do so because, in the early phase of the new small business, they're often required to do most of the work themselves. The new firm usually can't afford another salary (if, indeed, the owner himself is fortunate enough to be able to draw some modest salary from the outset!). Later on, despite the fact that the enterprise may be growing at a healthy rate, the retailer may postpone hiring even a part-timer until there appears to be no other way out. There's possibly another reason: Inexperienced shopkeepers typically lack knowledge about the hiring, training, and supervising of employees, and they are frequently unfamiliar with labor laws and regulations. Nevertheless, it's not enough to be the buyer, the salesperson, and the controller handling the financial end of the retail operation. Eventually, the burden becomes too great for one person. Store owners need to find others with whom to share the tasks and responsibilities, and they must take on the duties of a personnel administrator as well.

## SOME MANAGEMENT FUNDAMENTALS

Before proceeding with an expanded discussion of *personnel* management, it might prove insightful first to consider a definition or two of management itself—and then review some basic management tenets.

"Management," according to one source, "is the process undertaken by one or more persons to coordinate the activities of other persons to achieve results not attainable by any one person acting alone."* Another text describes management as "the process of planning, organizing, directing, and controlling the activities of employees in combination with other organizational resources to accomplish stated organizational goals."**

Thus, we may conclude that in a business organization: (1) management is a process; (2) two or more employees are involved; (3) their activities are "coordinated"; and (4) the managerial functions of planning, organizing, directing, and controlling are exercised.

Put more simply, a manager works with others to get the required job done.

Here's a distillation of some basic management concepts:

**Organization.** Ordinarily, we apply this term to the structured network of job positions within a company. Typically, the firm is structured or arranged in the form of a hierarchy, or "ladder." At the top of the ladder is the firm's owner or president.

An **organizational chart.** This is a schematic of the relationships among organizational positions. Positions are depicted by boxes, and the lines on the chart that connect the boxes represent lines of authority.

**Authority.** This is the power to make decisions and to take action. An organization's "chain of command" begins at the top and flows down through the hierarchy to the bottom—those employees at the lowest level in the organization.

**Line and staff.** In the retail company, most employees are *line* personnel. This means that they are in the firm's chain of command and "managed," or "supervised" by their superiors. In turn, they supervise their own subordinates.

Some employees are *staff* personnel: specialists and assistants who have no line responsibility within the organization. An assistant to the corporation's president is a staff person; so are window trimmers, security personnel, or maintenance employees.

**Unity of command.** Plainly stated, this tenet holds that each employee should report to only one superior—and not to more than one. This avoids confusion among workers and makes it easier to give direction.

**Span of management (span of control).** This bit of managerial philosophy holds that management should avoid assigning too many subordinates to a supervisor. There's a limit to how many people whose work interlocks can be supervised effectively by a single manager. The extent of the span may, of course, vary as a result of such factors as the supervisor's capabilities, the caliber of the employees being supervised, and the nature of the work itself.

The wider the span, the greater the danger of the manager losing control; the narrower the span, the more costly the job of supervision.

**Decentralization.** In an organization, to *centralize* is to keep all authority and power in a central place, usually at the firm's headquarters. Top management makes decisions in all areas of the business: finance, buying, merchandising, promotion, personnel, and so on.

---

* John M. Ivancevich, James H. Donnelly, Jr., and James L. Gibson, *Managing for Performance*, 3d ed. (Plano, Tex.: Business Publications, 1986), 7.
** Richard M. Steers, Gerardo R. Ungson, and Richard T. Mowday, *Managing Effective Organizations: An Introduction*. (Boston: Kent Publishing, 1985), 29.

When a company *decentralizes*, management delegates some of its authority and decision-making power, assigning some responsibilities to others in the organization. These others are then able to operate with some degree of autonomy. Of course, top management will still hold them accountable for the results of their actions.

As an example, the management of a drugstore or supermarket chain may decide to delegate the entire staffing procedure to the individual store managers. These executives will then be responsible for hiring, training, and, when necessary, firing their own store employees.

## PERSONNEL ADMINISTRATION

There are two distinct phases to personnel management. First is the purely mechanical, almost cut-and-dried handling of the more impersonal methods and techniques: creating plans, formulating policies, and setting up procedures so that the personnel function operates smoothly. This general area involves recruitment, selection, hiring, compensation, employee health and welfare, maintaining personnel records, and the like. Then there are the human aspects of administration: developing and training employees, managing their activities, counseling them, motivating and supervising them, and so on.

In your first year or two of business activity, you'll experience little need for long-range personnel planning. You know your employees well as individuals, and you learn how to handle them and get the most out of them by simple trial and error. But as the business grows larger, you find that layers of supervision are interposed between you as owner and your rank-and-file workers. By that time, you need an established set of specific personnel policies to run your operation properly. You also need a paperwork system that includes files containing employee application forms, letters of reference, evaluation forms, information for withholding taxes, notices of promotion or termination, and the like.

Insights into employee training, motivation, and supervision are offered in the next chapter. The balance of this chapter is devoted to the more impersonal aspects of personnel administration: the staffing process, compensating employees, and the more significant labor legislation with which the business organization needs to comply. As a prelude to the general topic area, you might be interested in the information presented in table 13–1. The data summarize the results of just part of a survey I made some years ago of department store personnel administrators located in California and New York.

## STAFFING YOUR STORE

Upon analysis, we can readily break down the staffing process into such activities as:

- Developing sources of prospective employees
- Establishing effective selection procedures
- Making use of employment application forms

### TABLE 13–1. CHARACTERISTICS SOUGHT IN SALES APPLICANTS

| Rank | Characteristic | Number of Stores Reporting | Percentage of Total |
|------|----------------|----------------------------|---------------------|
| 1 | Honest | 45 | 77.6 |
| 2 | Dependable | 35 | 60.3 |
| 3 | Enthusiastic | 31 | 53.4 |
| 4 | Neat | 30 | 51.7 |
| 5 | Self-motivating | 28 | 48.3 |
| 6 | Hardworking | 24 | 41.4 |
| 7 | Friendly | 23 | 39.7 |
| 8.5 | Alert | 21 | 36.2 |
| 8.5 | Cooperative | 21 | 36.2 |
| 10 | Intelligent | 20 | 34.5 |

*Source:* Irving Burstiner, "Current Personnel Practices in Department Stores," *Journal of Retailing* **51** (Winter 1975–76), 3–14, 86.

- Interviewing the more promising applicants
- Checking references
- Testing (when necessary)
- Orienting newly hired personnel

## Locating Prospective Employees

A natural tendency of many new retailers is to hire family members (children, nephews and nieces, cousins, in-laws) and/or friends as soon as job openings develop. If at all possible, you should try to avoid doing this. Your relationships with these individuals may interfere seriously with your in-store supervision of them, as well as impair their own contributions to your business. In the difficult, initial stage when you're trying to carve out a niche for yourself in the community, you certainly don't need additional headaches!

**Sources of Prospective Employees.** Most independent retailers experience little difficulty in attracting help for basic entry-level positions, such as those of salesclerk, stockperson, or delivery clerk. Usually, a simple "Help Wanted" sign in the window is all that's necessary. Even without a sign, applicants come in asking about jobs from time to time. These "walk-ins" constitute the single biggest—and, of course, the most inexpensive—source of potential employees in the retail trades. You can also reach prospects by telephoning or visiting local high schools (especially for part-time help), nearby colleges, and employment agencies. You can list your job openings with your local branch of the State Employment Service. Finally, if these common sources don't yield the desired results, you can resort to the classified section of your local daily or weekly newspaper and count on getting a number of replies.

When the time arrives to seek higher-level employees, such as store managers, assistant managers, part- or full-time buyers, and the like, you need to be more imaginative and aggressive in your pursuit of qualified personnel. Then you can resort to placing display advertisements in the newspaper or in a trade journal, contacting your independent buying office for assistance (if you have contracted with one), approaching "headhunters," or discussing your needs with suppliers and with other friendly retailers.

## HOW TO SELECT THE BEST CANDIDATES

Whether job seekers walk in your front door, come recommended by others, or reply to one of your ads, you would be wise to set up a screening and selection procedure. Preferably, this should be one that can grow into established company policy and that assures the best possible candidate for every opening. Common tools in the selection process are the application form, personal interview, reference check, and (in some instances) testing. We recommend one more for your protection: a two-or three-week "tryout" period.

### Beware of Discrimination

Before you begin preparing your selection procedure, bear in mind that federal law enjoins you from discriminating among job applicants on the basis of sex, age, race, or national origin. Make certain that you *always* comply with the letter of the law in *all* your employment practices: hiring, interviewing, reference checking, compensation, training, promotions, and so on.*

### How to Handle "Walk-Ins"

Even if you don't need anyone when job applicants come by, you owe these persons—and yourself as well—the courtesy of an informal chat. Try to determine if they're the kind of people you would like to have work for you and what skills they can bring to your organization. If your impression is favorable, take down their names, addresses, telephone numbers, and a few pertinent details for future reference. Advise them that you'll be sure to contact them should a need arise. Keep the information handy in a "future resource" file.

---

* For some worthwhile suggestions regarding employment practices, see Barry M. Farrell, "The Art and Science of Employment Interviews," *Personnel Journal* 65 (May 1986), 91–94; James D. Bell, James Castagnera, and Jane Patterson Young, "Employment References: Do You Know the Law?" *Personnel Journal* 63 (February 1984), 32–36; Philip S. Heller, "EEOC Standards: What Makes for a Good Test?" *Personnel Journal* 65 (July 1986), 102*ff.*

## The Employment Application Form

This form, when completed, serves two purposes: (1) it acts as a screening device, to help you decide whether the applicant meets your job requirements; and (2) it enables you to conduct a sensible employment interview. The form provides room for the applicant's name and address, educational background, previous job experience, pertinent abilities and skills, and personal information. You can avoid the time and expense of creating your own application forms by picking up the standard forms available at any business stationery store.

## The Employment Interview

The interview is a dialogue between the job applicant and the owner or manager that typically runs between ten and twenty minutes. Its major purpose is to help the interviewer gain insights into the applicant's speech, way of thinking, and personality, all of which complements the information already available on the application form. Larger retail firms, such as department and chain-store organizations, often require at least two interviews per applicant, each conducted by a different individual. The interviewer also attempts to assess other characteristics of the prospective employee: poise, tactfulness, posture, control of emotions, ability to communicate, and the like. It's wise to query gaps in the applicant's employment record, frequent changes in residence, evidence of job-hopping, and so on.

Reading a good book on how to conduct interviews will help you to improve your technique and give you some thoughts on ways to rate job applicants more objectively.*

## The Reference Check

You can generally expect that the personal references submitted by job hopefuls will reflect most positively on them. Perhaps the more important references to be checked are the former employers, particularly those who have directly supervised the worker in question. The best and quickest approach is to telephone those individuals personally, asking about your applicant and what the former supervisor thinks about him or her. A telephone call is preferable to a letter because most people dislike putting down negative comments in writing. It's fairly easy to discern any hesitancy on the part of the person at the other end of the telephone. A key question you may wish to ask toward the end of the conversation is, "Would you rehire him (or her) if you had another opening?"

---

* In addition to the Farrell article mentioned in the footnote on p. 193, you might find it useful to refer to Robert J. Solomon, "Using the Interview in Small Business," *Journal of Small Business Management* 22 (October 1984), 17–23.

## Testing

Although many books on personnel administration suggest that testing is a popular tool in selection, it's generally not indicated for the small retail operation because of the nature of typical store positions. Only if you plan to hire a secretary or typist, for example, might you find it worthwhile to have job applicants demonstrate their proficiency in relevant skills on standard tests.

## Tryout Period

Finally, you should adhere to a policy of placing all new employees "on probation" for two or three weeks before making your final commitment. For no matter how good your interviewing skills or your personal judgment might be, you can make mistakes in choosing among applicants. No screening technique can be better than observing the candidate's performance on the job.

## Orienting the New Employee

The Small Business Administration advises:

> Once you hire your employees, orient them to your business. Ask yourself: What does the employee *need to know?* What does the employee *wish to know?* Typically, the answers will point to three types of information employees should have:
>
> 1. *The job.* Training in his or her new job, introducing to fellow workers, touring the facility, explaining the work schedule or describing new equipment are examples of this type of information.
> 2. *Policy.* Procedures, rules, and regulations governing employment and items such as benefits and parking privileges are some you could cover under this topic.
> 3. *Background information.* The employee should be given a general organizational briefing that explains the history of the company, its objectives, its market, its customers, and the identity of executives and supervisors.
>
> Make new employees feel welcome. They are now part of your team. By taking the time to answer any questions in the early stage of their employment, you may save yourself problems later with employee relations. Let employees know what is expected of them and what they can expect from the job and your company.*

The first ten days on the job probably constitute the most critical period for the new employee in terms of developing good work habits, fostering attitudes, and ensuring adequate productivity. Instruction during this time needs to be thorough, precise, and clear, and it must be provided in a positive manner. If you're too busy to orient your new

---

* Terry L. Maris and Robert L. Mathis, "Organizing and Staffing a Small Business," *Management Aid 238* (Washington, D.C.: U.S. Small Business Administration, 1979), 5–6.

worker properly, then you need to delegate this responsibility to your top assistant or to your most experienced employee. Ask someone qualified to act as "Big Brother" or "Big Sister" to the newcomer. The employee needs to know a great deal about your store and its policies, about the merchandise you sell, about *how* to sell it, about your prices, and about your customers.

When your retail business has grown considerably larger, you may alleviate much of the orientation problem by distributing an employees' handbook to your new people. For the time being, you can use the sample table of contents of a typical handbook, listed in exhibit 13–1, for ideas of what "new hires" are interested in knowing about working for you.

## PAYING YOUR EMPLOYEES

Another decision area for you to explore is that of how best to compensate your employees. You need to devise a prudent compensation plan suited to your business long before you hire your first worker. The plan should:

- Be seen by your employees as a fair and just reward for their efforts
- Instill in them a feeling of security
- Compare favorably with the prevailing pay scales in the community
- Encourage good workers to remain with your store, instead of gravitating to your competitors

Further, your employees want to know how much they can expect to earn from Day 1. They would also like to have some idea of when and how often they can look forward to pay increases and if there's a future for them with your firm. Assuming satisfactory performance along the way, how soon will they be given additional responsibilities? When may they expect a promotion? How high can they go?

### Pay Plans

Well entrenched in the field of retailing, the *straight-salary method* is the typical approach to employee compensation—and the one most suited to the needs of the vast majority of retail establishments. Other approaches—such as the *straight-commission, salary-plus-commission,* and *commission-and-bonus* plans—are relatively rare in small-scale retailing. Of course, there are exceptions: For example, the commission-only and the salary-plus-commission methods are found among stores that sell furniture, automobiles, floor coverings, men's clothing, and some other types of merchandise.

**EXHIBIT 13–1. A SAMPLE TABLE OF CONTENTS FOR AN EMPLOYEES' HANDBOOK**

Employee Handbook
SAMPLE TABLE OF CONTENTS

1—WELCOME MESSAGE
2—HISTORY OF THE COMPANY
3—THIS IS OUR BUSINESS
4—YOU AND YOUR FUTURE
5—WHAT YOU WILL NEED TO KNOW
- Working Hours
- Reporting to Work
- "Time Clock"
- Rest Periods
- Absence from Work
- Reporting Absences
- Employment Record
- Pay Period
- Shift Premiums
- Safety and Accident Prevention
- Use of Telephones
- How to Air Complaints

6—THESE ARE YOUR BENEFITS
- Vacations
- Holidays
- Group Insurance
- Hospitalization and Surgical Benefits
- Free Parking
- Training Program
- Christmas Bonus
- Savings Plan
- Profit-Sharing Plan
- Suggestion Awards
- Jury Duty
- Military Leave
- U.S. Old Age Benefits
- Unemployment Compensation
- Equal Employment Opportunity

7—THESE SPECIAL SERVICES ARE FOR YOU
- Credit Union
- Education Plans
- Medical Dispensary
- Employee Purchases
- Company Cafeteria
- Monthly Magazine
- Annual Outing
- Bowling League
- Baseball Team

8—INDEX or TABLE OF CONTENTS

*Source:* "Pointers on Preparing an Employee Handbook," *Management Aid No. 197* (Washington, D.C.: U.S. Small Business Administration, 1975), 3.

Proponents of commission-only plans maintain that they bring out the best in their salespeople, that money is a great—indeed the only—motivator, and that good salespeople "trade up" their customers in order to earn higher commissions. They believe that although paying people salaries may make them feel more secure, it robs them of their drive. "What's the sense of pushing?" says the salaried individual, according to those who favor commission. "My salary's the same whether I try hard or take it easy." Commission-only advocates also point out the unfairness of compensating high and low producers alike with the same pay. When the commission plan is used, management may also derive comfort from the thought that not a dollar is paid out to employees until sales are made for the firm.

In my judgment, however, it's debatable whether high-pressure tactics such as those evidenced by some salespeople paid on a commission basis should ever be used in the retail store. Without the artificial stimulus of the straight-commission approach, weeding out the poorer producers and maintaining an adequate level of productivity throughout the selling staff are still possible through good supervision. I prefer the straight-salary method, which provides steady, week-in and week-out income to the employee. It's also without question the best plan for nonselling employees.

To encourage more courteous and prompt attention to customers, you can perhaps "sweeten the pie" even more for your store's salespeople by tacking on a small percentage of sales to their regular salaries. This additional commission of, say, 0.5 to 1 percent of sales, when shared by two or three people as a "bonus" at the end of the month, is a morale booster. If you have a manager who is responsible for the entire operation of the store, you might want to consider a similar arrangement for that person as well.

## Fixing Salary Levels

Having decided that you'll use the straight-salary approach, your next problem is to determine specific salary ranges for each position in your retail organization. These must be set with an eye toward the type of work performed, the level of responsibility, typical salaries for equivalent positions in your area, and so on.

To assist you in this task, prepare complete *job descriptions* for all positions in your firm: stock clerk, salesperson, cashier, assistant manager, store manager, assistant buyer, and so forth. These will help you in estimating the kind of salaries you should pay. You then need to decide on a minimum and maximum compensation figure for each job: what to pay the employee in that position when first hired, with a bit of built-in leeway for negotiation; how much to give that person for a first raise; the amount and timing of subsequent increases; and the "cap" or top figure you'll pay in that job. For example, a part-time salesperson whom you intend to start at $5.00 an hour might be bracketed to rise to a maximum of $8.50 an hour within two years. The job holder then remains at that level until promoted to a higher position in your store. You might schedule the first hourly increase of, perhaps, 50¢ or $1.00 for three months after employment to encourage continued good performance. After that, raises may be given every six months, following performance evaluations.

Although many of the department stores and larger chain-store organizations rate their employees' performance annually, your personnel contingent is tiny by comparison, and you ought to review their contributions more often. Six months is long enough to wait; besides, it's only fair to let people know about below-par performance to give them the opportunity to improve before it's too late! Also, if the evaluation turns out to be a rave review, this official pat on the back is marvelous for morale!

## Fringe Benefits to Think About

You'll come to realize that salary isn't everything to an employee. Pleasant working conditions, good interpersonal relations, fair and effective supervision, recognition for a job well done, the learning of new tasks, and opportunities for promotion are also essential to employee job satisfaction and morale. In addition, no compensation package is complete without incorporating some "fringe benefits." Today's workers expect them, no matter how small their employers. Even when not unionized, employees look for such basic benefits as holidays off with pay, paid vacations, and sick days.

**Paid Holidays.** In our nation's factories, offices, and retail stores, workers expect to spend certain holidays during the year at home. If these happen to fall during the week, they do not want to lose a day's pay. In the retailing field, unfortunately (or fortunately, depending on your point of view!), holidays such as Christmas, Columbus Day, Thanksgiving Day, and others can be important selling days. Indeed, the mass merchandisers often run special sales events on these dates, and the stores are crowded. The stores must be staffed to cope with the heavy traffic. Should you need to have your employees work in the store on such holidays, you'll find that "double-time pay" is expected at the very least.

**Vacations.** A rather common rule-of-thumb approach is to offer a three-day vacation with pay to employees who have worked for six months in your store—and a one-week vacation to those who have had a full year of experience. After a year, you may decide to offer two weeks with pay following two or three years of steady employment and, perhaps, up to three weeks for those who have been in your employ for seven to ten years.

**Sick Days.** People do get sick occasionally. Some independent retailers are penny-wise and pound-foolish in this regard, refusing to pay their employees for any days lost due to illness. The wiser approach is to cater to your employees' need for security and compensate them for time lost because of illness. An acceptable rule of thumb, and one by which you most certainly can live, is to allow up to three sick days for each six months of steady employment in your business. After a year, of course, you need to limit sick time to no more than a week of absence, except perhaps for your top employees.

**Other Fringes.** In time, you may want to investigate other kinds of employee benefits: group insurance (life and/or accident and health), retirement plans, profit-sharing, stock ownership (if you have a corporation), bonuses, and so on.* One "extra" that you can grant to your people immediately is the employee discount. Giving your employees a discount (10 to 15 percent is the average, but some retailers go as high as 20 or 25 percent) on whatever merchandise they purchase in your store isn't only a good human-relations gesture, it can also be a boon to your sales picture.

## LABOR LEGISLATION

To run their operations properly, small store owners need to know the details of the following federal laws, enacted over the years to aid and protect employees:

- *National Labor Relations Act (1935).* Gave workers the right to organize and engage in collective bargaining.
- *Fair Labor Standards Act (1938).* Established a minimum hourly wage, pay for overtime work, and outlined regulations for minors who are employed.
- *Equal Pay Act (1963).* Prohibited pay discrimination in the workplace: Men and women who do the same work must receive identical compensation.
- *Civil Rights Act (1964).* Banned discrimination in a firm's hiring approaches because of race, color, sex, national origin, or religion.
- *Age Discrimination in Employment Act (1967).* Banned discrimination in the employment process because of age.
- *Occupational Safety and Health Act (1970).* Mandated that companies maintain a safe workplace for their employees.
- *Equal Employment Opportunity Act (1972).* Amended the earlier Civil Rights Act to cover firms employing fifteen or more people.
- *Employee Retirement Income Security Act (1974).* Protected the pension rights of employees, including the accrual of benefits and vesting rights.
- *Mandatory Retirement Act (1978).* Barred the practice of requiring workers to retire at age sixty-five.
- *Job Training Partnership Act (1983).* Facilitated grants to states for the training of economically disadvantaged persons.

## FOR FURTHER INFORMATION

### Books

Beach, Dale S. *Personnel: The Management of People at Work.* New York: Macmillan, 1985.

Dubrin, Andrew J. *Contemporary Applied Management,* 2d ed. Plano, Tex.: Business Publications, 1985.

---

* For an interesting "menu" of employee benefit programs available to small companies, see Thomas J. Murray, "Flexible Benefits for Small Firms," *Duns Business Monthly* 128 (August 1986), 76*ff.*

Flippo, Edwin B. *Personnel Management,* 6th ed. New York: McGraw-Hill, 1984.

French, Wendell L. *Human Resources Management.* Boston: Houghton Mifflin, 1986.

Halloran, Jack. *Personnel and Human Resource Management.* Englewood Cliffs, N.J.: Prentice-Hall, 1986.

Henderson, R. *Compensation Management: Rewarding Performance,* 4th ed. Englewood Cliffs, N.J.: Prentice-Hall, 1985.

Hitt, Michael A., R. Dennis Middlemast, and Robert L. Mathis. *Management: Concepts and Effective Practice,* 2d ed. St. Paul, Minn.: West, 1986.

Ivancevich, John M., and William F. Glueck. *Foundations of Personnel: Human Resource Management,* 3d ed. Plano, Tex.: Business Publications, 1986.

Kennedy, J., and K. Grace. *Selection Interviewing.* Englewood Cliffs, N.J.: Prentice-Hall, 1986.

Novit, M. *Essentials of Personnel Management,* 2d ed. Englewood Cliffs, N.J.: Prentice-Hall, 1986.

Robbins, Stephen P. *Personnel: The Management of Human Resources,* 2d ed. Englewood Cliffs, N.J.: Prentice-Hall, 1982.

Rosenbloom, J., and G. Hallman. *Employee Benefit Planning,* 2d ed., Englewood Cliffs, N.J.: Prentice-Hall, 1986.

Sayles, L., and G. Strauss. *Managing Human Resources,* 2d ed. Englewood Cliffs, N.J.: Prentice-Hall, 1981.

Steers, Richard M., Gerardo R. Ungson, and Richard T. Mowday. *Managing Effective Organizations: An Introduction.* Boston: Kent, 1985.

Stoner, James A. *Management,* 3d ed. Englewood Cliffs, N.J.: Prentice-Hall, 1986.

Terry, George R., and Stephen G. Franklin. *Principles of Management,* 8th ed. Homewood, Ill.: Irwin, 1982.

Twomey, David P. *A Concise Guide to Employment Law: EEO and OSHA.* Cincinnati: South-Western, 1986.

Werther, William B., Jr., and Keith Davis. *Personnel Management and Human Resources,* 2d ed. New York: McGraw-Hill, 1985.

## Pamphlets Available from the Small Business Administration

### Management Aids

MA 2.010—"Planning and Goal Setting for Small Business"

MA 2.020—"Business Plan for Small Retailers"

MA 2.022—"Business Plan for Small Service Firms"

MA 5.001—"Checklist for Developing a Training Program"

MA 5.007—"Staffing Your Stores"

MA 5.008—"Managing Employee Benefits"

## Booklets Available from the Superintendent of Documents

S/N 045-000-00185-7—*Job Analysis, Job Specifications, and Job Descriptions*— $4.50.

S/N 045-000-00186-5—*Recruiting and Selecting Employees*—$4.50.

S/N 045-000-00189-0—*Managing Retail Salespeople*—$4.75.

S/N 045-000-00191-1—*Training and Developing Employees*—$4.50.

S/N 045-000-00196-2—*Employee Relations and Personnel Policies*—$4.50.

# 14

# Training and Motivating Your Employees

A new business, if it's successful, invariably grows. The quantity of work to be performed expands. As it does, additional personnel must be sought, hired, and trained to fill the newly created job openings. Relationships among the employees multiply rapidly. Coincidentally, the web of internal communications needed to ensure the smooth operation of the growing enterprise becomes ever more intricate. Yet, all along the way, the necessary work activities must progress without interruption. This development presents a challenge for the store owner.

## BUILDING YOUR ORGANIZATION

To meet the challenge, you need to organize your "personnel resources" just as skillfully as you organize your financial resources, your store, your merchandising and promotion, and other aspects of the business. You need to think about grouping similar work responsibilities and determine to whom they ought to be allocated. You have to decide how much authority to delegate and who should receive it. You need to match people to duties, to responsibilities, to authority, and to each other as well, so that an atmosphere of harmony and spirited productivity characterizes your place of business.

You need to think and plan ahead. You should know what your organization looks like at this very moment and, if all goes well, what it ought to look like in, say, three years from this date.

### Work on Your Organizational Chart

To obtain a useful picture of your present organization, draw an organizational chart that shows the major work activities now performed in your store, and fill in the names and perhaps titles of the people in charge of these activities. The chart may look something like the one in exhibit 14–1, if yours is just a one-person operation, or like the one in exhibit 14–2, if you have several employees. The organization of a still larger retail firm is displayed in exhibit 14–3.

**EXHIBIT 14–1. FUNCTIONAL ORGANIZATION FOR A ONE-PERSON RETAIL STORE**

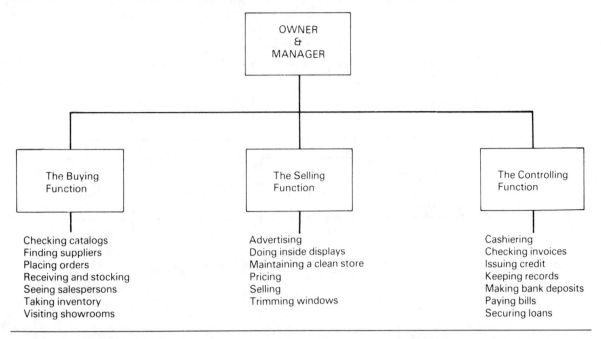

*Source:* Irving Burstiner, *The Small Business Handbook: A Comprehensive Guide to Starting and Running Your Own Business,* rev. ed. (New York: Prentice Hall Press, 1989), 99.

**EXHIBIT 14–2. ORGANIZATION CHART FOR A SMALL RETAIL FIRM**

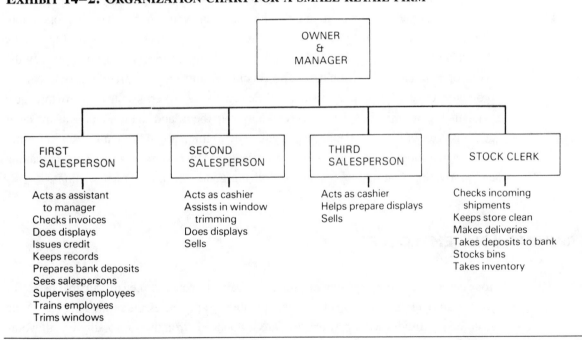

*Source:* Irving Burstiner, *The Small Business Handbook: A Comprehensive Guide to Starting and Running Your Own Business,* rev. ed. (New York: Prentice Hall Press, 1989), 100.

**EXHIBIT 14–3. ORGANIZATION OF THE GROWING STORE**

```
                              ┌──────────┐
                              │  Owner   │
                              └────┬─────┘
         ┌──────────┬──────────────┼──────────────┐
    ┌────┴────┐ ┌───┴────┐    │          ┌────┴─────┐
    │ Finance │ │Budgets │    │          │Personnel │
    └─────────┘ └────────┘    │          └──────────┘
```

| Department managers (buyers) as required | Operating superintendent | Sales promotion manager | Office manager |
|---|---|---|---|
| | Maintenance<br>Protection<br>Receiving<br>Marking<br>Storage<br>Delivery | Copywriting<br>Artwork<br>Production<br>Display | Pay records<br>Accounting<br>Correspondence<br>Insurance<br>Cash<br>Tax reports<br>Credit |

*Source:* John W. Wingate and Seymour Helfant, "Small Store Planning for Growth," *Small Business Management Series No. 33* (Washington, D.C.: U.S. Small Business Administration, 1977), 30.

Now you should consider what you expect your organization to look like in three years in light of the long-range planning you have done. Draw a chart corresponding to this new, enlarged organization, and put down the date you expect to have it in operation. This then becomes your "goal"; you need to devise ways of reaching your objective by the scheduled time, as well as a detailed timetable, of course. You need to specify the types of new employees you'll require, decide if any of your present people can be promoted or shifted to new responsibilities, estimate when you'll have to hire new personnel, determine how long it will take to train them, and so on. Finally, as the chief administrator of your retail enterprise, you need to think about both initial and refresher training, developing knowledgeable and effective supervisors to assist you, managing and motivating your employees, and exercising good, sensible human relations.

## TRAINING YOUR EMPLOYEES

Your employees are extensions of yourself. Trained properly, they're valuable assets to your retail operation, perhaps the most valuable of all your assets in the long run. Your customers' attitudes toward your store are influenced strongly—favorably or unfavorably—by their contacts with your salespeople. Indeed, these interactions represent one of the most powerful components of store image. Moreover, effective training and development programs are bound to improve employee performance.*

Frankly, half the job of motivating your employees is accomplished once they have had the right training. When you train employees, they feel that you're interested in them and that they can look forward to a future with you.

## Does Training Pay?

Actual, on-the-job studies of the contributions made by salespeople in retail businesses are rarely found in the literature. However, an article published some two decades ago reported the results of sales training in a midwestern department store (a member of Allied Stores). One small group of store salespeople were given eight half-hour training sessions; a similar group did not participate in the training, thus serving as a "control" for the test. The two groups' productivity was investigated by comparing their respective *average hourly rate of sales* (the total sales volume earned divided by the total number of hours worked). The trained group increased their sales during the training period by 40 percent. Moreover, when the total sales gains were measured against the total training costs, the return in sales measured an astounding 1,657.9 percent.**

Training pays. Training your people properly should help to:

- Increase your sales
- Lower your costs
- Develop your employees' skills more rapidly
- Lower your rate of employee turnover
- Improve worker morale
- Lead to better teamwork
- Raise employee productivity

To train your people properly, you need to:

- Ascertain the training needs of your employees
- Set specific goals for the training to accomplish
- Plan the training program(s)
- Choose appropriate training methods
- Train your people well
- Evaluate the outcome
- Make improvements in your program(s) for the next time around

---

* George H. Lucas, Jr., "The Relationships Between Job Attitudes, Personality Characteristics, and Job Outcomes: A Study of Retail Store Managers," *Journal of Retailing* **61** (Spring 1985), 35–62.

** Ann Karlson, "Does Retail Training Pay?" *Training in Business and Industry* (February 1969), 25–28.

In the early, formative stage of your organization, there's little need to develop a comprehensive training program in the formal sense, using classroom (*vestibule*) training. Eventually, however, sufficient expansion may take place to prompt you into thinking about formal training programs and about management development as well. You'll become eager to develop one or more "middle managers" to help you guide and supervise the growing organization.

When your firm is large enough, you can profit by reading the "Checklist for Developing a Training Program" (MA 5.001), listed in the bibliography at the end of this chapter. Though designed originally for the small manufacturing firm, the material it contains can be invaluable to the small retail organization as well. For example, each of the questions below serves as a heading for a series of thought-stimulating questions to help you prepare a worthwhile program:

- What is the goal of the training?
- What does the employee need to learn?
- What type of training?
- What method of instruction?
- What audio-visual aids will you use?
- What physical facilities will you need?
- What about the timing?
- Who will be selected as instructor?
- Who should be selected?
- What will the program cost?
- What checks or controls will you use?
- How should the program be publicized?

## But What About Right Now?

In the meantime, though, your organization is still a small one. What do you do in such circumstances? For the new worker, you may find a useful modus operandi in the checklist shown in exhibit 14–4. You can also tackle the problem head-on, simply by devoting one or two hours to devising an informal on-the-job training program for current and future employees. Exhibit 14–5 may be of assistance in this regard. Devised by the owners of a small chain of confectionery stores, it depicts a six-week schedule of the topics to be learned by new salesclerks and to be taught by the store manager. You can use the identical approach, substituting your own work details for those in the chart and shortening or lengthening the number of weeks. It's a good idea to make up one of these charts for each different job title in your retail firm.

In your first year or two of business, your training approaches will be for the most part on-the-job training, including demonstration and coaching. Plan to develop man-

## EXHIBIT 14–4. CHECKLIST FOR INSTRUCTING A WORKER

Four steps are necessary for giving a worker proper instructions about a new task:

1. *Prepare the learner* by:
   Putting him at ease
   Telling him what you are going to teach him
   Getting him interested in learning
   Finding out what he already knows
   Giving him credit for what he already knows

2. *Present the task to be learned* by:
   Giving him one step at a time
   Telling him how to do the task
   Showing him how the task is done
   Stressing key points of the task
   Presenting no more than he can master

3. *Let the learner do the task under supervision* by:
   Having him explain the task
   Having him show you how the task is done
   Correcting his mistakes

4. *Test the learner* by:
   Asking him for information about the task
   Checking on his performance and speed
   Checking on his quality
   Correcting mistakes—reteaching the points he may have missed
   Being sure that he can do the task without help

*Source:* William B. Logan, "Training the Technical Serviceman," *Small Marketers Aid No. 117* (Washington, D.C.: U.S. Small Business Administration, 1973), 3.

agers and specialized personnel eventually; this goal may involve other instructional techniques, such as:

| | |
|---|---|
| assigned readings | job rotation |
| college courses | management seminars |
| group discussions | programmed instruction |
| home-study courses | sensitivity training |
| instructional cassettes | special assignments |

## STORE LEADERSHIP

Managing employees isn't just a question of hiring, assigning duties, issuing orders, preparing work schedules, and the like. Directing the behavior of store personnel calls for skilled interpersonal relations, a familiarity with the dynamics of groups at work, proficiency in communication, substantial teaching capability, lots of empathy, and a good-humored sense of proportion. You see, one doesn't really *manage* people. You manage things and perhaps wild beasts. You *lead* people. The difference isn't at all subtle.

**EXHIBIT 14–5. SALESCLERK TRAINING GUIDE FOR A SMALL CONFECTIONERY CHAIN**

| WEEK I | WEEK II | WEEK III |
|---|---|---|
| Job duties (give typed job description).<br>Company history (where we stand; our strengths).<br>Our merchandise and prices (give inventory sheet).<br>Location of merchandise.<br>Bagging and wrapping.<br>Using the scales.<br>Filling bulk candy trays.<br><br>SALES TRAINING (assign to sponsor). | Sales slip procedure.<br>Register procedure.<br>Want-slip procedure.<br>Charge accounts.<br>Freshening up displays.<br>Store lighting, awning and strips, air conditioning, etc.<br>Stock rotation, bins.<br>Showcase and counter care.<br><br>SALES TRAINING/Selling | Cashiering.<br>Receiving procedure.<br>Helps in checking incoming deliveries.<br>Customer returns and exchanges.<br>Credit slips.<br>Store bank procedure.<br>Making bows.<br>Gift wrapping.<br><br>SALES TRAINING/Selling. |

| WEEK IV | WEEK V | WEEK VI |
|---|---|---|
| Checks incoming deliveries.<br>Prepares bank deposits.<br>Inventory procedure.<br>Merchandise transfers.<br>Parcel post procedures.<br>Initial display training.<br>Helps prepare displays.<br><br>SALES TRAINING/Selling. | Store opening procedure.<br>Store closing procedure.<br>Helps take inventory.<br>Makes bank deposits under supervision.<br>Display training.<br>Puts up interior display under supervision.<br><br>SALES TRAINING/Selling. | (Give store keys).<br>Opens store.<br>Closes store.<br>Makes bank deposits.<br>Creates and puts up interior display.<br>Helps in preparing window displays.<br>Gift basket preparation.<br><br>SALES TRAINING/Selling. |

*Source:* Compiled by the author.

Here are just a few of the literally dozens of active verbs in our language that bear connotations linked to the *leading* of people:

| | | |
|---|---|---|
| advising | encouraging | orienting |
| clarifying | explaining | persuading |
| communicating | facilitating | showing |
| complimenting | guiding | stimulating |
| convincing | inducing | suggesting |
| counseling | instructing | telling |
| demonstrating | motivating | training |

Leaders are individuals who guide others. As the leader of your store personnel, your task is to direct your employees so that the necessary tasks are done and your objectives are met.

## Leadership Styles

Much has appeared in print about leadership "styles." Leaders may be highly autocratic in their behavior, highly democratic, or somewhere in between the two extremes. What works well for one leader in a given environment with one group of people may not work at all for another leader in a different setting with a second group—or, for that matter, for a different leader in the original environment with the first group. The great diversity of leadership types boils down to the thesis, generally accepted nowadays, that leadership is a complex set of behaviors that involves three ultracomplex dimensions: the person who is doing the leading, those who follow, and the situation itself.

Frequently, when the pros and cons of several styles are expounded, the reader tends to imitate the style described as yielding the best overall results. This conclusion is foolish; the big problem in doing so is that it's usually *not* the individual's "natural" style. Not only does such copying tend to create a strained situation for the leader and for followers, but employees can sense the unreality of their boss's behavior and become confused. I suggest that you follow your own native bent in "handling" your employees, always bearing in mind the necessity for observing fairness, consistency, and good human relations. Along these lines, you can profit by looking over the suggestions listed in exhibit 14–6.

---

### EXHIBIT 14–6. SUGGESTIONS FOR IMPROVING HUMAN RELATIONS

1. Improve your own general understanding of human behavior.
2. Accept the fact that others do not always see things as you do.
3. In any differences of opinion, consider the possibility that you may not have the right answer.
4. Show your employees that you are interested in them and that you want their ideas on how conditions can be improved.
5. Treat your employees as individuals; never deal with them impersonally.
6. Respect differences of opinion.
7. Insofar as possible, give explanations for management actions.
8. Provide information and guidance on matters affecting employees' security.
9. Make reasonable efforts to keep jobs interesting.
10. Encourage promotion from within.
11. Express appreciation publicly for jobs well done.
12. Offer criticism privately, in the form of constructive suggestions for improvement.
13. Train supervisors to be concerned about the people they supervise, the same as they would be about merchandise or materials or equipment.
14. Keep your staff up-to-date on matters that affect them.
15. Quell false rumors, and provide correct information.
16. Be fair!

---

*Source:* Martin M. Bruce, "Human Relations in Small Business," *Small Business Management Series No. 3*, 3d ed. (Washington, D.C.: U.S. Small Business Administration, 1969), 14–15.

---

## HOW TO MOTIVATE YOUR EMPLOYEES

Managing, or rather *leading,* your people to want to work at their tasks with enthusiasm and spirit calls for your understanding and appreciation of that energizing concept called *motivation.* A motive is an impetus, a force, a drive that pushes a person. Motives lie behind all of our behaviors, though often we're not aware of them. As the owner of a small store, you will quickly learn that you can't motivate an employee with salary alone, nor even by offering special financial incentives. Much more is needed; for instance, ponder this thought, offered in an article about job design in the retail setting:

> Managers need to promote a sense of accomplishment in a job well done among their employees through positive reinforcement. Employees should have opportunities for growth and advancement, increasing responsibility, and a work situation which fosters positive attitudes about the supervision they receive.*

Studies of the motivational aspects of worker behavior reveal that employees may be motivated ("turned on") or demotivated ("turned off") by a number of factors, such as:

- Clarity and attainability of work goals
- Co-workers
- Firm's policies and procedures
- Handling of discipline
- Internal communications
- Job security
- Management's interest in its employees
- Nature of the work
- One's immediate supervisor
- Opportunity for advancement
- Participation in decision making**
- Recognition
- Salary or other compensation
- Training
- Working conditions

An article in *Personnel Journal* suggested that familiarity with the various sets of basic needs of individuals is helpful in learning how to motivate employees. Some techniques that supervisors can employ in light of those needs are listed in exhibit 14–7.

---

* Carol H. Anderson, "Job Design: Employee Satisfaction and Performance in Retail Stores," *Journal of Small Business Management* 22 (October 1984), 14–15. For further insights into worker motivation, see also Kenneth A. Kovach, "What Motivates Employees? Workers and Supervisors Give Different Answers," *Business Horizons* 30 (September–October 1987), 58–65.

** A well-known characteristic of Japanese-style management thinking, this approach can be "more easily introduced into American small businesses than into big businesses." See Matthew C. Sonfield, "Can Japanese Management Techniques Be Applied to American Small Business?" *Journal of Small Business Management* 22 (July 1984), 21–22.

## EXHIBIT 14–7. MOTIVATION: APPEALING TO PEOPLE'S BASIC NEEDS

*Recognition*

Call people by name when you speak to them.

Treat them with the friendly politeness that you do a friend.

Show interest in their family and other things they are particularly interested in.

Listen to what they have to say.

Watch for anything they do well and compliment them on it. (Sometimes compliment them when others can hear.)

Compliment them on specific things, not just generalities.

Notice things that other people don't notice and compliment them on these unexpected things. Above all, the compliment must be genuine and sincere.

Smile!

*Opportunity*

Encourage employees to look for new and better ways of doing work. Expand work by enrichment.

Listen to any new idea anyone has. (Use it if it's sound. If you can't use it, explain why you can't and urge them to develop another one.)

Give employees as much freedom as they can handle.

Encourage them to feel responsible for seeing that their work is carried out well.

Give them full credit for anything good they have done when you talk to their supervisors.

If they are good workers, help them get a promotion.

*Belonging*

Explain to new workers their job, the section, and the company.

Take them around and introduce them to other employees, explaining who each one is and what their jobs are.

Try to make each person feel needed by the company.

Get someone to buddy with a new employee while learning the ropes.

Explain to employees why their job is important and how it fits into the big operation, so they will be proud of their job.

Encourage social and recreational get-togethers for all the people under you and their families.

Encourage your people to eat, talk, play together.

Never, never blame "the company" for things your people don't like. Set an example of loyalty!

*Security*

Keep them as well-informed as you can about what is going on in the company. Help them feel that they are "in the know." (This cuts down rumors.)

Especially, tell them when there are going to be changes, and explain why and what the effects will be.

Be consistent yourself! Don't be one way today, another tomorrow.

When you have to reprimand someone, end it with some encouragement that they can be successful!

Suggest a better procedure, wherever possible, instead of criticizing a poor one.

*Source:* "Motivation—The State of the Art," by Haluk Bekiroglu and Turan Gonen. Reprinted with permission, *Personnel Journal,* copyright November 1977.

## EVALUATING PERFORMANCE

Small store owners typically encounter few problems in appraising the performance of their employees. This is so because of the close contact that normally takes place each day between employer and employee. Yet, simply to evaluate your people and keep your findings to yourself is poor management practice. All employees are entitled to feedback—to know how they are doing and how they are progressing. Soon after you have successfully launched your new retail enterprise, you should devote some time to devising an effective program for measuring performance. Periodic evaluations of your personnel become even more important as your retail firm grows in size.*

You'll need these for ascertaining the strengths and weaknesses of your employees, for guidance as to their training needs, to encourage a higher level of morale within the store, and to make sensible decisions about salary increases and/or promotions.

A useful procedure is to construct a simple *rating scale* by which you can rate each employee—numerically—on a number of criteria. A scale of 1 to 5, as follows, would be perfectly suitable for your purposes:

> 1—Poor
> 2—Fair
> 3—Good
> 4—Very Good
> 5—Excellent

You can employ a variety of "subjective" measures, such as appearance, courtesy, initiative, job knowledge, loyalty, relations with customers, resourcefulness, and sales ability. You can also select a few "objective" criteria; examples would be average sales per hour (total sales volume completed by the employee divided by the number of hours worked), the number of latenesses or absences, or the number of customer complaints.

Try to rate new employees at least quarterly during their first year with you; after that, a semiannual evaluation should be adequate.

## IMPROVING INTERNAL COMMUNICATIONS

One of the intangibles that influences your employees' level of motivation, positively or negatively, is your adeptness at communicating with them. To increase your proficiency, try to practice the following:

- Know what you want to say; think it through beforehand.

---

*For some useful insights into this topic area, see Martin G. Friedman, "10 Steps to Objective Appraisals," *Personnel Journal* 65 (June 1986), 66–71; Terry R. Lowe, "Eight Ways to Ruin a Performance Review," *Personnel Journal* 65 (January 1986), 60–62; Paul R. Reed and Mark J. Kroll, "A Two-Perspective Approach to Performance Appraisal," *Personnel* 62 (October 1985), 51–57.

- Organize your thoughts well in advance, and plan how you're going to present them.
- Always bear in mind that individuals differ from one another in family background, education, prior work experience, personality, intelligence, and the like. Consequently, each may need to be treated differently.
- Couch your messages in language your employees will understand.
- Keep your oral or written communications simple, clear, and complete.
- Encourage questions—to make certain that your messages are understood.
- Listen attentively to what your employees have to say.
- Avoid issuing orders; instead, *suggest* that the employee do whatever it is you wish him or her to do.

As a last, though extremely significant, point, bear in mind that all of us convey information to others in nonverbal fashion as well. Try to learn as much as you can about the significance of gestures, grimaces, smiles, frowns, winks, and the like—and about the use of "body language."*

## FOR FURTHER INFORMATION

### Books

Adelstein, Michael E., and W. Keats Sparrow. *Business Communications.* San Diego, Cal.: Harcourt Brace Jovanovich, 1983.

Atwater, W. *Human Relations.* Englewood Cliffs, N.J.: Prentice-Hall, 1986.

Brief, Arthur P., ed. *Managing Human Resources in Retail Organizations.* Lexington, Mass.: D. C. Heath, 1984.

Brown, L. *Communicating Facts and Ideas in Business,* 3d ed. Englewood Cliffs, N.J.: Prentice-Hall, 1982.

Chruden, Herbert J., and Arthur W. Sherman. *Managing Human Resources,* 7th ed. Cincinnati: South-Western, 1984.

Dessler, G. *Improving Productivity at Work: Motivating Today's Employees.* Englewood Cliffs, N.J.: Prentice-Hall, 1983.

Douglass, John, Stuart Klein, and David Hunt. *The Strategic Management of Human Resources.* New York: Wiley, 1985.

Eggland, Steven A., and John W. Williams. *Human Relations at Work,* 3d ed. Cincinnati: South-Western, 1987.

Fulmer, Robert M. *Practical Human Relations,* rev. ed. Homewood, Ill.: Irwin, 1983.

George, Claude S., Jr. *Supervision in Action,* 4th ed. Englewood Cliffs, N.J.: Prentice-Hall, 1985.

Haimann, Theo, and Raymond Hilgert. *Supervision: Concepts and Practices of Management,* 4th ed. Cincinnati: South-Western, 1987.

Halloran, J., and G. Frunzi. *Supervision: The Art of Management,* 2d ed. Englewood Cliffs, N.J.: Prentice-Hall, 1986.

Ivancevich, John M., James H. Donnelly, Jr., and James L. Gibson. *Managing for Performance,* 3d ed. Plano, Tex.: Business Publications, 1986.

---

* See Walter D. St. John, "You Are What You Communicate," *Personnel Journal* 64 (October 1985), 40–43.

Mescon, Michael H., Michael Albert, and Franklin Khedouri. *Individual and Organizational Effectiveness*. New York: Harper & Row, 1985.

Mosley, Donald C., and Paul H. Pietri. *Supervisory Management: The Art of Working With and Through People*. Cincinnati: South-Western, 1985.

Newman, Ruth, Marie Danziger, and Mark Cohen. *Communicating in Business Today*. Lexington, Mass.: D. C. Heath, 1987.

Portnoy, Robert A. *Leadership: What Every Leader Should Know About People*. Englewood Cliffs, N.J.: Prentice-Hall, 1986.

Preston, Paul, and Thomas Zimmerer. *Management for Supervisors*, 2d ed. Englewood Cliffs, N.J.: Prentice-Hall, 1983.

Reece, Barry L., and Rhonda G. Brandt. *Effective Human Relations in Organizations*, 2d ed. Boston: Houghton Mifflin, 1984.

Rosenblatt, S., T. Cheatham, and J. Watt. *Communication in Business*, 2d ed. Englewood Cliffs, N.J.: Prentice-Hall, 1982.

Sims, J., and P. Peterson. *Better Listening Skills*. Englewood Cliffs, N.J.: Prentice-Hall, 1981.

Stout, Vickie J., and Edward A. Perkins, Jr. *Practical Management Communication*. Cincinnati: South-Western, 1987.

Williams, J. Clifton, and George P. Huber. *Human Behavior in Organizations*, 3d ed. Cincinnati: South-Western, 1986.

## Pamphlets Available from the Small Business Administration

### Management Aids

MA 5.001—"Checklist for Developing a Training Program"
MA 5.008—"Managing Employee Benefits"
MA 5.009—"Techniques for Productivity Improvement"

## Booklets Available from the Superintendent of Documents

S/N 045-000-00189-0—*Managing Retail Salespeople*—$4.75.
S/N 045-000-00191-1—*Training and Developing Employees*—$4.50.
S/N 045-000-00196-2—*Employee Relations and Personnel Policies*—$4.50.

# VI

# Promoting Sales

# 15

# Successful Store Promotion

You're justifiably proud of your new store. Its decor, layout, and fixturization have been well planned and convey a pleasant image. Bins are fully stocked with well-chosen merchandise that's priced just right for your intended clientele. Displays are attractive and look most professional. Now the time has come for you to tell your story to the public—to promote your store, its wares, and its services.

From the marketing point of view, the term *promotion* encompasses several different sets of activities:

- Sales promotion
- Advertising (and its not-paid-for counterpart, publicity)
- Personal selling

In store retailing, each of these three elements in the "promotional mix" makes a significant contribution to the overall sales picture. For the retail firm, however, more time, effort, and expense are, of course, assigned to sales promotion—of which the most prominent aspect is display—and to personal selling than to advertising. That's because the retailer's total promotion budget is rather limited. Nowadays, the dollars you allocate to advertising never seem to go far enough, what with the sky-high rates of the mass media. Perhaps the only exceptions are the rates for local newspaper advertising and direct mail (see chapter 17).

For the sake of helping you make every one of your promotion dollars count, I prefer to devote an entire chapter to each of these elements. This chapter therefore deals almost exclusively with the area of sales promotion; the other segments of the promotion mix are covered in detail in the next two chapters.

## PROMOTION: ITS SIGNIFICANCE AND SCOPE

The cardinal purpose of all forms of promotion is to communicate. In retailing, we communicate with the public to bring shoppers into the store, to stimulate buying, and to

217

build goodwill for our business. *Advertising* is paid communication through one or more advertising media with large numbers of people. *Publicity* and *public relations* are also forms of communication en masse, but they're generally cost-free. Most often, *personal selling* in retailing is communication on a one-to-one, face-to-face basis inside the store itself. Finally, *sales promotion* is a catchall term that encompasses a variety of sales tools ranging from interior and window displays, through posters and sign tickets, to contests, sales events, premiums, and so forth.

Let's follow the typical small shopkeeper as he or she arrives at the store early on a weekday morning. Frequently, it's fifteen or twenty minutes before the scheduled opening time. The proprietor checks quickly through the store and the back room to make sure that all is in order, then takes out the "store bank" from wherever it has been hidden and puts the money into the cash register. Next, the lights are fully turned on, the front door is unlocked, and the owner waits patiently (?) for the first shopper to arrive.

At first blush, waiting seems like an extremely passive approach to promotion on the retailer's part, but the use of a long hook to pull shoppers in off the street would certainly be frowned upon! Nevertheless, the "hook" is there. Our typical shopkeeper is relying on the storefront, the show window and its displays, and perhaps the view of the interior through the glass entrance door. For the most part, the retailer is depending on a form of sales promotion to do the job of attracting shoppers and persuading them to enter the store.

## DISPLAY FUNDAMENTALS

In general, your show-window treatments are your chief means of generating store traffic. Your in-store displays act as "silent salespeople" to assist you and your actual salespeople in selling merchandise to your customers. Because of its importance to both sales and store image, the window display merits a great deal of thoughtful attention. To be successful, you need to:

**Know your store operation well.** Know what you and your business stand for; the kinds of products you carry; their quality; the prices and your pricing policies; and the services you offer.

**Know your customers well.** Be familiar with their likes and dislikes, along with their preferences as to styles, price level, and quality of merchandise; their response to special sales or promotions; and the services they expect of you.

**Know the rudiments of display.** Learn how to select items for display; the coordination of props, display materials, and fixtures; the use of lighting and motion to enhance display effectiveness; proper color coordination; how to strive for interest, balance, and harmony; and arranging and grouping items.

**Create an inspired six-month "promotion plan."** Combine your knowledge of the other three areas and prepare your plan well in advance. Work out the details of all the major elements—displays, advertising, sales promotion, and publicity and prepare a separate schedule of dates and activities for each of these phases.

The "display" section of your six-month promotion plan should be broken down into two separate categories: *interiors* and *windows*.

## Interior Displays

Use all interior displays as valuable "silent salespeople"—to provoke shopper interest, to create excitement in your store, and to instill the desire to buy. Study every nook and cranny of your store for potential display areas. Think about how to make the best use of both location and space with an eye to developing distinctive arrangements. Plan each setup in advance on paper, using scale drawings of the display area. Pay special attention to "key spots," such as around your register(s) or checkout(s), near sections that bear the heaviest traffic, and the main aisle. These locations are excellent for impulse items, seasonal goods, and promotional merchandise—whether they're grouped, in baskets or bins, on aisle tables or floor stands.

Change displays frequently for shopper interest. Keep them fresh-looking and clean. Use display cards or posters to help "tell the story." These should always look professional; either have them made for you or buy yourself a sign-making kit or machine. If possible, try to "departmentalize" the premises. As a general rule, goods that are bought by customers on impulse should be located toward the front of the store, and specialty or shopping goods (those goods for which consumers are willing to spend more time "shopping" for best price and quality) should be placed toward the rear. Small, expensive merchandise should be displayed in enclosed glass showcases and kept under lock and key.

## Your Window Displays

For many store retailers, the show window is the most significant promotional tool of all. The annual advertising appropriation, if an advertising budget exists, is usually small. On the other hand, the window-display budget is frequently three to five times larger than the advertising budget in order to accommodate ten to fifteen or more "window changes" during the year.

Physically, an empty window doesn't look like much: one or more glass panes, a window base or raised platform, one or two walls, perhaps a shelf or two, and a back. Yet this is as valuable an area as you can ever hope to obtain for your retail shop. It all depends, of course, on what you do with it.

Some retail stores have no windows at all. The glass front permits passersby to look right into the store interior, thus converting the interior into one big showroom and display. Others, most notably the many different types in our larger shopping malls, may have no glass in the front at all. At closing time, a gate is dropped down or pulled sideways to shut the store. The purpose of such an arrangement appears to be to encourage the shopping-center traffic to come in and look around. Other stores are fortunate enough to have two, three, or even more windows. What opportunities!

Your show window is your store's "face." It's also a setting—a stage on which you can set up an exciting scenario to tell your story. This stage on which your "play" unfolds should always be treated with enthusiasm and imagination. You need to think about casting the "actors" for the performance—that is, the merchandise to be shown. Use the background, props, materials, and signage to establish the atmosphere and the desired mood. Build drama through position, movement, and lighting. Arouse emotions in the "viewers." Avoid the natural tendency of the new retailer to throw just about everything carried in stock into the window; such displays are cluttered, confusing, and unproductive. Think in terms of a basic *theme* for each window change. Build around that theme— make it readily apparent to the viewer. Then group your merchandise and set up these groups with plenty of "air space" around them. Check over the pointers in exhibit 15–1 for ideas. Refer also to the list in exhibit 15–2 every time you change the window.

---

### EXHIBIT 15–1. SOME THOUGHTS FOR WINDOW DISPLAYS

- Shoppers will regard your storefront and show window as the "face" of your retail business. Therefore, the window treatments should always convey the impressions of quality, style, and distinctiveness that you would like to project.

- Displays should be kept clean and neat in appearance at all times. A crowded display contributes nothing but clutter; instead, use air (or "breathing space") between merchandise groupings.

- Whether you engage the services of a professional window trimmer or you do the displays yourself, your windows should be changed frequently. At least ten to fifteen changes each year are recommended. (Hint: You might be able to hire someone with display training from the local high school's distributive education program.)

- Window displays are generally more effective when built around a single, unifying theme (Going-Back-to-School, Mother's Day, Christmas, Springtime, Vacation Fun, Travel, and so forth).

- Merchandise, materials, display stands, mannequins (if required), and signs or posters should be carefully selected and prepared ahead of time so that the window may be completely trimmed without incident within a few hours' time.

- In selecting appropriate merchandise to put into the window, pay careful attention to the seasonality factor, to product sales appeal, and to individual gross markups.

- Color is an essential ingredient of display. The color combinations used in the window should be attractive and harmonious.

- Window bases (platforms) are usually covered with appropriate materials which contribute to the overall effect of the display—satins, netting, burlap, paper, artificial grass mats, and so forth. The retailer ought to build up a stock of such materials, over time.

- All point-of-purchase materials, such as sign tickets, posters, banners, and the like, should look professional and be kept perfectly clean.

- Special effects, such as motion, lighting, and sound, can be used profitably in connection with your display to draw attention to your window. As a simple example, motion can be imparted to a section of your display through the use of a small electric (or battery-operated) turntable or ceiling turner.

*Source:* Irving Burstiner, *The Small Business Handbook: A Comprehensive Guide to Starting and Running Your Own Business*, rev. ed. (New York: Prentice Hall Press, 1989), 192.

In the interim, here are a few themes for consideration that are not indicated in exhibit 15–1:

| | | |
|---|---|---|
| June in January | Bargain Days | Valentine's Day |
| January in June | Open House | On the Farm |
| Lincoln's Birthday | Graduation | Harvest Time |
| Paris in the Spring | Thanksgiving Day | Let's Go Hawaiian |
| At the Beach | Secretaries' Week | Election Day Sale |
| Halloween | Summertime | Fourth of July |
| Grandpop's Day | Sweepstakes | The World Series |
| Washington's Birthday | Springtime | Happy New Year |
| Jazztime | Latin America | Cruising |

---

**EXHIBIT 15–2. CHECKLIST FOR WINDOW DISPLAY**

I. Merchandise selected

1. Is the merchandise timely?
2. Is it representative of the stock assortment?
3. Are the articles harmonious—in type, color, texture, use?
4. Are the price lines of the merchandise suited to the interests of passersby?
5. Is the quantity on display suitable (that is, neither overcrowded nor sparse)?

II. Setting

1. Are glass, floor, props, and merchandise clean?
2. Is the lighting adequate (so that reflection from the street is avoided)?
3. Are spotlights used to highlight certain parts of the display?
4. Is every piece of merchandise carefully draped, pinned, or arranged?
5. Is the background suitable, enhancing the merchandise?
6. Are the props well suited to the merchandise?
7. Are window cards used, and are they neat and well placed?
8. Is the entire composition balanced?
9. Does the composition suggest rhythm and movement?

III. Selling power

1. Does the window present a readily recognized central theme?
2. Does the window exhibit power to stop passersby through the dramatic use of light, color, size, motion, composition, and/or item selection?
3. Does the window arouse a desire to buy (as measured by shoppers entering the store)?

---

*Source:* John W. Wingate and Seymour Helfant, "Small Store Planning for Growth," *Small Business Management Series No. 33,* 2d ed. (Washington, D.C.: U.S. Small Business Administration, 1977), 77.

## THOSE OTHER BENEFICIAL SALES-PROMOTION TOOLS

In this section is a list of other sales-promotion techniques for you to choose from in your advance planning. Some, you'll find, will not seem suitable to your particular type of retailing; others may look promising to you. Some, of course, will "pull" better than others. You should take pains to explore a variety of these approaches over the next six months:

**Anniversary promotions.** You start the ball rolling, of course, with your grand-opening promotion. After that, each succeeding store birthday provides a festive occasion for a storewide sale, contest, or other type of promotion. You have an entire year to plan for this event!

**Catalogs.** More properly included with your advertising plans, these are worthy of inclusion under the "sales promotion" heading because of their value in generating additional store traffic and selling merchandise. Fliers, package enclosures, and brochures also fall into this category.

**Contests.** Excellent for generating excitement throughout the neighborhood, these are among the more favored promotional techniques. You may draw from well-known types: jingle writing, art or drawing contests, prettiest baby (or grandmother), "count-the-beans-in-the-jar," "Why I like this store (or item)" in twenty-five words or less, "name-the-new-product," the sweepstakes (simple drawing of names or telephone numbers), and so forth. Note that it's relatively easy to tie your contest into local movie houses, restaurants, and other retail shops for prizes to award your winners. Other retailers are generally happy to provide you with free passes, dinners for two, and all kinds of merchandise in exchange for your offer to place signs featuring their businesses in your store window. Of course, you first need to "sell" them on the benefits (to *them!*) of this mutual promotion.

**Coupons.** From time to time, depending on the type of store you have, your customers will bring in manufacturers' coupons for redemption. In their most common form, they carry "cents-off" or discount offers; sometimes they may be used in connection with inexpensive "giveaway" items. Consumers love coupons! Perhaps you can take advantage of this knowledge by printing up your own coupons in circulars that you hand-deliver to homes in the neighborhood or that you offer through an ad in your local newspaper. If your store is in a shopping center, advertise in the shopping circulars the management distributes several times throughout the year. Introductory specials for new items and substantial discounts on popular merchandise generally have surprisingly strong "pulling power."

**Credit.** As you'll note in chapter 12, credit can be useful as a promotional tool not only for selling more to your customers but also for wooing people away from competitors who don't extend credit. It's true that charge-account customers buy more over the years than those who don't have such accounts. What's more, you can profit by resorting, periodically, to your charge files for direct-mail or telephone solicitation.

**Demonstrations.** Some types of merchandise are admirably suited to in-store demonstrations. Examples that come readily to mind include sports equipment, electric organs, fudge- or candy-making machines, toiletries and perfumes, vegetable-slicing utensils, electronic TV games, cookware, stereos, and floor-cleaning compounds or machines. Scheduled in advance and well publicized, in-store promotions can bring in crowds and sell goods.

**"Early-bird" and preseason sales events.** Such promotions may be used to stimulate sales three or four times each year. Of course, they need considerable planning and attention both to the selection and pricing of merchandise and to display.

**Giveaways and premiums.** This category includes an extensive variety of merchandise items that are either given out free to store customers or sold to them at well below the customary selling prices. They're offered to stimulate the sales of other store merchandise, to bring in shoppers, to build goodwill for the enterprise, to encourage continued patronage, and the like. Some are "advertising specialities," inexpensive products that carry the name of the issuing store and perhaps a brief advertising message. Specialties include balloons, pencils, matchbooks, rain bonnets, mini-sewing kits, and key chains. You can locate premium houses (by checking the Yellow Pages under "Premium Goods" or through trade directories or publications) that supply all kinds of premium merchandise, from items priced under $1 to some that go as high as $100 and more. Sets of dishes, bicycles, records and phonographs, encyclopedias, and luggage have been popular choices among retailers.

**Incentives for salesclerks.** Well-motivated salespeople in your store can push your slow movers, sell additional merchandise to customers through "suggestion selling," trade up shoppers to better-quality goods, and generally bring you higher daily sales figures. (Read the section in chapter 14 that's entitled "How to Motivate Your Employees.")

In addition, you can think about introducing *PM*s from time to time. The initials stand for *Push Money.* You announce to your salespeople, for example, that for this week only, you'll contribute a PM of 20 cents for each unit of Item X they sell. (This arrangement naturally means that you have to set up some kind of record-keeping system.) Occasionally you may find that your suppliers will contribute push money for certain of their products; this is, of course, passed on to your employees painlessly!

In-store contests are also quite popular among retailers. The individual salesclerk who either sells the most of a featured product or perhaps attains an established quota receives a prize in cash or in merchandise. Prizes can run the gamut from a pair of tickets for the theater or a ball game to an entire wardrobe, a color television, or an all-expenses-paid vacation.

**Price promotions.** Here, you have your choice of a number of promotional pricing techniques: leader pricing, multiple pricing, trade-in allowances, and so forth. These are discussed more fully in chapter 11.

**Publicity events.** Guest appearances of local or national celebrities, noteworthy displays of old costumes, art exhibits, Santas and clowns, kiddie rides, lectures on topics of general consumer interest, and a host of other "happenings" can be brought into play to create excitement in your neighborhood and store. You're limited only by the size of your promotion budget and your imagination. Included in this category, too, are the occasional neighborhood sale days, block parties, anniversaries, festivals, and other promotions offered cooperatively by the merchants in the area.

**Sampling.** A reliable old standby, the particular promotional technique of offering free samples of your merchandise is readily and pleasantly received by browsers and shoppers alike. It's especially suited to bakeries, confectionery shops, delicatessens, and other food stores.

**Shows.** Perhaps the best-known of all in this classification are the fashion shows, presented by retailers of better-quality women's clothing, sophisticated sportswear, children's apparel, and similar specialty lines. There are interesting possibilities here in this kind of promotion for many other retail-store types. Here are but a few: wigs or new hairstyles; antiques; paintings, sculptures, and other art forms; handicrafts of every description; stamps and coins; new furniture; giftware.

Show success is often contingent on the degree of creativity exercised in conception and preparation, as well as the professionalism demonstrated in the actual production. Close attention needs to be paid to time, place, and atmosphere as well as to the choice and scheduling of activities.

**Special sales.** Besides the more customary sales events, such as Washington's Birthday or Columbus Day sales and the popular Back-to-School, After-Christmas, or White Sale promotions, any number of special sales are available to the retailer for generating in-store traffic. Here are just a few suggestions: store manager's (or assistant manager's) sales, buyers'/assistant buyers' sales, warm- or cold-weather sales, moonlight or midnight sales, early-bird sales, clearance sales, and end-of-season sales.

## PUBLIC RELATIONS: ANOTHER PROMOTIONAL TOOL

Properly managed, the entire public relations area can constitute another major element in your promotion plans. It's all the more attractive because of its relatively insignificant cost. Your displays and certainly your paid media advertising use up most of the funds you set aside each year for promoting your retail enterprise. Yet a well-planned PR program can help your business grow, and it can cost you little except some time for planning plus a few petty-cash dollars.

One source defines public relations as "a management function that uses two-way communication to match the needs and interests of an institution or person with the needs and interests of the various publics with which that institution or person must communicate."* Another major textbook describes it as "the planned effort to influence opinion through good character and responsible performance, based upon mutually satisfactory two-way communications."**

Translated into retail terminology, those two definitions mean that good public relations starts with running a good store that offers needed merchandise at fair prices, with both employees and management committed to consumer satisfaction. The store must then seek to project that image honestly through open communication between the store and its various "publics"—both the internal public (the store personnel) and the external public (suppliers, the local community, other retailers, and so on).

### Your Public Relations Program

Planning your ongoing, year-round public/community relations program necessitates your following approximately the same procedure used to develop your display program: (1) know your store operation well; (2) know your customers well; (3) know the rudiments of public relations; and (4) combine all of this knowledge into an inspired six-month public relations plan. In connection with this planning, study the questions listed in exhibit 15–3. These should help to clarify your thinking and set the foundation for good public relations.

What kinds of activities foster closer ties with your community? You might consider

---

* S. Watson Dunn, *Public Relations: A Contemporary Approach* (Homewood, Ill.: Irwin, 1986), 5.
** Scott M. Cutlip and Allen H. Center, *Effective Public Relations,* 5th ed. (Englewood Cliffs, N.J.: Prentice-Hall, 1978), 16.

selecting some of those suggested in exhibit 15–4. By no means, however, should you limit yourself to these. Some solid thinking and the exercise of your creative bent can probably lead to more fertile and productive ideas.

---

### EXHIBIT 15–3. SIXTEEN SEARCHING QUESTIONS TO ASK YOURSELF

1. Do you have a policy that good community relations is a matter of top management concern?
2. Do you constantly guard against your business activities conflicting with public policy?
3. Do you recognize each of the groups that make up an important segment of your firm's public?
4. Do you take regular steps to see that each group receives the appreciation it deserves?
5. Do you maintain sympathetic and wholesome employee relations even with temporary help?
6. Do you have an established system for informing employees on what your firm stands for and how it functions?
7. Do you try to keep informed on what the public thinks of your firm?
8. Do you try to check what you hear and make improvements where needed?
9. Do you avoid high-pressure tactics in your community relations activities?
10. Do you make continuous and consistent efforts to improve your community relations skills instead of merely putting on sporadic drives?
11. Do you make a conscious effort to understand how government affects your business and to improve your relations with government agencies?
12. Do you insist that all your company's actions be completely honest and sincere?
13. Do you remind your employees constantly that selling, serving, and good community relations are inseparable?
14. Do you make it a point to consider what is best for the public at large as well as for your own private interest when major business decisions are being made?
15. Are your premises well kept and pleasing to the eye?
16. Do you have a policy of encouraging your employees to be active in community organizations of their choosing?

---

*Source:* Robert W. Miller, "Profitable Community Relations for Small Business," *Small Business Management Series No. 27* (Washington, D.C.: U.S. Small Business Administration, 1961), 29–33.

---

### EXHIBIT 15–4. COMMUNITY-RELATIONS ACTIVITIES FOR THE SMALL FIRM

1. Charitable contributions and participation in community fund-raising drives; for example, Community Chest, Red Cross.
2. Blood donor programs.
3. Membership and active participation in community organizations; for example—in addition to the civic, service, political, and religious groups already mentioned—veterans' and parent-teacher associations.
4. Sponsorship of activities in the fields of fire protection, water purification, noise abatement, smoke-fume elimination, accident prevention.
5. Speechmaking by owner and employees before community groups.
6. Plant tours and open-house events.

---

**Exhibit 15–4. Continued**

7. Community-oriented institutional advertising.

8. Sponsorship of cultural and sport activities of the community; for example, promotion of "little theater" groups, library-enlargement campaigns, park and civic statute improvements, "Little League" baseball, industrial bowling team sponsorship.

9. Membership and active participation in professional groups—especially local and regional chapters of such groups.

10. Student on-the-job training and summer employment for local students.

11. Participation in special days and/or weeks; community-sponsored events and celebrations; for example, junior government days, National Employ the Physically Handicapped Week, picnics for underprivileged children, Christmas toy distributions.

12. Publicity for achievements by local citizens—especially your own employees; for example, years-of-service pins, awards for the accumulation of sick leave, "Young-Man-of-the-Year" presentations.

*Source:* Robert W. Miller, "Profitable Community Relations for Small Business," *Small Business Management Series No. 27* (Washington, D.C.: U.S. Small Business Administration, 1961), 34.

## YOUR GRAND-OPENING PROMOTION

No event can play a more significant role in launching your new retail enterprise than your grand-opening promotion. Up to this point, most consumers who live, work, or shop in the vicinity of your store know little or nothing about you. Hopefully, though, you were astute enough to alert some of these people to your forthcoming grand opening—through signs or banners on your window(s) or perhaps through advertisements you placed in the local paper.

This initial promotional event should aim at delivering a strongly favorable message about your firm. This is when you need to begin fostering that all-important goodwill required for success in business. You need to let shoppers know that you and your store are ready to serve them. You need to tell them what you and your firm stand for, about the kinds of merchandise you carry, about your pricing approaches, and so on. You should seek the widest possible dissemination of information about your business. You need to reach as many potential buyers as you can.

### Planning Your Grand-Opening Event

Devising a grand-opening program is no easy task. Be sure to start working on it many months in advance. It will take time to think up good ideas and then to solidify your thinking, to work out the right approaches, to prepare the needed materials, to conceive of attractive window and interior displays, and so forth.

For best results, strive to attain two goals simultaneously: (1) to create excitement in the neighborhood; and (2) to convey your "story" fully and to as many people as possible. Think in terms of what you can do both *outside* and *inside* your store. What can you do with your show window(s), the store's interior, your salespeople?

Here are some helpful promotion tools you might consider utilizing; use this brief list to trigger your imagination:

| | |
|---|---|
| advertising specialties | handbills |
| balloons | kiddie rides |
| clown | newspaper advertising |
| contest | premiums |
| coupons | publicity releases |
| demonstrations | radio advertising |
| exhibit | ribbon-cutting ceremony |
| giveaways | sampling |
| guest celebrities | tie-in promotion |

## FOR FURTHER INFORMATION

### Books

Brannen, W. *Advertising and Sales Promotion: Cost-Effective Techniques for Your Small Business.* Englewood Cliffs, N.J.: Prentice-Hall, 1983.

Cutlip, Scott M., and A. Broom Center. *Effective Public Relations,* 6th ed. Englewood Cliffs, N.J.: Prentice-Hall, 1985.

Diamond, J., and G. Pintel. *Principles of Marketing,* 3d ed. Englewood Cliffs, N.J.: Prentice-Hall, 1986.

Edwards, C., and C. Lebowitz. *Retail Advertising and Sales Promotion,* 4th ed. Englewood Cliffs, N.J.: Prentice-Hall, 1981.

Govoni, N., et al. *Promotional Management.* Englewood Cliffs, N.J.: Prentice-Hall, 1986.

Mills, Kenneth H., and Judith E. Paul. *Applied Visual Merchandising.* Englewood Cliffs, N.J.: Prentice-Hall, 1982.

Moriarty, S. *Creative Advertising: Theory and Practice.* Englewood Cliffs, N.J.: Prentice-Hall, 1986.

Norris, James S. *Public Relations.* Englewood Cliffs, N.J.: Prentice-Hall, 1984.

Phillips, Pamela M., Ellye Bloom, and John D. Mattingly. *Fashion Sales Promotion: The Selling Behind the Selling.* New York: Wiley, 1985.

Shimp, Terence A., and M. Wayne Delozier. *Promotion Management and Marketing Communications.* New York: Dryden, 1986.

Simon, Raymond. *Public Relations: Concepts and Practices,* 3d ed. New York: Wiley, 1985.

Spitzer, Harry, and F. Richard Schwartz. *Inside Retail Sales Promotion and Advertising.* New York: Harper & Row, 1982.

Stanley, Richard E. *Promotion: Advertising, Publicity, Personal Selling, Sales Promotion,* 2d ed. Englewood Cliffs, N.J.: Prentice-Hall, 1982.

## Pamphlets Available from the Small Business Administration

### Management Aids

MA 4.012—"Marketing Checklist for Small Retailers"

## Booklets Available from the Superintendent of Documents

S/N 045-000-00152-1—*Small Store Planning for Growth*—$5.50.
S/N 045-000-00188-1—*Marketing Strategy*—$4.75.

# 16

# How to Upgrade Your Employees' Selling Skills

For most retail firms, the cost of labor is perhaps the single highest operating expense. It's therefore not surprising that customer self-service has taken over so frequently today. Once almost entirely reserved for five-and-dime stores and variety outlets (and later on for supermarkets and discount houses), self-service has found its way into department stores, drugstores and other chains, and many independent retail establishments. This trend has become increasingly popular during the past twenty-five years.

Nowadays, many retailers, unfortunately, view the salesclerk as an occasionally necessary evil—someone who's regarded for the most part as an order-filler-cum-stock-handler, merchandise arranger, and part-time cashier. Hopefully, the salesperson is honest, dependable (i.e., seldom absent or late), efficient at assigned tasks, and courteous to shoppers. What a piteous, effete philosophy!

Nevertheless, salespeople are still frequently found in merchandise lines where self-service can put the retail firm at a disadvantage. Major appliances, better jewelry, draperies, men's clothing, and floor coverings are but a few such products that come readily to mind.

## SALESPERSONSHIP IN SMALL-SCALE RETAILING

Energetic, skilled selling should be sought after by the small independent retailer. Where it exists, it distinguishes the fortunate store from those of nearby competitors and, even more, from the impersonal ambience of the department store or large chain-store unit. Your salespeople can and should build a steady, permanent clientele for you, over time. (Conversely, it's also possible for them to drive customers away from your establishment.)

Often, the salesperson serving the shopper is the only in-store individual that shopper meets and gets to know. Your customers tend to form opinions about your

228

business mostly from their contacts and interactions with your employees. People are rarely frustrated by—or become angered at—a showcase, counter, merchandise display, or the color scheme you have chosen for the store interior. They do, however, react to salespeople. Of course, you want their reactions to be strongly positive, not negative.

## The Significance of Selling

Advertising, sales promotion, publicity, and personal selling are all familiar approaches used by the retail company to communicate with prospective and actual customers and to persuade them in favor of the store, its merchandise, and its services. Your promotional efforts in the media and in your window displays may indeed succeed in attracting shoppers to your premises. Some of these consumers may even be predisposed to buy, when they come in, even without the intervention or participation of a salesperson. The majority of shoppers, however, enter a store not as a result of advertising or the window display but simply because of the "pulling power" of the store's location, the merchandise "mix," and the salespeople.

Personal selling, on a one-to-one, eyeball-to-eyeball basis, is by far the most powerful medium of all for such persuasion. The capable salesperson makes customers out of browsers. Indeed, from many on-the-spot observations made time and time again, I can vouchsafe the fact that a top sales producer outsells the "average" salesperson by 50 percent or more. In the area of suggestion selling alone (discussed later in this chapter), some salespeople are capable of selling additional merchandise to as many as three out of every ten purchasers on a fairly consistent basis. On the other hand, the "batting averages" for others may only be one out of twenty or twenty-five. This sort of information should convince you, after a bit of reflection, that capable sales employees can indeed make a difference in your business. It's true, of course, that some types of stores don't require much in the way of selling ability; for example, self-service operations or fast-food places that primarily sell hamburgers, French fries, and soft drinks. In most specialty-goods and shopping-goods retailing, however, a more adept sales staff makes for higher sales.

## Get and Train the Right People

Clearly, you owe it to yourself as a store owner to strive for near-perfection in the sales area. Top salespeople convert far more of the "lookers," "browsers," and "undecideds" into immediate cash sales and future "regulars." What makes the difference between mediocre performers and stars? Really only three things:

1. Hiring the right people in the first place
2. Training them properly
3. Motivating them to do their best

**Hiring the Right People.** Ideally, a salesperson should be someone your customers like and not someone who turns them off. This means that the individual should be neat, well-groomed, and pleasant—and that he or she should project the image of being an attentive and informed aide.

**Proper Training.** Once you have succeeded in hiring salespeople who appear to match the desired profile, you then need to train them to be effective and productive. You need to teach them where all the merchandise is located in the store. You must also have them learn the prices of the items, your firm's policies and systems, the details of product warranties and guarantees, and so on. More importantly, you have to teach them *how to sell.* Surprisingly, many new store owners assume that just about everyone can sell, and they therefore conduct no training. "Go out on the floor and take care of the customer," they advise the new salesperson. "You'll learn quickly enough by trial and error." (See chapter 14 for more on training employees.) To set the mood for yourself, read through the "Missed Opportunities" in exhibit 16–1.

---

### EXHIBIT 16–1. MISSED OPPORTUNITIES

"Sorry, we don't carry that brand," the sales clerk said to the customer who asked for a certain kind of fishing rod. He didn't offer to show the customer the brand which the store did carry.

The store's brand had features (for the same price) which the competing brand did not have. But the customer never knew it—unless he heard about it elsewhere.

"Do you have that one in the window in a 8½ triple A?" the woman asked. The shoe salesman shook his head. She turned and left the store.

Later she told her friends, "I'll never go in there again. The least he could have done was to offer to show me some other styles."

"Make up your mind," was the expression on the salesman's face as he waited for a customer to decide which washing machine she liked best. His message got through because she walked out without buying.

"I know she must have thought that I had all day to wait on her," he said. He was right, but what he didn't know was that she planned to buy a dryer also.

---

*Source:* Kenneth Grubb, "Are Your Salespeople Missing Opportunities?" *Small Marketers Aid No. 95* (Washington, D.C.: U.S. Small Business Administration, 1963), 1.

**Motivating Salespeople.** Effective training methods and procedures can go far toward raising the morale level in an organization and toward increasing the self-motivation of an employee. Many other factors, of course, play a role in the motivation process; among them are suitable working conditions, an adequate and competitive pay plan (and benefits), the opportunity for advancement, and good-quality supervision. Company rules, regulations, and policies should be fair, impartial, and clearly spelled out. Management needs to subscribe to, and at all times practice, good interpersonal relations. It must respond to its employees' needs for security and recognition. (For additional information, see the section on "How to Motivate Your Employees" in chapter 14.)

To boost the productivity of salespeople on a short-term basis, retailers often resort to special promotional techniques such as contests, special bonuses, and the issuance of PMs.

## SELLING IN THE STORE

While retail selling is in many respects akin to other types of selling, such as industrial sales or "door-to-door" selling, it's unique in one respect: No "prospecting" for potential customers is necessary. The store location itself—along with window (and interior) merchandise displays, store decor, and store layout—attracts prospective buyers.

Measures you can take to improve selling effectiveness in your store include:

- Showing the new salesperson how to sell through actual demonstrations by you and/ or your top sales producer
- Following up on such presentations with thorough discussions
- Using the technique of *role playing* to broaden the employee's outlook. This approach permits the inexperienced or weak salesperson to see things from the shopper's point of view by wearing, figuratively, the customer's hat. Have one employee try to sell another who is acting as the customer; then reverse their roles and repeat the procedure.
- Appointing a seasoned salesperson as "Big Brother" or "Big Sister" to the newcomer, not only for initial indoctrination and task training but also with the specific charge of encouraging, developing, and improving that person's selling efforts
- Encouraging your salespeople to read one or more books on selling, such as those listed at the end of this chapter, enrolling them in a course in selling at a local college, and so on
- Familiarizing your sales staff with the selling process itself (described in the next section), discussing with them each of the steps involved, and then deciding with them on the best methods to use in each step

## THE RETAIL SELLING PROCESS

Over the past few decades, the selling process used by sales representatives has been widely treated in many books on salesmanship. Many sales managers pinpoint six basic steps in that process:

- Prospecting for potential buyers
- Qualifying prospects
- Making the sales presentation
- Overcoming objections raised
- Closing the sale
- Following up the sale

The *retail* selling process differs. As we noted earlier, for example, prospecting isn't needed in the retail-store environment.

In my college textbook, *Basic Retailing,* I pointed out that the retail selling process appears to involve these four sequential phases:

1. Shopper contact
2. The sales dialogue
3. Completing the sale
4. Suggestion selling*

Each of these phases is discussed in some detail in the next section.

## Shopper Contact

Every shopper who enters your store expects of your sales staff the following (as a *minimum*):

- That they be alert and ready to assist as the shopper wishes
- That attention to the shopper be placed before all other activities, such as cleaning, arranging stock or displays, talking to each other, or telephone conversations
- That they show interest in and quickly comprehend the consumer's needs, and wants
- That they be knowledgeable about the store, its merchandise and prices, and the systems and services offered

Many shoppers plan to make a purchase but do not like to be rushed. They prefer to look about first, and they intensely dislike being pounced upon by an overzealous salesclerk. Others stride directly over to a salesperson and ask to be served. Still others enter to browse. Though their intentions differ, all require attention. What to do?

Teach your sales personnel to develop the ability to "size up" shoppers quickly in order to classify them as to "type." The key in this situation is the salesperson's alertness to the cues in the situation. Often, eye-to-eye contact with the consumer, a quick and ready smile, and a "Good morning!" (or "Good afternoon!") are all that's needed to convey the salesclerk's attention and readiness to help.

In any event, the silence needs to be broken in order to start building salesperson-shopper rapport. When the shopper is looking at a particular article of merchandise, an excellent way of initiating conversation is to make an appropriate comment about the item. Many retail merchants instruct their salespeople to ask, "May I help you?" to indicate their readiness. It might be better to say, "How may I help you?" Even better, you might preface the question with a friendly, "Good morning, Mrs. Ellis!" or a warm "How are you today, Mr. Farrell?" People love to hear their own names. Hearing their

---

* Irving Burstiner, *Basic Retailing* (Homewood, Ill.: Irwin, 1986), 630.

names makes them feel good—even important. Of course, store salesclerks can use this approach only if they know the shopper's name. It would be wise to encourage your sales personnel to learn their customers' names, perhaps from sales slips or from a "guest register," which some forward-looking store owners use to gather names and addresses. Another way to learn names might be through the very greeting itself: for example, "Good afternoon. My name's Helen. How can I help you, Miss . . . ?"

## The Sales Dialogue

This is the heart of the retail selling process. Here, the salesperson swings into action: to determine, first of all, what the shopper may be looking for and then to present suitable merchandise that will meet the shopper's needs. As the dialogue continues, the salesperson will stress the selling points of those items presented and try to anticipate—and successfully overcome—any objections that the shopper may voice.

**"Sizing Up the Shopper."** Obviously, it is to both the customer's and the store's advantage for the salesperson to pinpoint the kind of merchandise the customer is seeking as rapidly as possible. This, by the way, is frequently no mean accomplishment; many shoppers have in mind little more than a general feeling as to what they may need. For these individuals, your salespeople need: (1) a working knowledge of psychology; (2) considerable observational skill; and (3) the ability to listen attentively.

Adult and social psychology, as well as the relatively newer "science" of consumer behavior, tell us that all of us are born blessed with powerful basic needs and that we acquire other needs and wants as we go through life. Thus, we seek to satisfy our physiological (bodily) needs, our psychological (mental and emotional) needs, and our social needs. Our needs and wants are translated into the motives that are responsible for our behavior. Most of our actions are the result of the interplay of several motives within us. Sometimes these motives reinforce each other, and sometimes they conflict. This "psychology" is as applicable to our shopping behavior as it is to all the other things we do.

What, then, motivates shoppers to buy? More precisely, what needs and wants are they looking to satisfy? Here are some of the possibilities:

| | | |
|---|---|---|
| adventure | fun | recognition |
| affection | hope | romance |
| approval | hunger | self-fulfillment |
| care | love | self-gratification |
| comfort | mental health | self-preservation |
| convenience | physical health | sense of achievement |
| emulation | popularity | sense of belonging |
| esteem | prestige | status |
| excitement | pride | thirst |
| friendship | profit | |

With regard to specific product attributes, we're usually looking for such things as durability, ease of operation, economy of price, fashion, good performance, high quality, and availability of service. For insights into why customers buy hardware, for instance, refer to exhibit 16–2.

Hence, the salesperson needs to "size up" shoppers in terms of their dress, manner, and facial expression for clues. Such observations, complemented by two or three well-phrased questions, are often enough to establish the type of merchandise sought.

---

### EXHIBIT 16–2. WHY CUSTOMERS BUY HARDWARE

Why Do Customers Buy?

Customers buy because they would rather have products than the money with which they pay for them. In more detail, here are five reasons which should help you understand customers and how to deal with them:

1. Customers buy because *they need the product*. Most items purchased in a hardware store, for example, are bought to fill an immediate need. Pots and pans are needed in every home. A do-it-yourselfer needs hammers and nails. A painter needs paint, brushes, and supplies. But even though a customer needs such things, he has a choice among several brands and styles of products. It is your job to show him how a specific kind of product, which you have in your store, will best fill these needs.

2. Customers buy because *they can use a product*. They could easily get along without certain items because they do not really need them. Yet they often buy the items anyway. A large percentage of sales in hardware stores, for example, involve such items—they are desirable but not essential.

Therefore, the successful hardwareman puts extra effort into promoting and selling items such as electric can openers and ice crushers. Customers buy them for the convenience and satisfaction they provide rather than because they are necessary. In addition to adding a convenience that most families enjoy, such products help put spice into living.

3. Customers buy because the *purchase will add to their wealth*. For example, home owners buy materials and tools which they use to increase the value of their homes or to protect the investment which they have made in it. Seed for the lawn, and the awnings, and fences also add to property values. Moreover, some tools are purchased by customers to help them produce items which can be sold, or render services for which they will be paid.

4. Customers buy *to satisfy their pride of ownership*. Many customers like to keep up with their neighbors. Thus they buy the latest items in order to build up their status with neighbors and friends, as well as for the greater living comfort which the products offer.

5. Customers sometimes buy *as a safety precaution*. Home owners, for example, want safe homes so they buy items for precautionary purposes. Sometimes, they buy new stepladders to replace rickety old ones. Sometimes they buy materials for building fences around backyards to protect their children.

---

*Source:* Dwayne Laws, "Pleasing Your Boss, the Customer," *Small Marketers Aid No. 114* (Washington, D.C.: U.S. Small Business Administration, 1965), 1.

---

**Showing the Goods.** During the sales dialogue, the salesperson obtains additional clues from the shopper's reactions and uses them to pinpoint exactly the right merchandise. Having focused on the approximate nature of the customer's need, the salesperson must then seek to present the proper goods effectively. An effective presentation holds prospects' attention, arouses their interest in the items shown, and contributes to the shoppers' desire to buy. These functions suggest that the salesperson needs to continue building a fine rapport with the prospect. In addition to displaying a pleasant and agreeable manner, then, the salesperson ought to:

- Know everything there is to know about the merchandise
- Stress the benefits the item will bring to the shopper in terms of his needs
- Point out the major product attributes that can help the sale
- Demonstrate these selling points
- Involve the shopper if possible, in holding, touching, and working with the article
- Couch the presentation in good English, using terms that the shopper understands, that are positive and descriptive, and that convey pleasant associations

**Meeting Shopper Objections.** Objections proffered by the prospective buyer occur in retailing less often than they do in other forms of direct selling. Nevertheless, they are frequent enough. Experienced salespeople gain familiarity quite readily with the more common types of objections. Indeed, they learn easily how to anticipate them and to direct their conversation during the sales dialogue so that objections are seldom raised.

The majority of shoppers' objections seem to fall into two categories: objections to the price of the article or to certain features of the product or brand. Here are some examples of each:

### Price Objections

"It's too expensive for my pocketbook."
"I didn't plan to spend that much."
"The merchandise doesn't seem like good value for that price."
"I can't afford it."

### Product Objections

"This shade of blue doesn't flatter me at all."
"The jacket's too bulky; I feel cumbersome wearing it."
"Something tells me this material won't wear well."
"My previous experience with this model [or brand] was poor."
"I'm not satisfied with the warranty."

One thing is certain: All objections should be answered directly and not avoided. Objections to the price of an article (the most common type) can be countered by building the shopper's appreciation of the benefits of owning the product, by accenting its major attributes, and by stressing other facets, such as the quality of the materials used, product durability, and so on. Another technique, excellent for expensive appliances or other high-ticket items, is to point out how the merchandise renders satisfaction over a long period of time and how the shopper would only be spending a few dollars per week or month for that satisfaction.

Most books on selling describe a variety of techniques for meeting objections. Intriguing labels are often affixed to these methods. Unfortunately, the scope of this book precludes the mention of more than the following few examples:

**The question approach.** The salesperson requests that the prospect repeat the objection and then seeks further clarification through the use of simple questions, such as: "What makes you believe that?" or "Why do you feel that way?" During the resulting dialogue, the salesperson attempts to persuade the shopper (in a tactful manner, of course) that his or her line of reasoning may not be quite logical. At the very least, the shopper may well realize this without the help of the salesperson.

**The "yes, but . . ." technique.** This approach involves placing the shopper off guard by appearing to agree with the objection raised instead of attempting to deny it. The salesperson then brings up one or more previously unmentioned selling points or benefits to strengthen the presentation.

**The boomerang method.** This strong technique is usually associated with the "hard sell" type of sales presentation. It's therefore infrequently used in retail selling situations. It's sometimes referred to as "the turnaround technique" because the salesperson takes the objection and attempts to "turn it around" into a selling point. As an example, a prospect gives voice to the objection, "I don't think this winter coat will keep me warm enough; it's too light in weight." The salesperson counters with, "Mr. Hughes, you won't *want* to wear a coat that weighs you down! What's the point in carrying around an extra seven or eight pounds with you all day? I assure you, this material will provide as much warmth, if not more, as the heaviest coat you could find."

## Completing the Sale

As the sales dialogue draws to a close, the prospect is most likely psychologically "prepped" to buy. Then, through the use of one or two well-structured questions, the salesperson tests this readiness to buy. Two examples are: "When would you like this to be delivered—next Tuesday or next Friday?" or "Which do you prefer, the tan or the blue?" Such questions are known as *trial closes;* they enable the salesperson to make the decision as to whether or not to close the sale. The sale's "close," or "closing," consummates the presentation.

Again, your perusal of sales texts will yield perhaps a dozen or more different types of "closes," each with its own application and rationale. Like the techniques of overcoming objections, these closing methods usually bear interesting names. A representative sampling follows.

**The assumptive close.** This is the most commonly used technique for closing sales. The salesperson merely assumes that the shopper is ready and starts to write up the sales slip or wrap the merchandise (as the case may be). It's usually preceded by one or more trial closes.

**The balance-sheet close.** This method is often used in the sale of expensive goods or services, such as major appliances, automobiles, real estate, boats, home repairs, or swimming pools. The salesperson draws a line down the center of a sheet of paper, then lists for the prospective buyer the advantages/benefits of ownership on one side and the disadvantages on the other. The purpose is, of course, to convince the prospect that the former outweigh the latter, by far.

**The hook.** This technique involves overcoming any last-minute resistance to the close by offering a special inducement to the shopper, such as:

- "If you order it now, we can deliver it to you by the day after tomorrow."
- "I'll give you a 5 percent discount if you buy it tonight."
- "You'll receive a pair of stockings as a gift if you purchase it today."

**The SRO close.** The initials stand for "Standing Room Only"—which should give you a good idea of what this approach entails. To help clinch the sale, the salesperson may say something like:

- "We only have four left; if you don't purchase it now, we may not have it for you tomorrow."
- "The price is due to be increased on this item on Saturday."
- "I don't think we'll be getting any more of these in."

**The summary close.** The salesperson ticks off all the advantages of owning the article in question, making certain to secure the prospective customer's agreement on each in turn. This results in shoppers coming up with a list of affirmative responses, thus placing them in a most receptive mood for the actual closing.

## Suggestion Selling

I like to refer to this step as one that can help make "two customers out of one." Upon closing the primary sale, your sales personnel should never ask, "Will there be something else?" This is a useless phrase, entirely devoid of meaning. Instead, they should be trained to attempt to interest the customer in a *specific* additional item. Perhaps another article of merchandise complements the one purchased. Alternatively, the salesperson might suggest a totally unrelated item such as an advertised special or a recent addition to the store merchandise. In brief, salespeople should suggest, show, and, if possible, demonstrate the product. Believe it or not, insisting that your salespeople use suggestion selling can add 10 percent or more to your sales!

In most retail lines, there are certain "natural" suggestions of follow-up goods. Here's an abbreviated list, by way of illustration:

| To Go With | Suggest |
| --- | --- |
| a bathrobe | slippers |
| a coat | a scarf, a pocketbook |
| coffee | milk, cream, sugar |

| To Go With | Suggest |
|---|---|
| curtains | a curtain rod |
| a hammer | a screwdriver, a pair of pliers |
| a house plant | plant food, potting soil, a planter |
| liquor | cocktail mixes, wines |
| a shirt | a necktie |
| shoes | slippers, hosiery, a belt |
| slacks | a blouse, a shirt, a belt |

As a final thought, a fifth entry should be appended to the list of phases in the retail selling process: the *follow-up*. Completing the sales slip properly, bagging or wrapping the merchandise with dispatch, thanking customers, and reassuring them in a friendly manner of the wisdom of their choices all constitute essential follow-up steps to suggestion selling. Accompanying the customer to the door, if at all possible, is even better, as is inviting that individual to come back again, soon.

## FOR FURTHER INFORMATION

### Books

Diamond, J., and G. Pintel. *Principles of Selling*. Englewood Cliffs, N.J.: Prentice-Hall, 1985.

Futrell, Charles M. *ABC's of Selling*. Homewood, Ill.: Irwin, 1985.

Johnson, H. Webster, and Anthony J. Faria. *Creative Selling*, 4th ed. Cincinnati: South-Western, 1987.

Kurtz, David L., H. Robert Dodge, and Jay E. Klompmaker. *Professional Selling*, 4th ed. Plano, Tex.: Business Publications, 1985.

Masser, B., and W. Leeds. *Power Selling by Telephone*. Englewood Cliffs, N.J.: Prentice-Hall, 1983.

Mills, K., and J. Paul. *Successful Retail Sales*. Englewood Cliffs, N.J.: Prentice-Hall, 1979.

Pederson, Carlton A., and Milburn D. Wright. *Selling: Principles and Methods*, 8th ed. Homewood, Ill.: Irwin, 1984.

Shimp, Terence A., and M. Wayne Delozier. *Promotion Management and Marketing Communications*. New York: Dryden, 1986.

Stanley, Richard E. *Promotion: Advertising, Publicity, Personal Selling, Sales Promotion*, 2d ed. Englewood Cliffs, N.J.: Prentice-Hall, 1982.

Storholm, Gordon, and Louis C. Kaufman. *Principles of Selling*. Englewood Cliffs, N.J.: Prentice-Hall, 1985.

### Pamphlets Available from the Small Business Administration

#### Management Aids

MA 4.002—"Creative Selling: The Competitive Edge"
MA 4.012—"Marketing Checklist for Small Retailers"
MA 4.023—"Selling by Mail Order"

### Booklets Available from the Superintendent of Documents

S/N 045-000-00189-0—*Managing Retail Salespeople*—$4.75.

----- 17 -----

# Getting the Most Out of Your Advertising Dollars

Is advertising necessary?

Large-scale retailers apparently think so. Check your daily newspaper; you'll discover page after page filled with advertisements from department and chain stores, supermarkets, and mass merchandisers. Nationally known firms like K Mart and Sears, Roebuck and Company spend hundreds of millions annually on advertising.

Yet many small store owners do absolutely no media advertising at all. This fact shouldn't surprise you, for shopkeepers are notoriously tightfisted—and rightly so, considering that their net profits can be measured in no more than a few pennies per dollar rung up at the register. (The average retail enterprise nets only 2 or 3 percent of sales, after taxes.)

In the mid-1970s I surveyed some 195 independent retail establishments in a metropolitan area.* In all, about thirty different types of stores were represented in the group. More than half of them were neighborhood stores; the other locations ranged from central and secondary business districts to various types of shopping centers. I discovered that the median annual advertising expenditure for these outlets came to approximately $475—not what you would call a princely sum. Considering their median yearly sales of $110,000 (above the national average for those days!), this expenditure meant that the retailers, on average, spent less than 0.5 percent of their sales on advertising.

The majority of the store owners admitted that they did not advertise. On the other hand, some relied rather heavily on newspaper advertising, occasionally to the tune of ten times the median figure and more. These latter stores included, among other types, home furnishings and furniture stores, outlets selling major appliances, and menswear shops.

---

\* Irving Burstiner, "The Small Retailer and His Problems," *Journal of Business Education* 50 (March 1975), 243–45.

## Advertising Is an Investment

Many independent retailers rely entirely on their store locations and window displays to attract prospective customers. This shortsighted attitude can perhaps be attributed to the retail merchant's mistaken belief that advertising expenses represent just another operating cost to worry about and to control vigilantly. This just isn't so. The astute business manager regards such monies as a long-term investment and recognizes their contribution toward sales volume and business growth.

Your storefront, the sign you had erected above your entrance, your shop's display window(s), and a well-stocked and tastefully arranged store interior—which people manage to glimpse as they walk or drive past your location—these are all powerful promotional tools. Yet the contribution they make is necessarily limited, for they can only attract the attention of passersby. When you advertise, on the other hand, you *reach out* not only into the surrounding neighborhood and trading area but beyond, into the outlying community. Advertising's scope and its potential are far, far greater than interior and storefront displays.

## Your New Store *Must* Be Advertised

Advertising is an absolute necessity for the new retail enterprise. At the outset, both you and your store represent completely unknown quantities to the area's residents. For a successful business launch, you need to tell your story—to acquaint the public with the facts: the kind of store you have opened; the quality, breadth, and depth of the merchandise you carry in stock; your prices and the services you offer; the kind of prompt, courteous attention the customers can expect of your employees; and what you stand for generally.

My considered opinion is that *even the established store must continue to advertise,* if only to keep the image the owner is constantly seeking to build before the public. This is an image of a place where things are happening, where real contributions are made to the community, where people can purchase the things they want at fair prices, where shopping can be enjoyable, and so on. Moreover, advertising is needed to help maintain sales volume in the face of local competition—or when the economy begins to slide.

It should be pointed out, as a cautionary note, that no amount spent for advertising can support an inferior product for very long. Indeed, the statement that "good advertising starts with a good product" is practically an axiom in the advertising field. Your promotional efforts must convey the story of a healthy, viable business: a favorable location, attractive decor, satisfactory merchandise and prices, capable employees, and the like. Also, generating store traffic is not enough. You need to convert browsers into buyers and buyers into steady customers.

## MANAGE YOUR ADVERTISING: DON'T LET IT MANAGE YOU

To maximize the effectiveness of your advertising budget, you need to plan this phase of store administration just as carefully as you plan your buying, merchandising, or financing. Planning involves setting goals or objectives, then thinking through various methods of accomplishing those goals and choosing the better ones.

## Clarify Your Objectives

You have a wide range of choices when it comes to your advertising objectives: popularizing your new store, creating store traffic, announcing events such as preseason or clearance sales, introducing a fashionable new product or line, and so forth. To help you set your sights in the preopening stage of your retail business, arrange your advertising goals into three categories: (1) *immediate* (the first six months or so); (2) *near future* (the first two years); and (3) *distant future* (beyond that time).

Until your new store has successfully secured a foothold in the area, your basic challenge is clear: You need to gain the attention of likely prospects for your merchandise. You must somehow arouse their curiosity and their interest, create as much excitement among them as you can (in a positive sense, of course), and convince sizable numbers of shoppers to come into your store and, you hope, to make purchases. *You need to build a loyal clientele.* Your initial advertising activity thus contributes to the formation of your "store image." This image is built up over time from many impressions garnered by both shoppers and nonshoppers from just about every phase of your store operations.

Within perhaps two or three months of your grand opening, you might consider switching your outlook from this "pioneering" type of *institutional advertising* toward specific *product advertising*. The goals of this new phase in your promotion plans are to bring shoppers in to buy specific items of merchandise, to take advantage of special offers, to help you move inventory off your shelves, and to command immediate sales results. As time goes by, you may decide to bring into play still other objectives: clearing out leftover goods after Easter or Christmas, generating more sales dollars in periods of tight cash flow, disposing of slow-moving items, and the like.

## A Suggested Modus Operandi

Here's a logical progression for you to follow in managing your advertising efforts, adapted from recommendations in SBA publications. Some of these steps are treated in more detail later on in this chapter.

1. Settle on a first year's total expenditure you believe is appropriate to your needs.
2. Break down this overall total into planned monthly expenditures. (For details, see page 244.)
3. Analyze your retail operation. List the good and the not-so-good features, and use this knowledge to help shape the image you want to project in your advertising.
4. Decide on your most likely prospects. Study their characteristics, their needs, and their wants. Derive a sharply focused mental picture of your "target audience."
5. Review your store's merchandise and the services you offer. Select those you want to tell your prospects about.
6. Choose the most promising media for your particular purposes.

7. Strive to prepare advertisements that get results.
8. Evaluate, as best you can, the performance of every single ad. (In time, you can look forward to repeating the more successful ones.)

## DECIDING HOW MUCH TO SPEND

Setting an annual advertising budget is always a thorny problem, for no one can tell you whether a given sum is too large, too small, or just right. There's no one tried-and-proven method I could label successful. The problem is that, within the entrepreneurial mentality, two diametrically opposed motives wrestle with each other for a retailer's advertising dollars: (1) a pervasive impulse to clamp down on expenses with an iron glove; and (2) a just-as-fervent desire to increase sales and expand the business. The situation is further complicated because, as a rule, the results of advertising cannot easily be measured. A sane approach that can perhaps help you resolve this dilemma is to review briefly the ways other business organizations make their advertising-budget decisions. These are:

- The arbitrary approach
- The "affordable" method
- The "check-the-competition" technique
- The job-estimation method
- The "percentage-of-sales" approach

### The Arbitrary Approach

This method, whereby the store owner appears to pull a figure out of thin air, is the refuge of entrepreneurs who have little confidence in what advertising can do for their businesses and who are unclear as to their goals or, for that matter, the purposes of advertising. The technique is akin to gambling; indeed, the decision is occasionally made by rolling dice, by flipping a coin, or by tossing a dart at a board on the wall.

### The "Affordable" Method

A close relative of the arbitrary approach, this technique is used by business owners who lack self-confidence and who aren't quite convinced of the benefits of advertising. When asked about next year's advertising budget amount, they steadfastly maintain that they'll assign only what they can "spare" from the business. This amount is loosely defined as the funds that might be left over after tallying up the monies needed to take care of all other aspects of the operations: procuring merchandise and supplies, salaries, rent, utilities, store maintenance, and so forth.

### The "Check-the-Competition" Technique

This method is based on the assumption that the local competition knows what it's doing. You watch their advertising and estimate how much they have been spending (per store).

You then plan to spend an equivalent amount on your own advertising. If this approach proves to be too difficult for you, you can always check the national averages for your particular line of trade and go by that figure. Generally, this kind of information is available from your trade association.

## The Job-Estimation Method

This technique is rarely used, mainly because it's so difficult to work out. It does, however, make considerable sense as an exercise in logic: First you set specific goals for your advertising, and then you do some strenuous thinking about how much money you need to spend to achieve those goals satisfactorily. This approach is similar to the general contractor's way of operating. Before contracting with you to add a room to your house, put in a swimming pool or a patio, or erect a garage in back, the contractor considers your objectives, estimates the time needed for construction, the materials to be used, and the labor that needs to be hired. Then the contractor adds a desired profit margin before quoting an estimate of how much the job will cost you. The trouble with this technique is that, regardless of how smart you are, any estimate you might come up with could be considerably off target due to such unknowns as the amount of sales the advertising will produce and what your competitors are doing.

## The "Percentage-of-Sales" Approach

Your best bet—and the method I recommend most strongly—is the practical, heuristic technique termed the *percentage-of-sales* technique. The majority of independent retailers appears to favor this method, probably because it enables them to relate costs to sales and thereby keep their expenses from getting out of hand. When you think about it, though, the logic seems to be in error; it points up advertising as a function of *sales*, instead of the other way around.

The retail merchant first tallies up last year's sales, then totals all the funds allocated during that year to advertising, and compares the two, forming a ratio as shown:

$$\frac{\text{Advertising}}{\text{Percentage of Sales}} = \frac{\text{Total Advertising Cost}}{\text{Net Sales for Year}}$$

For example, with last-year sales of $180,000 and an advertising expenditure of $4,500, the percentage-of-sales figure is calculated in this fashion:

$$\frac{\text{Advertising}}{\text{Percentage of Sales}} = \frac{\$4,500}{\$180,000} = 2.5\%$$

This percentage figure of 2.5 then forms the guideline for the following year's advertising budget.

Of course, it's impossible to calculate this percentage when just starting out, since no prior year's figures are available. Still, as previously mentioned, you might well check with your trade association for the typical percentage-of-sales figure in your line of trade. (Just as a point of information, though, you should plan to spend more during the first year than the trade's average would indicate, to help you get your business off the ground.) There'll be no problem, though, the second year in business.

This approach can be improved upon. After your new store has been established, you can resort to two- or three-year averages of actual sales performance and advertising expenditures to derive an average percentage-of-sales figure. Averages are generally more accurate, since any one year's sales (or advertising expenses, for that matter) can be atypical because of unusual circumstances. Moreover, you'll be able to make a more realistic appraisal of your advertising needs with three years of experience behind you. You can also project next year's sales, which may be higher or lower than this year's in your expectations, and combine these figures with those three-year averages. Perhaps in this way you'll come closer to a more dependable percentage.

As a last suggestion, you should aim at spending *at least twice* the typical percentage-of-sales figure for your type of store during the first two or three years of business activity. You need to assume that competitive stores in your area have been conducting business successfully for a number of years and that they have already acquired a regular clientele. You, on the other hand, must first secure, and then consolidate, your position in the community. If 2 percent of sales happens to be typical for your kind of store, then you should budget at least 4, if not 5, percent for advertising.

## BREAKING DOWN THE ANNUAL BUDGET

Having set the annual appropriation, you next need to break this figure down into monthly statistics, also on a percentage-of-sales basis. You'll find that, for just about all retailing lines, sales for each month during the year vary considerably. The month of December, for example, may account for as much as 20 or 25 percent of the entire year's sales—and sometimes more. The summer months may each represent no more than 4 or 5 percent of sales. (Of course, the situation might be reversed, should your store be an ice cream parlor!) Let's assume that your expected monthly percentages of total sales are as follows:

| January | 4% | July | 4% |
|---------|-----|-----------|-----|
| February | 7 | August | 4 |
| March | 8 | September | 8 |
| April | 10 | October | 9 |
| May | 7 | November | 10 |
| June | 5 | December | 24 |

Before you proceed with your calculations, you should first set aside perhaps 5 or 10 percent of the yearly appropriation for a "contingency fund" that could be tapped for special circumstances, such as to meet an unexpected competitive situation, to launch a new line of merchandise or a new fashion, to take care of "cooperative advertising" offers from your suppliers, and the like. This is a healthy measure to take. If you decide to set aside, let's say, 10 percent of your first year's advertising appropriation of $5,000, you will still have $4,500 ($5,000 − $500) to distribute over the twelve months. Your planned monthly expenditures for advertising would then be as follows:

| | | | |
|---|---|---|---|
| January | $180 | July | $180 |
| February | 315 | August | 180 |
| March | 360 | September | 360 |
| April | 450 | October | 405 |
| May | 315 | November | 450 |
| June | 225 | December | 1,080 |

It may, however, be advisable for you to "steal from Peter to pay Paul." You might consider "borrowing" several hundred dollars from the December budget and using this money to prop up sales in one or two of the slower months. Likewise, you could reduce the allocations for other busy months (April, October, November) for the same purpose. This switch is supportable on the strength of the fact that street (or shopping-center) traffic is heavy enough during the pre-Christmas season and other busy periods that you can expect to do a brisk business even without much advertising. Some retailers feel differently; they believe that it's better to spend *more* advertising dollars during the busier months of the year because so many more consumers are "in the mood" to spend. This method is akin to chumming a stream to catch more fish. A case can be made for either approach. The decision is yours alone; you'll learn which way is best for you through trial and error.

## THE ADVERTISING MEDIA

Once you decide on how much to spend and when to spend it, you must ask yourself just how much advertising you can do with that $180 you have allotted to January. How much TV time can you purchase? More likely than not, not a blessed minute! What about going on radio? Yes, you just might be able to buy a brief spot announcement or two on a local station. Small wonder, then, that small retailers need to be ultracautious in their advertising plans. You must make every cent you spend count; there's never much money to fling about freely. Not only *how much,* but also *where* and *when* you spend your advertising dollars becomes vitally important.

Allocating your funds to the media that are right for you and determining the correct proportions are important considerations. Among the factors you can use to compare media are production costs, size of audience, media costs, extent of penetration of your store's trading area, immediacy of the reaction to your advertising, and the lead time needed from preparing the ad to its exposure to the public. Available media include:

- The *print media,* such as newspapers and magazines
- The *broadcast media* (radio, television)
- *Direct mail*
- The *position media* (billboards, bus and subway posters, and the like)
- A variety of so-called *supplemental media* (skywriting or matchbook covers, for example)

Most small retailers depend primarily on the newspapers, with perhaps occasional use of local radio and direct mail. Television is often ruled out because of its excessive cost and is therefore left almost exclusively to the manufacturer and to a few large-scale retail organizations. (A number of nonstore, "direct" retailers purvey a variety of products and services over TV, such as records and tapes, kitchen utensils, home fire and burglar alarms, personal loans, and home mortgages. This use of direct marketing via TV is nearly the equivalent of mail-order retailing, but the familiar magazine advertisement is replaced by the medium of television.)

## Newspapers

Nearly every locale in the country is blessed with a newspaper, usually a daily. It has been estimated that more than four out of five adults read a newspaper every day. In effect, then, you can count on reaching most of the homes and apartments in your trading area through advertising in this medium. Indeed, the same paper may be read by several family members in the typical household. In other words, your ad gets a lot more mileage than indicated by the "audited circulation" figures displayed on the newspaper's rate card.

As a retailer, you enjoy the "local" rate, which is below the rate charged the national advertiser. Your costs of preparation are minimal. The newspaper helps you plan your ads; it suggests headlines, copy, and layout. It can even supply standard illustrations (*cuts*) to help you dress them up.

Newspaper ads bring quick results, often on the very day they appear. This medium also has considerable flexibility: You can make last-minute copy changes, you can select the best day(s) of the week for your ad to appear, you can even request a special position within the paper. (Often, there's an additional charge for this request, but it may well be worth it.)

Prices for newspaper space are quoted on a per-line or per-inch basis; there are fourteen *agate lines* to one column inch. Display advertisements may be purchased in units of various sizes up to a full page. Costs quoted are generally for *run-of-paper* (R.O.P.) position; this means that the newspaper has the freedom to place the ad wherever they deem best. Should you want your ad to run on the second or third page, or in the upper right-hand corner of a page (a desirable position!), you may have to pay an additional charge. In addition, you should know that costs also depend on total linage used, as well as on circulation figures, and that you can negotiate with the newspaper for a lower rate based on the quantity of space used.

**Now for the Negatives** . . . This medium also has some drawbacks. For one thing, a newspaper will usually be distributed far beyond your trading area, so that there will be scads of "waste circulation." (For this reason, a local weekly paper may often be of more benefit to you than a more broad-based daily.) Your ad may not be noticed by the majority of the newspaper's readers, simply because so many advertisements in every issue compete for reader attention. Finally, the life of a single issue (per reader) is probably less than an hour; consequently, your message's exposure might be only a minute or less.

## You Can Benefit by Using Direct Mail

The extraordinarily versatile medium of direct mail enables you to target in on specific persons, groups, or organizations within your trading area, *all* of whom may be likely prospects for your retail business. Mailing pieces come in all formats, shapes, and sizes, ranging from the simple "penny postcard" (now 15 cents) through sales letters, flyers, envelope stuffers, brochures, cut-out and pop-up pieces, and the like—all the way to full-color, multipage catalogs. Direct mail is conducted on a one-to-one basis, a most effective means of communication and persuasion. This medium should be used far more in retailing than it is today.

You can profitably use direct mail to invite previously untapped shopper segments to come in to see a new line you're putting out, to persuade your regular customers to visit your store more often, to get people to "shop at home," and so forth. If your store atmosphere is, in your opinion, well suited to certain types—car owners, lawyers, golfers, or teachers, for example—or if certain goods you stock appeal to those types, then a good mailing piece sent to a list of those individuals may bring you additional new business. As an example, a large variety store in a southeastern corner of the country carried in its extensive merchandise inventory three or four popular novelties that seemed suitable for fund-raising efforts. The owners obtained a list of some fifty groups and organizations in the area and built an active little business through the mails.

An up-to-date mailing list is the basic key to direct-mail profits. You can develop your own list in several ways. If your policy is to fill out sales slips for all transactions, the names and addresses on these can help initiate your mailing list. Retailers in downtown, transient areas sometimes make use of a "Guest Register" where shoppers, especially out-of-towners, can record this information. Another source is the very customers whose charge cards you honor. You can also tap directories: the telephone book, town directory, voter lists, tax lists, and so on. Then, too, you may decide to run a contest or sweepstakes during the year; in this case, you can collect the names and addresses shown on the entry blanks.

Lists of every type and description are available for rent or purchase from mailing-list houses or brokers. These lists are often broken down geographically and demographically. The names and addresses are continually updated and usually guaranteed to be 95 percent accurate by the list house. Direct-mail specialists can help you to prepare your materials professionally and to print them; mailing houses address your envelopes (mechanically or electronically), collate and fold the literature that is to go into them, seal and stamp the envelopes, and cart your complete mailing off to the post office for you.

Visit your local post office for information regarding such mailings, bulk mailing permits, Form 3547 (Address Correction Requested), postage costs, and other pertinent details.

## Local Radio

Radio advertising is another possibility for the small retailer, for local rates are usually within the reach of the modest advertising budget. In practice, though, radio is used rather infrequently and generally as a supplement to newspaper advertising. It's normally reserved for special occasions such as a pre-Easter sale, a fashion show, or some special publicity event (like Santa's appearance).

Like television, radio is another "universal" medium; there are at least two radios for every man, woman, and child in the United States. Many people carry them on their person, and nearly every automobile comes equipped with one—all of which means that your messages can be carried into every nook and cranny of your store's trading area. You will find your biggest audiences during morning drive time; evening hours, for the most part, are devoted to television.

**The Advantages of Radio.** Radio offers the retail advertiser many of the same benefits found in the newspaper medium: extensive penetration of the market area, quick action, the flexibility to make last-minute changes in copy, and minimal production costs. Radio, however, is more efficient than newspapers in reaching select groups, for each station has its own group of loyal listeners. There are stations that cater almost exclusively to young people, to black people, to certain nationalities (often broadcasting, for the most part, in a foreign tongue), to lovers of classical or country music, and so on.

Sometimes it's possible to work out a "barter arrangement" with a radio station, whereby you pay for your advertising time with a combination of cash and merchandise. In turn, the items you supply may be used by the station, for example, as prizes in a contest or as awards on a giveaway show.

**The Disadvantages of Radio.** As a medium, radio also has its drawbacks. For one thing, the lack of any "video" rules out the possibility of displaying your merchandise or, for that matter, your store. Then there's the tremendous handicap of *fractionalization:* Any one area is usually covered by several different radio stations—and by ten or more in our larger cities. Fractionalization means that the chances are rather small that (1) your particular station is being listened to at any one time, and that (2) your own messages are being heard. For this reason, firms using radio think in terms of *flights,* or packages, of announcements, as well as of frequency and repetition.

To be effective, radio commercials need to be short and to the point. They also have to be dramatic enough to catch the listener's attention, because radio talk is often just "background noise" to many people.

## Other Useful Media

Other media can be helpful to your advertising efforts. (*Note:* Since both television and magazine advertising are most likely far down the pike for you, we won't be discussing them here.)

**Position Advertising.** Outdoor and transit advertising (on buses, trains, and taxicabs), posters, billboards, and signs constitute the *position media.* These may be profitably used by certain types of retail businesses, especially those that cater to travelers or transients. Such enterprises include skating rinks, amusement parks, gasoline service stations, restaurants, motels, and hotels. Space is generally rented on a monthly basis. Since exposure to the advertised message is often no more than a few seconds, the art, layout, and colors used must be striking—and the copy especially short. Frequently, such gimmicks as misspelled words, wry humor, fluorescent printing, and motion are used to gain attention.

**The "Yellow Pages."** Another important medium for many kinds of businesses is the "Yellow Pages" of the telephone directory. A listing in bold type costs you only a few dollars a month; the cost of a small display ad is also well within the reach of the typical small retail establishment. Newcomers to your neighborhood frequently resort to "letting their fingers do the walking through the 'Yellow Pages.' " Over time, this medium can bring you a considerable number of new customers. It's especially valuable for stores that sell home furnishings, lighting fixtures, floor coverings, major appliances, and the like.

## HOW TO PREPARE NEWSPAPER ADS THAT GET RESULTS

The elements that go into a newspaper advertisement are the layout, the artwork, the copy, and the store signature. Yet before you begin to put all the elements together, there are a number of things you should consider. For a starter, read through the checklist in exhibit 17–1. Then digest carefully the guidelines given in exhibits 17–2 and 17–3.

---

**EXHIBIT 17–1. PROFILING YOURSELF AND YOUR CUSTOMER**

The first step in evaluating the various ways of telling your story to your public is that of deciding *who you are* and *who your public is*. This "profile" checklist may be helpful:

1. *What Quality of Merchandise Do I Sell?* Are my price lines high? In the middle? Too low? Are my customers' incomes increasing rapidly so that they are prospects for higher price lines?

2. *How Do I Compare with Competition?* Am I priced competitively? Or do I stress quality and service? Are my merchandise lines as broad and varied as my competitors'?

3. *What Selling Techniques Do I Use?* Are my employees trained to sell related items? To sell higher-profit lines? Or are they just friendly clerks?

4. *What Customer Services Do I Feature?* Do I extend credit? Do I deliver? Do I offer a money-back guarantee, or item substitution? Do I repair merchandise? Do I stay open nights? Do I offer adequate parking space?

5. *Am I Accessible to the Public?* Am I located on a busy street with lots of foot traffic? Or do I have to promote harder so as to *pull* people to an out-of-the-way location? Am I long-in-business and well-known? Are there many people who still don't know me?

6. *Who Makes Up My Market?* Do I sell to men? Women? Teenagers? Tots? Do they have pronounced tastes? Are my customers' incomes high, low, or average? Are more young families with more children moving into my neighborhood? Do they all live near the store? Within a one-mile radius? Do they come from all over the city?

7. *Why Do People Buy from Me?* Do I know why my *best* customers continue to buy from me? Have I asked them why? Do they like me for reasons that could be featured in my advertising?

8. *Why Don't People Buy from Me?* Have I ever asked a customer who *stopped* shopping why he quit my store? Do I take an objective look at my windows, my displays, counters, lighting? Is the store clean? Are the employees courteous and well-informed?

After you've studied these questions, fix the things you don't like about your store. Capitalize on what you *do* like. Decide who your customers should be. Then decide what kind of "face" you're going to present to them in your advertising.

---

*Source:* Charles T. Lipscomb, Jr., "Checklist for Successful Retail Advertising," *Small Marketers Aid No. 96* (Washington, D.C.: U.S. Small Business Administration, 1974), 1–2.

---

**EXHIBIT 17–2. PLANNING FOR RESULTS**

Certain things are basic to planning advertisements whose results can be measured. First of all, *advertise products or services that have merit in themselves.* Unless a product or service is good, few customers will make repeat purchases no matter how much advertising the store does.

Many people will not make an initial purchase of a shoddy item because of doubt or unfavorable word-of-mouth publicity. The ad that successfully sells inferior merchandise usually loses customers in the long run.

Small marketers, as a rule, *should treat their messages seriously.* Humor is risky as well as difficult to write. Be on the safe side and tell people the facts about your merchandise and services.

Another basic element in planning advertisements is to know *exactly what you wish a particular ad to accomplish.* In an immediate-response ad, you want customers to come in and

**Exhibit 17–2. Continued**

buy a certain item or items in the next several days. In attitude advertising, you decide which attitude you are trying to create and plan each individual ad to that end. In a small operation, the ads usually feature merchandise rather than store policies.

*Plan the ad around only one idea.* Each ad should have a single message. If the message needs reinforcing with other ideas, keep them in the background. If you have several important things to say, use a different ad for each one and run the ads on succeeding days or weeks.

The pointers that follow are designed to help you plan ads so they will make your store stand out consistently when people read or hear about it.

*Identify your store fully and clearly.* Logotypes or signatures in printed ads should be clean-lined, uncluttered, and prominently displayed. Give your address and telephone number.

*Pick illustrations that are all similar in character.* Graphics—that is, drawings, photos, borders, and layout—that are similar in character help people to recognize your advertising immediately.

*Pick a printing typeface and stick to it.* Using the same typeface . . . helps people to recognize your ads. Also, using the same sort of type and illustrations in all ads allows you to concentrate on the message when examining changes in response to ads.

*Make copy easy to read.* The printed message should be broken up with white space to allow the reader to see the lines quickly.

*Use coupons for direct-mail advertising response as often as possible.* Coupons give an immediate sales check. Key the coupon in some manner so that you can measure the response easily.

*Source:* Elizabeth M. Sorbet, "Measuring the Results of Advertising," *Small Marketers Aid No. 121* (Washington, D.C.: U.S. Small Business Administration, 1966), 2.

## Exhibit 17–3. Pack your ads with selling punch

- *Make your ads easy to recognize.* Give your copy and layout a consistent personality and style.
- *Use a simple layout.* Your layout should lead the reader's eye easily through the message from the art and headline to the copy and price to the signature.
- *Use dominant illustrations.* Show the featured merchandise in dominant illustrations. Whenever possible, show the product in use.
- *Show the benefit to the reader.* Prospective customers want to know "what's in it for me." But, do not try to pack the ad with reasons to buy—give the customer one primary reason, then back it up with one or two secondary reasons.
- *Feature the "right" item.* Select an item that is wanted, timely, stocked in depth, and typical of your store. Specify brand merchandise and take advantage of advertising allowances and cooperative advertising whenever you can.
- *State a price or range of prices.* Don't be afraid to quote high prices. If the price is low, support it with statements which create belief, such as clearance or special purchase.
- *Include store name and address.* Double check every ad to make sure that it contains store name, address, telephone number, and store hours.

*Source:* Ovid Riso, "Advertising Guidelines for Small Retail Firms," *Management Aid No. 4.015* (Washington, D.C.: U.S. Small Business Administration, n.d.), 4–5.

## Additional Thoughts

The most effective method of persuading people to buy is, of course, direct selling. In the hands of the professional salesperson, a likely prospect is led step by step through the sales presentation to a successful closing. The salesperson often follows the *AIDA Principle;* the acronym *AIDA* is derived from the initial letters of four words: *Attention, Interest, Desire, Action.* The principle works as follows:

1. Secure the prospect's *Attention.*
2. Arouse his or her *Interest* in what you're selling.
3. Build *Desire* in the prospect to have what you offer.
4. Get *Action* in the form of a signed order.

As a selling device, then, the newspaper advertisement must be regarded as inferior to the one-to-one sales presentation. You're usually confined to a relatively small area of the printed page by virtue of the small retailer's limited advertising budget. Yet within that space you still need to do essentially the same kind of selling job as the salesperson. The only way to profit under such constraints, then, is to be ruthlessly—and cleverly—selective in your choice of the ad's ingredients. Each and every ad you place should be designed to help you sell your merchandise, your services, your special promotions, your store. Let this "selling orientation" become second nature with you. This way, you prepare all your ads with the AIDA Principle in mind, and you work out in advance *how best* to accomplish each of those four steps.

Here are some of the "tricks of the trade" you can use to draw readers' attention to *your* ad, even though it may be buried among other, often larger ads:

- Heavy or unusual borders
- An actual photograph
- Lively artwork/illustration
- Wide, white-space margins around the copy
- Bold, provocative headlines
- Printing in reverse (white letters, black background)

With regard to your copy:

- Keep it short.
- Get to the point.
- Use basic English.
- Avoid the passive tense.
- Build in, if you can, an emotional appeal.
- Stress one or two major selling points.
- Promise benefits.
- Avoid exaggeration.

As a final thought, you should know that doubling the size of a newspaper ad doesn't double the number of readers. In the majority of instances, several repeat insertions of the same small ad produce better results than a one-shot large ad.

## SHOULD YOU USE AN ADVERTISING AGENCY?

Frankly, for your first two or three years in business, your total annual advertising budget won't be sufficient to interest any but the smallest of ad agencies. Even the small agency may not want to work with you on the usual commission basis; instead, it may ask you for a minimum fee. Perhaps after a few years, after an ascending sales curve or when you have added several units and become a small chain, you might give some consideration to searching for a good agency.

## FOR FURTHER INFORMATION

### Books

Bovee, Courtland L., and William F. Arens. *Contemporary Advertising*, 2d ed. Homewood, Ill.: Irwin, 1986.

Caples, John. *How to Make Your Advertising Make Money*. Englewood Cliffs, N.J.: Prentice-Hall, 1983.

Cohen, William. *Direct Response Marketing*. New York: Wiley, 1984.

David, Bruce E. *The Profitable Advertising Manual: A Handbook for Small Business*, 2d ed. Twinsburg, Ohio: Worthprinting, 1986.

Edwards, C., and C. Lebowitz. *Retail Advertising and Sales Promotion*, 4th ed. Englewood Cliffs, N.J.: Prentice-Hall, 1981.

Gray, Ernest A. *Profitable Methods for Small Business Advertising*. New York: Wiley, 1984.

Moriarty, S. *Creative Advertising: Theory and Practice*. Englewood Cliffs, N.J.: Prentice-Hall, 1986.

Norris, J. *Advertising*, 3d ed. Englewood Cliffs, N.J.: Prentice-Hall, 1984.

Nylen, David W. *Advertising: Planning, Implementation, and Control*, 3d ed. Cincinnati: South-Western, 1986.

Rothschild, Michael. *Advertising: From Fundamentals to Strategies*. Lexington, Mass.: D. C. Heath, 1987.

Russell, J., and G. Verrill. *Otto Kleppner's Advertising Procedure*, 9th ed. Englewood Cliffs, N.J.: Prentice-Hall, 1986.

Sutton, C. *Advertising Your Way to Success: How to Create Best-Selling Advertisements in All Media*. Englewood Cliffs, N.J.: Prentice-Hall, 1981.

### Pamphlets Available from the Small Business Administration

#### Management Aids

MA 4.015—"Advertising Guidelines for Small Retail Firms"
MA 4.018—"Plan Your Advertising Budget"
MA 4.023—"Selling by Mail Order"

# VII

# Managing the Financial Aspects

# 18

# Managing Your Business's Finances

The small store owner is quick to concede that record keeping is a tedious, at times quite annoying, task. Nonetheless, it's a necessary task; you must keep records to be able to document and support the statements made on your tax forms and to comply with various governmental regulations. Yet this continuous chore need not turn you off, because a properly-set-up, accurate record-keeping system contributes to business success. It helps you know where you are, where you have been, and where you're going.

## KEEPING RECORDS: SOME BASICS

Like many independent retail merchants, you may plan to handle your books personally during the first year or two of business. If so, be sure to have an accountant set them up so that you'll be able to generate readily the kinds of facts you need to run your operation. On the other hand, you may decide to employ a part-time bookkeeper or turn the entire problem over to a bookkeeping service. Simplified bookkeeping systems are available for store owners; your business stationer probably stocks several of them.

### Required Records

In reality, the sole proprietorship needs only four basic records for income-tax purposes:

- A checkbook
- A cash-receipts journal
- A cash-disbursements journal
- A petty-cash fund

With the checkbook, you keep track of those business expenses paid by check. You use the cash-receipts journal to enter, on a daily basis, all monies received—and you record each day's cash outlay for purchases and expenses in the cash-disbursements journal. Finally, you keep track of minor amounts paid out from your petty-cash fund.

257

Naturally, you also need to save all supporting documents for those records. These include, among other items, all invoices, purchase orders, daily cash-receipt forms, and petty-cash vouchers. In addition, your record-keeping system probably also needs to include the following:

- An accounts receivable ledger (if you extend credit)
- A general ledger (in which you record assets, liabilities, and capital)
- An employees' payroll record book
- Various internal forms

*Journals* are used as books of original entry—to record daily transactions. Each journal entry generally indicates the date of the transaction, a brief description of it, and the amount of money involved. *Ledgers* are books or files in which a number of accounts are kept together. Each journal entry is later posted to a ledger account. In your ledger, you also want to keep a list of the equipment you have, together with the dates of purchase and purchase costs, for purposes of calculating depreciation.

Store sales should be tallied up at the close of each day and a form similar to that shown in exhibit 18–1 completed. More information relative to financial record keeping is provided in exhibits 18–2 to 18–4.

## BUDGETING LEADS TO EFFECTIVE MANAGEMENT

Budgets are plans—blueprints for managerial action over specified periods of time. They're guides to follow; at the same time, they're targets to shoot for. As one SBA publication has put it:

> Briefly, budgeting requires you to consider your basic objectives, policies, plans, resources, and so forth. It requires you to make sure your company is properly organized. It requires you and your key people to undertake a coordinated, comprehensive, and informative effort to achieve common objectives. It helps you insure that proper controls and evaluative procedures are established throughout your company. It encourages and motivates everyone concerned to put forth a good effort. It provides a plan so that all of you know where you are going—as well as why, how, when, and with whom. In short, the budgeting process is a valuable tool in planning for profits.*

As you observed in chapter 5, serious planning of any kind calls for considerable self-discipline and much hard work. Making a budget not only involves analyzing the present situation and making a forecast of the future situation but also establishing goals and subgoals and then providing the linkage between *now* and *then* in terms of scheduling events, strategies, and tactics. Naturally, since budgets are targets to be reached in the

---

* Charles J. Woelfel, "Basic Budgets for Profit Planning," *Management Aid 220* (Washington, D.C.: Small Business Administration, 1979), 2.

## EXHIBIT 18–1. SAMPLE DAILY CASH SUMMARY FORM

### DAILY SUMMARY OF SALES AND CASH RECEIPTS

DATE MARCH 23, 19—

#### CASH RECEIPTS

| | |
|---|---|
| 1. Cash sales .................................................................. | $435.00 |
| 2. Collections on account ............................................. | 100.00 |
| 3. Miscellaneous receipts* .......................................... | 15.00 |
| 4. TOTAL RECEIPTS TO BE ACCOUNTED FOR .......... | $550.00 |

#### CASH ON HAND

| | | |
|---|---|---|
| 5. Cash in register till: | | |
|     Coins ................................................. | $ 25.00 | |
|     Bills .................................................... | 510.00 | |
|     Checks ............................................... | 95.00 | |
|       Total cash in register or till .......... | | $630.00 |
| 6. Petty-cash slips ........................................... | | 14.00 |
| 7. TOTAL CASH ACCOUNTED FOR ................ | | $644.00 |
| 8. Less change and petty-cash fund: | | |
|     Petty-cash slips ................................ | $ 14.00 | |
|     Coins and bills .................................. | 86.00 | |
|       Change and petty-cash fund (fixed amount) ...... | | 100.00 |
| 9. TOTAL CASH DEPOSIT ............................ | | $544.00 |
| 10. CASH SHORT (Item 4 less item 9 if item 4 is larger) .......... | | $ 6.00 |
| 11. CASH OVER (Item 9 less item 4 if item 9 is larger) .......... | | |

#### TOTAL SALES

| | |
|---|---|
| 12. Cash sales .................................................................. | $435.00 |
| 13. Charge sales (sales checks #262 to #316) ..................... | 225.00 |
| 14. TOTAL SALES ......................................................... | $660.00 |

BY JOHN DOE

---

*Source:* Robert C. Ragan, "Financial Recordkeeping for Small Stores," *Small Business Management Series No. 32* (Washington, D.C.: U.S. Small Business Administration, 1976), 16.

*Note to appear on back of summary: "Miscellaneous receipts: Refund on merchandise $15.00."

---

## EXHIBIT 18–2. FINANCIAL CHECKLIST FOR THE OWNER-MANAGER

### SMALL BUSINESS FINANCIAL STATUS CHECKLIST
(What an Owner-Manager Should Know)

DAILY

1. Cash on hand.
2. Bank balance (keep business and personal funds separate).
3. Daily Summary of sales and cash receipts (see attached).
4. That all errors in recording collections on accounts are corrected.
5. That a record of all monies paid out, by cash or check, is maintained.

WEEKLY

1. Accounts Receivable (take action on slow payers).

2. Accounts Payable (take advantage of discounts).

3. Payroll (records should include name and address of employee, social security number, number of exemptions, date ending the pay period, hours worked, rate of pay, total wages, deductions, net pay, check number).

4. Taxes and reports to State and Federal Government (sales, withholding, social security, etc.).

MONTHLY

1. That all Journal entries are classified according to like elements (these should be generally accepted and standardized for both income and expense) and posted to General Ledger.

2. That a Profit and Loss Statement for the month is available within a reasonable time, usually 10 to 15 days following the close of the month. This shows the income of the business for the month, the expense incurred in obtaining the income, and the profit or loss resulting. From this, take action to eliminate loss (adjust mark-up? reduce overhead expense? pilferage? incorrect tax reporting? incorrect buying procedures? failure to take advantage of cash discounts?).

3. That a Balance Sheet accompanies the Profit and Loss Statement. This shows assets (what the business has), liabilities (what the business owes), and the investment of the owner.

4. The Bank Statement is reconciled. (That is, the owner's books are in agreement with the bank's record of the cash balance.)

5. The Petty Cash Account is in balance. (The actual cash in the Petty Cash Box plus the total of the paid-out slips that have not been charged to expense total the amount set aside as petty cash.)

6. That all Federal Tax Deposits, Withheld Income and FICA Taxes (Form 501) and State Taxes are made.

7. That Accounts Receivable are aged, i.e., 30, 60, 90 days, etc., past due. (Work all bad and slow accounts.)

8. That Inventory Control is worked to remove dead stock and order new stock. (What moves slowly? Reduce. What moves fast? Increase.)

*Source:* John Cotton, "Keeping Records in Small Business," *Small Marketers Aid No. 155* (Washington, D.C.: U.S. Small Business Administration, 1974), 8.

## EXHIBIT 18–3. SOME COMMON BUSINESS-EXPENSE CATEGORIES

Expenses are the cost of goods sold and services used in the process of selling goods or services. Some common expenses for all businesses are:

- Cost of goods sold (Cost of Goods Sold = Beginning Inventory − Purchases − Ending Inventory)

- Wages and salaries (Don't forget to include your own—at the actual rate you'd have to pay someone else to do your job.)

- Rent

- Utilities (electricity, gas, telephone, water, etc.)

- Supplies (office, cleaning, and the like)

- Delivery expenses

- Insurance

## Exhibit 18–3. Continued

- Advertising and promotional costs
- Maintenance and upkeep
- Depreciation (Here you need to make sure your depreciation policies are realistic and that all depreciable items are included.)
- Taxes and licenses
- Interest
- Bad debts
- Professional assistance (accountant, attorney, etc.)

There are, of course, many other types of expenses, but the point is that *every* expense must be recorded and deducted from your revenues before you know what your profit is. Understanding your expenses is the first step toward *controlling them* and *increasing your profit*.

*Source:* Narendra C. Bhandari, "Checklist for Profit Watching," *Small Marketers Aid No. 165* (Washington, D.C.: U.S. Small Business Administration, 1978), 3.

## Exhibit 18–4. Records: how long to keep them

| Retain for at least | Type of records |
|---|---|
| Two years | Order, billing, and shipping records. |
| | Pension records (after death of pensioner). |
| Three years | Records of sales, use taxes (state, local). |
| | Routine purchasing records. |
| Six to seven years | Accounts payable records. |
| | Accounts receivable records. |
| | Cancelled checks. |
| | Contracts (after expiration date). |
| | Income tax returns, and attendant records. |
| | Inventory schedules. |
| | Leases (after expiration date). |
| | Payroll records. |
| | Records of lawsuits. |
| Ten years | Cancelled stock certificates. |
| | Cash books. |
| Indefinitely | Audit reports. |
| | Copyrights. |
| | Corporation by-laws, minutes of stockholders' meetings, annual reports. |
| | Deeds. |
| | Depreciation schedules. |
| | Easement records. |
| | Financial statements. |
| | General ledgers. |
| | Patents. |
| | Records of major purchases. |
| | Trademark registrations. |

*Source:* Various publications of the U.S. Small Business Administration.

future, they must be flexible. Further, methods of monitoring these plans need to be set up, so you can make adjustments where necessary as time goes by.

As the owner of a retail store, you need to think in terms of budget planning for each of your business's major functional areas. In so doing, you're simply thinking ahead—trying to introduce a touch of rational management. Without a plan, you *let* things happen to your business, instead of *making* them happen. A useful reference in this regard is a short article in the April 1978 issue of the *Journal of Small Business Management*. It provides an illuminating treatment of the budgeting process for the small businessperson, including the target profit goal, sales forecast, pro forma accounting statements, and cash-flow statements.*

## EXPENSE MANAGEMENT

For optimum usefulness, prepare your budgets on a quarterly basis (at the very minimum). Some, like your pro forma profit-and-loss and your cash-flow statements, should be made out monthly. Deviations from budgets should be noted and acted on immediately: Therein lies their value. Perhaps several of your expenses need to be cut back to bring you more in line with your projected figures. In this connection, a comparison of your expenses with those of other, similar retailers may be helpful; a useful form for this purpose is provided in exhibit 18–5. Or you may need to do a bit more advertising or sales promotion to boost your sales to your planned figures for the period.

Finally, a thoughtfully constructed *cash budget* helps you to anticipate periods when you need additional funds to operate your business, as well as those when you have a temporary surplus on hand, which you may want to capitalize on through some type of investment. Exhibit 18–6 contains an illustration of a simplified cash-budget forecast. Note that such items as (4) ("Expected Cash Sales") and (5) ("Expected Collections") are taken right from your monthly pro forma operating statements.**

### A Few Words About Major Purchases

Occasionally, a beginning retailer invests too heavily in fixed assets. This can be a perilous mistake because the new enterprise is typically launched with a minimum of capital. It's more prudent to seek a flexible cash position at the outset by consigning a portion of your resources to a *reserve fund* for unexpected contingencies. As your business takes root and begins to grow, however, you will soon discover a need for a nodding acquaintance with *capital budgeting*—the allocating of substantial sums for

---

* James D. Suver and Galen D. Hadley, "Budgeting—Key to Survival in the Small Business," *Journal of Small Business Management* 16 (April 1978) 46–52.

** For a useful discussion of cash-flow management, see Ray Thompson, "Understanding Cash Flow: A System Dynamics Analysis," *Journal of Small Business Management* 24 (April 1986) 23–30.

---

## EXHIBIT 18–5. EXPENSE COMPARISON FORM

| | Your Figures | | Averages Figures |
|---|---|---|---|
| | Dollars | % of Sales | |
| NET SALES | | 100% | 100% |
| Cost of Goods Sold | | | |
| GROSS PROFIT or MARGIN | | | |
| | | | |
| OPERATING EXPENSES: | | | |
| | | | |
| | | | |
| | | | |
| | | | |
| | | | |
| | | | |
| | | | |
| | | | |
| | | | |
| | | | |
| | | | |
| | | | |
| | | | |
| TOTAL EXPENSES | | | |
| NET PROFIT | | | |
| | | | |
| Rate of Stockturn | | | |
| | | | |

Use this form to make your own comparisons with typical operating experiences of other retailers in your line of business.

Find the average operating ratios for your line of business and copy them in the column headed "Average Figures."

Then place your sales figure on the Net Sales line in the "Dollars" column.

Next place the dollar amount of each of your expenses in the "Dollars" column.

When you have filled in the remaining items on the form, convert the dollar amounts into percentages by dividing the net sales figure into each of the item amounts. Place these percentages in the "% of Sales" column.

You can now compare the operating ratios of your store with the ratios of the average store. This comparison can assist you in uncovering conditions in your business which need further investigation and possible corrective action.

*Source:* "Expenses in Retail Business," a publication of NCR Corporation, Dayton, Ohio.

## EXHIBIT 18–6. FORECASTING YOUR CASH BUDGET

| | January Est. | January Actual | February Est. | February Actual |
|---|---|---|---|---|
| 1. Cash in Bank (Start of Month) | $1,400 | $1,400* | $1,850 | $2,090* |
| 2. Cash in Register (Start of Month) | 100 | 100 | 150 | 70 |
| 3. Total Cash [add (1) and (2)] | $1,500 | $1,500 | $2,000 | $2,160 |
| 4. Expected Cash Sales | 1,200 | 1,420 | 900 | |
| 5. Expected Collections | 400 | 380 | 350 | |
| 6. Other Money Expected | 100 | 52 | 50 | |
| 7. Total Receipts [add (4), (5) and (6)] | $1,700 | $1,852 | $1,300 | |
| 8. Total Cash Receipts [add (3) and (7)] | $3,200 | $3,352 | $3,300 | |
| 9. All Disbursements (for Month) | 1,200 | 1,192 | 1,000 | |
| 10. Cash Balance at End of Month in Bank Account and Register [Subtract (9) from (8)] | $2,000 | $2,160 | $2,300 | |

*Source:* John F. Murphy, "Sound Cash Management and Borrowing," *Small Marketers Aid No. 147* (Washington, D.C.: U.S. Small Business Administration, 1978), 3.

*The owner-manager writes in these figures as they become available.

major purchases. Such planning is precipitated by the desire either to cut costs or increase sales. Capital budgeting is usually a more vital concern for the manufacturing plant; decisions need to be made regarding the replacement of outmoded machinery, the purchase of additional equipment, the developing and marketing of new products, expansion, and the like. Yet even the small store owner, from time to time, needs to face decisions that involve large capital expenditures. Examples include:

- Renovating or remodeling the storefront
- Refurbishing the store interior
- Opening a second store
- Purchasing new cash registers or other equipment
- Merchandise management by EDP

Such investments cannot readily be financed from current profits. Loan or equity capital is usually involved, although leasing may sometimes be of value. Such decisions must be made with caution and the aid of your accountant, because a wrong move can jeopardize your business.

Among the considerations to bear in mind in your decision making are the following:

- Borrowed funds cost you more than either accumulated profits or fresh equity capital.
- In inflationary times, you need to spend more next year for the item you're considering this year.

- Calculating the payback on your investment becomes more difficult in the light of fluctuating interest rates and the erosion of the dollar.
- The potential of other alternatives (including not doing anything at all) should always be estimated simultaneously with the problem at hand.

## RATIO ANALYSIS: A VALUABLE TOOL

Large corporations usually maintain sufficient capital in their coffers to compensate for serious errors in managerial judgment. With limited financial resources, the small retail firm needs to monitor its operation with consummate care. A most helpful technique for analyzing the results of business activity is that of *ratio analysis*. Ratios express the relationship of one thing to another. Ratios are fractions, and fractions are ratios. So are percentages. The fraction $1/3$ means *one part out of a total of three parts*. It may also be interpreted as *one to three* (generally written as *1:3*), as *0.33*, or as *33 1/3%*. So you see, the quotient that results when one quantity is divided by a second is also a ratio.

Practically every entry on your store's operating statement can be converted into a useful ratio, simply by dividing it by the *net sales figure*.

*Example:* Your first year's P&L indicates net sales of $150,000 and shows the following expenses (among others, of course):

| | |
|---|---|
| Cost of goods sold | $88,000 |
| Rent | 7,800 |
| Labor | 26,400 |
| Supplies | 4,200 |
| Delivery expense | 3,600 |

Dividing each of these figures in turn by $150,000, we come up with these percentages of net sales:

| | |
|---|---|
| Cost of goods sold | 58.7% |
| Rent | 5.2 |
| Labor | 17.6 |
| Supplies | 2.8 |
| Delivery expense | 2.4 |

In ratio analysis, you can either compare current ratios with past ratios to uncover trends or your ratios with those of other retailers in the same line as yourself. (Operating results are usually available through your trade association.) For instance, a review of your monthly operating statements along ratio lines may convince you that your labor, delivery, or other expenses are getting out of hand or that your cost of goods keeps rising. You can then take steps to bring these situations more in line. (Of course, you could just as easily discover that you're doing a mite better than other retailers of your type!)

Astute businesspeople employ a variety of other ratios to maintain firm financial control over their enterprises and to make decisions. Both the balance sheet and the operating statement provide this information. For a *liquidity measure,* that is, a test of the business's ability to pay off its debts, there's the *current ratio:*

$$\text{Current Ratio} = \frac{\text{Current Assets}}{\text{Current Liabilities}}$$

Usually, your current ratio should be at least 2:1, meaning that your balance sheet should show at least twice as much in current assets as in current liabilities. This ratio is, of course, a simple and rough rule of thumb; it may differ from one type of business to the next. (Your best approach is to follow the norm in your line of retailing.)

A more exacting ratio to ascertain liquidity is the *quick ratio* or the *acid-test ratio.* This is much the same as the current ratio except that the inventory value is omitted from the current assets:

$$\text{Quick Ratio} = \frac{\text{Cash} + \text{Negotiable Securities} + \text{Accounts Receivable}}{\text{Current Liabilities}}$$

In this case, the rule-of-thumb guide is 1:1. When these ratios fall so low as to become worrisome, you can change the picture by plowing back profits into your business, paying off some current debt, adding to current assets by means of long-term borrowing or additional equity capital, and so on.

## Profitability and Efficiency Ratios

A host of other ratios demonstrate whether a business is producing the kind of profit it should or whether operations are being conducted as efficiently as they can be. Some of the more popular are:

| | | |
|---|---|---|
| Return on Assets | = | Net Profit ÷ Total Assets |
| Return on Equity | = | Net Profit ÷ Owner's Equity |
| Return on Net Worth | = | Net Profit ÷ Tangible Net Worth |
| Profit to Sales | = | Net Operating Profit ÷ Net Sales |
| Sales to Net Worth | = | Net Sales ÷ Tangible Net Worth |
| Stockturn | = | Sales ÷ Average Inventory at Retail |

To repeat, the chief value of ratio analysis lies in comparing your results with those of other, similar firms or with former ratios in your business. Compute ratios every time you have a new basic accounting statement.

## IS THE COMPUTER FOR YOU?

During the infancy of your new retail enterprise, the answer to this question has to be a resounding *no*. (Of course, if you purchase someone else's big, strapping business, your response might well be in the affirmative.) Even though micro- and minicomputers are now available to the small business owner at relatively low prices, you're better off allocating that kind of money to your store's inventory—or holding it in abeyance as reserve capital for unexpected contingencies. A common error of the beginner is to invest too much in long-term capital assets.

## Should You Automate?

Automation comes in time. Given initial success and a modicum of growth, you'll begin thinking about it. At first, think in terms of equipment designed to save both time and labor, such as typewriters, bookkeeping machines, and copiers. Eventually, you may consider the advantages and disadvantages of the computer for your retail business.

If you decide that a computer can be helpful, you still need not buy your own. The smaller firm can enjoy the benefits of electronic data processing by using a computer service bureau or a time-sharing arrangement.

**Computer Service Bureaus.** You can locate a service bureau through your accountant, your banker, your trade association, or the "Yellow Pages" (look under "Data Processing Service"). The service bureau processes your information and produces the results you request. Among other services, such a firm can handle your check and payroll registers, sales journals, and ledgers (general, accounts payable, and so on), as well as your income statements and balance sheets. Another useful management aid for many types of retail concerns is the inventory report. You mail or deliver your *source documents* (checks, sales slips, receipts, journal entries, and the like) to the service bureau according to a set schedule. In turn, they keypunch the transactions, process the input you have supplied, and print the reports you request.

In using a service bureau, you will encounter two types of charges: a programming charge and a processing charge. The former is generally a one-time charge (unless you later request changes in the program), and its cost depends on your needs. If you take a standard programming package, of course, your cost is considerably less than that for a custom-made program. Your processing charge is based on the number and length of the reports you require.

**Time-Sharing Arrangements.** The time-sharing approach works differently. A computer terminal is installed in your place of business and connected to a computer through telephone lines. The costs involve a monthly charge for the rental of the terminal, plus a

---

charge for the amount of time used. Its major advantage is the fast turnaround time, measured in hours instead of days, as is the case with the computer service bureau. Your own operator enters the source information on the terminal, and the information reports are transmitted back. If lengthy printouts are required, the service bureau may be the more economical approach.

## THE PC (PERSONAL COMPUTER)

Microcomputers are also known as *PCs;* the initials stand for *personal computer.* In the past few years, the prices of PCs have come down so drastically that they now lie well within affordable range for the majority of small business owners. The PC is small, lightweight, and easy to set up on a desk or table.

The U.S. Small Business Administration advises: "With its business applications, a microcomputer system gives you professional management planning and control capability that can maximize your personal management abilities and goals and your company's growth and profit potentials."*

What kinds of "business applications" are referred to here? Below are just a few of the things your PC can do for you:

- Maintain your accounts (receivables, payables)
- Prepare profit and loss statements and balance sheets
- Make up payroll checks
- Keep payroll records
- Store and print all correspondence
- Maintain files
- Print needed business forms
- Hold and update mailing lists
- Manage your inventory
- Prepare purchase orders

Before you decide to buy a PC of your own, you'll need to find answers to the following questions:

- The "Hardware" Question: What kind of PC will best meet my business's needs?
- The "Software" Question: How do I choose the programs that will enable my computer to perform well for me?
- Do I have sufficient time (and interest) to follow the detailed instructions (and/or undergo the training) required to operate a PC? (Or, can I afford to put an experienced PC operator on my payroll?)

---

* Michael M. Stewart and Alan C. Shulman, "How to Get Started with a Small Business Computer," *Management Aid No. 2.027* (Washington, D.C.: U.S. Small Business Administration, 1984), 2.

# FOR FURTHER INFORMATION

## Books

Carey, O., and D. Olson. *Financial Tools for Small Businesses.* Englewood Cliffs, N.J.: Prentice-Hall, 1982.

Hartley, W. C., and Yale Meltzer. *Cash Management: Planning, Forecasting, and Control.* Englewood Cliffs, N.J.: Prentice-Hall, 1979.

Horngren, Charles T. *Introduction to Management Accounting,* 6th ed. Englewood Cliffs, N.J.: Prentice-Hall, 1984.

Hylsop, D., and I. Place. *Records Management: Controlling Business Information.* Englewood Cliffs, N.J.: Prentice-Hall, 1982.

Keith, L., and R. Keith. *Accounting: A Management Perspective,* 2d ed. Englewood Cliffs, N.J.: Prentice-Hall, 1985.

Krevolin, N. *Records/Information Management and Filing.* Englewood Cliffs, N.J.: Prentice-Hall, 1986.

Neveu, Raymond. *Fundamentals of Managerial Finance,* 2d ed. Cincinnati: South-Western, 1985.

Scharf, Charles A., et al. *Acquisitions, Mergers, Sales, Buyouts and Takeovers: A Handbook with Forms,* 3d ed. Englewood Cliffs, N.J.: Prentice-Hall, 1985.

Van Horne, J. *Fundamentals of Financial Management,* 6th ed. Englewood Cliffs, N.J.: Prentice-Hall, 1986.

## Pamphlets Available from the Small Business Administration

### Management Aids

MA 1.001—"The ABC's of Borrowing"

MA 1.004—"Basic Budgets for Profit Planning"

MA 1.011—"Analyze Your Records to Reduce Costs"

MA 1.015—"Budgeting in a Small Service Firm"

MA 1.016—"Sound Cash Management and Borrowing"

MA 2.014—"Should You Lease or Buy Equipment?"

MA 2.027—"How to Get Started with a Small Business Computer"

## Booklets Available from the Superintendent of Documents

S/N 045-000-00137-7—*Guides for Profit Planning*—$4.50.

S/N 045-000-00142-3—*Financial Recordkeeping for Small Stores*—$5.50.

S/N 045-000-00150-4—*Ratio Analysis for Small Business*—$4.50.

S/N 045-000-00175-0—*Asset Management*—$2.75.

S/N 045-000-00176-8—*Managing Fixed Assets*—$4.75.

S/N 045-000-00187-3—*Cost Control*—$4.75.

S/N 045-000-00193-8—*Capital Planning*—$4.50.

S/N 045-000-00208-0—*Handbook of Small Business Finance*—$4.50.

# 19

# Safety Measures for Your Store

The mere mention of the word "security" to the department-store manager conjures up visions of merchandise shortages, shoplifting, employee theft, and possibly, burglary and robbery. Methods of crime detection and prevention appear to be central to the theme. Yet for the small independent retailer I recommend a broadening of the security concept to include any and all measures to impede or to prevent the occurrence of events that can injure one's business.

Securing your store involves so much more than simply installing better locks on all doors, placing convex mirrors around the selling area, or hiring a guard to stand near the exit. It must include *all* the procedures and systems that you establish to reduce the possibility of fire, all other casualty losses, and the accidental injury of employees, shoppers, or other individuals. You can also take positive steps to guard against the undesirable events that can take place in the handling of money (bad checks, counterfeit bills, short-changing at the register), as well as against shoplifting, employee theft, and even robbery or burglary.

## WAYS TO REDUCE YOUR RISK

Knowledge and advance preparation are helpful in your precautions against the perils of both fire and accidents. Exhibit 19–1, for example, provides you with a useful checklist for locating hazards in your store. Exhibit 19–2 contains a set of instructions you can give to your employees to help prevent injuries.

Here are some additional pointers:

- In rainy weather, keep the entrance area dry. Lay down a nonskid mat for your shoppers to walk on.
- Instill good housekeeping attitudes in your employees; don't permit trash to accumulate on your premises.
- Be careful when raising or lowering the awning. Sometimes, water or snow accumulates on top; passersby may be unpleasantly surprised by a sudden shower.

270

- Consider installing a sprinkler system in the store and stockroom.
- Buy a first-aid kit. Keep it well stocked and make certain all employees know where it's located.
- Install several approved fire extinguishers in appropriate spots. Teach your personnel how to operate them.
- Mount smoke alarms in the back of the store and in all storage areas. Check on them occasionally to make sure the batteries still operate.
- Advise your store people of the procedures to be followed in the event of accidental injury on the premises.

---

### EXHIBIT 19–1. LOCATING HAZARDS IN THE STORE

Look for the following kinds of danger spots when you check your store for hazards that can cause accidents:

*Falls*

> Highly polished floors
> A single stairstep in an unexpected location
> Dark stairs
> Unanchored or torn rugs
> Wet or slippery floors
> Unused display fixtures
> Projecting objects, such as open drawers behind counters
> Wastebaskets, stock cartons, and ladders
> Loose wires

*Stockroom Hazards*

Check for improper storage, or improper use of papercutters, scissors, and razor blades. (Be sure that employees use proper knife for opening cartons.)
> Dollies, carts, and other materials-handling equipment
> Goods improperly stacked, especially on high shelves
> Ladders in bad repair

*Aisles*

Narrow, or crowded, aisles are dangerous, especially when employees are in a hurry. For one-way traffic, an aisle should be two feet wider than your widest stockcart. For two-way traffic, the aisle should be three feet wider than twice the width of your widest cart. Eliminate wherever possible sharp inclines, narrow passageways, and low ceilings. Even when you have taken these precautions, you have to be on the lookout for the following hazards:
> Obstructions in aisles
> Protruding valves and pipes
> Blind corners

*Fire Hazards*

Even though your local fire department may inspect retail stores periodically, include fire hazards in your check. Thus you can be sure that the recommendations of the fire department are in force. Look for the following:
> Accumulations of waste paper, rags, and so on
> Smoking in areas containing flammable materials

---

## EXHIBIT 19–1. CONTINUED

Insufficient ashtrays for smokers
Unmarked fire exits
Blocked fire exits
Fire doors that need repairs
Wrong-size electrical fuses
Frayed or exposed electrical wires
Fire hose that has been weakened by rot
Extinguishers that need recharging (A store should have one for paper fires and another for electrical fires.)

*Miscellaneous Hazards*

Loose overhead plaster
Loose overhead light fixtures
Elevators (If you have one, has it been inspected recently?)

*Source:* S. J. (Bob) Curtis, "Preventing Accidents in Small Stores," *Small Marketers Aid No. 104* (Washington, D.C.: U.S. Small Business Administration, 1974), 2.

## EXHIBIT 19–2. PREVENTING INJURIES IN THE STORE

The best rules for preventing injuries are those that are specific. Keep in mind that employees are more willing to observe your rules when they know the reason behind them. Here are fifteen rules that will apply to practically all small stores:

1. If you smoke, smoke only in authorized areas and use an ashtray. Don't throw matches or ashes into the wastebasket or into an empty carton.
2. Open doors slowly to avoid hitting anyone coming from the other side.
3. When moving tanks and carts, watch out for customers and fellow workers.
4. Don't stand in front of a closed door.
5. Clean up liquid spilt on the floor immediately.
6. Use handrails when going up or down stairs. Never carry anything so heavy or bulky that you don't have one hand free to hold the railing. Carry so you can see where you are going.
7. Don't run—walk.
8. Never indulge in horseplay.
9. Never stand on an open drawer or climb on stock shelves.
10. When using a ladder, make sure that it is steady.
11. Don't leave drawers or cabinet doors open.
12. Remove staples with a staple remover.
13. Open cartons with the proper tool.
14. Keep selling and nonselling areas neat at all times.
15. When a repairman is working in your area, move out of his way and warn customers.

*Source:* S. J. (Bob) Curtis, "Preventing Accidents in Small Stores," *Small Marketers Aid No. 104* (Washington, D.C.: U.S. Small Business Administration, 1974), 3.

## EMPLOYEE THEFT

It has been estimated that retailers lose more money each year through internal (employee) theft than from shoplifting, robbery, and burglary combined. The majority of workers think nothing of taking home inexpensive items such as pencils, tape, stationery, and other supplies. They may think twice before carrying out regular store merchandise with them; nevertheless, some do. They may also pass articles over the counter to friends or family members, sometimes without charging at all for the merchandise or perhaps ringing up a reduced amount on the register. Many salesclerks filch change or bills from the cash drawer.

Sometimes salesclerks don't even ring up a sale and pocket the money instead. This particular type of theft often happens when customers, in an obvious hurry, depart with their packages, leaving temptation by the register in the form of the exact amount of the purchase. One way of avoiding such situations is to insist that all sales be rung up promptly and register receipts issued to every customer. Another useful technique is the sales slip, filled out in duplicate so that you retain a record of each sale. These slips must be completed legibly, of course, and numbered in sequence.

Other steps you can take to lessen the problem include the following:

- Require your personal approval on all discounts extended to customers or employees.
- Require your approval, too, on all cash disbursements, such as those made to the window washer, porter, or others.
- Carefully investigate the background of each new employee you hire.
- Show your employees that you expect honesty at all times. Set an example with your own behavior.
- While embezzlement is relatively rare in small-scale retailing, it still remains a possibility. One way of protecting your business is to bond employees who handle large amounts of money. (See the section on fidelity bonds in chapter 3.)
- Each month, reconcile your bank statement with your records. At the same time, review all canceled checks and the endorsements on them.
- If you suspect one of your employees of "tapping the till," hire a store shopping service. Such a firm sends investigators to your store; these individuals, like ordinary shoppers, make purchases from your salespeople. At the same time, they look for signs of suspicious behavior, such as not ringing the register promptly or ringing up a lower amount.

## PROPER MONEY-HANDLING PROCEDURES

Tighten up your store security by implementing a few commonsense measures with regard to the handling of money.* Here are some of the procedures you can follow to reduce your losses:

- The glimpse of a register crammed with bills can be tempting to a holdup specialist. Keep emptying bills from your register throughout the day.
- Along the same lines, make bank deposits several times each day, preferably at different hours from one day to the next.

---

* Some of this material is based on the following: S. J. (Bob) Curtis, "Preventing Burglary and Robbery Loss," *Small Marketers Aid No. 134* (Washington, D.C.: U.S. Small Business Administration, 1973).

- Send two of your people to the bank, rather than a lone individual. Vary their route to the bank so that no set pattern can be observed.
- Instead of balancing your register at closing time, do so an hour or more earlier.
- Leave the cash drawer open (and, of course, empty) overnight. A closed register is an invitation to the burglar to use force in opening it, causing damage to the equipment.
- Alert your employees to the methods used by short-change artists and to the possibility of being handed counterfeit bills (see exhibit 19–3).
- When accepting checks from customers, consider the advice presented in exhibit 19–4.

---

### EXHIBIT 19–3. INFORMATION ABOUT "BAD MONEY"

Be alert to recognize bad money. This may be authentic money that has been altered to increase its apparent value, or it may be counterfeit money.

Sometimes a large-denomination bill will be split into two pieces. One half of the large-denomination bill is pasted to the side of a real $1 bill, and the other half to another $1 bill. These bills are presented at a busy time with the large-denomination side up. Another trick is to cut a large-denomination bill in half and paste one half on one end of a $1 bill and the other half on the end of another. Each bill is then folded so only the large-denomination end shows.

To prevent such swindles, make a habit of unfolding all paper money and looking at both sides of large bills.

To detect counterfeit currency, compare the suspected bill with a genuine bill of the same denomination.

*Faults of Counterfeit Money*

The fine lines will be irregular, broken, and scratchy.

The points on the rim of the printed seal may be broken and irregular.

Portions of the designs may appear unusually white or dark and perhaps smudgy.

Serial numbers probably will be unevenly spaced.

There will be no tiny red and blue silk threads scattered about in the paper.

*Secret-Service Suggestions Are:*

Do not return it.

Telephone the police at once.

Delay the passer under a pretext.

Avoid argument; if necessary say that police will handle the matter.

If the passer leaves, write down his description.

Write down the license numbers of any cars involved.

---

*Source:* "Money Safeguarding Procedures," a publication of NCR Corporation, Dayton, Ohio.

## THE SHOPLIFTING PROBLEM

Shoplifting has been on the upsurge for years. The retail store, regardless of its size, is a most attractive hunting ground for this type of criminal activity. Self-service stores are even more attractive. While the typical incident generally involves no more than a few

**EXHIBIT 19–4. A PROCEDURE FOR ACCEPTING CHECKS**

When presented with a check, insist on good identification, such as:

Driver's license.

Auto registration.

Employee identification card.

Passport.

Do not accept:

Social security cards.

Selective service cards.

Club or membership cards.

Follow your store's policy for accepting checks; and when a check is presented, examine it carefully to be sure:

It is written in ink with no erasures or alterations on it.

All blank lines are filled in.

It has MICR encoding along the bottom of the check.

It is neither more than thirty days old, nor dated ahead.

The written and figure amounts agree.

The signature is legible.

The name of the person to whom the check is made is legible.

The name of the bank and its city and state are printed on the face of the check.

All payroll checks have the firm name printed (not typed) on the face of the check. This also applies to other types of checks issued by businesses, governments, and commercial establishments.

If the check is presented by anyone other than the originator, it is endorsed (signed) on the back with the name of the person presenting it.

The endorser signs his name exactly as it appears on the front of the check.

If a check is made out to two people, both must endorse it before you can cash the check.

It does not have a restrictive endorsement.

Follow any special rules your store may have for cashing Travelers' Checks or United States Postal Money Orders. Be careful, but not suspicious, in cashing checks. Most checks are good and the person who presents a check should be treated with as much courtesy as the person who presents cash.

*Source:* "Money Safeguarding Procedures," a publication of NCR Corporation, Dayton, Ohio.

dollars' worth of merchandise, the cumulative effect on retailers' operating statements across the country is staggering.

Note this observation made by the SBA *two decades ago:*

> Petty thievery may not seem like major crime to the casual crook who pockets a ball-point pen here, a pocket calendar there. But to the small business fighting for survival, it's murder. There is a retail theft committed every five seconds in this country. These thefts cost each American $150 a year. No store is immune.

A store operating at 3 percent profit on sales would have to sell $1,216.66 worth of merchandise a year to make up for the daily loss of a 10-cent candy bar. Just to cover a yearly loss of $1,000 in thefts, a retailer would have to sell each day over 900 candy bars, or 130 packs of cigarettes, or 380 cans of soup. Faced with such unreasonable selling volumes most small business people are forced instead to raise their prices and lower their ability to compete.*

There are two kinds of shoplifters: the professionals and the amateurs. Skilled thieves, who are in the minority, are adept at sleight-of-hand maneuvers and practiced in the special "tools of the trade," such as coats fitted with hooks, secret slits, or pockets, as well as boxes built with hinged tops or ends. Professionals are difficult to detect, but luckily they account for only a small percentage of shoplifted goods. Of more importance to the average small store owner are the amateurs, for these individuals are responsible for the bulk of stolen merchandise. A sizable number are juveniles; some estimates range as high as 60 to 65 percent. Young women and housewives are also represented in considerable numbers. Then there are the more obvious types, easy to spot, such as vagrants and drunks.

Among the more common methods of safeguarding the store against shoplifting are:

- Placing convex mirrors in selected spots throughout the store so that the salespeople can see around corners and into every nook and cranny
- Posting signs with the warning that shoplifters, if caught, will be prosecuted
- Training employees to be alert and to watch shoppers who come in with bulky clothing, packages, or shopping bags, or who otherwise act suspicious
- More recently, using electronic wafers, attached to garments, that send out signals when the shoplifter tries to leave the store.**

To prevent "ticket switching," you might consider these methods:

- *Tamper-proof gummed labels* that rip apart when an attempt is made to remove them
- Hard-to-break *plastic string* for soft-goods tickets
- *Special staple patterns* that are recognizable to store personnel, for tickets that are stapled on
- *Extra price tickets* concealed elsewhere on merchandise†

Additional suggestions for curbing your losses to shoplifters are listed in exhibit 19–5.

---

* Addison H. Verrill, "Reducing Shoplifting Losses," *Management Aid No. 3.006* (Washington, D.C.: U.S. Small Business Administration, first printed 1967, reprinted 1984), 2.

** See Addison H. Verrill, "Reducing Shoplifting Losses," *Small Marketers Aid No. 129* (Washington, D.C.: U.S. Small Business Administration, 1967), 3–4.

† Ibid., 5.

## EXHIBIT 19–5. SOME SUGGESTIONS FOR CURBING SHOPLIFTING LOSSES

1. Serve all customers as promptly as possible. Honest customers generally appreciate the quick service. The shoplifter does not want sales help, and good, quick attention will generally motivate him to practice his trade elsewhere.

2. When another customer enters, the busy salesperson should acknowledge his presence by saying, "I'll be with you in a moment." Again, the good customer appreciates the service while the shoplifter knows he has been seen and is being thought of.

3. The salesperson should not turn his back on a customer. This is an open invitation to the shoplifter.

4. Keep an eye on people loitering around the entrances and exits of the store.

5. Never leave the store or department unattended.

6. Develop a warning system so that all employees can be alerted when the presence of shoplifters is suspected.

7. Lock up expensive merchandise that is attractive to shoplifters.

8. Do not stack merchandise so high on counters and in aisles that it blocks your view.

9. Do not arrange merchandise so that it can easily be pushed off counters into some type of container.

10. When merchandise is made up of pairs, display only one of the pair. A shoplifter does not want one earring, one shoe, or one glove.

11. Whenever possible, attach merchandise to displays so that it is not easily removed. Although a coat, for example, may look nice leisurely draped over a mannequin's arm, it is far more difficult for the shoplifter to take it if the mannequin's arms are in it.

12. Keep counters and tables neat and orderly.

13. Place telephones in such a way that salespeople can view their selling area when using the phone.

14. Examine your records to spot high shrinkage areas.

15. Return to stock any merchandise that was brought out for a customer's inspection but not sold.

16. Destroy discarded sales slips. Shoplifters may use them as evidence of purchase.

*Source:* Anthony J. Faria, "Minimizing Shoplifting Losses: Some Practical Guidelines," *Journal of Small Business Management* 15 (October 1977), 40.

## ROBBERY AND BURGLARY

While no store can ever be entirely immune to these two crimes, you can certainly better your chances of reducing possible losses or of remaining relatively unscathed for long periods of time by taking a number of precautionary measures. These measures include locks, burglar alarms, and other methods of protecting your premises, as well as store lighting and personnel instruction. They are listed below for your consideration:

- Be careful in assigning keys. Issue only the few you need, and keep track of them.
- Never attach your store's name or address to keys or key chains.
- If a key is lost, replace the cylinder in the lock immediately.

- Use pin-tumbler cylinder locks with at least five pins. Of course, two locks are often better than one.
- Doors can be pried or jimmied open. Have your doors and door frames (as well as your locks) inspected by a good locksmith.
- Use dead-bolt locks for back doors.
- Equip your premises with an effective burglar-alarm system such as the silent central-station alarm. You'll need to contact a security firm for details.
- Avoid the old-fashioned "ringing bell" type of alarm that goes off when the door is opened by an intruder. While it's relatively inexpensive and simple to install, it doesn't offer much in the way of protection.
- Keep your cash in a strong safe, one that is both fire- and burglar-resistant. Keep it locked at all times.
- Place your safe so that it can be seen from outside the store; bolt it to the building itself.
- In high-risk areas, heavy metal screens or gratings are one way of protecting your show windows. An alternate method, especially with stores that sell expensive merchandise, is to install burglar-resistant glass in windows, doors, and showcases.
- Train your employees to remain as calm as possible if confronted with a robber. Emphasize the fact that lives are more important than money and that you want no "heroes." Advise them to cooperate with the criminal in every way.
- Burglaries usually occur at night. Light is a strong deterrent to crime. Your store's interior should be illuminated after dark so that police, on foot or in patrol cars, can quickly ascertain if anything is amiss.
- Similarly, the exterior of your store premises should be illuminated. Many retailers set up this lighting on a timer so that lights go on and off automatically.
- Make a complete check of your store and back room before closing while an employee waits outside for you. Two people should close the store.

## FOR FURTHER INFORMATION

### Books

Baumer, Terry L., and Dennis P. Rosenbaum. *Combating Retail Theft: Programs and Strategies.* Stoneham, Mass.: Butterworth, 1984.

Curtis, Bob. *Retail Security: Controlling Loss for Profit.* Stoneham, Mass.: Butterworth, 1983.

————. *Security Control: External Theft.* New York: Lebhar Friedman, 1971.

Farrell, Kathleen L., and John A. Ferrara. *Shoplifting: The Antishoplifting Guidebook.* New York: Praeger, 1985.

### Pamphlets Available from the Small Business Administration

#### Management Aids

MA 3.006—"Reducing Shoplifting Losses"

MA 5.005—"Preventing Employee Pilferage"

# 20

# Highlights of Business Law and Taxation for the Small Store Owner

In our society, every person and organizations of all types have to comply with, and are constrained by, the existing body (and framework) of U.S. law. Moreover, just as individuals are required to pay taxes of various kinds, so are business enterprises.

In the first part of this chapter, we offer a brief introduction to our legal environment; the balance is devoted to explaining some of the intricacies of the federal tax on income as well as other taxes for which business owners may be liable. Anything more than a general discussion of those aspects of business law that retail store owners need to be familiar with is, of course, beyond the scope of this book. (For further information on legal aspects, you'll find some helpful reference works in the "For Further Information" section at the end of this chapter.)

## BUSINESS LAW

Terms like *business law* and *commercial law* are usually applied to those bodies of *statutory law* (passed by governments—at all levels) and *common law* (carried over from English law and, beyond that, from Roman law) that govern business activity. Included are laws that pertain to:

- *Legal forms of business.* The formation and dissolution of business enterprises (sole proprietorships, partnerships, and corporations).
- *Property.* Collectively, this substantial body of law is often referred to as the *Law of Property.* It deals with buildings and other *real property* as well as with personal assets. It covers real estate transactions, relationships between property owners and their tenants, personal wills and estates, copyrights and trademarks, bankruptcy, and so on.
- *Torts.* Torts are *civil wrongs* that are committed against individuals. Thus, they're not *criminal wrongs*—a term that is applied where a wrong is committed against the public. The *Law of Torts* deals with such acts as assault, battery, defamation of character, misrepresentation, negligence, trespassing, and the like.

- *Agency.* An agent is a person (or organization) who legally represents another party. The *Law of Agency* covers the authorization of agents to represent other individuals or firms. To some degree, it also impinges on the *Law of Contracts* (discussed next).
- *Contracts.* Properly executed legal contracts are enforceable in our courts. A legal contract is a voluntary agreement concluded by two or more parties. The agreement must involve an offer, the purpose of which must be a legal one. Each party to the contract must be mentally sound and of legal age.

    Some examples of contracts commonly seen in the retail sector are those that involve purchasing a car, boat, or house; buying a refrigerator, television set, or other major item on the installment plan; securing a bank loan; applying for a Visa, MasterCard, or American Express credit card; hiring a construction firm to rebuild the exterior of a store; or securing a fire-insurance policy.

## TAXES AND YOUR BUSINESS

Taxes are a way of life today. They are the cost we pay for the privileges we enjoy as citizens within this society. Because of our unique, three-tiered governmental structure, business owners face tax liabilities on all three levels: federal, state, and local.

With regard to that paramount of federal tax, the income tax, our Internal Revenue Service stresses the fact that it wants you to pay only what you're required to—no more, no less. Revenue personnel suggest that you take all your permissible deductions. Moreover, they want you to keep abreast of your tax liability and set aside funds to pay it. Finally, they advise you to pay up in a timely fashion in order to avoid any penalties.

When starting out, seek the services of a competent tax counselor, because you need to set up your records in such a manner that you can obtain all necessary facts for taxation purposes.

Here is a list of the kinds of taxes for which you may be liable:

*Federal*   Employee income tax, Social Security tax, excise tax, unemployment tax, and, of course, income tax
*State*     Income tax, unemployment tax, sales tax, franchise tax, and possibly others
*Local*     Sales tax, real estate tax, personal property tax, licenses, and possibly income tax and others

As a new small business owner, you'll discover that you must play two roles with regard to taxes: that of a *debtor,* one who is liable for taxes, and that of an *agent,* one who must collect various taxes and pass them on to the appropriate agency. As an agent, you make deductions from employees' wages for income and Social Security taxes, collect sales taxes, and perform other functions on behalf of the government. You need to apply to the IRS (on Form SS-4) for an Employer Identification Number (EIN), obtain a sales-tax authorization certificate (in most states and in some cities), and consult various agencies for information—such as the state departments of labor and taxation and certain county or municipal departments, depending on your type of business.

# THE FEDERAL INCOME TAX

Income-tax regulations differ, depending on the legal form you choose for your new business operation.

## Sole Proprietorships

Chances are that you've formed your new business as a sole proprietor; the typical new retail store owner does. If so, then for purposes of establishing your tax liability, whatever income the operation brings you each year must be added to your other personal gross income for that year. From a pessimistic point of view, any loss incurred can be subtracted from your other income. This merger of personal and business income takes place because, unlike the corporation, both the sole proprietorship and the partnership are not considered separate "taxable persons." Of course, the Internal Revenue Service does want to be kept apprised of your business's progress, and so it requires an *information return* in both cases, explanations of which follow.

If yours is a sole proprietorship that's set up on the calendar-year basis, your income tax return is due on or before April 15 of each year. If you follow a fiscal year, then your return is due on or before the fifteenth day of the fourth month after your year's close. Requesting an extension of time for your return is entirely possible; you can apply for an additional four months by submitting Form 4868—Application for Automatic Extension of Time to File U.S. Individual Income Tax Return. You should know, however, that this form must reach the IRS before the deadline for your return and that you're also required to estimate your tax, and pay any tax you will owe, with the form.

**Which Forms to Submit.** You file your tax return on Form 1040—Individual Income Tax Return. This is the same form you used as an employee. Now, however, since you're also the owner of a business, you need to submit along with your 1040 the information return already mentioned. This is Schedule C—Profit (or Loss) from Business or Profession—Sole Proprietorship. A sample Schedule C appears in exhibit 20–1. In addition to submitting other information on this form, you're required to:

- Show your gross receipts and all other business income
- Detail the operating expenses you've incurred
- Explain how you arrived at your cost of goods sold
- Indicate your method of arriving at depreciation costs
- Supply information about expense-account allocations

**Estimated Tax.** The regulations concerning withholding taxes put individual taxpayers on a "pay-as-you-go" plan. Nevertheless, you'll probably need to file an estimated tax form if you expect the total of your estimated federal income and self-employment taxes

Exhibit 20–1. Schedule C (form 1040)

| SCHEDULE C (Form 1040) Department of the Treasury Internal Revenue Service | **Profit or Loss From Business** (Sole Proprietorship) Partnerships, Joint Ventures, Etc., Must File Form 1065. ▶ Attach to Form 1040, Form 1041, or Form 1041S. ▶ See Instructions for Schedule C (Form 1040). | OMB No. 1545-0074 **1988** Attachment Sequence No. 09 |
|---|---|---|

| Name of proprietor Susan J. Brown | Social security number (SSN) 111 : 00 : 1111 |
|---|---|

| A Principal business or profession, including product or service (see Instructions) Retail, ladies apparel | B Principal business code (from Part IV) ▶ 3 9 1 3 |
|---|---|

| C Business name and address ▶ Milady Fashions 725 Big Sur Drive Franklin, N.Y. 18725 | D Employer ID number (Not SSN) 1 0 1 2 3 4 5 6 7 |
|---|---|

E  Method(s) used to value closing inventory:
   (1) ☐ Cost   (2) ☐ Lower of cost or market   (3) ☐ Other (attach explanation)

|  |  | Yes | No |
|---|---|---|---|
| F  Accounting method: (1) ☐ Cash  (2) ☐ Accrual  (3) ☐ Other (specify) ▶ ............................. | | | |
| G  Was there any change in determining quantities, costs, or valuations between opening and closing inventory? (If "Yes," attach explanation.) | | | ✓ |
| H  Are you deducting expenses for business use of your home? (If "Yes," see Instructions for limitations.) | | | ✓ |
| I  Did you "materially participate" in the operation of this business during 1988? (If "No," see Instructions for limitations on losses.) | | ✓ | |

J  If this schedule includes a loss, credit, deduction, income, or other tax benefit relating to a tax shelter required to be registered, check here. ▶ ☐
   If you check this box, you MUST attach Form 8271.

## Part I  Income

| | | |
|---|---|---|
| 1a Gross receipts or sales | 1a | 397,742 |
| b Less: Returns and allowances | 1b | 1,442 |
| c Subtract line 1b from line 1a. Enter the result here | 1c | 396,300 |
| 2 Cost of goods sold and/or operations (from Part III, line 8) | 2 | 239,349 |
| 3 Subtract line 2 from line 1c and enter the **gross profit** here | 3 | 156,951 |
| 4 Other income (including windfall profit tax credit or refund received in 1988) | 4 | –0– |
| 5 Add lines 3 and 4. This is the **gross income** ▶ | 5 | 156,951 |

## Part II  Deductions

| | | | | | | |
|---|---|---|---|---|---|---|
| 6 Advertising | 6 | 3,500 | 23 Repairs | 23 | 1,776 | |
| 7 Bad debts from sales or services (see Instructions) | 7 | 479 | 24 Supplies (not included in Part III) | 24 | 1,203 | |
| 8 Bank service charges | 8 | 180 | 25 Taxes | 25 | 5,802 | |
| 9 Car and truck expenses | 9 | 2,250 | 26 Travel, meals, and entertainment: | | | |
| 10 Commissions | 10 | | a Travel | 26a | | |
| 11 Depletion | 11 | | b Meals and entertainment | | | |
| 12 Depreciation and section 179 deduction from Form 4562 (not included in Part III) | 12 | 2,731 | c Enter 20% of line 26b subject to limitations (see Instructions) | | | |
| 13 Dues and publications | 13 | | d Subtract line 26c from 26b | 26d | | |
| 14 Employee benefit programs | 14 | | 27 Utilities and telephone | 27 | 3,570 | |
| 15 Freight (not included in Part III) | 15 | | 28a Wages | 63,450 | | |
| 16 Insurance | 16 | 950 | b Jobs credit | 4,400 | | |
| 17 Interest: | | | c Subtract line 28b from 28a | 28c | 59,050 | |
| a Mortgage (paid to banks, etc.) | 17a | | 29 Other expenses (list type and amount): | | | |
| b Other | 17b | 2,633 | Chamber of Commerce $60 | | | |
| 18 Laundry and cleaning | 18 | | Fee Credit Card Co  6,000 | | | |
| 19 Legal and professional services | 19 | | Trash Removal  1,600 | | | |
| 20 Office expense | 20 | 216 | Window Washing  238 | | | |
| 21 Pension and profit-sharing plans | 21 | | | | | |
| 22 Rent on business property | 22 | 12,000 | | 29 | 7,898 | |

| | | |
|---|---|---|
| 30 Add amounts in columns for lines 6 through 29. These are the **total deductions** ▶ | 30 | 104,238 |
| 31 Net profit or (loss). Subtract line 30 from line 5. If a profit, enter here and on Form 1040, line 12, and on Schedule SE, line 2. If a loss, you MUST go on to line 32. (Fiduciaries, see instructions.) | 31 | 52,713 |

32 If you have a loss, you MUST check the box that describes your investment in this activity (see Instructions)
   32a ☐ All investment is at risk.
   32b ☐ Some investment is not at risk.
   If you checked 32a, enter the loss on Form 1040, line 12, and Schedule SE, line 2. If you checked 32b, you MUST attach Form 6198.

For Paperwork Reduction Act Notice, see Form 1040 Instructions.         Schedule C (Form 1040) 1988

*Source:* "Tax Guide for Small Business—1988 Edition," *Publication 334* (Washington, D.C.: Internal Revenue Service, November 1988), 140–41.

# EXHIBIT 20-1. CONTINUED

## Part III Cost of Goods Sold and/or Operations (See Schedule C Instructions for Part III)

| | | |
|---|---|---:|
| 1 | Inventory at beginning of year. (If different from last year's closing inventory, attach explanation.) | **42,843** |
| 2 | Purchases less cost of items withdrawn for personal use | **240,252** |
| 3 | Cost of labor. (Do not include salary paid to yourself.) | **-0-** |
| 4 | Materials and supplies | **-0-** |
| 5 | Other costs | **-0-** |
| 6 | Add lines 1 through 5 | **283,095** |
| 7 | Less: Inventory at end of year | **43,746** |
| 8 | Cost of goods sold and/or operations. Subtract line 7 from line 6. Enter the result here and in Part I, line 2. | **239,349** |

## Part IV Codes for Principal Business or Professional Activity

Locate the major business category that best describes your activity (for example, Retail Trade, Services, etc.). Within the major category, select the activity code that identifies (or most closely identifies) the business or profession that is the principal source of your sales or receipts. Enter this 4-digit code on line B on page 1 of Schedule C. (Note: *If your principal source of income is from farming activities, you should file **Schedule F (Form 1040)**, Farm Income and Expenses.*)

### Construction

Code
- 0018 Operative builders (building for own account)

**General contractors**
- 0034 Residential building
- 0059 Nonresidential building
- 0075 Highway and street construction
- 3889 Other heavy construction (pipe laying, bridge construction, etc.)

**Building trade contractors, including repairs**
- 0232 Plumbing, heating, air conditioning
- 0257 Painting and paper hanging
- 0273 Electrical work
- 0299 Masonry, dry wall, stone, tile
- 0414 Carpentering and flooring
- 0430 Roofing, siding, and sheet metal
- 0455 Concrete work
- 0471 Water well drilling
- 0885 Other building trade contractors (excavation, glazing, etc.)

### Manufacturing, Including Printing and Publishing
- 0612 Bakeries selling at retail
- 0638 Other food products and beverages
- 0653 Textile mill products
- 0679 Apparel and other textile products
- 0695 Leather, footware, handbags, etc.
- 0810 Furniture and fixtures
- 0836 Lumber and other wood products
- 0851 Printing and publishing
- 0877 Paper and allied products
- 0893 Chemicals and allied products
- 1016 Rubber and plastics products
- 1032 Stone, clay, and glass products
- 1057 Primary metal industries
- 1073 Fabricated metal products
- 1099 Machinery and machine shops
- 1115 Electric and electronic equipment
- 1313 Transportation equipment
- 1339 Instruments and related products
- 1883 Other manufacturing industries

### Mining and Mineral Extraction
- 1511 Metal mining
- 1537 Coal mining
- 1552 Oil and gas
- 1719 Quarrying and nonmetallic mining

### Agricultural Services, Forestry, and Fishing
- 1917 Soil preparation services
- 1933 Crop services
- 1958 Veterinary services, including pets
- 1974 Livestock breeding
- 1990 Other animal services
- 2113 Farm labor and management services
- 2212 Horticulture and landscaping
- 2238 Forestry, except logging
- 0836 Logging
- 2279 Fishing, hunting, and trapping

### Wholesale Trade—Selling Goods to Other Businesses, Government, or Institutions, Etc.

**Durable goods, including machinery, equipment, wood, metals, etc.**
- 2618 Selling for your own account

Code
- 2634 Agent or broker for other firms—more than 50% of gross sales on commission

**Nondurable goods, including food, fiber, chemicals, etc.**
- 2659 Selling for your own account
- 2675 Agent or broker for other firms—more than 50% of gross sales on commission

### Retail Trade—Selling Goods to Individuals and Households
- 3012 Selling door-to-door, by telephone or party plan, or from mobile unit
- 3038 Catalog or mail order
- 3053 Vending machine selling

**Selling From Store, Showroom, or Other Fixed Location**

*Food, beverages, and drugs*
- 3079 Eating places (meals or snacks)
- 3095 Drinking places (alcoholic beverages)
- 3210 Grocery stores (general line)
- 0612 Bakeries selling at retail
- 3236 Other food stores (meat, produce, candy, etc.)
- 3251 Liquor stores
- 3277 Drug stores

*Automotive and service stations*
- 3319 New car dealers (franchised)
- 3335 Used car dealers
- 3517 Other automotive dealers (motorcycles, recreational vehicles, etc.)
- 3533 Tires, accessories, and parts
- 3558 Gasoline service stations

*General merchandise, apparel, and furniture*
- 3715 Variety stores
- 3731 Other general merchandise stores
- 3756 Shoe stores
- 3772 Men's and boys' clothing stores
- 3913 Women's ready-to-wear stores
- 3921 Women's accessory and specialty stores and furriers
- 3939 Family clothing stores
- 3954 Other apparel and accessory stores
- 3970 Furniture stores
- 3996 TV, audio, and electronics
- 3988 Computer and software stores
- 4119 Household appliance stores
- 4317 Other home furnishing stores (china, floor coverings, drapes, etc.)
- 4333 Music and record stores

*Building, hardware, and garden supply*
- 4416 Building materials dealers
- 4432 Paint, glass, and wallpaper stores
- 4457 Hardware stores
- 4473 Nurseries and garden supply stores

*Other retail stores*
- 4614 Used merchandise and antique stores (except used motor vehicle parts)
- 4630 Gift, novelty, and souvenir shops
- 4655 Florists
- 4671 Jewelry stores

Code
- 4697 Sporting goods and bicycle shops
- 4812 Boat dealers
- 4838 Hobby, toy, and game shops
- 4853 Camera and photo supply stores
- 4879 Optical goods stores
- 4895 Luggage and leather goods stores
- 5017 Book stores, excluding newsstands
- 5033 Stationery stores
- 5058 Fabric and needlework stores
- 5074 Mobile home dealers
- 5090 Fuel dealers (except gasoline)
- 5884 Other retail stores

### Real Estate, Insurance, Finance, and Related Services
- 5512 Real estate agents and managers
- 5538 Operators and lessors of buildings (except developers)
- 5553 Operators and lessors of other real property (except developers)
- 5710 Subdividers and developers, except cemeteries
- 5736 Insurance agents and services
- 5751 Security and commodity brokers, dealers, and investment services
- 5777 Other real estate, insurance, and financial activities

### Transportation, Communications, Public Utilities, and Related Services
- 6114 Taxicabs
- 6312 Bus and limousine transportation
- 6338 Trucking (except trash collection)
- 6510 Trash collection without own dump
- 6536 Public warehousing
- 6551 Water transportation
- 6619 Air transportation
- 6635 Travel agents and tour operators
- 6650 Other transportation and related services
- 6676 Communication services
- 6692 Utilities, including dumps, snowplowing, road cleaning, etc.

### Services (Providing Personal, Professional, and Business Services)

**Hotels and other lodging places**
- 7096 Hotels, motels, and tourist homes
- 7211 Rooming and boarding houses
- 7237 Camps and camping parks

**Laundry and cleaning services**
- 7419 Coin-operated laundries and dry cleaning
- 7435 Other laundry, dry cleaning, and garment services
- 7450 Carpet and upholstery cleaning
- 7476 Janitorial and related services (building, house, and window cleaning)

**Business and/or personal services**
- 7617 Legal services (or lawyer)
- 7633 Income tax preparation
- 7658 Accounting and bookkeeping
- 7674 Engineering, surveying, and architectural

Code
- 7690 Management, consulting, and public relations
- 7716 Advertising, except direct mail
- 7732 Employment agencies and personnel supply
- 7757 Computer and data processing, including repair and leasing
- 7773 Equipment rental and leasing (except computer or automotive)
- 7914 Investigative and protective services
- 7880 Other business services

**Personal services**
- 8110 Beauty shops (or beautician)
- 8318 Barber shop (or barber)
- 8334 Photographic portrait studios
- 8516 Shoe repair and shine services
- 8532 Funeral services and crematories
- 8714 Child day care
- 8730 Teaching or tutoring
- 8755 Counseling (except health practitioners)
- 8771 Ministers and chaplains
- 6882 Other personal services

**Automotive services**
- 8813 Automotive rental or leasing, without driver
- 8839 Parking, except valet
- 8854 General automotive repairs
- 8870 Specialized automotive repairs (brake, body repairs, paint, etc.)
- 8896 Other automotive services (wash, towing, etc.)

**Miscellaneous repair, except computers**
- 9019 TV and audio equipment repair
- 9035 Other electrical equipment repair
- 9050 Reupholstery and furniture repair
- 2881 Other equipment repair

**Medical and health services**
- 9217 Offices and clinics of medical doctors (MDs)
- 9233 Offices and clinics of dentists
- 9258 Osteopathic physicians and surgeons
- 9274 Chiropractors
- 9290 Optometrists
- 9415 Registered and practical nurses
- 9431 Other licensed health practitioners
- 9456 Dental laboratories
- 9472 Nursing and personal care facilities
- 9886 Other health services

**Amusement and recreational services**
- 8557 Physical fitness facilities
- 9613 Videotape rental stores
- 9639 Motion picture theaters
- 9654 Other motion picture and TV film and tape activities
- 9670 Bowling alleys
- 9696 Professional sports and racing, including promoters and managers
- 9811 Theatrical performers, musicians, agents, producers, and related services
- 9837 Other amusement and recreational services

- 8888 Unable to classify

for the year to exceed the total withheld from your wages by $500 or more. Form 1040ES—Estimated Tax for Individuals—consists of instructions, an estimated-tax worksheet, and four declaration vouchers. The vouchers are due four times a year: by the fifteenth of April, June, September, and January. Payments of estimated taxes may be made in full with the first voucher or in four equal payments. If changes in your tax status occur during the year, you may amend your declaration.

## Partnerships

Although the partnership itself isn't subject to income tax, it is required to determine its earned income and to file an information return for its tax year. In this case, you'll need to file Form 1065—U.S. Partnership Return of Income. Here, you list the firm's income and business deductions and then complete various schedules, as described briefly below:

Schedule A—Computation of the cost of goods sold and/or operations
Schedule H—Income (loss) from rental real estate activity(ies)
Schedules K and K1—Partners' shares of income, credits, deductions, etc.
Schedule L—Balance sheets for the beginning and end of the tax year.
Schedule M—Reconciliation of partners' capital accounts

A completed Form 1065 can be seen in exhibits 20–2 and 20–3.

Like the sole proprietor, you and each of your partners must file individually on the ubiquitous Form 1040. On your 1040, you need to report your *distributive share* of the partnership's income or loss—whether or not actual distributions were made. In other words, you can't just put down what you drew out of the business!

## Corporations

If you've incorporated your new business, be prepared for a more complex taxing structure. You need to file a corporation tax return every year, even if the business has no taxable income. Ask the IRS to send you Publication 542—Tax Information on Corporations. If you've elected the S-corporation form, ask for Publication 589—Tax Information on S Corporations. (For more on S corporations, see page 291.) Then get yourself a competent tax accountant.

Let's get this business of your personal income-tax liability out of the way first. If you're a wage-earning employee of your corporation, even if you're the firm's president or other officer, then you must file Form 1040. You need to respect all the rules and deadlines that any American worker does. That's your personal responsibility.

Then, just like any other taxpayer, your corporation must attend to its responsibilities by filing its own tax return. Generally, corporations submit Form 1120—U.S. Corporation Income Tax Return. For the S corporation, the proper return to file is Form 1120S—U.S. Income Tax Return for an S Corporation. Certain small corporations (not

EXHIBIT 20–2. FORM 1065

| Form **1065** | **U.S. Partnership Return of Income** | OMB No. 1545-0099 |
|---|---|---|
| Department of the Treasury Internal Revenue Service | ▶ For Paperwork Reduction Act Notice, see Form 1065 Instructions. For calendar year 1988, or fiscal year beginning_ _ _ _ _ _ _, 1988, and ending_ _ _ _ _ _ _, 19_ _ _ | **1988** |

| A Principal business activity | Use IRS label. Other-wise, please print or type. | Name | D Employer identification number |
|---|---|---|---|
| *Wholesale* | | 10-9876543          DEC88          D71 | I R S |
| B Principal product or service | | A&B DISTRIBUTING COMPANY | E Date business started |
| *Sundries* | | 334 WEST MAIN STREET | *10-1-78* |
| C Business code number | | ANYTOWN     MD          20904 | F Enter total assets at end of tax year |
| *5001* | | | $ *44,152* |

|  |  | Yes | No |
|---|---|---|---|
| G Check accounting method: (1) ☐ Cash  (2) ☑ Accrual (3) ☐ Other | | | |
| H Check applicable boxes: (1) ☐ Final return (2) ☐ Change in address  (3) ☐ Amended return | | | |
| I Number of partners in this partnership ▶   **2** | | | |
| J Is this partnership a limited partnership (see the Instructions)? | | | ✓ |
| K Are any partners in this partnership also partnerships? | | | ✓ |
| L Is this partnership a partner in another partnership? | | | ✓ |
| M Does the partnership meet all the requirements shown in the Instructions for Question M? | | | ✓ |
| N Was there a distribution of property or a transfer (for example, by sale or death) of a partnership interest during the tax year? If "Yes," see the Instructions concerning an election to adjust the basis of the partnership's assets under section 754 | | | ✓ |
| O (1) Does the partnership have any foreign partners? | | | ✓ |
| (2) If so, were any distributions made to foreign partners during the tax year? | | | |
| P At any time during the tax year, did the partnership have an interest in or a signature or other authority over a financial account in a foreign country (such as a bank account, securities account, or other financial account)? (See the Instructions for exceptions and filing requirements for Form TD F 90-22.1.) If "Yes," write the name of the foreign country. ▶ _ _ _ _ _ _ _ _ | | | ✓ |
| Q Was the partnership the grantor of, or transferor to, a foreign trust which existed during the current tax year, whether or not the partnership or any partner has any beneficial interest in it? If "Yes," you may have to file Form 3520, 3520-A, or 926 | | | ✓ |
| R Check this box if the partnership has filed or is required to file Form 8264, Application for Registration of a Tax Shelter | | | ☐ |
| S Check this box if this is a partnership subject to the consolidated partnership audit procedures of TEFRA. (See the Instructions.) | | | ☐ |
| T Check this box if the partnership is a publicly traded partnership as defined in section 469(k)(2) | | | ☐ |

**Caution:** *Include only trade or business income and expenses on lines 1a–21 below. See the instructions for more information.*

### Income

| | | | |
|---|---|---|---|
| 1a Gross receipts or sales $_ *410,024*_   1b Minus returns and allowances $_ *3,365*_ Balance ▶ | 1c | 406,659 | |
| 2 Cost of goods sold and/or operations (Schedule A, line 7) | 2 | 267,641 | |
| 3 Gross profit (subtract line 2 from line 1c) | 3 | 139,018 | |
| 4 Ordinary income (loss) from other partnerships and fiduciaries (attach schedule) | 4 | | |
| 5 Net farm profit (loss) (attach Schedule F (Form 1040)) | 5 | | |
| 6 Net gain (loss) (Form 4797, line 18) | 6 | 1,195 | |
| 7 Other income (loss) | 7 | | |
| 8 **TOTAL** income (loss) (combine lines 3 through 7) | 8 | 140,213 | |

### Deductions (see instructions for limitations)

| | | | |
|---|---|---|---|
| 9a Salaries and wages (other than to partners) $ *29,350*   9b Minus jobs credit $_ — _ Balance ▶ | 9c | 29,350 | |
| 10 Guaranteed payments to partners | 10 | 25,000 | |
| 11 Rent | 11 | 9,000 | |
| 12 Deductible interest expense not claimed elsewhere on return (see Instructions) | 12 | 871 | |
| 13 Taxes | 13 | 2,208 | |
| 14 Bad debts | 14 | 2,250 | |
| 15 Repairs | 15 | 2,235 | |
| 16a Depreciation from Form 4562 (attach Form 4562) $_ *2,083*_ 16b Minus depreciation claimed on Schedule A and elsewhere on return  $_ — _ Balance ▶ | 16c | 2,083 | |
| 17 Depletion (**Do not deduct oil and gas depletion.**) | 17 | | |
| 18a Retirement plans, etc. | 18a | | |
| b Employee benefit programs | 18b | | |
| 19 Other deductions (attach schedule) | 19 | 13,947 | |
| 20 **TOTAL** deductions (add amounts in column for lines 9c through 19) | 20 | 86,944 | |
| 21 Ordinary income (loss) from trade or business activity(ies) (subtract line 20 from line 8) | 21 | 53,269 | |

**Please Sign Here**

Under penalties of perjury, I declare that I have examined this return, including accompanying schedules and statements, and to the best of my knowledge and belief, it is true, correct, and complete. Declaration of preparer (other than taxpayer) is based on all information of which preparer has any knowledge.

*Frank W. Able*                   ▶ *4-3-89*
Signature of general partner          Date

**Paid Preparer's Use Only**

| Preparer's signature ▶ | Date | Check if self-employed ▶ ☐ | Preparer's social security no. |
|---|---|---|---|
| Firm's name (or yours if self-employed) and address ▶ | | E.I. No. ▶ | |
| | | ZIP code ▶ | |

*Source:* "Tax Guide for Small Business—1988 Edition," *Publication 334* (Washington, D.C.: Internal Revenue Service, November 1988), 148–51.

# EXHIBIT 20–2. CONTINUED

Form 1065 (1988)

## Schedule A  Cost of Goods Sold and/or Operations

| | | | |
|---|---|---|---|
| 1 | Inventory at beginning of year. | 1 | 18,125 |
| 2 | Purchases minus cost of items withdrawn for personal use | 2 | 268,741 |
| 3 | Cost of labor. | 3 | |
| 4a | Additional section 263A costs (attach schedule) (see instructions) | 4a | |
| b | Other costs (attach schedule) | 4b | |
| 5 | Total (add lines 1 through 4b). | 5 | 286,866 |
| 6 | Inventory at end of year. | 6 | 19,225 |
| 7 | Cost of goods sold (subtract line 6 from line 5). Enter here and on page 1, line 2 | 7 | 267,641 |

8a Check all methods used for valuing closing inventory:
   (I)  ☐ Cost
   (II) ☑ Lower of cost or market as described in regulations section 1.471-4
   (III) ☐ Writedown of "subnormal" goods as described in regulations section 1.471-2(c)
   (Iv) ☐ Other (specify method used and attach explanation) ▶ .............................................................

   b Check if the LIFO inventory method was adopted this tax year for any goods (if checked, attach Form 970) . . . . ☐
   c Do the rules of section 263A (with respect to property produced or acquired for resale) apply to the partnership?  . . ☐ Yes  ☑ No
   d Was there any change in determining quantities, cost, or valuations between opening and closing inventory? If "Yes," attach explanation . . . . . . . . . . . . . . . . . . . . . . . . . . . . . . . . . . . . . . . . . . ☐ Yes  ☑ No

## Schedule H  Income (Loss) From Rental Real Estate Activity(ies)

1  In the space provided below, show the kind and location of each rental property. Attach a schedule if more space is needed.
   Property A  .................................................................................................................
   Property B  .................................................................................................................
   Property C

| Rental Real Estate Income | | Properties | | | Totals (Add columns A, B, C, and amounts from any attached schedule) |
|---|---|---|---|---|---|
| | | A | B | C | |
| 2 Gross income | 2 | | | | 2 |
| Rental Real Estate Expenses | | | | | |
| 3 Advertising | 3 | | | | |
| 4 Auto and travel | 4 | | | | |
| 5 Cleaning and maintenance | 5 | | | | |
| 6 Commissions | 6 | | | | |
| 7 Insurance | 7 | | | | |
| 8 Legal and other professional fees | 8 | | | | |
| 9 Interest expense | 9 | | | | |
| 10 Repairs | 10 | | | | |
| 11 Taxes | 11 | | | | |
| 12 Utilities | 12 | | | | |
| 13 Wages and salaries | 13 | | | | |
| 14 Depreciation from Form 4562 | 14 | | | | |
| 15 Other (list) ................ | | | | | |
| ................ | | | | | |
| ................ | | | | | |
| 16 Total expenses. Add lines 3 through 15 | 16 | | | | 16 |
| 17 Net income (loss) from rental real estate activity(ies). Subtract line 16 from line 2. Enter total net income (loss) from all properties on Schedule K, line 2. | 17 | | | | 17 |

EXHIBIT 20–2. CONTINUED

Form 1065 (1988)

Page 3

| Schedule K | Partners' Shares of Income, Credits, Deductions, etc. | | |
|---|---|---|---|
| | **(a) Distributive share items** | | **(b) Total amount** |

| | | | |
|---|---|---|---|
| **Income (Loss)** | 1 Ordinary income (loss) from trade or business activity(ies) (page 1, line 21) . . . . . . | 1 | 53,269 |
| | 2 Net income (loss) from rental real estate activity(ies) (Schedule H, line 17) . . . . . | 2 | |
| | 3a Gross income from other rental activity(ies) . . . . . . | 3a | |
| | b Minus expenses (attach schedule) . . . . . . . . . | 3b | |
| | c Balance: net income (loss) from other rental activity(ies) . . . . . . . . . . ▶ | 3c | |
| | 4 Portfolio income (loss) (see instructions): | | |
| | a Interest income . . . . . . . . . . . . . . . . . . . . . . . . | 4a | |
| | b Dividend income . . . . . . . . . . . . . . . . . . . . . . . | 4b | 150 |
| | c Royalty income . . . . . . . . . . . . . . . . . . . . . . . | 4c | |
| | d Net short-term capital gain (loss) (Schedule D, line 4) . . . . . . . . . . . . | 4d | 100 |
| | e Net long-term capital gain (loss) (Schedule D, line 9) . . . . . . . . . . . . | 4e | 200 |
| | f Other portfolio income (loss) (attach schedule) . . . . . . . . . . . . | 4f | |
| | 5 Guaranteed payments . . . . . . . . . . . . . . . . . . . . | 5 | 25,000 |
| | 6 Net gain (loss) under section 1231 (other than due to casualty or theft) (see instructions) | 6 | 1,051 |
| | 7 Other (attach schedule). . . . . . . . . . . . . . . . . . . . . | 7 | |
| **Deductions** | 8 Charitable contributions (attach list) . . . . . . . . . . . . . . . | 8 | 650 |
| | 9 Expense deduction for recovery property (section 179) (attach schedule) . . . . | 9 | |
| | 10 Deductions related to portfolio income (do not include investment interest expense) . . | 10 | |
| | 11 Other (attach schedule). . . . . . . . . . . . . . . . . . . . | 11 | |
| **Credits** | 12a Credit for income tax withheld . . . . . . . . . . . . . . . . | 12a | |
| | b Low-income housing credit: (1) Partnerships to which section 42(j)(5) applies . . . . | 12b(1) | |
| | (2) Other . . . . . . . . . . . . . . . . . . . . . | 12b(2) | |
| | c Qualified rehabilitation expenditures related to rental real estate activity(ies) (attach schedule) | 12c | |
| | d Credit(s) related to rental real estate activity(ies) other than 12b and 12c (attach schedule) . | 12d | |
| | e Credit(s) related to other rental activity(ies) (see instructions) (attach schedule) . . . . | 12e | |
| | 13 Other (attach schedule). . . . . . . . . . . . . . . . . . | 13 | |
| **Self-Employment** | 14a Net earnings (loss) from self-employment . . . . . . . . . . . . . | 14a | 77,074 |
| | b Gross farming or fishing income . . . . . . . . . . . . . . . | 14b | |
| | c Gross nonfarm income . . . . . . . . . . . . . . . . . . | 14c | 77,074 |
| **Tax Preference Items** | 15a Accelerated depreciation of real property placed in service before 1/1/87 . . . . | 15a | |
| | b Accelerated depreciation of leased personal property placed in service before 1/1/87 | 15b | |
| | c Depreciation adjustment on property placed in service after 12/31/86 . . . . . | 15c | |
| | d Depletion (other than oil and gas) . . . . . . . . . . . . . . | 15d | |
| | e (1) Gross income from oil, gas, and geothermal properties . . . . . . . . | 15e(1) | |
| | (2) Deductions allocable to oil, gas, and geothermal properties . . . . . . | 15e(2) | |
| | f Other (attach schedule). . . . . . . . . . . . . . . . . . | 15f | |
| **Investment Interest** | 16a Interest expense on investment debts . . . . . . . . . . . . . . | 16a | |
| | b (1) Investment income included on lines 4a through 4f, Schedule K . . . . . . | 16b(1) | 450 |
| | (2) Investment expenses included on line 10, Schedule K . . . . . . . . | 16b(2) | |
| **Foreign Taxes** | 17a Type of income _____ | | |
| | b Foreign country or U.S. possession _____ | | |
| | c Total gross income from sources outside the U.S. (attach schedule) . . . . . . | 17c | |
| | d Total applicable deductions and losses (attach schedule) . . . . . . . . . | 17d | |
| | e Total foreign taxes (check one): ▶ ☐ Paid ☐ Accrued . . . . . . . | 17e | |
| | f Reduction in taxes available for credit (attach schedule) . . . . . . . . . | 17f | |
| | g Other (attach schedule). . . . . . . . . . . . . . . . . . | 17g | |
| **Other** | 18a Total expenditures to which a section 59(e) election may apply (attach schedule) . . . | 18a | |
| | b Attach schedule for other items and amounts not reported above (see instructions) . . | | |
| **Analysis** | 19a Total distributive income/payment items (combine lines 1 through 5, above) . . . . . | 19a | |
| | b Analysis by type of partner: | | |

| | (a) Corporate | (b) Individual | | (c) Partnership | (d) Exempt organization | (e) Nominee/Other |
|---|---|---|---|---|---|---|
| | | i. active | ii. passive | | | |
| 1. General partners | | | | | | |
| 2. Limited partners | | | | | | |

EXHIBIT 20–2. CONTINUED

Form 1065 (1988)

## Schedule L Balance Sheets
(See the Instructions for Question M Before Completing Schedules L and M.)

| Assets | Beginning of tax year (a) | (b) | End of tax year (c) | (d) |
|---|---|---|---|---|
| 1 Cash | | 405 | | 8,620 |
| 2 Trade notes and accounts receivable | 7,150 | | 10,990 | |
| a Minus allowance for bad debts | | 7,150 | | 10,990 |
| 3 Inventories | | 18,125 | | 19,225 |
| 4 Federal and state government obligations | | 1,000 | | 1,000 |
| 5 Other current assets (attach schedule) | | | | |
| 6 Mortgage and real estate loans | | | | |
| 7 Other investments (attach schedule) | | 1,000 | | — |
| 8 Buildings and other depreciable assets | 16,000 | | 8,900 | |
| a Minus accumulated depreciation | 4,000 | 12,000 | 5,583 | 3,317 |
| 9 Depletable assets | | | | |
| a Minus accumulated depletion | | | | |
| 10 Land (net of any amortization) | | 500 | | 1,000 |
| 11 Intangible assets (amortizable only) | | | | |
| a Minus accumulated amortization | | | | |
| 12 Other assets (attach schedule) | | 40,180 | | 44,152 |
| 13 TOTAL assets | | | | |
| **Liabilities and Capital** | | | | |
| 14 Accounts payable | | 9,180 | | 10,462 |
| 15 Mortgages, notes, bonds payable in less than 1 year | | 3,600 | | 4,000 |
| 16 Other current liabilities (attach schedule) | | | | |
| 17 All nonrecourse loans | | | | |
| 18 Mortgages, notes, bonds payable in 1 year or more | | 14,900 | | 14,900 |
| 19 Other liabilities (attach schedule) | | | | |
| 20 Partners' capital accounts | | 12,500 | | 14,790 |
| 21 TOTAL liabilities and capital | | 40,180 | | 44,152 |

## Schedule M Reconciliation of Partners' Capital Accounts
(Show reconciliation of each partner's capital account on Schedule K-1 (Form 1065), Question K.)

| (a) Capital account at beginning of year | (b) Capital contributed during year | (c) Income (loss) from lines 1,2, 3c, and 4 of Sch. K | (d) Income not included in column (c) plus nontaxable income | (e) Losses not included in column (c), plus unallowable deductions | (f) Withdrawals and distributions | (g) Capital account at end of year |
|---|---|---|---|---|---|---|
| 12,500 | 1,000 | 53,719 | 1,101 | 650 | 52,880 | 14,790 |

### Designation of Tax Matters Partner

The following general partner is hereby designated as the tax matters partner (TMP) for the tax year for which this partnership return is filed:

Name of
designated TMP ▶

Identifying
number of TMP ▶

Address of
designated TMP ▶

## EXHIBIT 20–3. SCHEDULE K–1 (FORM 1065)

| SCHEDULE K-1 (Form 1065) Department of the Treasury Internal Revenue Service | **Partner's Share of Income, Credits, Deductions, etc.** For calendar year 1988 or fiscal year beginning , 1988, and ending , 19 | OMB No. 1545-0099 **1988** |
|---|---|---|

| Partner's Identifying number ▶ 123 - 00 - 6789 | Partnership's Identifying number ▶ 10 - 9876543 |
|---|---|

| Partner's name, address, and ZIP code | Partnership's name, address, and ZIP code |
|---|---|
| Frank W. Able<br>10 Green Street<br>Anytown, MD 20904 | A & B Distributing Co.<br>334 West Main Street<br>Anytown, MD 20904 |

**A** Is this partner a general partner? . . . ☑ Yes ☐ No

**B** Partner's share of liabilities:
Nonrecourse. . . . . . . . $ _____
Other . . . . . . . . . . $ 14,681

**C** What type of entity is this partner? ▶ Individual

**D** Is this partner a ☑ domestic or a ☐ foreign partner?

**E** Enter partner's percentage of:
|  | (I) Before decrease or termination | (II) End of year |
|---|---|---|
| Profit sharing | _____ % | 50 % |
| Loss sharing | _____ % | 50 % |
| Ownership of capital | _____ % | 50 % |

**F** IRS Center where partnership filed return ▶ Philadelphia

**G** Tax Shelter Registration Number ▶ N/A

**H(1)** Did the partner's ownership interest in the partnership change after Oct. 22, 1986? . . . . . . . ☐ Yes ☑ No
If yes, attach statement. (See Form 1065 Instructions.)

**(2)** Did the partnership start or acquire a new activity after Oct. 22, 1986? . . . . . . . . ☐ Yes ☑ No
If yes, attach statement. (See Form 1065 Instructions.)

**I** Check here if this partnership is a publicly traded partnership as defined in section 469(k)(2) . . . . . . . ☐

**J** Check here if this is an amended Schedule K-1. . . . . ☐

**K** Reconciliation of partner's capital account:

| (a) Capital account at beginning of year | (b) Capital contributed during year | (c) Income (loss) from lines 1, 2, 3, and 4 below | (d) Income not included in column (c), plus nontaxable income | (e) Losses not included in column (c), plus unallowable deductions | (f) Withdrawals and distributions | (g) Capital account at end of year |
|---|---|---|---|---|---|---|
| 6,500 | -0- | 26,860 | 550 | 325 | 26,440 | 7,145 |

**Reminder:** If you received a 1987 Schedule K-1 that was for a short year and you chose to report the 1987 amounts over a 4-year period, be sure to include one-fourth of the short year amounts, in addition to the items reported on this Schedule K-1, on the appropriate lines of your 1988 Form 1040 and related schedules.

**Caution:** Refer to attached Partner's Instructions for Schedule K-1 (Form 1065) before entering information from this schedule on your tax return.

| | (a) Distributive share Item | | (b) Amount | (c) 1040 filers enter the amount In column (b) on: |
|---|---|---|---|---|
| **Income (Loss)** | 1 Ordinary income (loss) from trade or business activity(ies) . . | 1 | 26,635 | ⎫ (See Partner's Instructions for Schedule K-1 (Form 1065)) |
| | 2 Net income or loss from rental real estate activity(ies) . . . . | 2 | | |
| | 3 Net income or loss from other rental activity(ies). . . . . . | 3 | | |
| | 4 Portfolio income (loss): | | | |
| | a Interest . . . . . . . . . . . . . . . . . . . | 4a | | Sch. B, Part I, line 2 |
| | b Dividends . . . . . . . . . . . . . . . . . . | 4b | 75 | Sch. B, Part II, line 4 |
| | c Royalties . . . . . . . . . . . . . . . . . . | 4c | | Sch. E, Part I, line 5 |
| | d Net short-term capital gain (loss). . . . . . . . . . . | 4d | 50 | Sch. D, line 5, col. (f) or (g) |
| | e Net long-term capital gain (loss) . . . . . . . . . . | 4e | 100 | Sch. D, line 12, col. (f) or (g) |
| | f Other portfolio income (loss) (attach schedule) . . . . . | 4f | | (Enter on applicable lines of your return) |
| | 5 Guaranteed payments . . . . . . . . . . . . . . | 5 | 20,000 | ⎫ (See Partner's Instructions for Schedule K-1 (Form 1065)) |
| | 6 Net gain (loss) under section 1231 (other than due to casualty or theft) | 6 | 526 | |
| | 7 Other (attach schedule) . . . . . . . . . . . . | 7 | | (Enter on applicable lines of your return) |
| **Deduc-tions** | 8 Charitable contributions . . . . . . . . . . . . . | 8 | 325 | Sch. A, line 14 or 15 |
| | 9 Expense deduction for recovery property (section 179) (attach schedule) . . | 9 | | ⎫ (See Partner's Instructions for Schedule K-1 (Form 1065)) |
| | 10 Deductions related to portfolio income . . . . . . . . | 10 | | |
| | 11 Other (attach schedule) . . . . . . . . . . . . | 11 | | |
| **Credits** | 12a Credit for income tax withheld . . . . . . . . . . | 12a | | See Partner's Instructions for Schedule K-1 (Form 1065) |
| | b Low-income housing credit: (1) Partnerships to which section 42(j)(5) applies | b(1) | | ⎫ Form 8586, line 5 |
| | (2) Other . . . . . . . . . . . . . . . . . . | b(2) | | |
| | c Qualified rehabilitation expenditures related to rental real estate activity(ies) (attach schedule). . . . . . . . . . . . . | 12c | | ⎫ (See Partner's Instructions for Schedule K-1 (Form 1065)) |
| | d Credit(s) related to rental real estate activity(ies) other than 12b and 12c (attach schedule) . . . . . . . . . . . . | 12d | | |
| | e Credit(s) related to other rental activity(ies) (see instructions) (attach schedule) | 12e | | |
| | 13 Other credits (attach schedule) . . . . . . . . . . | 13 | | |

For Paperwork Reduction Act Notice, see Form 1065 Instructions.

Schedule K-1 (Form 1065) 1988

*Source:* "Tax Guide for Small Business—1988 Edition," *Publication 334* (Washington, D.C.: Internal Revenue Service, November 1988), 153–54.

EXHIBIT 20–3. CONTINUED

Schedule K-1 (Form 1065) (1988)                                                                 Page 2

| | | (a) Distributive share item | | (b) Amount | (c) 1040 filers enter the amount in column (b) on: |
|---|---|---|---|---|---|
| Self-employment | 14a | Net earnings (loss) from self-employment | 14a | 46,037 | Sch. SE, Section A or B |
| | b | Gross farming or fishing income | 14b | | } (See Partner's Instructions for Schedule K-1 (Form 1065)) |
| | c | Gross nonfarm income | 14c | 46,037 | |
| Tax Preference Items | 15a | Accelerated depreciation of real property placed in service before 1/1/87 | 15a | | Form 6251, line 5e |
| | b | Accelerated depreciation of leased personal property placed in service before 1/1/87 | 15b | | Form 6251, line 5f |
| | c | Depreciation adjustment on property placed in service after 12/31/86 | 15c | | Form 6251, line 4j |
| | d | Depletion (other than oil and gas) | 15d | | Form 6251, line 5c |
| | e | (1) Gross income from oil, gas, and geothermal properties | e(1) | | See Form 6251 Instructions |
| | | (2) Deductions allocable to oil, gas, and geothermal properties | e(2) | | See Form 6251 Instructions |
| | f | Other (attach schedule) | 15f | | (See Partner's Instructions for Schedule K-1 (Form 1065)) |
| Investment Interest | 16a | Interest expense on investment debts | 16a | | Form 4952, line 1 |
| | b | (1) Investment income included in Schedule K-1, lines 4a through 4f | b(1) | 225 | } (See Partner's Instructions for Schedule K-1 (Form 1065)) |
| | | (2) Investment expenses included in Schedule K-1, line 10 | b(2) | | |
| Foreign Taxes | 17a | Type of income _____ | | | Form 1116, Check boxes |
| | b | Name of foreign country or U.S. possession _____ | | | Form 1116, Part I |
| | c | Total gross income from sources outside the U.S. (attach schedule) | 17c | | Form 1116, Part I |
| | d | Total applicable deductions and losses (attach schedule) | 17d | | Form 1116, Part I |
| | e | Total foreign taxes (check one): ▶ ☐ Paid ☐ Accrued | 17e | | Form 1116, Part II |
| | f | Reduction in taxes available for credit (attach schedule) | 17f | | Form 1116, Part III |
| | g | Other (attach schedule) | 17g | | See Form 1116 Instructions |
| Other | 18a | Total expenditures to which a section 59(e) election (relating to the optional 10-year writeoff of certain tax preference items) may apply (attach schedule). | | | (See Partner's Instructions for Schedule K-1 (Form 1065)) |
| | b | Other items and amounts not reported on lines 1 through 17g, 19, and 20 that are required to be reported separately to you | | | |
| | 19a | Low-income housing credit: Partnerships to which section 42(j)(5) applies | 19a | | } Form 8611 |
| | b | Low-income housing credit: Other | 19b | | |

| | 20 | Investment Tax Credit Property: | A | B | C | |
|---|---|---|---|---|---|---|
| Recapture of Tax Credits | a | Description of property (State whether recovery or nonrecovery property. If recovery property, state whether regular percentage method or section 48(q) election used.) | | | | Form 4255, top |
| | b | Date placed in service | | | | Form 4255, line 2 |
| | c | Cost or other basis | | | | Form 4255, line 3 |
| | d | Class of recovery property or original estimated useful life | | | | Form 4255, line 4 |
| | e | Date item ceased to be investment credit property | | | | Form 4255, line 8 |

Other Information Provided by Partnership:

_____

_____

_____

_____

_____

the S type) may be able to save time and trouble by substituting Form 1120–A—U.S. Corporation Short-Form Income Tax Return.*

Corporate tax returns must be filed with the IRS center that serves the state where the corporation's principal office is located—where the books and records of the corporation are maintained. If the company follows the calendar year, then the tax return is due by March 15 of the following year; if the fiscal-year approach is used, then the tax return is due on or before the fifteenth day of the third month following the close of the fiscal year. Should more time be needed, the corporation may request an automatic six-month extension by submitting Form 7004—Application for Automatic Extension of Time to File Corporation Income Tax Return.

Exhibits 20–4 through 20–6 provide illustrations of Forms 1120, 1120–A, and 1120S.

**Tax Rates.** Current tax rates on a corporation's taxable income are given below:

| Taxable Income | Tax Rate |
|---|---|
| Not over $50,000 | 15% |
| Over $50,000 but not over $75,000 | 25 |
| Over $75,000 | 34 |

*Note:* An additional 5-percent tax, up to $11,750, is imposed on corporate taxable income over $100,000. Corporations with taxable incomes of at least $335,000 pay a flat rate of 34 percent.

**Estimated Tax Payments.** Corporations are also on a "pay-as-you-go" plan. Every corporation whose estimated tax is expected to be forty dollars or more is required to make payments of estimated tax. In the majority of cases, four installments are due each year. Payments must be deposited with an authorized financial institution or a Federal Reserve Bank. Each deposit must be accompanied by a federal tax-deposit coupon. Any income-tax balance, after installments on estimated tax have been considered, must be paid by the due date of your corporation income-tax return.

**The S Corporation.** Corporations with certain qualifications may elect not to be subject to the income tax, in which case any income they earn is taxed instead to the shareholders. These are S corporations. What happens, in effect, when a corporation becomes an S type, is that all income and net operating losses (with certain adjustments) are

---

* To be able to use Form 1120–A, a company must meet a number of specific requirements. Among them are (1) the firm's gross receipts, total income, and total assets must each be below $250,000; (2) the firm cannot hold ownership in a foreign corporation; and (3) it cannot have foreign shareholders who own 50 percent or more of its stock.

EXHIBIT 20–4. FORM 1120

| Form **1120** | | U.S. Corporation Income Tax Return | | OMB No. 1545-0123 |
|---|---|---|---|---|

Department of the Treasury
Internal Revenue Service

For calendar year 1988 or tax year beginning ............... , 1988, ending ............... , 19 ....
► For Paperwork Reduction Act Notice, see page 1 of the Instructions.

**1988**

**Check if a—**
A Consolidated return ☐
B Personal holding co. ☐
C Personal service corp (as defined in Temp. Regs sec. 1 441-4T—see instructions) ☐

Use IRS label. Otherwise, please print or type.

Name
10-0395674    DEC88    D71    3998
TENTEX TOYS,    INC
36 DIVISION STREET
ANYTOWN                    IL    60930

**D** Employer Identification number

**E** Date incorporated
3·1·72

**F** Total assets (See Specific Instructions.)
Dollars: $ 879,417   Cents:

**G** Check applicable boxes: (1) ☐ Initial return (2) ☐ Final return (3) ☐ Change in address

| | | | | | Line | Dollars | Cents |
|---|---|---|---|---|---|---|---|
| Income | 1a | Gross receipts or sales $2,010,000 | b Less returns and allowances $20,000 | c Bal ► | 1c | 1,990,000 | |
| | 2 | Cost of goods sold and/or operations (Schedule A) | | | 2 | 1,520,000 | |
| | 3 | Gross profit (line 1c less line 2) | | | 3 | 470,000 | |
| | 4 | Dividends (Schedule C, line 19) | | | 4 | 10,000 | |
| | 5 | Interest | | | 5 | 4,500 | |
| | 6 | Gross rents | | | 6 | | |
| | 7 | Gross royalties | | | 7 | | |
| | 8 | Capital gain net income (attach separate Schedule D) | | | 8 | | |
| | 9 | Net gain or (loss) from Form 4797, Part II, line 18 (attach Form 4797) | | | 9 | | |
| | 10 | Other income (see instructions—attach schedule) | | | 10 | 1,000 | |
| | 11 | Total income—Add lines 3 through 10 and enter here | | ► | 11 | 485,500 | |
| Deductions (See instructions for limitations on deductions) | 12 | Compensation of officers (Schedule E) | | | 12 | 70,000 | |
| | 13a | Salaries and wages 44,000 | b Less jobs credit 6,000 | c Balance ► | 13c | 38,000 | |
| | 14 | Repairs | | | 14 | 800 | |
| | 15 | Bad debts | | | 15 | 1,600 | |
| | 16 | Rents | | | 16 | 9,200 | |
| | 17 | Taxes | | | 17 | 15,000 | |
| | 18 | Interest | | | 18 | 27,200 | |
| | 19 | Contributions (see Instructions for 10% limitation) | | | 19 | 23,150 | |
| | 20 | Depreciation (attach Form 4562) | 20 | 17,600 | | | |
| | 21 | Less depreciation claimed in Schedule A and elsewhere on return | 21a | (12,400) | 21b | 5,200 | |
| | 22 | Depletion | | | 22 | | |
| | 23 | Advertising | | | 23 | 8,700 | |
| | 24 | Pension, profit-sharing, etc., plans | | | 24 | | |
| | 25 | Employee benefit programs | | | 25 | | |
| | 26 | Other deductions (attach schedule) | | | 26 | 78,300 | |
| | 27 | Total deductions—Add lines 12 through 26 and enter here | | ► | 27 | 277,150 | |
| | 28 | Taxable income before net operating loss deduction and special deductions (line 11 less line 27) | | | 28 | 208,350 | |
| | 29 | Less: a Net operating loss deduction (see instructions) | 29a | | | | |
| | | b Special deductions (Schedule C, line 20) | 29b | 8,000 | 29c | 8,000 | |
| Tax and Payments | 30 | Taxable income (line 28 less line 29c) | | | 30 | 200,350 | |
| | 31 | Total tax (Schedule J) | | | 31 | 55,387 | |
| | 32 | Payments: a 1987 overpayment credited to 1988 | 32a | | | | |
| | | b 1988 estimated tax payments | 32b | 69,117 | | | |
| | | c Less 1988 refund applied for on Form 4466 | 32c ( ) | d Bal ► 32d | 69,117 | | |
| | | e Tax deposited with Form 7004 | 32e | | | | |
| | | f Credit from regulated investment companies (attach Form 2439) | 32f | | | | |
| | | g Credit for Federal tax on fuels (attach Form 4136) | 32g | | 32h | 69,117 | |
| | 33 | Enter any penalty for underpayment of estimated tax—check ► ☐ if Form 2220 is attached | | | 33 | | |
| | 34 | Tax due—If the total of lines 31 and 33 is larger than line 32h, enter amount owed | | | 34 | | |
| | 35 | Overpayment—If line 32h is larger than the total of lines 31 and 33, enter amount overpaid | | | 35 | 13,730 | |
| | 36 | Enter amount of line 35 you want: Credited to 1989 estimated tax ► 13,731 | Refunded ► | | 36 | 13,730 | |

**Please Sign Here**

Under penalties of perjury, I declare that I have examined this return, including accompanying schedules and statements, and to the best of my knowledge and belief, it is true, correct, and complete. Declaration of preparer (other than taxpayer) is based on all information of which preparer has any knowledge.

► _James Q. Barclay_ Signature of officer    Date 3·7·89    Title _President_

**Paid Preparer's Use Only**

| Preparer's signature ► | | Date | Check if self-employed ☐ | Preparer's social security number |
| Firm's name (or yours if self-employed) and address ► | | | E.I. No. ► | ZIP code ► |

*Source:* "Tax Guide for Small Business—1988 Edition," *Publication 334* (Washington, D.C.: Internal Revenue Service, November 1988), 162–65.

EXHIBIT 20–4. CONTINUED

Form 1120 (1988)

**Schedule A** Cost of Goods Sold and/or Operations (See instructions for line 2, page 1.)

| | | |
|---|---|---|
| 1 Inventory at beginning of year | 1 | 126,000 |
| 2 Purchases | 2 | 1,127,100 |
| 3 Cost of labor | 3 | 402,000 |
| 4a Additional section 263A costs (see instructions—attach schedule) | 4a | |
| b Other costs (attach schedule) | 4b | 163,300 |
| 5 Total—Add lines 1 through 4b | 5 | 1,818,400 |
| 6 Inventory at end of year | 6 | 298,400 |
| 7 Cost of goods sold and/or operations—Line 5 less line 6. Enter here and on line 2, page 1 | 7 | 1,520,000 |

8a Check all methods used for valuing closing inventory:
(i) ☐ Cost  (ii) ☑ Lower of cost or market as described in Regulations section 1.471-4 (see instructions)
(iii) ☐ Writedown of "subnormal" goods as described in Regulations section 1.471-2(c) (see instructions)
(iv) ☐ Other (Specify method used and attach explanation.) ▶ _____

b Check if the LIFO inventory method was adopted this tax year for any goods (if checked, attach Form 970) . . . . . ☐

c If the LIFO inventory method was used for this tax year, enter percentage (or amounts) of closing inventory computed under LIFO | 8c |

d Do the rules of section 263A (with respect to property produced or acquired for resale) apply to the corporation? . ☑ Yes ☐ No

e Was there any change in determining quantities, cost, or valuations between opening and closing inventory? If "Yes," attach explanation . . . . . ☐ Yes ☑ No

**Schedule C** Dividends and Special Deductions (See Schedule C instructions.)

| | (a) Dividends received | (b) % | (c) Special deductions multiply (a) × (b) |
|---|---|---|---|
| 1 Dividends from less-than-20%-owned domestic corporations that are subject to the 70% deduction (other than debt-financed stock) | | 70 | |
| 2 Dividends from 20%-or-more-owned domestic corporations that are subject to the 80% deduction (other than debt-financed stock) | 10,000 | 80 | 8,000 |
| 3 Dividends on debt-financed stock of domestic and foreign corporations (section 246A) | | see instructions | |
| 4 Dividends on certain preferred stock of less-than-20%-owned public utilities | | 41.176 | |
| 5 Dividends on certain preferred stock of 20%-or-more-owned public utilities | | 47.059 | |
| 6 Dividends from less-than-20%-owned foreign corporations and certain FSCs that are subject to the 70% deduction | | 70 | |
| 7 Dividends from 20%-or-more-owned foreign corporations and certain FSCs that are subject to the 80% deduction | | 80 | |
| 8 Dividends from wholly owned foreign subsidiaries subject to the 100% deduction (section 245(b)) | | 100 | |
| 9 **Total**—Add lines 1 through 8. See instructions for limitation | | | 8,000 |
| 10 Dividends from domestic corporations received by a small business investment company operating under the Small Business Investment Act of 1958 | | 100 | |
| 11 Dividends from certain FSCs that are subject to the 100% deduction (section 245(c)(1)) | | 100 | |
| 12 Dividends from affiliated group members subject to the 100% deduction (section 243(a)(3)) | | 100 | |
| 13 Other dividends from foreign corporations not included in lines 3, 6, 7, 8, and 11 | | | |
| 14 Income from controlled foreign corporations under subpart F (attach Forms 5471) | | | |
| 15 Foreign dividend gross-up (section 78) | | | |
| 16 IC-DISC and former DISC dividends not included in lines 1, 2, and/or 3 (section 246(d)) | | | |
| 17 Other dividends | | | |
| 18 Deduction for dividends paid on certain preferred stock of public utilities (see instructions) | | | |
| 19 Total dividends—Add lines 1 through 17. Enter here and on line 4, page 1. ▶ | 10,000 | | |
| 20 Total deductions—Add lines 9, 10, 11, 12, and 18. Enter here and on line 29b, page 1 ▶ | | | 8,000 |

**Schedule E** Compensation of Officers (See instructions for line 12, page 1.)
Complete Schedule E only if total receipts (line 1a, plus lines 4 through 10, of page 1, Form 1120) are $150,000 or more.

| (a) Name of officer | (b) Social security number | (c) Percent of time devoted to business | Percent of corporation stock owned (d) Common | (e) Preferred | (f) Amount of compensation |
|---|---|---|---|---|---|
| 1 James Q. Barclay | 581·00·0936 | 100 % | 45 % | % | 40,000 |
| | | % | % | % | |
| George M. Collins | 447·00·2604 | 100 % | 15 % | % | 21,000 |
| | | % | % | % | |
| Samuel Adams | 401·00·2611 | 50 % | 2 % | % | 9,000 |
| 2 Total compensation of officers | | | | | 70,000 |
| 3 Less: Compensation of officers claimed in Schedule A and elsewhere on return | | | | | ( ) |
| 4 Compensation of officers deducted on line 12, page 1 | | | | | 70,000 |

# EXHIBIT 20–4. CONTINUED

**Schedule J**    **Tax Computation (See instructions.)**

1 Check if you are a member of a controlled group (see sections 1561 and 1563) . . . . . . . . ▶ ☐

2 If line 1 is checked:

  **a** Enter your share of the $50,000 and $25,000 taxable income bracket amounts (in that order):

    *(i)* ⌊$      ⌋    *(ii)* ⌊$      ⌋

  **b** Enter your share of the additional 5% tax (not to exceed $11,750) ⌊$      ⌋

3 Income tax (See instructions to figure the tax). Check this box if the corporation is a qualified personal service corporation (see instructions) ▶ ☐ . . . . . . . . . . . . . . . . | **3** | 61,387

4a Foreign tax credit (attach Form 1118) . . . . . . . . | 4a |

  **b** Possessions tax credit (attach Form 5735) . . . . . . | 4b |

  **c** Orphan drug credit (attach Form 6765) . . . . . . . | 4c |

  **d** Credit for fuel produced from a nonconventional source (see instructions) . . . . . . . . . . . . . . | 4d |

  **e** General business credit. Enter here and check which forms are attached:
    ☐ Form 3800    ☐ Form 3468    ☑ Form 5884
    ☐ Form 6478    ☐ Form 6765    ☐ Form 8586 . . . . | 4e | 6,000

  **f** Credit for prior year minimum tax (attach Form 8801) . . . . . | 4f |

5 Total—Add lines 4a through 4f . . . . . . . . . . . . . . | **5** | 6,000

6 Line 3 less line 5 . . . . . . . . . . . . . . . . . | **6** | 55,387

7 Personal holding company tax (attach Schedule PH (Form 1120)) . . . . . . | **7** |

8 Recapture taxes. Check if from: ☐ Form 4255   ☐ Form 8611 . . . . . | **8** |

9a Alternative minimum tax (see instructions—attach Form 4626) . . . . . | **9a** |

  **b** Environmental tax (see instructions—attach Form 4626) . . . . . | **9b** |

10 Total tax—Add lines 6 through 9b. Enter here and on line 31, page 1 . . . . . | **10** | 55,387

---

**Additional Information** (See instruction F.)

**H** Refer to the list in the instructions and state the principal:

  (1) Business activity code no. ▶ 3998

  (2) Business activity ▶ Manufacturing

  (3) Product or service ▶ Toys

**I** (1) Did the corporation at the end of the tax year own, directly or indirectly, 50% or more of the voting stock of a domestic corporation? (For rules of attribution, see section 267(c).) . — **No** ✓

    If "Yes," attach a schedule showing: (a) name, address, and identifying number; (b) percentage owned; and (c) taxable income or (loss) before NOL and special deductions of such corporation for the tax year ending with or within your tax year.

  (2) Did any individual, partnership, corporation, estate, or trust at the end of the tax year own, directly or indirectly, 50% or more of the corporation's voting stock? (For rules of attribution, see section 267(c).) If "Yes," complete (a) through (c) . — **No** ✓

    (a) Attach a schedule showing name, address, and identifying number.

    (b) Enter percentage owned ▶

    (c) Was the owner of such voting stock a person other than a U.S. person? (See instructions.) Note: *If "Yes," the corporation may have to file Form 5472.* . . .

      If "Yes," enter owner's country ▶

**J** Was the corporation a U.S. shareholder of any controlled foreign corporation? (See sections 951 and 957.) . . . — **No** ✓

  If "Yes," attach Form 5471 for each such corporation.

**K** At any time during the tax year, did the corporation have an interest in or a signature or other authority over a financial account in a foreign country (such as a bank account, securities account, or other financial account)? . . . . . . . . . — **No** ✓
(See instruction F and filing requirements for form TD F 90-22.1.)
If "Yes," enter name of foreign country ▶

**L** Was the corporation the grantor of, or transferor to, a foreign trust which existed during the current tax year, whether or not the corporation has any beneficial interest in it? . . . . — **No** ✓
If "Yes," the corporation may have to file Forms 3520, 3520-A, or 926.

**M** During this tax year, did the corporation pay dividends (other than stock dividends and distributions in exchange for stock) in excess of the corporation's current and accumulated earnings and profits? (See sections 301 and 316.) . . . . . . — **No** ✓
If "Yes," file Form 5452. If this is a consolidated return, answer here for parent corporation and on **Form 851**, Affiliations Schedule, for each subsidiary.

**N** During this tax year did the corporation maintain any part of its accounting/tax records on a computerized system? . . . . — **No** ✓

**O** Check method of accounting:
  (1) ☐ Cash
  (2) ☑ Accrual
  (3) ☐ Other (specify) ▶

**P** Check this box if the corporation issued publicly offered debt instruments with original issue discount . . . . . ☐
If so, the corporation may have to file Form 8281.

**Q** Enter the amount of tax-exempt interest received or accrued during the tax year ▶ ⌊ 5,000 ⌋

**R** Enter the number of shareholders at the end of the tax year if there were 35 or fewer shareholders ▶

EXHIBIT 20–4. CONTINUED

## Schedule L — Balance Sheets

| Assets | Beginning of tax year (a) | Beginning of tax year (b) | End of tax year (c) | End of tax year (d) |
|---|---|---|---|---|
| 1 Cash | | 14,700 | | 28,331 |
| 2 Trade notes and accounts receivable | 98,400 | | 103,700 | |
| a Less allowance for bad debts | | 98,400 | | 103,700 |
| 3 Inventories | | 126,000 | | 298,400 |
| 4 Federal and state government obligations | | 100,000 | | 120,000 |
| 5 Other current assets (attach schedule) | | 26,300 | | 17,266 |
| 6 Loans to stockholders | | | | |
| 7 Mortgage and real estate loans | | | | |
| 8 Other investments (attach schedule) | | 100,000 | | 80,000 |
| 9 Buildings and other depreciable assets | 272,400 | | 296,700 | |
| a Less accumulated depreciation | 88,300 | 184,100 | 104,280 | 192,420 |
| 10 Depletable assets | | | | |
| a Less accumulated depletion | | | | |
| 11 Land (net of any amortization) | | 20,000 | | 20,000 |
| 12 Intangible assets (amortizable only) | | | | |
| a Less accumulated amortization | | | | |
| 13 Other assets (attach schedule) | | 14,800 | | 19,300 |
| 14 Total assets | | 684,300 | | 879,417 |
| **Liabilities and Stockholders' Equity** | | | | |
| 15 Accounts payable | | 28,500 | | 34,834 |
| 16 Mortgages, notes, bonds payable in less than 1 year | | 4,300 | | 4,300 |
| 17 Other current liabilities (attach schedule) | | 6,800 | | 7,400 |
| 18 Loans from stockholders | | | | |
| 19 Mortgages, notes, bonds payable in 1 year or more | | 176,700 | | 264,100 |
| 20 Other liabilities (attach schedule) | | | | |
| 21 Capital stock: a Preferred stock | | | | |
| b Common stock | 200,000 | 200,000 | 200,000 | 200,000 |
| 22 Paid-in or capital surplus | | | | |
| 23 Retained earnings—Appropriated (attach schedule) | | 30,000 | | 40,000 |
| 24 Retained earnings—Unappropriated | | 238,000 | | 328,783 |
| 25 Less cost of treasury stock | | ( ) | | ( ) |
| 26 Total liabilities and stockholders' equity | | 684,300 | | 879,417 |

## Schedule M-1 — Reconciliation of Income per Books With Income per Return (You are not required to complete this schedule if the total assets on line 14, column (d), of Schedule L are less than $25,000.)

| | | | |
|---|---|---|---|
| 1 Net income per books | 147,783 | 7 Income recorded on books this year not included in this return (itemize): | |
| 2 Federal income tax | 55,387 | | |
| 3 Excess of capital losses over capital gains | 3,600 | a Tax-exempt interest $ 5,000 | |
| 4 Income subject to tax not recorded on books this year (itemize): | | b Insurance Proceeds 9,500 | 14,500 |
| 5 Expenses recorded on books this year not deducted in this return (itemize): | | 8 Deductions in this tax return not charged against book income this year (itemize): | |
| a Depreciation . . $ | | a Depreciation . . . $ 1,620 | |
| b Contributions carryover $ 850 | | b Contributions carryover $ | |
| c Travel and entertainment . $ See Itemized Statement Attached $16,850 | 17,700 | | 1,620 |
| 6 Total of lines 1 through 5 | 224,470 | 9 Total of lines 7 and 8 | 16,120 |
| | | 10 Income (line 28, page 1)—line 6 less line 9 | 208,350 |

## Schedule M-2 — Analysis of Unappropriated Retained Earnings per Books (line 24, Schedule L) (You are not required to complete this schedule if the total assets on line 14, column (d), of Schedule L are less than $25,000.)

| | | | |
|---|---|---|---|
| 1 Balance at beginning of year | 238,000 | 5 Distributions: a Cash | 65,000 |
| 2 Net income per books | 147,783 | b Stock | |
| 3 Other increases (itemize): Refund of 1987 Income Tax | 18,000 | c Property | |
| | | 6 Other decreases (itemize): Reserve for Contingencies | 10,000 |
| 4 Total of lines 1, 2, and 3 | 403,783 | 7 Total of lines 5 and 6 | 75,000 |
| | | 8 Balance at end of year (line 4 less line 7) | 328,783 |

EXHIBIT 20–5. FORM 1120–A

| Form **1120-A** | **U.S. Corporation Short-Form Income Tax Return** | OMB No. 1545-0890 |
|---|---|---|
| Department of the Treasury Internal Revenue Service | To see if you qualify to file Form 1120-A, see instructions. For calendar year 1988 or tax year beginning ............ , 1988, ending ............ , 19 .... | **1988** |

**A** Check this box if corp. is a personal service corp. (as defined in Temp. Regs. sec 1 441-4T—see instructions) ▶ ☐

Use IRS label. Otherwise, please print o type.

Name
10-2134657    DEC88    D89    5995
ROSE FLOWER SHOP, INC.
38 SUPERIOR LANE
FAIR CITY,    MD    20715

**B** Employer Identification number (EIN)

**C** Date incorporated  **7-1-82**

**D** Total assets (See Specific Instructions )
Dollars  $ **65,987**  | Cents

**E** Check applicable boxes:  (1) ☐ Initial return  (2) ☐ Change in address
**F** Check method of accounting:  (1) ☐ Cash  (2) ☑ Accrual  (3) ☐ Other (specify) ▶

| | | | |
|---|---|---|---|
| **Income** | **1a** Gross receipts or sales  **248,000**  **b** Less returns and allowances  **7,500**  Balance ▶ | **1c** | **240,500** |
| | **2** Cost of goods sold and/or operations (see instructions) | **2** | **144,000** |
| | **3** Gross profit (line 1c less line 2) | **3** | **96,500** |
| | **4** Domestic corporation dividends subject to the 70% deduction | **4** | |
| | **5** Interest | **5** | **942** |
| | **6** Gross rents | **6** | |
| | **7** Gross royalties | **7** | |
| | **8** Capital gain net income (attach separate Schedule D (Form 1120)) | **8** | |
| | **9** Net gain or (loss) from Form 4797, Part II, line 18 (attach Form 4797) | **9** | |
| | **10** Other income (see instructions) | **10** | |
| | **11** Total income—Add lines 3 through 10. ▶ | **11** | **97,442** |
| **Deductions** (See instructions for limitations on deductions.) | **12** Compensation of officers (see instructions) | **12** | **23,000** |
| | **13a** Salaries and wages  **24,320**  **b** Less jobs credit  Balance ▶ | **13c** | **24,320** |
| | **14** Repairs | **14** | |
| | **15** Bad debts | **15** | |
| | **16** Rents | **16** | **6,000** |
| | **17** Taxes | **17** | **3,320** |
| | **18** Interest | **18** | **1,340** |
| | **19** Contributions (see instructions for 10% limitation) | **19** | **1,820** |
| | **20** Depreciation (attach Form 4562)  **20** | | |
| | **21** Less depreciation claimed elsewhere on return  **21a** | **21b** | |
| | **22** Other deductions (attach schedule)  *(Advertising)* | **22** | **3,000** |
| | **23** Total deductions—Add lines 12 through 22. ▶ | **23** | **62,800** |
| | **24** Taxable income before net operating loss deduction and special deductions (line 11 less line 23) | **24** | **34,642** |
| | **25** Less: **a** Net operating loss deduction (see instructions)  **25a** | | |
| | **b** Special deductions (see instructions)  **25b** | **25c** | |
| | **26** Taxable income (line 24 less line 25c) | **26** | **34,642** |
| | **27** Total tax (from Part I, line 7 on page 2) | **27** | **5,196** |
| **Tax and Payments** | **28** Payments: | | |
| | **a** 1987 overpayment credited to 1988 .  **28a** | | |
| | **b** 1988 estimated tax payments .  **28b**  **6,000** | | |
| | **c** Less 1988 refund applied for on Form 4466  **28c** (    ) Bal ▶ **28d**  **6,000** | | |
| | **e** Tax deposited with Form 7004  **28e** | | |
| | **f** Credit from regulated investment companies (attach Form 2439)  **28f** | | |
| | **g** Credit for Federal tax on fuels (attach Form 4136)  **28g** | | |
| | **h** Total payments—Add lines 28d through 28g | **28h** | **6,000** |
| | **29** Enter any penalty for underpayment of estimated tax—Check ▶ ☐ if Form 2220 is attached. | **29** | |
| | **30** Tax due—if the total of lines 27 and 29 is larger than line 28h, enter amount owed | **30** | |
| | **31** Overpayment—if line 28h is larger than the total of lines 27 and 29, enter amount overpaid | **31** | **804** |
| | **32** Enter amount of line 31 you want: Credited to 1989 estimated tax ▶  **804**  Refunded ▶ | **32** | |

**Please Sign Here**

Under penalties of perjury, I declare that I have examined this return, including accompanying schedules and statements, and to the best of my knowledge and belief, it is true, correct, and complete. Declaration of preparer (other than taxpayer) is based on all information of which preparer has any knowledge.

*George Rose*  |  2-14-89  |
Signature of officer  |  Date  |  Title

**Paid Preparer's Use Only**

| Preparer's signature | Date | Check if self-employed ▶ ☐ | Preparer's social security number |
|---|---|---|---|
| Firm's name (or yours if self-employed) and address | | E.I. No. ▶ | ZIP code ▶ |

For Paperwork Reduction Act Notice, see page 1 of the Instructions.  |  Form **1120-A** (1988)

*Source:* "Tax Guide for Small Business—1988 Edition," *Publication 334* (Washington, D.C.: Internal Revenue Service, November 1988), 158–59.

# Exhibit 20–5. Continued

Form 1120-A (1988)  Page **2**

## Part I  Tax Computation (See Instructions.)

| | | | |
|---|---|---|---|
| 1 | Income tax (See instructions to figure the tax.) Check this box if the corp. is a qualified personal service corp. (See instructions.) ▶ ☐ | 1 | 5,196 |
| 2a | General business credit. Check if from: ☐ Form 3800 ☐ Form 3468 ☐ Form 5884 ☐ Form 6478 ☐ Form 6765 ☐ Form 8586  **2a** | | |
| b | Credit for prior year minimum tax (attach Form 8801) . . . . . . .  **2b** | | |
| 3 | Total credits—Add lines 2a and 2b . . . . . . . . . . . . | 3 | |
| 4 | Line 1 less line 3 . . . . . . . . . . . . . . . . . . | 4 | 5,196 |
| 5 | Recapture taxes. Check if from: ☐ Form 4255 ☐ Form 8611 . . . . . . . | 5 | |
| 6 | Alternative minimum tax (see instructions—attach Form 4626) . . . . . . . . | 6 | |
| 7 | Total tax—Add lines 4 through 6. Enter here and on line 27, page 1 . . . . | 7 | 5,196 |

## Additional Information (See instruction F.)

**G** Refer to the list in the instructions and state the principal:

(1) Business activity code no. ▶ 5995

(2) Business activity ▶ Flower Shop

(3) Product or service ▶ Flowers

**H** Did any individual, partnership, estate, or trust at the end of the tax year own, directly or indirectly, 50% or more of the corporation's voting stock? (For rules of attribution, see section 267(c).) . . Yes ☐  No ☑
If "Yes," attach schedule showing name, address, and identifying number.

**I** Enter the amount of tax-exempt interest received or accrued during the tax year ▶  – 0 –

**J** (1) If an amount for cost of goods sold and/or operations is entered on line 2, page 1, complete (a) through (c):

| | | |
|---|---|---|
| (a) Purchases (see instructions) ▶ . | 134,014 | |
| (b) Additional sec. 263A costs. (See instructions — attach schedule) ▶ | | |
| (c) Other costs (attach schedule) ▶. | 9,466 | |

(2) Do the rules of section 263A (with respect to property produced or acquired for resale) apply to the corporation? . . . Yes ☐  No ☑

**K** At any time during the tax year, did you have an interest in or a signature or other authority over a financial account in a foreign country (such as a bank account, securities account, or other financial account)? (See instruction F for filing requirements for form TD F 90-22.1.) . . . . Yes ☐  No ☑
If "Yes," write in the name of the foreign country ▶ ..................

**L** Enter amount of cash distributions and the book value of property (other than cash) distributions made in this tax year ▶  – 0 –

## Part II  Balance Sheets

| | | (a) Beginning of tax year | (b) End of tax year |
|---|---|---|---|
| **Assets** | | | |
| 1 | Cash . | 20,540 | 18,498 |
| 2 | Trade notes and accounts receivable . . . . . . . | | |
| a | Less: allowance for bad debts . . . . . . . . . . | ( ) | ( ) |
| 3 | Inventories . . . . . . . . . . . . . . . | 2,530 | 2,010 |
| 4 | Federal and state government obligations . . . . . . | 13,807 | 45,479 |
| 5 | Other current assets (attach schedule) . . . . . . . | | |
| 6 | Loans to stockholders . . . . . . . . . . . | | |
| 7 | Mortgage and real estate loans . . . . . . . . | | |
| 8 | Depreciable, depletable, and intangible assets . . . . . | | |
| a | Less: accumulated depreciation, depletion, and amortization . . | ( ) | ( ) |
| 9 | Land (net of any amortization) . . . . . . . . . | | |
| 10 | Other assets (attach schedule) . . . . . . . . | | |
| 11 | Total assets . . . . . . . . . . . | 36,877 | 65,987 |
| **Liabilities and Stockholders' Equity** | | | |
| 12 | Accounts payable . . . . . . . . . . . . | 6,415 | 6,079 |
| 13 | Other current liabilities (attach schedule) . . . . . . | | |
| 14 | Loans from stockholders . . . . . . . . . . | | |
| 15 | Mortgages, notes, bonds payable . . . . . . . . | | |
| 16 | Other liabilities (attach schedule) . . . . . . . . | | |
| 17 | Capital stock (preferred and common stock) . . . . . | 20,000 | 20,000 |
| 18 | Paid-in or capital surplus . . . . . . . . . . | | |
| 19 | Retained earnings . . . . . . . . . . . | 10,462 | 39,908 |
| 20 | Less cost of treasury stock . . . . . . . . . . | ( ) | ( ) |
| 21 | Total liabilities and stockholders' equity . . . . . | 36,877 | 65,987 |

## Part III  Reconciliation of Income per Books With Income per Return (Must be completed by all filers)

| | | | | |
|---|---|---|---|---|
| 1 | Enter net income per books . . . . . . . . | 29,446 | 5 | Income recorded on books this year not included in this return (itemize) |
| 2 | Federal income tax . . . . . . . . . . | 5,196 | | |
| 3 | Income subject to tax not recorded on books this year (itemize) | | 6 | Deductions in this tax return not charged against book income this year (itemize) |
| 4 | Expenses recorded on books this year not deducted in this return (itemize) | | 7 | Income (line 24, page 1). Enter the sum of lines 1, 2, and 3, and 4 less the sum of lines 5 and 6 . . . .  34,642 |

EXHIBIT 20–6. FORM 1120S

| | |
|---|---|
| Form **1120S** | **U.S. Income Tax Return for an S Corporation** |

Form **1120S**
Department of the Treasury
Internal Revenue Service

**U.S. Income Tax Return for an S Corporation**
For the calendar year 1988 or tax year beginning .............., 1988, ending .............., 19 ....
▶ For Paperwork Reduction Act Notice, see page 1 of the instructions.

OMB No. 1545-0130

**1988**

| A Date of election as an S corporation | Use IRS label. Other-wise, please print or type. | 10-4487964   DEC88   D74   3070<br>ESTEX FABRICATORS,   INC<br>482 WINSTON ST<br>METRO CITY        OH    43704 | C Employer Identification number |
|---|---|---|---|
| 12/1/87 | | | |
| B Business code no. (see Specific Instructions) | | | D Date Incorporated  3/1/72 |
| 3070 | | | E Total assets (see Specific Instructions) |

I R S

E Total assets — Dollars 925,714 | Cents

F Check applicable boxes: (1) ☒ Initial return  (2) ☐ Final return  (3) ☐ Change in address  (4) ☐ Amended return

G Check this box if this is an S corporation subject to the consolidated audit procedures of sections 6241 through 6245 (see instructions) ........ ▶ ☐

H Enter number of shareholders in the corporation at end of the tax year . . . . . . . . . . . . . . . . ▶ 5

Caution: Include only trade or business income and expenses on lines 1a through 21. See the instructions for more information.

**Income**

| | | | |
|---|---|---|---|
| 1a | Gross receipts or sales 2,010,000 — b Less returns and allowances 21,000 — c Bal ▶ | 1c | 1,989,000 |
| 2 | Cost of goods sold and/or operations (Schedule A, line 7) . . . . . | 2 | 1,520,000 |
| 3 | Gross profit (subtract line 2 from line 1c) . . . . . . . . . | 3 | 469,000 |
| 4 | Net gain (or loss) from Form 4797, line 18 (see Instructions) . . . | 4 | -0- |
| 5 | Other income (see instructions—attach schedule) . . . . . . | 5 | 1,000 |
| 6 | Total income (loss)—Combine lines 3, 4, and 5 and enter here . . . . ▶ | 6 | 470,000 |

**Deductions (See instructions for limitations.)**

| | | | |
|---|---|---|---|
| 7 | Compensation of officers . . . . . . . . . . . . . | 7 | 70,000 |
| 8a | Salaries and wages 44,000  b Less jobs credit 6,000  c Bal ▶ | 8c | 38,000 |
| 9 | Repairs . . . . . . . . . . . . . . . . . | 9 | 800 |
| 10 | Bad debts (see instructions) . . . . . . . . . . . | 10 | 1,600 |
| 11 | Rents . . . . . . . . . . . . . . . . . | 11 | 9,200 |
| 12 | Taxes . . . . . . . . . . . . . . . . . | 12 | 15,000 |
| 13 | Deductible interest expense not claimed or reported elsewhere on return (see instructions) | 13 | 24,200 |
| 14a | Depreciation from Form 4562 (attach Form 4562) . . . . . 14a 17,600 | | |
| b | Depreciation reported on Schedule A and elsewhere on return . . 14b 12,400 | | |
| c | Subtract line 14b from line 14a . . . . . . . . . . | 14c | 5,200 |
| 15 | Depletion (Do not deduct oil and gas depletion. See instructions.) . . . . | 15 | -0- |
| 16 | Advertising . . . . . . . . . . . . . . . . | 16 | 8,700 |
| 17 | Pension, profit-sharing, etc. plans . . . . . . . . . . | 17 | -0- |
| 18 | Employee benefit programs . . . . . . . . . . . | 18 | -0- |
| 19 | Other deductions (attach schedule) . . . . . . . . . | 19 | 78,300 |
| 20 | Total deductions—Add lines 7 through 19 and enter here . . . . . ▶ | 20 | 251,000 |
| 21 | Ordinary income (loss) from trade or business activity(ies)—Subtract line 20 from line 6 . . . | 21 | 219,000 |

**Tax and Payments**

| | | | |
|---|---|---|---|
| 22 | Tax: | | |
| a | Excess net passive income tax (attach schedule) . . . . . 22a | | |
| b | Tax from Schedule D (Form 1120S) . . . . . . . . 22b | | |
| c | Add lines 22a and 22b . . . . . . . . . . . . | 22c | -0- |
| 23 | Payments: | | |
| a | Tax deposited with Form 7004 . . . . . . . . . . 23a | | |
| b | Credit for Federal tax on fuels (attach Form 4136) . . . . . 23b | | |
| c | Add lines 23a and 23b . . . . . . . . . . . . | 23c | -0- |
| 24 | Tax due (subtract line 23c from line 22c). See instructions for Paying the Tax . . . . ▶ | 24 | -0- |
| 25 | Overpayment (subtract line 22c from line 23c) . . . . . . . . . . ▶ | 25 | -0- |

**Please Sign Here**

Under penalties of perjury, I declare that I have examined this return, including accompanying schedules and statements, and to the best of my knowledge and belief, it is true, correct, and complete. Declaration of preparer (other than taxpayer) is based on all information of which preparer has any knowledge.

▶ John L. Anders          3/9/89          ▶ President
Signature of officer        Date             Title

**Paid Preparer's Use Only**

| Preparer's signature ▶ | | Date | Check if self-employed ▶ ☐ | Preparer's social security number |
|---|---|---|---|---|
| Firm's name (or yours if self-employed) and address ▶ | | | E.I. No. ▶ | |
| | | | ZIP code ▶ | |

Form **1120S** (1988)

*Source:* "Tax Guide for Small Business—1988 Edition," *Publication 334* (Washington, D.C.: Internal Revenue Service, November 1988), 168–70, 173.

EXHIBIT 20–6. CONTINUED

Form 1120S (1988)                                                                                      Page 2

## Schedule A  Cost of Goods Sold and/or Operations (See Instructions for Schedule A.)

| | | |
|---|---|---:|
| 1 | Inventory at beginning of year | 1 | 126,000 |
| 2 | Purchases | 2 | 1,127,100 |
| 3 | Cost of labor | 3 | 402,000 |
| 4a | Additional section 263A costs (attach schedule) (see instructions) | 4a | 60,000 |
| b | Other costs (attach schedule) | 4b | 103,300 |
| 5 | Total—Add lines 1 through 4b | 5 | 1,818,400 |
| 6 | Inventory at end of year | 6 | 298,400 |
| 7 | Cost of goods sold and/or operations—Subtract line 6 from line 5. Enter here and on line 2, page 1 | 7 | 1,520,000 |

8a Check all methods used for valuing closing inventory:

(i) ☐ Cost

(ii) ☒ Lower of cost or market as described in Regulations section 1.471-4

(iii) ☐ Writedown of "subnormal" goods as described in Regulations section 1.471-2(c)

(iv) ☐ Other (Specify method used and attach explanation) ▶ ..............................................................

b Check this box if the LIFO inventory method was adopted this tax year for any goods (if checked, attach Form 970) . . . . ☐

c If the LIFO inventory method was used for this tax year, enter percentage (or amounts) of closing inventory computed under LIFO . . . . . . . . . . . . . . . . | 8c |

d Do the rules of section 263A (with respect to property produced or acquired for resale) apply to the corporation? . . . ☐ Yes  ☒ No

e Was there any change in determining quantities, cost, or valuations between opening and closing inventory? (If "Yes," attach explanation.) . . . . . . . . . . . . . . . . . . . ☐ Yes  ☒ No

## Additional Information Required

| | | Yes | No |
|---|---|---|---|
| I | Did you at the end of the tax year own, directly or indirectly, 50% or more of the voting stock of a domestic corporation? (For rules of attribution, see section 267(c).) If "Yes," attach a schedule showing: (1) name, address, and employer identification number; and (2) percentage owned. | | × |
| J | Refer to the listing of business activity codes at the end of the Instructions for Form 1120S and state your principal: (1) Business activity ▶ .............................; (2) Product or service ▶ ............................ | | |
| K | Were you a member of a controlled group subject to the provisions of section 1561? . . . . . . . . . . . . | | × |
| L | At any time during the tax year, did you have an interest in or a signature or other authority over a financial account in a foreign country (such as a bank account, securities account, or other financial account)? (See Instructions for exceptions and filing requirements for form TD F 90-22.1.) . . . . . . . . . . . . . . . . | | × |
| | If "Yes," enter the name of the foreign country ▶ ............................................................ | | |
| M | Were you the grantor of, or transferor to, a foreign trust which existed during the current tax year, whether or not you have any beneficial interest in it? If "Yes," you may have to file Forms 3520, 3520-A, or 926. . . . . . . . . . | | × |
| N | During this tax year did you maintain any part of your accounting/tax records on a computerized system? . . . . . | | × |

O Check method of accounting: (1) ☐ Cash  (2) ☒ Accrual  (3) ☐ Other (specify) ▶ ............................

P Check this box if the S corporation has filed or is required to file Form 8264, Application for Registration of a Tax Shelter . . . . . . . . . . . . . . . . . . . . . . . . . . . . . . . . . ▶ ☐

Q Check this box if the corporation issued publicly offered debt instruments with original issue discount . . . . . ▶ ☐

If so, the corporation may have to file Form 8281, Information Return for Publicly Offered Original Issue Discount Instruments.

R If the corporation: (1) filed its election to be an S corporation after December 31, 1986, (2) was a C corporation prior to making the election, and (3) at the beginning of the tax year has net unrealized built-in gain as defined in section 1374(d)(1), enter the net unrealized built-in gain (see instructions) ▶  37,200

## Designation of Tax Matters Person (See Instructions.)

The following shareholder is hereby designated as the tax matters person (TMP) for the tax year for which this tax return is filed:

| Name of designated TMP ▶ | John H. Anders | Identifying number of TMP ▶ | 458 - 00 - 0327 |
|---|---|---|---|

| Address of designated TMP ▶ | 4340 Holmes Parkway  Metro City, OH  43704 |
|---|---|

EXHIBIT 20–6. CONTINUED

Form 1120S (1988)                                                                                                           Page **3**

| Schedule K | Shareholders' Shares of Income, Credits, Deductions, Etc. (See Instructions.) | | |
|---|---|---|---|
| | **(a) Distributive share Items** | | **(b) Total amount** |

**Income (Loss) and Deductions**

| | | | |
|---|---|---|---|
| 1 | Ordinary income (loss) from trade or business activity(ies) (page 1, line 21) | 1 | 219,000 |
| 2a | Gross income from rental real estate activity(ies). | 2a | |
| b | Minus expenses (attach schedule) | 2b | |
| c | Balance: net income (loss) from rental real estate activity(ies). | 2c | |
| 3a | Gross income from other rental activity(ies) | 3a | |
| b | Minus expenses (attach schedule) | 3b | |
| c | Balance: net income (loss) from other rental activity(ies) | 3c | |
| 4 | Portfolio income (loss): | | |
| a | Interest income | 4a | 4,000 |
| b | Dividend income | 4b | 16,000 |
| c | Royalty income | 4c | |
| d | Net short-term capital gain (loss) (Schedule D (Form 1120S)). | 4d | |
| e | Net long-term capital gain (loss) (Schedule D (Form 1120S)) | 4e | |
| f | Other portfolio income (loss) (attach schedule) | 4f | |
| 5 | Net gain (loss) under section 1231 (other than due to casualty or theft) (see instructions) | 5 | |
| 6 | Other income (loss) (attach schedule) | 6 | |
| 7 | Charitable contributions (attach list) | 7 | 24,000 |
| 8 | Section 179 expense deduction (attach schedule) | 8 | |
| 9 | Expenses related to portfolio income (loss) (attach schedule) (see instructions) | 9 | |
| 10 | Other deductions (attach schedule) | 10 | |

**Credits**

| | | | |
|---|---|---|---|
| 11a | Jobs credit | 11a | 6,000 |
| b | Low-income housing credit: (1) Partnership to which section 42(j)(5) applies | 11b(1) | |
| | (2) Other. | 11b(2) | |
| c | Qualified rehabilitation expenditures related to rental real estate activity(ies) (attach schedule) | 11c | |
| d | Credits related to rental real estate activity(ies) other than on lines 11b and 11c (attach schedule) | 11d | |
| e | Credit(s) related to other rental activity(ies) (see instructions) (attach schedule) | 11e | |
| 12 | Other credits (attach schedule) | 12 | |

**Investment Interest**

| | | | |
|---|---|---|---|
| 13a | Interest expense on investment debts | 13a | 3,000 |
| b | (1) Investment income included on lines 4a through 4f, Schedule K | 13b(1) | 20,000 |
| | (2) Investment expenses included on line 9, Schedule K | 13b(2) | |

**Tax Preference and Adjustment Items**

| | | | |
|---|---|---|---|
| 14a | Accelerated depreciation of real property placed in service before 1987 | 14a | |
| b | Accelerated depreciation of leased personal property placed in service before 1987 | 14b | |
| c | Depreciation adjustment on property placed in service after 1986 | 14c | |
| d | Depletion (other than oil and gas) | 14d | |
| e | (1) Gross income from oil, gas, or geothermal properties | 14e(1) | |
| | (2) Gross deductions allocable to oil, gas, or geothermal properties | 14e(2) | |
| f | Other items (attach schedule) | 14f | |

**Foreign Taxes**

| | | | |
|---|---|---|---|
| 15a | Type of income | | |
| b | Name of foreign country or U.S. possession | | |
| c | Total gross income from sources outside the U.S. (attach schedule) | 15c | |
| d | Total applicable deductions and losses (attach schedule) | 15d | |
| e | Total foreign taxes (check one): ▶ ☐ Paid ☐ Accrued | 15e | |
| f | Reduction in taxes available for credit (attach schedule) | 15f | |
| g | Other (attach schedule) | 15g | |

**Other Items**

| | | | |
|---|---|---|---|
| 16 | Total property distributions (including cash) other than dividends reported on line 18, Schedule K | 16 | 65,000 |
| 17 | Other items and amounts not included in lines 1 through 16, Schedule K, that are required to be reported separately to shareholders (attach schedule). | | |
| 18 | Total dividend distributions paid from accumulated earnings and profits contained in other retained earnings (line 26 of Schedule L) | 18 | |

## EXHIBIT 20–6. CONTINUED

Form 1120S (1988)  Page 4

| Schedule L Balance Sheets | Beginning of tax year | | End of tax year | |
|---|---|---|---|---|
| **Assets** | (a) | (b) | (c) | (d) |
| 1 Cash | | 14,700 | | 64,514 |
| 2 Trade notes and accounts receivable | 98,400 | | 83,700 | |
| a Less allowance for bad debts | | 98,400 | | 83,700 |
| 3 Inventories | | 126,000 | | 298,400 |
| 4 Federal and state government obligations | | 100,000 | | 120,000 |
| 5 Other current assets (attach schedule) | | 26,300 | | 26,300 |
| 6 Loans to shareholders | | | | |
| 7 Mortgage and real estate loans | | | | |
| 8 Other investments (attach schedule) | | 100,000 | | 100,000 |
| 9 Buildings and other depreciable assets | 272,400 | | 299,400 | |
| a Less accumulated depreciation | 88,300 | 184,100 | 105,900 | 193,500 |
| 10 Depletable assets | | | | |
| a Less accumulated depletion | | | | |
| 11 Land (net of any amortization) | | 20,000 | | 20,000 |
| 12 Intangible assets (amortizable only) | | | | |
| a Less accumulated amortization | | | | |
| 13 Other assets (attach schedule) | | 14,800 | | 19,300 |
| 14 Total assets | | 684,300 | | 925,714 |
| **Liabilities and Shareholders' Equity** | | | | |
| 15 Accounts payable | | 28,500 | | 34,834 |
| 16 Mortgages, notes, bonds payable in less than 1 year | | 4,300 | | 4,300 |
| 17 Other current liabilities (attach schedule) | | 6,800 | | 7,400 |
| 18 Loans from shareholders | | | | |
| 19 Mortgages, notes, bonds payable in 1 year or more | | 176,700 | | 265,180 |
| 20 Other liabilities (attach schedule) | | | | |
| 21 Capital stock | | 200,000 | | 200,000 |
| 22 Paid-in or capital surplus | | | | |
| 23 Accumulated adjustments account | | | 141,000 | |
| 24 Other adjustments account | | | 5,000 | |
| 25 Shareholders' undistributed taxable income previously taxed | | | | |
| 26 Other retained earnings (see instructions) | 268,000 | | 268,000 | |
| Check this box if the corporation has subchapter C earnings and profits at the close of the tax year ▶ ☐ (see instructions) | | | | |
| 27 Total retained earnings per books—Combine amounts on lines 23 through 26, columns (a) and (c) (see instructions) | | 268,000 | | 414,000 |
| 28 Less cost of treasury stock | | ( ) | | ( ) |
| 29 Total liabilities and shareholders' equity | | 684,300 | | 925,714 |

**Schedule M** Analysis of Accumulated Adjustments Account, Other Adjustments Account, and Shareholders' Undistributed Taxable Income Previously Taxed (If Schedule L, column (c), amounts for lines 23, 24, or 25 are not the same as corresponding amounts on line 9 of Schedule M, attach a schedule explaining any differences. See instructions.)

| | Accumulated adjustments account | Other adjustments account | Shareholders' undistributed taxable income previously taxed |
|---|---|---|---|
| 1 Balance at beginning of year | -0- | -0- | |
| 2 Ordinary income from page 1, line 21 | 219,000 | | |
| 3 Other additions | 20,000 | 5,000 | |
| 4 Total of lines 1, 2, and 3 | 239,000 | 5,000 | |
| 5 Distributions other than dividend distributions | 65,000 | -0- | |
| 6 Loss from page 1, line 21 | -0- | | |
| 7 Other reductions | 33,000 | -0- | |
| 8 Add lines 5, 6, and 7 | 98,000 | -0- | |
| 9 Balance at end of tax year—Subtract line 8 from line 4 | 141,000 | 5,000 | |

passed on to the shareholders—whether or not the income is actually distributed. In turn, each shareholder must incorporate this information into his or her personal Form 1040. (Of course, the S corporation must still file Form 1120S.)

The following are some of the qualifications:

- It must be a domestic corporation.
- It must have only one class of stock.
- It may have not more than thirty-five shareholders (only individuals, estates, and certain trusts)
- Shareholders must be citizens or residents of the United States; nonresident aliens cannot be shareholders.

To indicate its choice of S-corporation status, the firm must file Form 2553—Election by a Small Business Corporation.

### The IRS Wants to Help You

Our tax laws aren't only lengthy and complex; they're continually being interpreted and modified. To reiterate an earlier suggestion, do yourself a favor. Find a competent tax professional to help you prepare your returns. The IRS has local offices all over the country, whose staffs are ready to answer all your questions. Don't fail to use their services. Secure a copy of the latest edition of Publication 334—*Tax Guide for Small Business.* A list of other useful IRS publications, all free of charge to you, is shown in exhibit 20–7.

## OTHER FEDERAL TAXES

### Social Security Taxes

The *Federal Insurance Contributions Act* (FICA) provides for a federal system for old age, survivors, disability, and hospital insurance to be financed through Social Security taxes. Taxes for these purposes are levied on both you and your employees. As an employer, you're liable for the collection and payment of your employees' taxes; you need to withhold them from wages, just as you do income tax. The rate in 1988 was 7.51 percent of each employee's wages, and the rate for the employer's tax was also 7.51 percent. There's a *wage base* for the employee; the 7.51 percent applies only to the first $45,000 of wages. (For more on FICA taxes, see the section on "Withholding" below.)

### Federal Unemployment Tax

In general, you are subject to the Federal Unemployment Tax Act tax (FUTA)

- If during the current or preceding calendar year you paid wages of $1,500 or more in any calendar quarter, *or*

---

**EXHIBIT 20–7. USEFUL IRS TAX PUBLICATIONS**

| Publication Number | Title |
|---|---|
| 15 | Employer's Tax Guide (Circular E) |
| 334 | Tax Guide for Small Business |
| 505 | Tax Withholding and Estimated Tax |
| 526 | Charitable Contributions |
| 533 | Self-Employment Tax |
| 534 | Depreciation |
| 535 | Business Expenses |
| 536 | Net Operating Losses |
| 537 | Installment Sales |
| 538 | Accounting Periods and Methods |
| 539 | Employment Taxes |
| 541 | Tax Information on Partnerships |
| 542 | Tax Information on Corporations |
| 548 | Deduction for Bad Debts |
| 560 | Self-Employed Retirement Plans |
| 572 | General Business Credit |
| 575 | Pension and Annuity Income |
| 587 | Business Use of Your Home |
| 589 | Tax Information on S Corporations |
| 590 | Individual Retirement Arrangements (IRAs) |
| 917 | Business Use of a Car |

*Source:* "Tax Guide for Small Business—1987," *Publication 334* (Washington, D.C.: Internal Revenue Service, 1987), 178.

- If you employed one or more employees for at least a part of a day during each of twenty different calendar weeks

This tax is imposed on the employer only. In 1988 the rate was 6.2 percent on the first $7,000 of wages paid to *each* employee during the year. However, partial but substantial credit may be received because of payments of state unemployment taxes.

Quarterly deposits of FUTA tax may have to be made in your case. If so, each must be accompanied by a federal tax deposit (FTD) coupon. On or before January 31 of the following year, you need to file Form 940—Employer's Annual Federal Unemployment (FUTA) Tax Return.

## USEFUL INFORMATION ABOUT WITHHOLDING

As you already know, your employees are compelled to "pay-as-they-go" on their federal income-tax obligations each time they are paid by you. To this end, all new employees, when hired, must complete a Form W–4—Employee's Withholding Allowance Certificate—which authorizes you to withhold income tax from their paychecks in accordance with tables available from the IRS. (See exhibit 20–8 for two sample sheets of these tables, for employees paid on a weekly basis.) The tables are published in *Publication 15—Employer's Tax Guide (Circular E)*. You may also apply the *percentage* method of withholding, which is also explained in *Publication 15*. Other duties follow:

- Near the end of each year, you need to ask your employees if they have any changes in their exemption status. If so, they must fill out new W–4s for you. After the year's close, you must furnish all employees with copies of Form W–2—Wage and Tax Statement.
- When you deduct the stipulated percentage of employee wages for the FICA tax, no withholding allowances are permitted, as they are with the withholding of income tax.
- The amounts you withhold from employee wages must be deposited in an authorized financial institution or a Federal Reserve bank. The amount of tax determines the frequency of your deposits.
- In addition, Form 941 (Employer's Quarterly Federal Tax Return) must be filed each quarter. These returns, combining Social Security taxes and income-tax withholding, are due by the end of the month following each calendar quarter.

## OTHER POINTERS REGARDING FEDERAL TAXES

### Self-Employment Tax

This is the Social Security tax paid by the self-employed. If you are in business for yourself—that is, if you own a sole proprietorship or are a partner—and if your annual earnings from self-employment are $400 or more, you're probably liable for the self-employment tax. Schedule SE of Form 1040 is used to compute this tax. (The schedule is illustrated in IRS Publication 533—Self-Employment Tax.) The net rate for 1988 was 13.02 percent of earnings, up to the wage base of $45,000. If you had wages subject to Social Security tax during the year from another source, such as a previous job, you must subtract the total of those earnings from the $45,000 base figure to determine the amount subject to the self-employment tax.

### Federal Excise Taxes

For the most part, federal excise taxes are more applicable to certain types of manufacturing companies and importers than to retailers. As a group, these taxes are levied on the sale of certain named articles, on certain transactions or occupations, and on the use of certain items. Examples of all three types in the retailing sphere include excise taxes on the sale of diesel and special motor fuels, the occupational tax imposed on dealers of beer or liquor, and the use tax on highway motor vehicles. To obtain more specifics, send for IRS Publication 510—Excise Taxes.

## Exhibit 20–8. Sample pages from "Circular E"

## SINGLE Persons–WEEKLY Payroll Period
### (For Wages Paid After December 1988)

| And the wages are– | | And the number of withholding allowances claimed is– | | | | | | | | | | |
|---|---|---|---|---|---|---|---|---|---|---|---|---|
| At least | But less than | 0 | 1 | 2 | 3 | 4 | 5 | 6 | 7 | 8 | 9 | 10 |
| | | The amount of income tax to be withheld shall be– | | | | | | | | | | |
| $0 | $25 | $0 | $0 | $0 | $0 | $0 | $0 | $0 | $0 | $0 | $0 | $0 |
| 25 | 30 | 1 | 0 | 0 | 0 | 0 | 0 | 0 | 0 | 0 | 0 | 0 |
| 30 | 35 | 2 | 0 | 0 | 0 | 0 | 0 | 0 | 0 | 0 | 0 | 0 |
| 35 | 40 | 2 | 0 | 0 | 0 | 0 | 0 | 0 | 0 | 0 | 0 | 0 |
| 40 | 45 | 3 | 0 | 0 | 0 | 0 | 0 | 0 | 0 | 0 | 0 | 0 |
| 45 | 50 | 4 | 0 | 0 | 0 | 0 | 0 | 0 | 0 | 0 | 0 | 0 |
| 50 | 55 | 5 | 0 | 0 | 0 | 0 | 0 | 0 | 0 | 0 | 0 | 0 |
| 55 | 60 | 5 | 0 | 0 | 0 | 0 | 0 | 0 | 0 | 0 | 0 | 0 |
| 60 | 65 | 6 | 0 | 0 | 0 | 0 | 0 | 0 | 0 | 0 | 0 | 0 |
| 65 | 70 | 7 | 1 | 0 | 0 | 0 | 0 | 0 | 0 | 0 | 0 | 0 |
| 70 | 75 | 8 | 2 | 0 | 0 | 0 | 0 | 0 | 0 | 0 | 0 | 0 |
| 75 | 80 | 8 | 3 | 0 | 0 | 0 | 0 | 0 | 0 | 0 | 0 | 0 |
| 80 | 85 | 9 | 3 | 0 | 0 | 0 | 0 | 0 | 0 | 0 | 0 | 0 |
| 85 | 90 | 10 | 4 | 0 | 0 | 0 | 0 | 0 | 0 | 0 | 0 | 0 |
| 90 | 95 | 11 | 5 | 0 | 0 | 0 | 0 | 0 | 0 | 0 | 0 | 0 |
| 95 | 100 | 11 | 6 | 0 | 0 | 0 | 0 | 0 | 0 | 0 | 0 | 0 |
| 100 | 105 | 12 | 6 | 1 | 0 | 0 | 0 | 0 | 0 | 0 | 0 | 0 |
| 105 | 110 | 13 | 7 | 1 | 0 | 0 | 0 | 0 | 0 | 0 | 0 | 0 |
| 110 | 115 | 14 | 8 | 2 | 0 | 0 | 0 | 0 | 0 | 0 | 0 | 0 |
| 115 | 120 | 14 | 9 | 3 | 0 | 0 | 0 | 0 | 0 | 0 | 0 | 0 |
| 120 | 125 | 15 | 9 | 4 | 0 | 0 | 0 | 0 | 0 | 0 | 0 | 0 |
| 125 | 130 | 16 | 10 | 4 | 0 | 0 | 0 | 0 | 0 | 0 | 0 | 0 |
| 130 | 135 | 17 | 11 | 5 | 0 | 0 | 0 | 0 | 0 | 0 | 0 | 0 |
| 135 | 140 | 17 | 12 | 6 | 0 | 0 | 0 | 0 | 0 | 0 | 0 | 0 |
| 140 | 145 | 18 | 12 | 7 | 1 | 0 | 0 | 0 | 0 | 0 | 0 | 0 |
| 145 | 150 | 19 | 13 | 7 | 2 | 0 | 0 | 0 | 0 | 0 | 0 | 0 |
| 150 | 155 | 20 | 14 | 8 | 2 | 0 | 0 | 0 | 0 | 0 | 0 | 0 |
| 155 | 160 | 20 | 15 | 9 | 3 | 0 | 0 | 0 | 0 | 0 | 0 | 0 |
| 160 | 165 | 21 | 15 | 10 | 4 | 0 | 0 | 0 | 0 | 0 | 0 | 0 |
| 165 | 170 | 22 | 16 | 10 | 5 | 0 | 0 | 0 | 0 | 0 | 0 | 0 |
| 170 | 175 | 23 | 17 | 11 | 5 | 0 | 0 | 0 | 0 | 0 | 0 | 0 |
| 175 | 180 | 23 | 18 | 12 | 6 | 0 | 0 | 0 | 0 | 0 | 0 | 0 |
| 180 | 185 | 24 | 18 | 13 | 7 | 1 | 0 | 0 | 0 | 0 | 0 | 0 |
| 185 | 190 | 25 | 19 | 13 | 8 | 2 | 0 | 0 | 0 | 0 | 0 | 0 |
| 190 | 195 | 26 | 20 | 14 | 8 | 3 | 0 | 0 | 0 | 0 | 0 | 0 |
| 195 | 200 | 26 | 21 | 15 | 9 | 3 | 0 | 0 | 0 | 0 | 0 | 0 |
| 200 | 210 | 28 | 22 | 16 | 10 | 5 | 0 | 0 | 0 | 0 | 0 | 0 |
| 210 | 220 | 29 | 23 | 18 | 12 | 6 | 0 | 0 | 0 | 0 | 0 | 0 |
| 220 | 230 | 31 | 25 | 19 | 13 | 8 | 2 | 0 | 0 | 0 | 0 | 0 |
| 230 | 240 | 32 | 26 | 21 | 15 | 9 | 3 | 0 | 0 | 0 | 0 | 0 |
| 240 | 250 | 34 | 28 | 22 | 16 | 11 | 5 | 0 | 0 | 0 | 0 | 0 |
| 250 | 260 | 35 | 29 | 24 | 18 | 12 | 6 | 0 | 0 | 0 | 0 | 0 |
| 260 | 270 | 37 | 31 | 25 | 19 | 14 | 8 | 2 | 0 | 0 | 0 | 0 |
| 270 | 280 | 38 | 32 | 27 | 21 | 15 | 9 | 3 | 0 | 0 | 0 | 0 |
| 280 | 290 | 40 | 34 | 28 | 22 | 17 | 11 | 5 | 0 | 0 | 0 | 0 |
| 290 | 300 | 41 | 35 | 30 | 24 | 18 | 12 | 6 | 1 | 0 | 0 | 0 |
| 300 | 310 | 43 | 37 | 31 | 25 | 20 | 14 | 8 | 2 | 0 | 0 | 0 |
| 310 | 320 | 44 | 38 | 33 | 27 | 21 | 15 | 9 | 4 | 0 | 0 | 0 |
| 320 | 330 | 46 | 40 | 34 | 28 | 23 | 17 | 11 | 5 | 0 | 0 | 0 |
| 330 | 340 | 47 | 41 | 36 | 30 | 24 | 18 | 12 | 7 | 1 | 0 | 0 |
| 340 | 350 | 49 | 43 | 37 | 31 | 26 | 20 | 14 | 8 | 2 | 0 | 0 |
| 350 | 360 | 50 | 44 | 39 | 33 | 27 | 21 | 15 | 10 | 4 | 0 | 0 |
| 360 | 370 | 52 | 46 | 40 | 34 | 29 | 23 | 17 | 11 | 5 | 0 | 0 |
| 370 | 380 | 53 | 47 | 42 | 36 | 30 | 24 | 18 | 13 | 7 | 1 | 0 |
| 380 | 390 | 56 | 49 | 43 | 37 | 32 | 26 | 20 | 14 | 8 | 3 | 0 |
| 390 | 400 | 58 | 50 | 45 | 39 | 33 | 27 | 21 | 16 | 10 | 4 | 0 |
| 400 | 410 | 61 | 52 | 46 | 40 | 35 | 29 | 23 | 17 | 11 | 6 | 0 |
| 410 | 420 | 64 | 53 | 48 | 42 | 36 | 30 | 24 | 19 | 13 | 7 | 1 |
| 420 | 430 | 67 | 56 | 49 | 43 | 38 | 32 | 26 | 20 | 14 | 9 | 3 |
| 430 | 440 | 70 | 59 | 51 | 45 | 39 | 33 | 27 | 22 | 16 | 10 | 4 |
| 440 | 450 | 72 | 62 | 52 | 46 | 41 | 35 | 29 | 23 | 17 | 12 | 6 |
| 450 | 460 | 75 | 64 | 54 | 48 | 42 | 36 | 30 | 25 | 19 | 13 | 7 |
| 460 | 470 | 78 | 67 | 56 | 49 | 44 | 38 | 32 | 26 | 20 | 15 | 9 |
| 470 | 480 | 81 | 70 | 59 | 51 | 45 | 39 | 33 | 28 | 22 | 16 | 10 |
| 480 | 490 | 84 | 73 | 62 | 52 | 47 | 41 | 35 | 29 | 23 | 18 | 12 |
| 490 | 500 | 86 | 76 | 65 | 54 | 48 | 42 | 36 | 31 | 25 | 19 | 13 |
| 500 | 510 | 89 | 78 | 68 | 57 | 50 | 44 | 38 | 32 | 26 | 21 | 15 |
| 510 | 520 | 92 | 81 | 70 | 60 | 51 | 45 | 39 | 34 | 28 | 22 | 16 |
| 520 | 530 | 95 | 84 | 73 | 62 | 53 | 47 | 41 | 35 | 29 | 24 | 18 |
| 530 | 540 | 98 | 87 | 76 | 65 | 54 | 48 | 42 | 37 | 31 | 25 | 19 |

*Source:* "Circular E—Employer's Tax Guide," *Publication 15* (Washington, D.C.: Internal Revenue Service, 1989).

EXHIBIT 20–8. CONTINUED

# MARRIED Persons–WEEKLY Payroll Period

## (For Wages Paid After December 1988)

| And the wages are– | | And the number of withholding allowances claimed is– | | | | | | | | | | |
|---|---|---|---|---|---|---|---|---|---|---|---|---|
| At least | But less than | 0 | 1 | 2 | 3 | 4 | 5 | 6 | 7 | 8 | 9 | 10 |
| | | The amount of income tax to be withheld shall be– | | | | | | | | | | |
| $0 | $65 | $0 | $0 | $0 | $0 | $0 | $0 | $0 | $0 | $0 | $0 | $0 |
| 65 | 70 | 1 | 0 | 0 | 0 | 0 | 0 | 0 | 0 | 0 | 0 | 0 |
| 70 | 75 | 2 | 0 | 0 | 0 | 0 | 0 | 0 | 0 | 0 | 0 | 0 |
| 75 | 80 | 2 | 0 | 0 | 0 | 0 | 0 | 0 | 0 | 0 | 0 | 0 |
| 80 | 85 | 3 | 0 | 0 | 0 | 0 | 0 | 0 | 0 | 0 | 0 | 0 |
| 85 | 90 | 4 | 0 | 0 | 0 | 0 | 0 | 0 | 0 | 0 | 0 | 0 |
| 90 | 95 | 5 | 0 | 0 | 0 | 0 | 0 | 0 | 0 | 0 | 0 | 0 |
| 95 | 100 | 5 | 0 | 0 | 0 | 0 | 0 | 0 | 0 | 0 | 0 | 0 |
| 100 | 105 | 6 | 0 | 0 | 0 | 0 | 0 | 0 | 0 | 0 | 0 | 0 |
| 105 | 110 | 7 | 1 | 0 | 0 | 0 | 0 | 0 | 0 | 0 | 0 | 0 |
| 110 | 115 | 8 | 2 | 0 | 0 | 0 | 0 | 0 | 0 | 0 | 0 | 0 |
| 115 | 120 | 8 | 3 | 0 | 0 | 0 | 0 | 0 | 0 | 0 | 0 | 0 |
| 120 | 125 | 9 | 3 | 0 | 0 | 0 | 0 | 0 | 0 | 0 | 0 | 0 |
| 125 | 130 | 10 | 4 | 0 | 0 | 0 | 0 | 0 | 0 | 0 | 0 | 0 |
| 130 | 135 | 11 | 5 | 0 | 0 | 0 | 0 | 0 | 0 | 0 | 0 | 0 |
| 135 | 140 | 11 | 6 | 0 | 0 | 0 | 0 | 0 | 0 | 0 | 0 | 0 |
| 140 | 145 | 12 | 6 | 1 | 0 | 0 | 0 | 0 | 0 | 0 | 0 | 0 |
| 145 | 150 | 13 | 7 | 1 | 0 | 0 | 0 | 0 | 0 | 0 | 0 | 0 |
| 150 | 155 | 14 | 8 | 2 | 0 | 0 | 0 | 0 | 0 | 0 | 0 | 0 |
| 155 | 160 | 14 | 9 | 3 | 0 | 0 | 0 | 0 | 0 | 0 | 0 | 0 |
| 160 | 165 | 15 | 9 | 4 | 0 | 0 | 0 | 0 | 0 | 0 | 0 | 0 |
| 165 | 170 | 16 | 10 | 4 | 0 | 0 | 0 | 0 | 0 | 0 | 0 | 0 |
| 170 | 175 | 17 | 11 | 5 | 0 | 0 | 0 | 0 | 0 | 0 | 0 | 0 |
| 175 | 180 | 17 | 12 | 6 | 0 | 0 | 0 | 0 | 0 | 0 | 0 | 0 |
| 180 | 185 | 18 | 12 | 7 | 1 | 0 | 0 | 0 | 0 | 0 | 0 | 0 |
| 185 | 190 | 19 | 13 | 7 | 2 | 0 | 0 | 0 | 0 | 0 | 0 | 0 |
| 190 | 195 | 20 | 14 | 8 | 2 | 0 | 0 | 0 | 0 | 0 | 0 | 0 |
| 195 | 200 | 20 | 15 | 9 | 3 | 0 | 0 | 0 | 0 | 0 | 0 | 0 |
| 200 | 210 | 22 | 16 | 10 | 4 | 0 | 0 | 0 | 0 | 0 | 0 | 0 |
| 210 | 220 | 23 | 17 | 11 | 6 | 0 | 0 | 0 | 0 | 0 | 0 | 0 |
| 220 | 230 | 25 | 19 | 13 | 7 | 1 | 0 | 0 | 0 | 0 | 0 | 0 |
| 230 | 240 | 26 | 20 | 14 | 9 | 3 | 0 | 0 | 0 | 0 | 0 | 0 |
| 240 | 250 | 28 | 22 | 16 | 10 | 4 | 0 | 0 | 0 | 0 | 0 | 0 |
| 250 | 260 | 29 | 23 | 17 | 12 | 6 | 0 | 0 | 0 | 0 | 0 | 0 |
| 260 | 270 | 31 | 25 | 19 | 13 | 7 | 2 | 0 | 0 | 0 | 0 | 0 |
| 270 | 280 | 32 | 26 | 20 | 15 | 9 | 3 | 0 | 0 | 0 | 0 | 0 |
| 280 | 290 | 34 | 28 | 22 | 16 | 10 | 5 | 0 | 0 | 0 | 0 | 0 |
| 290 | 300 | 35 | 29 | 23 | 18 | 12 | 6 | 0 | 0 | 0 | 0 | 0 |
| 300 | 310 | 37 | 31 | 25 | 19 | 13 | 8 | 2 | 0 | 0 | 0 | 0 |
| 310 | 320 | 38 | 32 | 26 | 21 | 15 | 9 | 3 | 0 | 0 | 0 | 0 |
| 320 | 330 | 40 | 34 | 28 | 22 | 16 | 11 | 5 | 0 | 0 | 0 | 0 |
| 330 | 340 | 41 | 35 | 29 | 24 | 18 | 12 | 6 | 1 | 0 | 0 | 0 |
| 340 | 350 | 43 | 37 | 31 | 25 | 19 | 14 | 8 | 2 | 0 | 0 | 0 |
| 350 | 360 | 44 | 38 | 32 | 27 | 21 | 15 | 9 | 4 | 0 | 0 | 0 |
| 360 | 370 | 46 | 40 | 34 | 28 | 22 | 17 | 11 | 5 | 0 | 0 | 0 |
| 370 | 380 | 47 | 41 | 35 | 30 | 24 | 18 | 12 | 7 | 1 | 0 | 0 |
| 380 | 390 | 49 | 43 | 37 | 31 | 25 | 20 | 14 | 8 | 2 | 0 | 0 |
| 390 | 400 | 50 | 44 | 38 | 33 | 27 | 21 | 15 | 10 | 4 | 0 | 0 |
| 400 | 410 | 52 | 46 | 40 | 34 | 28 | 23 | 17 | 11 | 5 | 0 | 0 |
| 410 | 420 | 53 | 47 | 41 | 36 | 30 | 24 | 18 | 13 | 7 | 1 | 0 |
| 420 | 430 | 55 | 49 | 43 | 37 | 31 | 26 | 20 | 14 | 8 | 3 | 0 |
| 430 | 440 | 56 | 50 | 44 | 39 | 33 | 27 | 21 | 16 | 10 | 4 | 0 |
| 440 | 450 | 58 | 52 | 46 | 40 | 34 | 29 | 23 | 17 | 11 | 6 | 0 |
| 450 | 460 | 59 | 53 | 47 | 42 | 36 | 30 | 24 | 19 | 13 | 7 | 1 |
| 460 | 470 | 61 | 55 | 49 | 43 | 37 | 32 | 26 | 20 | 14 | 9 | 3 |
| 470 | 480 | 62 | 56 | 50 | 45 | 39 | 33 | 27 | 22 | 16 | 10 | 4 |
| 480 | 490 | 64 | 58 | 52 | 46 | 40 | 35 | 29 | 23 | 17 | 12 | 6 |
| 490 | 500 | 65 | 59 | 53 | 48 | 42 | 36 | 30 | 25 | 19 | 13 | 7 |
| 500 | 510 | 67 | 61 | 55 | 49 | 43 | 38 | 32 | 26 | 20 | 15 | 9 |
| 510 | 520 | 68 | 62 | 56 | 51 | 45 | 39 | 33 | 28 | 22 | 16 | 10 |
| 520 | 530 | 70 | 64 | 58 | 52 | 46 | 41 | 35 | 29 | 23 | 18 | 12 |
| 530 | 540 | 71 | 65 | 59 | 54 | 48 | 42 | 36 | 31 | 25 | 19 | 13 |
| 540 | 550 | 73 | 67 | 61 | 55 | 49 | 44 | 38 | 32 | 26 | 21 | 15 |
| 550 | 560 | 74 | 68 | 62 | 57 | 51 | 45 | 39 | 34 | 28 | 22 | 16 |
| 560 | 570 | 76 | 70 | 64 | 58 | 52 | 47 | 41 | 35 | 29 | 24 | 18 |
| 570 | 580 | 77 | 71 | 65 | 60 | 54 | 48 | 42 | 37 | 31 | 25 | 19 |
| 580 | 590 | 79 | 73 | 67 | 61 | 55 | 50 | 44 | 38 | 32 | 27 | 21 |
| 590 | 600 | 80 | 74 | 68 | 63 | 57 | 51 | 45 | 40 | 34 | 28 | 22 |
| 600 | 610 | 82 | 76 | 70 | 64 | 58 | 53 | 47 | 41 | 35 | 30 | 24 |
| 610 | 620 | 83 | 77 | 71 | 66 | 60 | 54 | 48 | 43 | 37 | 31 | 25 |

# DEPRECIATING YOUR ASSETS

Whatever type of business you are in, you have to purchase property and equipment from time to time. Most property lasts for several years, so, with certain exceptions, it isn't realistic to consider the entire cost an expense in any one year. Therefore, when the property is purchased, it is entered in the books as a fixed, or plant, asset. The decrease in value over the life of the property, known as *depreciation,* is treated as an expense distributed over the period during which the asset is used.

According to the IRS:

Property is depreciable if it meets these requirements:

1. It must be used in business or held for the production of income.
2. It must have a determinable life, and that life must be longer than one year.
3. It must be something that wears out, decays, gets used up, becomes obsolete, or loses value from natural causes.*

Depreciable property may be *tangible* (that is, assets that can be seen or touched), or it may be *intangible*—copyrights or franchises, for example. Land is not depreciable; neither is the firm's "goodwill." You may be able to treat the costs of certain assets placed in service as one-time expenses, rather than as capital expenditures. Such deductions are known as *Section 179 deductions.* It's possible to write off such expenses up to a maximum of $10,000 during the year.**

**Calculating Depreciation Expense.** According to current tax law, you must follow a specific system when calculating your depreciation expense for any tangible business asset. This is the *modified accelerated cost recovery system,* or *MACRS.* Under MACRS, there are eight classes of property; these may be seen in exhibit 20–9.

There are several depreciation methods available; determining the proper method to use depends on the property class involved and other factors. Discussion of these methods is, of course, well beyond the scope of this book. For further assistance on the topic, I suggest you send for a copy of IRS Publication 534—Depreciation—and be sure to consult your accountant.

# FOR FURTHER INFORMATION

## Books

Adams, Paul. *The Complete Legal Guide for Small Business.* New York: Wiley, 1982.
Ashcroft, John D., and Janet E. Ashcroft. *College Law for Business,* 10th ed. Cincinnati: South-Western, 1987.

---

* "Tax Guide for Small Business—1987 Edition," *Publication 334* (Washington, D.C.: Internal Revenue Service, November 1987), 38.
** Ibid., 39.

## EXHIBIT 20-9. PROPERTY CLASSES UNDER MACRS

| Recovery Period Classes | Examples of Tangible Assets in Class |
|---|---|
| 3-year property | Tractor units for over-the-road, race horses over 2 years old when placed in service |
| 5-year property | Automobiles and trucks, computers, typewriters and other office machines |
| 7-year property | Office furniture and fixtures |
| 10-year property | Barges, tugboats, other vessels |
| 15-year property | Municipal wastewater treatment plant |
| 20-year property | Farm buildings, municipal sewers |
| Nonresidential rent property | Real property which is not residential rental property (*Note:* This is to be depreciated over 31.5 years.) |
| Residential rent property | Real property that is a rental building or structure (including mobile homes) for which 80% or more of the gross rental income for the tax year is rental income from dwelling units. (*Note:* This is to be depreciated over 27.5 years.) |

*Source:* "Tax Guide for Small Business—1988 Edition," *Publication 334* (Washington, D.C.: Internal Revenue Service, November 1988), 40.

Block, Julian. *Julian Block's Guide to Year Round Tax Savings,* rev. ed. Homewood, Ill.: Dow Jones-Irwin, 1987.

Bower, James B., and Harold Q. Langenderfer. *Income Tax Procedure.* Cincinnati: South-Western, 1986.

Brody, David Eliot. *Business and Its Legal Environment.* Lexington, Mass.: D. C. Heath, 1986.

Burke, Frank M., and Buford Berry. *Tax Practice Handbook.* Englewood Cliffs, N.J.: Prentice-Hall, 1986.

Cameron, George D., III, and Phillip J. Scaletta, Jr. *Business Law: Text and Cases,* 2d ed. Plano, Tex.: Business Publications, 1985.

Corley, Robert N., Peter J. Shedd, and Eric M. Holmes. *Principles of Business Law,* 13th ed. Englewood Cliffs, N.J.: Prentice-Hall, 1986.

Hemphill, C. *Basic Business Law.* Englewood Cliffs, N.J.: Prentice-Hall, 1984.

Lane, Marc J. *Taxation for Small Business.* New York: Wiley, 1982.

Lasser, J. K. *J. K. Lasser's How to Avoid A Tax Audit.* New York: Simon & Schuster, 1984.

Moran, John Jude. *Practical Business Law.* Englewood Cliffs, N.J.: Prentice-Hall, 1986.

Prentice-Hall Editorial Staff. *Federal Tax Handbook, 1986 Edition.* Englewood Cliffs, N.J.: Prentice-Hall, 1986.

Raby, William L., and Victor H. Tidwell. *Introduction to Federal Taxation, 1987 Edition.* Englewood Cliffs, N.J.: Prentice-Hall, 1986.

Ruland, William. *Managers' Guide to Corporate Tax.* New York: Wiley, 1984.

## Pamphlets Available from the Small Business Administration

### Management Aids

MA 6.005—"Introduction to Patents"

# VIII

# Business Expansion and Growth

# — 21 —

# Considerations for the Future

We all recognize that nothing remains the same for long. In our world change, not stasis, is the norm. People change over time. So do values, attitudes, interests, and wants. Neighborhoods develop; others deteriorate. Our entire economy passes through valleys and over peaks in long-term cycles. New legislation appears, and old laws are shelved. Governments at all levels are continually replaced by new cadres promising to provide what the outgoing politicians failed to provide.

## THE FUTURE OF YOUR BUSINESS

Over time, you may find that your store's activity bobs up and down like a float on an ocean wave. This behavior is perfectly normal. A business buoyed by good planning, competent management, and a sense of destiny will continue to move along. Another, beset by internal problems and lacking managerial flexibility, may sink quickly to the bottom of the sea like a lead weight. The successful business passes through a life cycle of its own over the long term, one that parallels our own lives: birth and infancy, adolescence, the maturity of adulthood, and finally, senescence and ultimate demise. Each of these phases carries its own inherent challenges. You must rethink your business's objectives at each stage—and make new plans. Since most of this book dealt only with the earliest phase of your new retail enterprise, the other stages merit some discussion, however brief, at this point.

### Growth and Maturation

Once established on a firm footing, a good store operation should look to consolidate its initial successes before embarking on a well-plotted growth track. Fight the temptation to expand hastily, whether by opening additional store units or by moving to larger quarters. Premature expansion can be dangerous to your business's health. Instead, consider the *internal* moves listed on the next page.

- Adding new merchandise lines
- Increasing your promotional efforts to attract new customers (while retaining your regular clientele)
- Renovating your store to yield more selling space
- Remodeling the storefront to attract more passersby
- Increasing the breadth and depth of your inventory
- Renting the store next door and pushing through the walls to create a larger store
- Exploring the possibilities of mail order selling to supplement your store business

Often, this kind of internal growth suffices for the retailer who prefers the comparative simplicity of managing a single profitable outlet to the headaches of directing a chain-store organization or launching an entirely new type of business.

Before undertaking further expansion (if desired), not only should your retail firm be functioning at a high level of efficiency but you'll also need to have on hand all the necessary resources—personnel, supervisory and managerial capability, merchandising talent, promotional skill, and sufficient capital as well. The thought of expanding either through the franchise route or through a merger with another, similar type of store may occur to you; you've read or heard about such actions. Defer thinking about these possibilities to a date well in the future; you're not yet ready to tackle such approaches. Indeed, you may never be ready.

## DIRECTIONS FOR EXPANSION

Let's assume that you found, and successfully established, your special niche in the retailing sector more than a year ago. Thanks to an expanding customer base, your store's monthly sales figures have been surpassing those of last year for the corresponding months by wide margins. Your quarterly operating statements reflect steadily increasing "bottom lines." If you're like most new retail entrepreneurs, you're probably beginning to think about future growth for your company. At this point in time, you'd be wise to undertake some serious long-range, or *strategic,* planning.* Despite its importance, planning of this nature isn't found all that often among small firm managements.**

As mentioned above, soon after discovering that their first store is a resounding success, many store owners typically begin to think about finding, and opening, another store just as soon as they can. They believe that by doing so, they'll most likely double their sales volume. Unfortunately, this just isn't the case; in fact, opening a second outlet

---

* For a useful outline of the strategic planning process, see John E. Van Kirk and Kathleen Noonan, "Key Factors in Strategic Planning," *Journal of Small Business Management* 20 (July 1982), 1–7; Reed Moyer, "Strategic Planning for the Small Firm," *Journal of Small Business Management* 20 (July 1982), 8–14.

** Donald L. Sexton and Philip Van Auken, "A Longitudinal Study of Small Business Strategic Planning," *Journal of Small Business Management* 23 (January 1985), 15.

without exercising extreme caution and good judgment can be downright dangerous. Just because the first location has proven profitable doesn't mean the next one will also be successful. Yes, it may—but then again, it may not. The new store will be located in another area and will need to serve a different clientele altogether.

Bear in mind that there are more choices open to you to accomplish company expansion than just by this customary routine.*

Here are some other pathways to growth:

- Open stores in other locations and become a chain-store organization.
- Franchise your retail operation.
- Acquire a second retail business (of the same or any other type).
- Merge with another retail company.
- Integrate backwards by setting up your own wholesaling firm and/or manufacturing plant.
- Diversify by starting (or buying) a different business.

## Franchising

Owners of successful retail enterprises are often tempted, sooner or later, to seek rapid expansion through franchising their operations. This route to expansion isn't as easy as it might appear, though. You should understand, first of all, that selling franchises can be an entirely new ball game, quite different from running a retail store.** You'll discover that you'll need to devote your energy and talents to such activities as:

- Developing an attractive and franchisable "package"
- Devising an effective marketing program to sell franchises
- Accumulating the requisite finances to launch the program
- Preparing a sensible timetable for your franchising effort
- Hiring, and then training, a field sales force to sell the package
- Searching for new store locations
- Securing competent legal and real estate advice
- Investigating, and then selecting, responsible and productive franchisees

The great appeal of franchising is, of course, the opportunity it offers for rapid business growth without the need to commit heavy financial resources of your own. Yet with courage, proper planning, and determination, you should be able to build your own chain over time without having to resort to the franchise mode of distribution.

---

* For insights into some approaches to company diversification, along with a helpful literature review, see Edward B. Roberts and Charles A. Berry, "Entering New Businesses: Selecting Strategies for Success," *Sloan Management Review* 26 (Spring 1985), 3–17.
** For some useful guidelines for the franchisor, see J. Donald Weinrauch, "Franchising the Established Business," *Journal of Small Business Management* 24 (July 1986), 1–7.

Of course, this might take you much longer, and you might have to borrow large sums of money or seek equity capital. By doing it yourself, though, you not only continue to run your own show, you're also able to keep all the profits for yourself!

## Mergers and Acquisitions

More often seen in the manufacturing sector than among retail firms, mergers and acquisitions are another pathway to rapid company growth. Sometimes a retailer merges with another firm of the same type or perhaps seeks to diversify by acquiring a totally unrelated kind of business.* Companies merge for various reasons: to bring in additional capital, machinery, equipment, or specialized personnel; to open up an entirely new geographical territory; to gain a larger market share; to increase overall sales volume; to protect their holdings by putting their eggs into more than one basket; and so on. Difficulties are, of course, to be expected when meshing two companies: problems in fusing the two complements of personnel, in combining systems and procedures, in blending merchandise and supply inventories, and so forth.

## PREREQUISITE: REVIEW YOUR FINANCES!

Whatever route to company expansion you choose to follow—adding more stores of your own, acquiring another firm, or franchising your operation—you'll need to anticipate the amount of capital required to stay on course. A healthy approach to planning for your financial needs is first to evaluate the current economic state of your business and then to work up plausible annual cash budgets for the first three to five years of your "growth plan." (See the section on cash budgets in chapter 19.) Remember that budgets are not only plans; they are also effective devices for controlling operations.

If you construct these cash budgets with consummate care, you'll be able to determine well in advance those time periods when you'll require additional funding. You'll know when the reinvestment of profits won't quite cover your needs, when you'll have to solicit bank loans, when you'll need to look for a partner (or sell some shares of stock in your corporation), and so on.

---

\* Some worthwhile suggestions for managements contemplating mergers or acquisitions appear in Edward B. Roberts and Charles A. Berry, "Entering New Businesses: Selecting Strategies for Success," *Sloan Management Review* 26 (Spring 1985), 3–17; George Hamilton, "Start Your Acquisition Program Ten Minutes from Now," *Business Horizons* 28 (September–October 1985), 12–15; Milton C. Lauenstein, "Diversification—The Hidden Explanation of Success," *Sloan Management Review* 27 (Fall 1985), 49–55; David E. Jemison and Sim B. Sitkin, "Acquisitions: The Process Can Be a Problem," *Harvard Business Review* 64 (March–April 1986), 107–116; Lee Tom Perry, "Merging Successfully: Sending the Right Signals," *Sloan Management Review* 27 (Spring 1986), 47–56.

## OUTLINE YOUR ORGANIZATIONAL NEEDS

Regardless of the direction in which your growth plans take you, you'll assuredly need to devote much thought to outlining company requirements for adding personnel all along the way. You should, of course, set plans in this area for a minimum of five years ahead. You'll need to devise a comprehensive human-resources program that will ensure a steady supply of lower-, middle-, and upper-management people as well as rank-and-file employees. Your program must embrace such activities as:

- Forecasting the numbers and types of people you'll need as you progress toward your goal
- Conducting job analyses, then preparing job descriptions and working up job specifications
- Recruiting job applicants to fill slots in your organization as they open up
- Training present employees for new duties and responsibilities within the organization
- Reviewing your approaches to employee compensation
- Selecting promising candidates for promotion
- Devising curricula for training
- Choosing appropriate training methods as well as trainers
- Evaluating employee performance

## MARKETING RESEARCH CAN HELP

Occasionally, business owners may face new problems for which immediate solutions are nearly impossible to discover. When this occurs, they may be able to apply marketing-research methods to gather enough pertinent information to help resolve the problem and facilitate appropriate decision making. Few small-scale entrepreneurs are familiar with these techniques, however. Fewer still have had actual experience in conducting formal studies.*

This is often not the case with larger business organizations. Over the years, their managements may have researched several different aspects of their operations, including the following:

- The nature, size, and approximate purchasing power of specific market segments
- The performance of sales representatives
- The state of employee morale
- The effectiveness of their advertising and sales promotions
- The feasibility of building, or relocating to, new premises
- The desirability of an acquisition or merger

---

* For a brief, though worthwhile, introduction to this subject area, see James G. Barnes, G. A. Pynn, and A. C. Noonan, "Marketing Research: Some Basics for Small Business," *Journal of Small Business Management* 20 (July 1982), 62–66.

## The Formal Research Process

Happily, the vast majority of problems encountered by business managers can be resolved without any need for formal research projects. An occasional, more complex, problem situation may, however, require further study.

The steps in the *formal research process* are:

1. Clarify, and then define, the problem.
2. Decide on the kinds of facts you need to be able to solve the problem.
3. Choose a method for collecting the facts.
4. Select a sample population from which to gather the information.
5. Collect the data.
6. Analyze the data.
7. Draw conclusions.
8. Take action, in light of those conclusions.

## Collecting the Data

The tendency in today's computerized business environment is to substitute the word *data* for any and all types of useful information. In actuality, data are facts; the singular is *datum,* meaning *a fact.*

Researchers seek two basic classes of data: primary and secondary. *Primary data* are facts that haven't as yet been collected by any person or agency. If you have need of this sort of information, you'll have to expend time, effort, and often money, to collect it. *Secondary data* are facts that are already available somewhere. Of course, the trick is to locate the information.

**Locating Secondary Data.** Information of this nature exists in abundance. Over the years, literally millions of facts of all kinds have been made available by many agencies as well as by countless thousands of individuals. You may be able to find helpful secondary data in business, trade, and consumer publications; at your trade association's headquarters; in public and university libraries; in directories of all kinds; and even in your own company's records.

The most prolific of all data sources is, of course, the federal government. Examples of their many useful publications include the different *Censuses (of Business, of Population,* and so on), the annual *Statistical Abstract of the United States,* and the *Survey of Current Business.*

**How to Gather Primary Data.** Three major approaches are available to the marketing researcher for the collection of primary data: observational techniques, experimentation, and survey methods. Of the three, survey methods (explained later on in this section) are the most widely used simply because they can be applied to many different types of problems.

*Observational techniques* usually require the use of trained observers or special equipment, such as movie cameras, tachistoscopes, and camcorders. These methods have one serious drawback: They can reveal *how* people behave, but they cannot tell us *why* they behave in this way. In the retail setting, for example, observation can be used to determine the direction of shopper traffic throughout the store, or the differing percentages of "lookers" who will be attracted to the various departments or merchandise displays.

On the other hand, observational methods would be of little value in attempting to ascertain shoppers' needs, preferences, or dislikes. Nor would they be of much help in determining consumer opinions of, or attitudes toward, any and all aspects of the retail operation. Neither can observation aid the retail decision maker in selecting the proper retail price to assign to a new item.

*Experimentation* is a more exacting and definitive method for gathering information than either observational techniques or surveys. Retail companies make use of this approach only occasionally, because it's far more difficult to set up an experiment in a real-life situation than in a laboratory. For one thing, it's necessary to control all the *extraneous variables* (factors outside the strict confines of the problem situation) that might affect the outcome of the experiment.

Here are three kinds of retail problems for which experimental approaches may prove useful:

- Choosing the most desirable selling price for a new article of merchandise
- Selecting the most effective version of a newspaper advertisement or television commercial
- Determining the effectiveness of an interior display

To illustrate the experimental method let's tackle that first problem in the above list. Assume that a home furnishings chain has just added an unusually attractive new table lamp to its regular assortment. The manufacturer's literature indicates a suggested retail price for the item of $79.95. After due consideration of the cost per piece, the accompanying freight expense, and the retailer's usual markup policies, management calculates that a retail price of $61.00 for the table lamp would be more than ample.

Some doubt remains, however. Is there a chance that some shoppers might feel the item is too cheap because of its low price, and not buy it? Would almost as many lamps be sold if they were priced at $79.95—or even higher? (If so, then the firm would earn substantially more gross-margin dollars!)

To solve this problem, management conceived of an actual experiment. Three store units were selected for the test. Care was taken to choose stores that were substantially similar in terms of size and weekly sales volume. A display of the new lamps was set up in each store on the same day, and each contained a large poster that described the lamp.

Displays, posters, and sign copy were all identical, *with the exception of the retail price shown*. A different price appeared in each store: $60.00, $70.00, and $85.00.

Sales slips were collected for all lamps sold for the next three weeks. At the end of the period, the special displays were taken down and the sales records compared.

Results indicated that more lamps were sold at $70 than at either the $60.00 or $85.00 figure. Moreover, sales at the $85.00 price were rather low. Management decided to place a price tag of $70 on the new lamps in all their stores.

*Survey Methods.* Persons and organizations can be surveyed by mail, over the telephone, or through personal interviews. Each approach has advantages and disadvantages. Personal interviews are the costliest and most time-consuming of the three; they can, however, result in the collection of a great deal of useful, in-depth information. Other problems with this method include the need for, and costs of, training capable interviewers and the possibility that *interviewer bias* may affect survey results. Nowadays, more surveys are conducted by mail or telephone than by personal interview.

Some type of survey instrument, or questionnaire, is used to help collect the information. In preparing questionnaires, careful consideration must be given to couching the questions in language that respondents will readily understand, as well as to the type, scope, and sequence of questions used.

Retail firms use surveys to determine customer demographics; to ascertain shopper interests, likes, and dislikes; to survey buyer intentions; and so on.

One of the most useful, and simple to understand, formats for the survey instrument is the *semantic differential*. Retailers can profitably use it to determine shoppers' attitudes toward their firms; to discover their strengths and weaknesses as perceived by the general public; to investigate the opinions that consumers hold regarding the depth, breadth, and quality of the merchandise they carry as well as their pricing policies, the caliber of their salespeople, their promotions, their newspaper or radio advertising; and so forth.

The typical semantic-differential questionnaire is comprised of carefully selected *scales*, perhaps ten or fifteen in all, printed on a single sheet of paper. Each scale consists of two contrasting or *polar* words or phrases that are separated by a series of dashes. For example, if you wished to probe your customers' opinions about the merchandise you carry, you might include the following two scales on the sheet:

|  | (1) | (2) | (3) | (4) | (5) | (6) | (7) |  |
|---|---|---|---|---|---|---|---|---|
| Top-quality merchandise | — | — | — | — | — | — | — | Shabby merchandise |
| Wide selection of goods | — | — | — | — | — | — | — | Narrow selection of goods |

Instructions as to how to complete this questionnaire are generally provided at the top of the sheet, along with one or two sample, checked-off scales to illustrate the procedure. For each scale, the respondent is to check off the blank that most closely approximates how he or she feels.

Column headings are generally given at the top; these indicate the relative "value" of each blank. For example, in the "top-quality merchandise . . . shabby merchandise" scale, the first blank (#1) would be checked by a person who believes that the store's merchandise is "*Extremely* top-quality." The other six blanks would be interpreted as follows:

# 2—Very (top-quality)

# 3—Somewhat (top quality)

# 4—Don't Know—or—Cannot Decide

# 5—Somewhat (shabby)

# 6—Very (shabby)

# 7—Extremely (shabby)

A few other scales of value to store retailers are shown below:

|  | (1) | (2) | (3) | (4) | (5) | (6) | (7) |  |
|---|---|---|---|---|---|---|---|---|
| A progressive firm | — | — | — | — | — | — | — | A backward firm |
| A reliable store | — | — | — | — | — | — | — | An unreliable store |
| Salespeople are friendly | — | — | — | — | — | — | — | Salespeople are unfriendly |
| Slow checkout | — | — | — | — | — | — | — | Speedy checkout |
| Displays are attractive | — | — | — | — | — | — | — | Displays are unattractive |
| Prices are high | — | — | — | — | — | — | — | Prices are low |

## MANAGEMENT SUCCESSION

Let's assume that you have already established and built up, through diligent effort and perseverance, your own successful retail enterprise. You find that sales continue to mount, end-of-period profits are increasing, and in general, things are going great. You've already selected your "growth track" and are thoroughly enmeshed in your expansion plans. Of late, however, you've been finding that your new responsibilities and steadily growing workload are starting to tax both your patience and your strength. Gradually, you're coming to realize that you need someone else to help you—someone who can act as your first assistant.

If this is true, then you're way behind schedule! Long before this point, you should have thought of finding, and training, a strong second-in-command. Why? Because, all along, you were caught in a perilous situation: What if you had become sick or incapacitated and couldn't attend to your duties? In that event, how would your business have been affected?

### Choosing Your Top Assistant

To select the one person who, you believe, will be a worthy "understudy" for you, begin by reviewing carefully your employees' capabilities. You need someone whom you can teach to think much like you do, and who—given the right training and your close supervision—would be competent enough to take over as your successor, should the need arise.

If you have no such candidate for promotion in your employ, you'll have to search for someone outside your organization. Look for a bright, energetic, self-motivated individual who has already had a few years of solid, management-level experience.

## Keeping Your Business in the Family

Of course, you may prefer to keep all assets of the business (and its cash flow, too!) entirely within your family. You may want your spouse, children, siblings, or other relatives to continue enjoying the benefits of your hard-won success. If this is so, try to make sure that your relatives are indeed interested in taking over the enterprise, should you some day relinquish the reins. One of the best ways of ensuring the interest of family members is to place them, early in the game, in "responsible positions."*

They may prove incompetent, or they may show a declining interest over time; in either case, it's important to discover this early in the game.

## FOR FURTHER INFORMATION

### Books

Carey, O., and D. Olson. *Opportunity Management: Strategic Planning for Smaller Businesses.* Englewood Cliffs, N.J.: Prentice-Hall, 1984.

Cooke, Terence E. *Mergers and Acquisitions.* New York: Basil Blackwell, 1986.

Gorton, Keith, and Isobel Carr. *Low-cost Marketing Research: A Guide for Small Businesses.* New York: Wiley, 1983.

Hagendorf, S. *Tax Guide for Buying and Selling A Business,* 6th ed. Englewood Cliffs, N.J.: Prentice-Hall, 1986.

Luck, David J., and Ronald S. Rubin. *Marketing Research,* 7th ed. Englewood Cliffs, N.J.: Prentice-Hall, Inc., 1987.

Marren, Joseph H. *Mergers and Acquisitions: Will You Overpay?* Homewood, Ill.: Dow Jones-Irwin, 1985.

O'Flaherty, Joseph S. *Going Public: The Entrepreneur's Guide.* New York: Wiley, 1984.

Rock, Milton L., ed. *The Mergers and Acquisitions Handbook.* New York: McGraw-Hill, 1987.

Scharf, Charles A., et al. *Acquisitions, Mergers, Sales, Buyouts, Takeovers: A Handbook with Forms,* 3d ed. Englewood Cliffs, N.J.: Prentice-Hall, 1985.

Siegel, William L. *Franchising.* New York: Wiley, 1983.

Weiers, Ronald M. *Marketing Research.* Englewood Cliffs, N.J.: Prentice-Hall, 1984.

---

* David M. Ambrose, "Transfer of the Family-Owned Business," *Journal of Small Business Management* 21 (January 1983), 55.

## Pamphlets Available from the Small Business Administration

### Management Aids

MA 2.004—"Problems in Managing a Family-owned Business"

MA 3.002—"Management Checklist for a Family Business"

MA 7.007—"Evaluating Franchise Opportunities"

# Appendix

---

**EXHIBIT A–1. ASK YOURSELF THESE QUESTIONS BEFORE YOU BEGIN**

**GETTING STARTED**

Your building

    Have you found a good building for your store?    _____

    Will you have enough room when your business gets bigger?    _____

    Can you fix the building the way you want it without spending too much money?    _____

    Can people get to it easily from parking spaces, bus stops, or their homes?    _____

    Have you had a lawyer check the lease and zoning?    _____

Equipment and supplies

    Do you know just what equipment and supplies you need and how much they will cost?    _____

    Can you save some money by buying secondhand equipment?    _____

Your merchandise

    Have you decided what things you will sell?    _____

    Do you know how much or how many of each you will buy to open your store with? _____

    Have you found suppliers who will sell you what you need at a good price?    _____

    Have you compared the prices and credit terms of different suppliers?    _____

Your records

    Have you planned a system of records that will keep track of your income and expenses, what you owe other people, and what other people owe you?    _____

    Have you worked out a way to keep track of your inventory so that you will always have enough on hand for your customers but not more than you can sell? _____

    Have you figured out how to keep your payroll records and take care of tax reports and payments?    _____

    Do you know what financial statements you should prepare?    _____

    Do you know how to use these financial statements?    _____

    Do you know an accountant who will help you with your records and financial statements?    _____

Your store and the law

    Do you know what licenses and permits you need?    _____

    Do you know what business laws you have to obey?    _____

    Do you know a lawyer you can go to for advice and for help with legal papers? _____

Protecting your store

Have you made plans for protecting your store against thefts of all kinds—
shoplifting, robbery, burglary, employee stealing? _____

Have you talked with an insurance agent about what kinds of insurance you need? _____

Buying a business someone else has started

Have you made a list of what you like and don't like about buying a business
someone else has started? _____

Are you sure you know the real reason why the owner wants to sell his business? _____

Have you compared the cost of buying the business with the cost of starting a
new business? _____

Is the stock up to date and in good condition? _____

Is the building in good condition? _____

Will the owner of the building transfer the lease to you? _____

Have you talked with other businessmen in the area to see what they think of
the business? _____

Have you talked with the company's suppliers? _____

Have you talked with a lawyer about it? _____

## MAKING IT GO

Advertising

Have you decided how you will advertise? (Newspapers—posters—handbills—
radio—by mail?) _____

Do you know where to get help with your ads? _____

Have you watched what other stores do to get people to buy? _____

The prices you charge

Do you know how to figure what you should charge for each item you sell? _____

Do you know what other stores like yours charge? _____

Buying

Do you have a plan for finding out what your customers want? _____

Will your plan for keeping track of your inventory tell you when it is time to
order more and how much to order? _____

Do you plan to buy most of your stock from a few suppliers rather than a little
from many, so that those you buy from will want to help you succeed? _____

Selling

Have you decided whether you will have salesclerks or self-service? _____

Do you know how to get customers to buy? _____

Have you thought about why you like to buy from some salesmen while others
turn you off? _____

Your employees

If you need to hire someone to help you, do you know where to look? _____

Do you know what kind of person you need? _____

Do you know how much to pay? _____

Do you have a plan for training your employees? _____

Credit for your customers

Have you decided whether to let your customers buy on credit? _____

Do you know the good and bad points about joining a credit-card plan? _____

Can you tell a deadbeat from a good credit customer? _____

### A FEW EXTRA QUESTIONS

Have you figured out whether you could make more money working for someone else? _____

Does your family go along with your plan to start a business of your own? _____

Do you know where to find out about new ideas and new products? _____

Do you have a work plan for yourself and your employees? _____

Have you gone to the nearest Small Business Administration office for help with your plans? _____

If you have answered all these questions carefully, you've done some hard work and serious thinking. That's good. But you have probably found some things you still need to know more about or do something about.

Do all you can for yourself, but don't hesitate to ask for help from people who can tell you what you need to know. Remember, running a business takes guts! You've got to be able to decide what you need and then go after it.

*Good luck!*

---

*Source:* "Checklist for Going into Business," *Small Marketers Aid No. 71* (Washington, D.C.: U.S. Small Business Administration, 1977).

---

### EXHIBIT A–2. CHECKLIST FOR INCREASING GROSS MARGIN

I. Increasing your markon
   A. Buying for less
      1. Do you take advantage of all discount opportunities?
      2. Do you watch purchases under seasonal rebate agreements so that they will not fall below limits?
      3. Do you keep your transportation costs to a minimum by using the most economical common carrier, packing methods, and consolidations?
      4. Do you concentrate your purchases with key suppliers?
      5. Do you actually use the facilities of a resident buying office to obtain better values?
      6. Could you realize savings by placing orders further ahead?
      7. Could you realize savings by placing blanket orders?
      8. Have you an undeveloped opportunity to use private brands to compete with national brands?
      9. Do you resist special quantity price concessions, for merchandise that will not turn over for a long period of time?
   B. Selling for more
      1. Do you take every opportunity to buy exclusive merchandise?
      2. Do you price every item on its merits (rather than applying an average markup on most goods)?
      3. Are goods costing the same put into stock at different prices when there is a difference in value in the customers' eyes?

      4. Could you raise price line endings slightly without detracting from your sales volume?

  C. Promoting higher-markup goods.

      1. Do you know the markup of each price line and in each classification?

      2. Do you make an adequate effort to feature in your advertising those price lines and items that bear a long markup?

      3. Is your long-markup merchandise adequately displayed in the store?

      4. Are your salespeople trained to give special attention to the higher-markup goods in stock?

      5. Do you give rewards for selling high-markup goods?

      6. Do you avoid giving valuable space to slow sellers?

II. Curtailing your reductions

  A. Buying

      1. Will your markdowns be reduced by rising wholesale prices?

      2. Do your buyers make careful buying plans before they go to market?

      3. Do your buyers frequently overbuy promotional merchandise, later forcing you to take heavy markdowns on remainders?

      4. Are your stocks peaked well in advance of the sales peak?

      5. Do you curtail reorders at the peak of the selling season?

      6. Are you developing classic lines with a long life?

      7. Are merchandise shortcomings leading to customer returns and markdowns? (If so, demand higher quality standards.)

      8. Do you place your orders on time so that you will have the proper merchandise in your store when the demand is great?

      9. Do you concentrate your buying on what you know will sell instead of experimenting with fringe sizes, colors, fabrics, and types of merchandise?

    10. Do you "test" new merchandise in small quantities before the beginning of a season and then concentrate heavily on the items that were successful?

    11. Do you buy "items," where possible, instead of full lines?

    12. Do you follow up your orders carefully to check for better deliveries?

    13. Do you refuse to accept past-due merchandise when the demand falls off?

    14. Do you receive merchandise at regular staggered intervals as opposed to receiving it "when ready"?

  B. Selling

      1. Are your salespeople adequately presenting the older goods in your stock?

      2. Do you have a good follow-up system to ensure that goods don't become slow sellers?

      3. Do you carefully instruct your salespeople in the selling points of merchandise that is slow-moving?

      4. Are your salespeople using forced selling methods that lead to returns and eventual markdowns?

      5. Do you provide your salespeople with proper rewards for selling slow-moving merchandise?

  C. Control

      1. Do you have any opportunities to increase your stockturn and reduce the length of time goods are on hand before being sold?

      2. Do you take your markdowns early enough?

      3. Do you take them too soon?

      4. Do you set the first markdown low enough to move most of the goods marked down?

      5. Have you established special markdown prices?

6. Do you have a system of good physical control of stock that avoids shortages?
7. Do you reorder well enough in advance to avoid being out of best-sellers?
8. Do you avoid unnecessary markdowns on staple merchandise that can be carried over to next year?
9. Do you keep a record of markdowns by sizes . . . to avoid errors in future ordering?

III. Increasing your cash discounts
    A. Are you getting the largest possible cash discounts from your suppliers?
    B. Do you pay all your bills on time so as to obtain the discounts offered?
    C. Are you taking advantage of anticipation opportunities?

IV. Lowering your workroom and alteration costs
    A. Are charges to your customers desirable, and are they adequate?
    B. Is your workroom being run as economically as possible?
    C. Would it be feasible to eliminate your workroom operation?

---

*Source:* John W. Wingate and Seymour Helfant, "Small Store Planning for Growth," *Small Business Management Series No. 33,* 2d ed. (Washington, D.C.: U.S. Small Business Administration, 1977), 96–99.

---

### EXHIBIT A–3. CHECKLIST FOR INTERIOR ARRANGEMENT AND DISPLAY

I. Layout
    1. Are your fixtures low enough and signs so placed that the customer can get a bird's-eye view of the store and tell in what direction to go for wanted goods?
    2. Do your aisle and counter arrangements tend to stimulate a circular traffic flow through the store?
    3. Do your fixtures (and their arrangement), signs, lettering, and colors all create a coordinated and unified effect?
    4. Before any supplier's fixtures are accepted, do you make sure they conform in color and design to what you already have?
    5. Do you limit the use of hanging signs to special sale events?
    6. Are your counters and aisle table *not* overcrowded with merchandise?
    7. Are your ledges and cashier/wrapping stations kept free of boxes, unneeded wrapping materials, personal effects, and odds and ends?
    8. Do you keep trash bins out of sight?

II. Merchandise emphasis
    1. Do your signs referring to specific goods tell the customer something significant about them, rather than simply naming the products and their prices?
    2. For your advertised goods, do you have prominent signs, including tear sheets at the entrances, to inform and guide customers to their exact location in the store?
    3. Do you prominently display both advertised and nonadvertised specials at the ends of counters as well as at the point of sale?
    4. Are both your national and private brands highlighted in your arrangement and window display?
    5. Wherever feasible, do you give the more colorful merchandise in your stock preference in display?
    6. In the case of apparel and home furnishings, do the items that reflect your store's fashion sense or fashion leadership get special display attention at all times?
    7. In locating merchandise in your store, do you always consider the productivity of space—vertical as well as horizontal?

8. Is your self-service merchandise arranged so as to attract the customer and assist in selection by the means indicated below:
   a. Is each category grouped under a separate sign?
   b. Is the merchandise in each category arranged according to its most significant characteristic—whether color, style, size, or price?
   c. In apparel categories, is the merchandise arranged by price lines or zones to assist the customer to make a selection quickly?
   d. Is horizontal space usually devoted to different items and styles within a category (vertical space being used for different sizes—smallest at the top, largest at the bottom)?
   e. Are impulse items interspersed with demand items and *not* placed across the aisle from them, where many customers will not see them?
9. Do you plan your windows and displays in advance?
10. Do you meet with your salesforce after windows are trimmed to discuss the items displayed?
11. Do you use seasonal, monthly, and weekly plans for interior and window displays, determining the fixtures to be used and merchandise to be displayed?
12. Do your displays reflect the image of your store?
13. Do you budget the dollars you will set aside for fixtures and props to be used in your displays, as well as the expense of setting them up and maintaining them?
14. Do you keep your fixtures and windows clean and dust-free?
15. Do you replace burned-out light bulbs immediately?
16. Do you take safety precautions in setting up your fixtures?
17. Do garments fit properly on mannequins and fixtures?

*Source:* John W. Wingate and Seymour Helfant, "Small Store Planning for Growth," *Small Business Management Series No. 33,* 2d ed. (Washington, D.C.: U.S. Small Business Administration, 1977), 100–102.

### EXHIBIT A–4. CHECKLIST FOR INCREASING TRANSACTIONS

I. Stock assortment
  A. Unit control systems
    1. Do you have an adequate system for checking on staple items?
    2. For other than staple items, do you have an adequate unit control system in operation?
    3. Do you have an effective system for checking on slow-selling stock?
    4. Do you have an effective system for spotting potential fast-selling stock?
    5. Do you keep a close check on customer demand by a want-slip system?
    6. Do you keep adequate records to help you plan for next year's purchases?
    7. Do you plan your inventory so that you will always be "in stock" at peak periods?
    8. Do you make use of electronic data processing (EDP) to ensure good inventory control, at the low rates available to small retailers?
  B. Balance of stock
    1. Is the stock in each of your merchandise classifications balanced to the rate of sale in each?
    2. Is your stock balanced by price line, color, size, and type?
    3. Do you have too many price lines?
    4. Are your prices and price lines the right choice to meet your competition?
    5. Do you carry deep stocks in each of the running styles?

6. Do you carry deep stocks in heart sizes, colors, and materials?

7. In fringe sizes, colors, etc., do you deliberately keep low stocks and depend on substitution to avoid lost sales at these points?

8. Do you keep a proper balance among the following classes of stock: staple, assortment, prestige, and clearance?

9. Do you maintain a basic stock assortment even in dull months?

C. Selection

1. Do you avoid stocking items from different suppliers and in different brands that virtually duplicate one another?

2. Do you select each item in stock with a distinct customer group or target in mind?

3. Do you choose items for promotion that have outstanding merit in price, fashion, or utility?

4. Do you place adequate emphasis on special value promotions, neither too much nor too little?

5. Do the characteristics of the stock give your store a clearly defined personality or image that attracts people in the trading area?

6. Do you keep in close touch with all new market developments by cooperating with a buying office or voluntary group and by seeing all salesmen who call?

7. Do you carefully select the lines you carry since you can't be all things to all people?

8. Do you know your competition, their strengths and weaknesses?

II. Promotion

A. Outside publicity

1. Do you promote best-sellers?

2. Do you make adequate use of the appropriate media: newspapers, direct mail, signs, radio-TV, press publicity, stunts, special sales inducements, sampling, house-to-house selling, home and club demonstrations, mail and telephone selling?

3. Do you use the most appropriate newspapers?

4. Do you have adequate promotion each month of the year?

5. Do you advertise on the right days of the week?

6. Are your ad layouts eye-catching?

7. Does the ad copy inspire interest, desire, and action; and, above all, is the copy believable?

8. Does your store have adequate window space?

9. Are your show windows well planned and compelling?

10. Do you use one large ad for better effectiveness rather than a number of small ads?

11. Do you keep a record of what your competitors advertise?

12. Do you tie in with local merchants' community sales efforts?

13. Do you promote your store as the type of store you want it to be to the kind of customers you want to attract?

14. Do you promote your strong points in the types of merchandise you carry and the services you offer?

15. Do you maintain an excellent relationship with your regular customers, while still going after new customers?

16. Does your advertising copy sell your store as well as the item?

17. Do you include related merchandise, when possible, in all your ads?

18. Do you present the main benefits of the merchandise you advertise?

19. Do you include your store's name and address in all your advertising?

B. In-store publicity

1. Do you maintain adequate ensemble displays that coordinate items?

2. Do your salespeople suggest to customers the coordinations featured in displays?

3. Do you make effective use of advertising blowups?
4. Are your signs effective?
5. Do you use handbills at store entrances to attract customers to specials in the store?
6. Do you take the best advantage of interdepartmental selling?

C. Layout

1. Are the merchandise lines properly located in your store and easily accessible?
2. Is each merchandise line adequately serviced?
3. Are your fixtures up-to-date?
4. Is the lighting good?
5. Is the majority of your fast-selling merchandise always on display, available for customer inspection without the intervention of a salesclerk?
6. Are informative labels, listing major selling points, attached to all items for which customers may need the information?
7. Are your impulse goods so placed as to be seen by customers shopping for demand items?
8. Do you limit your reserve stock area if you are paying a high rental?

D. Sales

1. Is your salesforce well chosen?
2. Is your salesforce adequately trained in merchandise information and in customer handling?
3. Do your salespeople get adequate merchandise information?
4. Do you provide your salespeople with sufficient premiums, rewards, and contests to maintain their interest?
5. Do you give considerate attention to their suggestions and grievances?
6. Is each of your buyers a good leader?
7. Do you train your salesforce to substitute items when styles and sizes are sold out?
8. Do you get on the floor often enough to stimulate your salesforce—and learn what your customers are demanding?
9. Do you motivate your salesforce to do an outstanding job?
10. Do you teach your salesforce to increase the size of their sales through the use of multiple unit pricing, when it is available?

E. Customer Services

1. Do you make it convenient for customers to exchange merchandise or obtain refunds?
2. Do you have a liberal refund policy?
3. Do you offer gift wrapping?
4. Do you sell gift certificates?
5. Do you encourage charge accounts?
6. Do you have lay-away services?
7. Do you accept telephone orders?

*Source:* John W. Wingate and Seymour Helfant, "Small Store Planning for Growth," *Small Business Management Series No. 33*, 2d ed. (Washington, D.C.: U.S. Small Business Administration, 1977), 90–95.

# Index